ATTRIBUTION, COMMUNICATION BEHAVIOR, AND CLOSE RELATIONSHIPS

The field of close relationships is one of the most fertile areas of work in the social and behavioral sciences. Central to theoretical developments in the study of close relationships is a focus on people's interpretive activities and communication behavior. Theories of attribution and of communication styles are prominent in contemporary explanations of why and how people begin close relationships, maintain and enhance closeness, and sometimes terminate close relationships. This volume brings together leading scholars to explain how attribution and communication behavior can help us to understand the nature of close relationships. As a comprehensive and up-to-date reference, *Attribution, Communication Behavior, and Close Relationships* will appeal to scholars in communication studies, family studies, human development, social and clinical psychology, family socialogy, and social work.

Valerie Manusov is an Associate Professor of Speech Communication at the University of Washington.

John H. Harvey is Professor of Psychology at the University of Iowa.

ADVANCES IN PERSONAL RELATIONSHIPS

Series Editors
HARRY T. REIS
University of Rochester

MARY ANNE FITZPATRICK
University of Wisconsin, Madison

ANITA L. VANGELISTI
University of Texas, Austin

Advances in Personal Relationships represents the culmination of years of multidisciplinary and interdisciplinary work on personal relationships. Sponsored by the International Society for the Study of Personal Relationships (ISSPR), the series offers readers cutting-edge research and theory in the field. Contributing authors are internationally known scholars from a variety of disciplines, including social psychology, clinical psychology, communication, history, sociology, gerontology, and family studies. Volumes include integrative reviews, conceptual pieces, summaries of research programs, and major theoretical works.

Attribution, Communication Behavior, and Close Relationships

Edited by

VALERIE MANUSOV
University of Washington

JOHN H. HARVEY
University of Iowa

PUBLISHED BY THE PRESS SYNDICATE OF THE UNIVERSITY OF CAMBRIDGE
The Pitt Building, Trumpington Street, Cambridge, United Kingdom

CAMBRIDGE UNIVERSITY PRESS
The Edinburgh Building, Cambridge CB2 2RU, United Kingdom
40 West 20th Street, New York, NY 10011-4211, USA
10 Stamford Road, Oakleigh, Melbourne 3166, Australia
Ruiz de Alarcón 13, 28014 Madrid, Spain
Dock House, The Waterfront, Cape Town 8001, South Africa

http://www.cambridge.org

First published 2001

Printed in the United States of America

Typefaces Palatino 10/13   *System* Quark XPress™   [HT]

A catalogue record for this book is available from the British Library

Library of Congress Cataloguing-in-Publication Data

Attribution, communication behavior, and close relationships /
[edited by] Valerie Manusov, John H. Harvey.
     p. cm.—(Advances in personal relations)
     ISBN 0 521 77089 0
     1. Attribution (Social psychology) 2. Interpersonal communication.
    3. Interpersonal relations. I. Manusov, Valerie Lynn. II. Harvey, John H., 1943–
III. Series.
HM1076 .A77 2000
158.2—dc21   00-028951

ISBN 0 521 77089 0 hardback

This book is dedicated to pioneering scholars of communication behavior and of attribution processes, especially Harold Kelley and the late Neil Jacobson, whose collective work contributed greatly to the development of the interface between attribution and communication behavior in close relationships.

Contents

List of Contributors

Hilary Ammazzalorso, Department of Psychology, University of Minnesota

David Atkins, Center for Clinical Research, University of Washington

Denise S. Bartell, Department of Human Ecology, University of Texas at Austin

Ellen Berscheid, Department of Psychology, University of Minnesota

Anita Blakeley-Smith, Department of Psychology, University of Queensland, Australia

Thomas N. Bradbury, Department of Psychology, University of California, Los Angeles

Daphne Blunt Bugental, Department of Psychology, University of California, Santa Barbara

Valerian J. Derlega, Department of Psychology, Old Dominion University

Sona Dimidjian, Center for Clinical Research, University of Washington

Tim Dun, Department of Communication, University of Iowa

Michael E. Eidenmuller, Department of Speech Communication, University of Texas at Tyler

Paul Ekman, Department of Psychology, University of California, San Francisco

Judith Feeney, Department of Psychology, University of Queensland, Australia

Frank D. Fincham, Department of Psychology, State University of New York, Buffalo

Jeanne Flora, Department of Communication, California State University, Fullerton

Joseph P. Forgas, School of Psychology, University of New South Wales, Sydney, Australia

Mark Frank, Department of Communication, Rutgers University

Cynthia Gallois, Department of Psychology, University of Queensland, Australia

John H. Harvey, Department of Psychology, University of Iowa

James M. Honeycutt, Department of Studies Communication, Louisiana State University

Neil Jacobson *(deceased),* Center for Clinical Research, University of Washington

Matthew D. Johnson, Department of Psychology, State University of New York at Binghamton

Benjamin R. Karney, Department of Psychology, University of California, Los Angeles

Jody Koenig, Department of Speech Communication, University of Washington

Nora Langenfeld, Department of Psychology, University of Minnesota

Kenneth Leonard, Research Institute on Addictions, Buffalo, New York

Jason Lopes, Department of Psychology, University of Minnesota

Valerie Manusov, Department of Speech Communication, University of Washington

Sandra Metts, Department of Communication, Illinois State University

Patricia Noller, Department of Psychology, University of Queensland, Australia

Julia Ormazu, Department of Psychology, University of Iowa

Candida C. Peterson, Department of Psychology, University of Queensland, Australia

Linda J. Roberts, Department of Psychology, University of Wisconsin, Madison

Ronald Rogge, Department of Psychology, University of California, Los Angeles

Alan M. Rubin, School of Communication Studies, Kent State University, Ohio

Rebecca B. Rubin, School of Communication Studies, Kent State University, Ohio

Chris Segrin, Department of Communication, University of Arizona

William Shennum, Five Acres Boys' and Girls' Aid Society, Altadena, California

Alan Sillars, Department of Communication, University of Montana

Denise Haunani Solomon, Department of Communication Arts, University of Wisconsin, Madison

Brian H. Spitzberg, School of Communication, San Diego State University

Catherine A. Surra, Department of Human Ecology, University of Texas at Austin

Ashlea Troth, Department of Psychology, University of Queensland, Australia

Anita L. Vangelisti, College of Communication, University of Texas at Austin

Ellen E. Whipple, School of Social Work, Michigan State University

Steven R. Wilson, Department of Communication, Purdue University, Illinois

Barbara A. Winstead, Department of Psychology, Old Dominion University, Virginia

Introduction

Valerie Manusov

Our close relationships provide the context for many of our most important – and most mundane – experiences. Because personal relationships are where so much that we value happens, understanding the nature and processes of close relationships is critical. This book is meant to aid in the journey to learn more about what occurs in and around personal relationships. In particular, it focuses on two processes – attributions and communication. In some chapters, the two are discussed as separately occurring activities; in other chapters, the link is much closer. Indeed, looking over the ways that these chapters envision attributions and communication behavior in close relationships enhances our understanding of what the processes entail.

Some of the authors in the current volume conceptualize attributions as the explanations that are given for social actions, including communication behaviors. This perspective on the attribution – communication link identifies attributions as a general form of sense making, which is likely to occur when the cause or origin of behaviors needs to be identified. For example, in her chapter Anita Vangelisti describes attributions as "explanations for why [people's] emotions are evoked." Attributions, for these authors, are people's *verbal descriptions* of why a communicative event occurred. This conceptualization of attribution as explanation for communication (or other) behaviors reveals attributions as social creations used by people to help them understand and describe their own or others' actions. They are utterances elicited by researchers, but also presumably used in everyday life, that provide descriptions of people's answers to "why" questions.

This perspective on attributions equates to some researchers' view of accounts, and indeed, Jeanne Flora and Chris Segrin discuss attributions as *accounts* for relational development. Likewise, David Atkins,

Sona Dimidjian, and Neil Jacobson, in seeking research on people's explanations for extramarital involvement, label the attributions they found as *justifications,* a common form of account. Also, Cathy Surra and Denise Bartell captured causal explanations in the reasons (accounts) people gave for their commitment to their relationships. The authors who analyze attributions as communicated accounts provide a function for attributions not usually discussed when attributions are seen as a private form of sense making (but see Sandra Metts' commentary for some caution about using this approach).

Other authors conceptualize attributions as tied specifically to cause and/or responsibility and use rating scales to assess the structure of the attributions; this rating approach is more consistent with traditional attribution work. These authors differ, however, in the degree to which they rely on previously identified attribution dimensions. Ellen Berscheid, Jason Lopes, Hilary Ammazzalorso, and Nora Langenfeld, for example, provide an analysis that rests firmly in – while simultaneously extending – Kelley's discussion of personal and environmental causes. Steven Wilson and Ellen Whipple use four attribution dimensions, namely, locus, generality (similar to stability), blame, and knowledge. The knowledge attribution was an extension of previous research made relevant by the object of the attributions, children's misbehavior. Likewise, Daphne Bugental, William Shennum, Mark Frank, and Paul Ekman, through the Picture Attribution Test, determined the extent to which the children they were studying or someone else (actor versus other) was the primary causal agent.

These authors show that traditional attribution dimensions may need to be expanded according to the type of relationship and the nature of the behavior that are under investigation. Indeed, Candida Peterson, Ashlea Troth, Cynthia Gallois, and Judith Feeney use a set of attribution dimensions unique to their interest in assessments of communication difficulty. They look at the extent to which people perceived their own and their partner's motivations and conversational strategies during the interaction task as having friendly or hostile intent, being open or closed communication, revealing topic avoidance or involvement, reflecting a competitive or cooperative orientation, and reflecting a calm or emotional mood.

Others, such as Valerian Derlega and Barbara Winstead, use their data to establish potential new categories of attributions. These authors found a large variety of reasons (e.g., similarity of background or privacy concerns) that people offer as attributions for why they did or did not disclose their human immunodeficiency virus (HIV) status to others. Similarly, Patricia Noller, Judith Feeney, and Anita Blakeley-Smith provide both responsibility and causal attributions that reveal the types of explanations people give for changes in their relationship. These include such causes of change as having children, maturity, time together, and alterations in the needs of the couple members. In general, the authors who focus on attribution structure in this book do so in a way that broadens what the term structure or nature has meant in past research. They help show that the nature of the relationship in which the attributions are made and the topic of the research study affect the types of attribution dimensions that are likely to be relevant. However, in his commentary Frank Fincham has pointed out some caveats about exploring too may dimensions of attributions.

Several authors in this volume reveal an even closer link between attributions and communication. Valerie Manusov and Jody Koenig, for instance, look at the attributions couples provide for nonverbal interaction behaviors as the meanings that they have ascribed to the communication cues. Thus, unlike the previous groups of authors, who presume that communication behaviors, such as hurtful messages, changes in relationships, or choosing not to communicate, need attributions to make sense of the message itself, these authors operationalize the attribution *as* the message. Alan Sillars, Linda Roberts, Tim Dun, and Kenneth Leonard also focus on attributions as communication. In their extensive coding of real-time interactions, Sillars et al. accessed the attributions people gave to what they are their partners were likely thinking at the time of the interaction. Individual members of couples stated what they thought they and their partner were attempting to communicate or what was probably going on in their minds as they interacted; thus, the attributions reflected the couples' assessments of the meanings for the communication behaviors in which they or their partner engaged.

The variety of possible ways presented by the authors to investigate the ties between attributions and communication in close relationships provides an important benefit of the current volume. In general, the chapters reveal at least three ways of thinking about this link. First, attributions are seen as a form of communication that involves explanations for behaviors or events. Second, attributions are seen as necessary *for* communication cues (i.e., causal or other explanations are given for why someone communicated what or how he or she did). Third, attributions may be seen as an important part of the communicated message itself, with causal explanations becoming the meaning ascribed to or communicated by behaviors.

In addition to conceiving the attribution–communication link in multiple and interesting ways, several other chapter authors attempt to expand our understanding of how attribution or communication processes work. Matthew Johnson, Benjamin Karney, Ronald Rogge, and Thomas Bradbury, for instance, review an organized line of research that seeks to determine whether attributions vary as a function of other cognitions, such as marital satisfaction, or vice versa. They determine, and make a compelling case, that attribution making tends to precede satisfaction, a causal order that is not usually discussed in models of the process. Even more importantly for the goals of this book, however, Johnson et al. offer some preliminary data suggesting a moderating (i.e., interaction) effect between communication behavior and attributions in affecting satisfaction. This role for communication and other behavior differs from that in other models in which attributions are presumed to cause behaviors, which in turn affect satisfaction.

Similarly, Joseph Forgas reviews a series of studies that attempt to determine the role that mood plays in shaping attributions. He asserts that moods are likely to affect both what people think (the content of their attributions) and how they think (the process of attribution). Forgas argues that the "affect infusion" of moods may be even more pervasive than the effects of larger emotions, and this perspective gives attribution making a permeable quality not seen commonly in other attribution work. According to Forgas, "precisely because of their low intensity and limited cognitive structure, moods may often have a more long-lasting, subtle, and unconscious influence on thinking, attribution, and communication in relationships than do distinct emotions."

Interestingly, other authors in the volume (e.g., James Honeycutt and Michael Eidenmuller in their assessment of the effects of and attributions for music on mood) provide additional support for Forgas' contentions. Denise Solomon's commentary reveals some additional important elaborations and clarifications of the role emotion plays in cognition and behavior. Rebecca Rubin and Alan Rubin also detail the connection between attributions and another cognitive and behavioral process, uncertainty reduction. They show possible ways in which people form attributions for media characters and personalities as part of increasing the closeness in their "parasocial relationships."

Brian Spitzberg also offers an opportunity to explore the boundaries and processes of attributions, but he does so in a way that is different from those of our other authors. Spitzberg uses this forum to suggest a list of criteria by which the efficacy of theories, including attribution theories, can be judged. He then employs the criteria to assess how well attribution theories stand the test of viability. In doing so, he offers a number of challenges for researchers using attributional models. John Harvey and Julia Ormazu temper Spitzberg's critique somewhat but help show the value of looking more broadly and critically at attribution theory, particularly as applied to communication in close relationships.

In addition to a desire to explore the possible connections between attributions and communication, however, this volume provides a chance to see research that crosses interdisciplinary boundaries. Our goal was to find authors from a number of backgrounds who all are doing work relevant to the book's topic. While social psychology and communication are the primary disciplines represented, the authors in this collection also show the relevance of this research for people studying human development, family relationships, and clinical psychology. The fact that most of the researchers in this book use one another's work is testament to our belief that multiple disciplines provide important perspectives on the study of close relationships.

We hope you find this collection stimulating and useful for the work you are doing. Both John and I have found working together and with these authors to be an exciting experience. We thank them for their good work and contribution to this volume. We also are indebted to Julia Hough, Editor at Cambridge University Press, for her faith in this project. On a more personal note, John Harvey thanks Pamela and Patrick Harvey for their support. I send thanks to Chuck McSween for the time he has given me many evenings and weekends to put this collection together. During those hours, he watched over our son Cameron, who was born just as the idea for this book was conceived.

PART ONE

ATTRIBUTION, AFFECT, AND WELL-BEING IN RELATIONSHIPS

CHAPTER ONE

Affective Influences on Communication and Attribution in Relationships

Joseph P. Forgas

Human beings are intensely social creatures. Our remarkable ability to relate to others has much to do with our evolutionary success as a species, and personal relationships are also responsible for most of the significant affective experiences in our lives (Argyle & Henderson, 1985). Affect, emotions, and mood thus represent a critical feature of human relationships (Forgas, 1979). Indeed, as Zajonc (1980) suggested, feelings may well be *the* primary currency of interpersonal behavior.

Although affect lies at the heart of most relationships, our understanding of how feelings influence our thoughts, judgments, and communication with significant others remained little understood until recently (Bradbury & Fincham, 1987). This chapter reviews some of the most recent evidence for the role of affect in relationship judgments and behaviors. It will suggest that affective influences on relationships are most likely when partners need to engage in open, constructive thinking about a complex, ambiguous, or unusual issue. The role of cognitive information processing strategies in mediating mood effects on relationship judgments and behaviors will be discussed, and a general integrative theory accounting for such effects, the Affect Infusion Model (Forgas, 1995a), will be outlined.

AFFECT, THINKING, AND BEHAVIOR

Traditionally, psychologists assumed that social thinking and behavior were best analyzed in terms of cold, rational cognitive and behavioral

Support from a Special Investigator Award by the Australian Research Foundation and from the Research Prize by the Alexander von Humboldt Foundation is gratefully acknowledged. Please address all correspondence to Joseph P. Forgas, School of Psychology, University of New South Wales, Sydney 2052, Australia; e-mail *jp.forgas@unsw.edu.au*; Internet: *http://www.psy.unsw.edu.au/~joef/jforgas.htm*.

principles, where affect is either irrelevant or appears only as a source of noise or disruption. This view has been fundamentally challenged by recent psychological and neuropsychological evidence (Bower & Forgas, 2000; Damasio, 1994; LeDoux, 1996). It now appears that cognition, judgment, and social behavior are almost always affectively loaded. Indeed, the evidence suggests that absence of affective reactions significantly impairs social decisions (Damasio, 1994), confirming that affect is an integral and necessary part of our adaptive reactions to the social world (Frijda, 1986).

Emotions and Moods in Relationships

People experience a wide variety of affective states in their relationships, from subtle moods to intense emotions. Moods may be defined as low-intensity, diffuse, and relatively enduring affective states without a salient antecedent cause and therefore with little cognitive content (e.g., feeling good or feeling badly). Emotions, in contrast, are more intense, are short-lived, and usually have a definite cause and clear cognitive content (e.g., anger or fear) (Forgas, 1992a).

One line of research on affect in relationships seeks to explore the rich framework of cognitive knowledge structures within which relationship emotions are embedded. Such emotion scripts have important consequences for the way partners think, feel, and behave toward each other. To the extent that distinct emotions, unlike moods, are rich in cognitive content (Smith & Kirby, 2000), they typically trigger responses that are directed by their specific appraisal qualities. Emotion scripts thus have a predictable and highly visible influence on what partners think, do, and remember (Gottman & Levenson, 1986).

Although research on emotion prototypes is a thriving area, there are also some problems with this approach. It is recognized by several writers that in the absence of complete agreement about the particular kinds of appraisals that generate particular kinds of emotions, some of the predictions are based solely on intuitive analysis (Fletcher & Fincham, 1991). Although emotion schemata can clearly influence how relationship knowledge is structured (Niedenthal & Halberstadt, 2000), there is an obvious need for a complementary research strategy exploring the dynamic, *functional* consequences for relationship judgments and behaviors of less noticeable, milder affective states such as moods. This is one of my objectives here.

Moods, unlike emotions, are typically not in the focus of our consciousness and have little cognitive content and structure. Yet precisely because of their low intensity and limited cognitive structure, moods may often have a longer lasting, subtle, and unconscious influence on thinking, attribution, and communication in relationships than do distinct emotions (Forgas, 1992a, 1993, 2000; Sedikides, 1995). This chapter explores the conditions likely to facilitate or hinder affect infusion—the gradual coloring of thoughts and judgments by a prevailing affective state—in relationships, and it outlines an information processing theory likely to account for the presence or absence of these effects.

Early Evidence for Mood Effects on Relationships

Historically, only a handful of researchers have studied affective influences on relationships. In one of the earliest studies, Feshbach and Singer (1957) demonstrated that fearful subjects are likely to perceive more anxiety in others, a finding that was interpreted by the authors as evidence for the psychodynamic notion of projection. In a series of classic studies, Schachter (1959) showed that induced aversive emotions can influence interpersonal preferences: Anxious people made highly targeted partner choices consistent with a motivated strategy to control and repair their aversive mood. Other experiments in the 1960s and 1970s relied on associationist, conditioning theories when investigating the influence of affect on relationship judgments and behaviors (e.g., Clore & Byrne, 1974; Griffitt, 1970). Results showed that an affective state could become readily associated with how a partner is perceived and evaluated, even if the affect was elicited by a completely irrelevant *prior* cause (such as being in an unpleasant room).

More recent theories rely on cognitive principles to account for affective influences on relationship judgments and behaviors. The emerging social cognition paradigm in the early 1980s provided a promising framework for understanding the subtle links between thinking and feeling in relationships (Bradbury & Fincham, 1992; Fletcher & Fincham, 1991). Recent theories thus rely on information processing principles to explain how and why affect can influence the way people select, learn, process, and remember relationship information (e.g., Bower, 1991; Bower & Forgas, 2000; Clore, Schwarz, & Conway, 1994; Forgas, 1992a, 1995a). The cognitive approach also yielded important new insights about relationship dynamics and dysfunctions (Fletcher, Fitness, & Blampied, 1990; Gottman, 1979; Noller & Ruzzene, 1991).

MOOD EFFECTS ON RELATIONSHIP COGNITION
AND BEHAVIORS: THE AFFECT INFUSION MODEL

Interpreting and managing social relationships is an inherently complex and demanding cognitive task (cf. Fletcher & Fincham, 1991; Forgas, 1985a, 1991a). There is now strong evidence suggesting that moods can influence both *what* people think (the content of cognition) and *how* people think (the process of cognition). A recent integrative theory, the Affect Infusion Model (AIM; Forgas, 1995a), seeks to account for both informational and processing mood effects, and it explains both the presence and the absence of mood congruity in terms of the different information processing strategies people use.

Affect infusion occurs when information stored in memory that is associated with a prevailing mood is selectively primed to exert an influence on and become incorporated into ongoing cognitive and behavioral processes, eventually coloring their outcome (Forgas, 1995a, 2000). As this definition suggests, affect infusion is dependent on the nature of the task and the kind of processing strategy used. The AIM predicts that affect infusion should only occur when a person is engaged in genuinely constructive information processing that involves an open information search strategy and the elaboration of the available stimulus details. Thus, as Fiedler (1991) suggested, affect should only influence cognitive processes when the task involves the active generation of new information.

Four distinct information processing strategies are identified by the AIM: direct access, motivated, heuristic, and substantive processing. Each processing strategy is characterized by different affect infusion potentials. For example, when a cognitive task can be solved through the direct access and retrieval of a preexisting, stored response or when a response is generated through a targeted, motivated search driven by a preexisting goal, affect infusion is unlikely, because these strategies require little open and constructive processing. Indeed, in terms of the AIM, motivated processing can be a major vehicle for reducing mood effects and even producing mood-incongruent outcomes, especially when people are motivated to achieve mood repair or mood control (Berkowitz, Jaffee, & Troccoli, 2000; Forgas, 1991a; Sedikides, 1994).

Of course, many responses in relationships require some degree of constructive processing. The AIM distinguishes between (a) heuristic, simplified and (b) substantive, generative processing as the two main alternatives when constructive processing is required. These are high affect infusion strategies, as they involve some degree of open information search and constructive thinking (Fiedler, 1991, Forgas, 1992a). The AIM predicts that affect infusion and mood congruence in thinking and judgments should be limited to conditions that recruit either heuristic or substantive processing.

Affect infusion occurs in the course of heuristic processing, because mood itself may be mistakenly used as a source of heuristic information according to the *affect-as-information* principle. For example, people may rely on a "How do I feel about it?" heuristic to infer their response (Clore et al., 1994; Schwarz & Clore, 1988). Given the complex and involved nature of relationships, heuristic processing is probably rarely used when dealing with personally meaningful relationship information (Forgas, 1994). It is more likely that during substantive processing, affect may infuse our thoughts and behaviors owing to its selective priming effects on how relationship information is selected, learned, recalled, and interpreted (Bower, 1991; Bower & Forgas, 2000; Forgas & Bower, 1987). There is strong evidence for the effects of moods on many complex and realistic social and relationship judgments due to such *affect-priming* effects (Forgas, 1991b, 1993, 1995b; Forgas & Bower, 1987; Mayer, Gaschke, Braverman, & Evans, 1992; Salovey, O'Leary, Stretton, Fishkin, & Drake, 1991; Sedikides, 1995).

The AIM regards affect-as-information and affect priming as complementary avenues of affect infusion. Affect-as-information is most likely to be involved during heuristic processing, and affect priming is likely during substantive processing. These mechanisms are empirically distinguishable in terms of processing latency, judgmental latency, memory, and other cognitive measures (Forgas, 1992a, 1995a). Further, choice of processing strategy depends on three kinds of variables: the characteristics of the person (e.g., personality, personal relevance, motivation, cognitive capacity, and affect), the characteristics of the task (familiarity, complexity, typicality, novelty), and the features of the situation (publicity, accountability, scrutiny, etc.). As the AIM has been adequately described previously (Forgas, 1992a, 1995a), it will not be discussed in greater detail here. Rather, I shall now turn to a review of some of the specific evidence showing affect infusion in relationship judgments, attributions, and behaviors.

MOOD EFFECTS ON RELATIONSHIP EVALUATION

Relationship evaluations may show a mood-congruent bias, as people in a good mood may selectively recall mood-congruent, enjoyable, and pleasant episodes, whereas sad mood facilitates the recall of sad, depressing relationship events. In other words, activation of a mood "also spreads activation throughout the memory structures to which it is connected" (Bower, 1981, p. 135), producing a mood-congruent bias in attention, learning, recall, and associations. Fluctuating affective states may therefore have an important influence on marital satisfaction, as happy partners often produce attributions that "enhance relationship quality, whereas unhappy partners produce attributions that maintain their current levels of distress" (Fletcher, Fitness, & Blampied, 1990, p. 251).

To test these ideas, my colleagues and I performed a series of experiments to assess whether affect infuses the way partners think about their personal relationship under conditions conducive to substantive, elaborate processing strategies. We were also interested in assessing whether these mood effects continue to be important even in long established relationships (Forgas, Levinger, & Moylan, 1994). Intuitively, one would expect mood to have less of an influence on evaluations of well established relationships. However, information processing analyses based on the AIM have contrary implications. As relationship longevity increases and affective involvement becomes deeper, partners also tend to develop a wider range of increasingly complex and heterogenous experiences. The more complex the informational base relevant to a social judgment, the more likely that temporary mood will have a significant influence on what is selectively remembered and used in judgments (Forgas, 1994). As long established relationships provide a richer and more elaborate informational base, the effects of mood on relationship judgments may not decline; they may even increase with relationship longevity.

Our first study was carried out in a realistic field setting. Based on prior work on relationship cognition (Fitness & Strongman, 1991; Noller & Ruzzene, 1991), and the AIM (Forgas, 1992a, 1995a), we predicted that positive mood should enhance and negative mood should decrease relationship evaluation, irrespective of relationship longevity. We used an unobtrusive method. Outside movie theaters, about 190 male and female subjects (mean length of relationships 50.42 months) who had just seen a happy or a sad film (the unobtrusive mood induction) were asked to evaluate the quality of their current, or most recent, romantic relationship on a number of dimensions.

As predicted, those in a temporary good mood judged their relationship significantly more positively than did those in a neutral or a bad mood irrespective of the sex of the respondent or the length of the relationship. These results establish that a temporary mood, generated by the experience of seeing a happy or a sad film, had a highly significant impact on the way people evaluate their intimate relationships. The counterintuitive finding of undiminished mood effects even in long-term relationships in particular is consistent with the AIM and shows that mood effects persist as long as the information base is sufficiently rich and complex and requires substantive processing.

Our second experiment used a laboratory procedure and more elaborate dependent measures, including evaluations of the relationship, the partner, and judgments about preferred conflict resolution strategies. Following exposure to happy, sad, or neutral video films, in an allegedly unrelated study 84 participants rated their current or most recent intimate relationship, their partner, and their preferred ways of dealing with relationship conflict. Mood significantly influenced all these judgments irrespective of relationship longevity. Results also showed that people in a positive mood evaluated their partners more positively and reported more intimacy than did control, or sad, subjects. As is consistent with the AIM, these results show that mood is more likely to bias judgments that require elaborate, constructive information processing.

The link between more complex information recruiting more substantive processing and greater mood effects was also confirmed in several later experiments. In these studies, happy or sad subjects were asked to form impressions about more or less typical relationships that required more or less substantive processing (Forgas, 1993, 1995b). Results showed a clear pattern of mood congruence, and the extent of mood effects was consistently greater when the relationship judged was more complex, ambiguous, or unusual. In terms of the AIM, such atypical relationships require longer and more constructive processing, allowing greater scope for affect-based associations to infuse the judgment (Forgas, 1995b, Exp. 3).

These studies confirm that affect infusion into relationship judgments crucially depends on the kind of information processing strategy people use. These results also explain the cognitive mechanisms whereby temporary moods may well give rise to an escalating spiral of negativity (or positivity) in relationship judgments, especially when both partners tend to get caught up in each other's moods (Gottman, 1979). A prior history of trust (Holmes, 1991), on the other hand, is likely to help couples to withstand the other's temporary affective oscillations. Affect may also have an impact on causal attributions for specific relationship conflicts, as our further studies found.

MOOD EFFECTS ON ATTRIBUTIONS FOR COMMUNICATION IN RELATIONSHIPS

Effective functioning in intimate relationships requires the accurate perception and interpretation of the actions of partners. Surprisingly, experimental research indicates that even this most basic attribution task may be subject to mood-based influences. In one experiment, we asked happy or sad participants to view and judge their videotaped interactions with a partner (Forgas, Bower, & Krantz, 1984). There was clear evidence for a mood-congruent bias in these judgments. The very same actions and behaviors that were seen as positive, skilled, and poised in a happy mood were interpreted as awkward, unskilled, and negative when in a bad mood. Later experiments also measured the time it took for such judgments to be produced. We found that mood-induced biases were indeed greater when longer and more construc-tive, elaborate processing strategies were used by judges (Forgas & Bower, 1987). Such mood effects also influence the way people explain more complex social behaviors, such as successes and failures. It turns out that happy people tend to find more lenient, generous explana-tions for such outcomes, whereas sad people consistently make more pessimistic, negative interpretations (Forgas, Bower, & Moylan, 1990).

Moods can also influence the likelihood of people committing attri-butional errors, according to some more recent studies (Forgas, 1998c). It turns out that happy people are more likely to think superficially and commit the fundamental attribution error (incorrectly inferring intentionality), whereas sad people pay more attention to situational constraints on behavior. These results suggest that mood may play a critical role in real-life relationship conflicts and partner communica-tion, as the next section will show.

Mood Effects on Attributions for Relationship Conflict

Dealing with conflict is an inevitable part of relationships, and explain-ing the causes of conflict is one of the more complex and demanding cognitive tasks partners face in everyday life. In several experiments, we examined one of the major counterintuitive predictions of the AIM: that mood should have a greater influence on attributions about complex and serious than on those about simple, relationship conflicts, because such events require more elaborate and constructive processing.

In each of these studies, people in happy, sad, or control moods made attributions for more or less serious real-life conflicts they experienced in their close relationships. In the first study, a field experiment (Forgas, 1994), 48 volunteer subjects read three short passages inducing a happy, sad, or neutral mood, before making attributions for happy and unhappy events in their current intimate relationships. People in a negative mood were more likely to blame themselves for conflict episodes, whereas happy subjects identified the causes of conflict in external factors such as their partners and the situation. Attributions for happy events showed a reverse pattern, with more internal attributions by happy rather than sad subjects for rewarding episodes. This pattern is consistent with our prediction of mood congruency in conflict attributions: Even slight variations in temporary mood, brought about by such everyday occurrences as reading a literary passage, can have a marked effect on attributions for real-life events in our relationships.

Experiment 2 (Forgas, 1994) used a different, unobtrusive mood induction. Subjects ($N = 162$) were approached on the street, immediately after (experimental groups) or before (control group) they saw selected happy or sad films. They were asked to complete a brief questionnaire attributing the causes of six common types of more or less serious conflicts in their intimate relationships. Sad subjects were again more likely to attribute conflict to internal, stable, and global causes, in effect blaming themselves, whereas happy subjects were less likely to blame themselves than were controls. Further, both positive and negative mood effects were greater on attributions for serious rather than simple conflicts. This pattern suggests that affect infusion is enhanced when more substantive processing is required to deal with problematic information.

In the third experiment (Forgas, 1994) mood was induced through happy, sad, or neutral videofilms. Subjects ($N = 96$) made attributions for real-life serious and simple conflicts recalled from their relationships. The processing latency for performing these judgments was also measured by a computer-administered procedure. Sad subjects were more likely to make internal, stable, and global attributions for conflict. There was also a two-way interaction between mood and conflict severity: Mood had a much greater impact on attributions for serious rather than simple conflicts. Such mood-induced biases in explaining serious conflicts may be a major source of difficulty in personal relationships (Fitness & Strongman, 1991; Forgas, 1991a; Noller & Ruzzene, 1991).

These three experiments produced convergent evidence that happy people are more likely to focus on external, unstable, and specific causes in their explanations of conflict, whereas the same incidents tend to be attributed to internal, stable, and global causes by sad partners. This attributional pattern is consistent with memory-based affect-priming explanations (Bower, 1991; Forgas, Bower, & Moylan, 1990). Of particular interest is the counterintuitive result that the more extensive processing required to think about complex and serious conflicts increased rather than reduced these mood effects. Because conflict is an inevitable feature of social relationships, these results suggest that sad partners are more likely to feel guilty and to blame internal, stable, and global causes for their conflicts, a strategy that is somewhat reminiscent of "learned helplessness" responses. Such affective distortions in conflict explanations may also be characteristic of chronic mood disorders such as depression.

Mood Effects on Strategic Communication

Language is the dominant medium of interpersonal behavior, and strategic messages such as requests play a crucial role in coordinating and maintaining our personal relationships. It is through the judicious use of requests that we achieve our goals, satisfy our needs, manage social situations, and coordinate social behaviors. Despite the great variety of requests in terms of content and form, most requests can be characterized in terms of a single critical dimension, their level of politeness or directness (Clark & Schunk, 1980; Gibbs, 1985).

Mood Effects on Communicating Requests

The everyday use of requests is dominated by one key pragmatic constraint: Requests must be sufficiently polite so as not to give offense yet be sufficiently direct to maximize compliance (Clark, 1989; Forgas, 1985b). Requesting in relationships can thus be an inherently problematic task in which the instrumental objectives (e.g., obtaining compliance) must be carefully balanced against interpersonal considerations (e.g., avoiding causing upset). To the extent that requesting involves substantive processing (Clark, 1989; Gibbs, 1985), mood should influence these communication strategies. In several experiments we predicted that people should adopt a more confident, direct request strategy when experiencing a positive mood, owing to the selective priming of positive thoughts and associations (Forgas, 1998b, 1999a,b). Negative mood, in turn, should produce more cautious, polite, and indirect requests. Furthermore these effects should be greater when the situation is complex and demanding and thus calls for more elaborate processing.

In the first study (Forgas, 1999a, Exp. 1), participants (N = 120) were asked to recall and write about happy and sad experiences to induce good and bad moods. Next, in what they believed was an unrelated study, they were asked to select more or less polite request forms they would prefer to use in easy and in difficult interpersonal situations. Mood had a marked influence: Happy participants preferred markedly more direct, impolite requests, whereas sad persons chose more indirect, polite request alternatives. Further, mood effects were greater in more difficult and demanding request situations that required more extensive, substantive processing. We obtained very similar results in a follow-up experiment (Forgas, 1999a, Exp. 2), in which participants (N = 96) could formulate their own open-ended requests, which were subsequently rated for politeness and directness.

Experiment 3 (Forgas, 1999a) sought to confirm and extend these findings in several directions. After a mood induction using happy or sad films, participants wrote down in their own words the requests they would use in a variety of more or less difficult interpersonal situations. Their words were subsequently rated and analyzed in terms of a number of features, such as their politeness and elaboration. We also assessed their recall memory for their requests, as a measure of the kind of processing strategies used.

Results showed that happy people used more direct and impolite and less elaborate requests than did control or sad subjects. As predicted, mood effects on request politeness were also significantly greater in more difficult situations. An analysis of recall data confirmed that requests formulated in difficult and demanding situations were processed more extensively and were remembered better, and it is precisely these requests that were most influenced by mood. These findings establish that moods can influence not only people's thoughts, judgments, and attributions, but also their strategic communication in relationships. The results support the prediction that sad persons form more pessimistic associations and thus use more cautious and polite forms, whereas happy people adopt more direct and confident communication strategies.

In a further study, we asked participants to select more or less polite request alternatives they would use in each of 16 different realistic situations (Forgas, 1999b, Exp. 1). Mood effects were greatest on preferences for direct, unconventional requests that were most likely to violate cultural conventions of politeness and should recruit the most substantive, elaborate processing strategies. These findings further confirm that mood effects on communication are highly dependent on processing strategies.

Similar effects were also obtained in unobtrusive experiments looking at naturally produced requests of the kind that frequently occur in real-life relationships (Forgas, 1999b, Exp. 2). Sad people used more polite, friendly, and elaborate forms, and happy people used more direct and less polite forms. Sad persons also delayed their requests longer, and they used more indirect and hedging forms, as was consistent with their more cautious, defensive behavioral strategies primed by their mood. The analysis of recall showed that mood effects were greater when requests received more elaborate processing, as indicated by superior memory. These studies offer clear evidence that verbal communication in relationships is likely to show marked mood dependence as long as a degree of open, constructive processing is required.

Mood Effects on Responding to Requests

Affective states may not only influence strategic communication but can also have an impact on how people respond to verbal messages directed at them. Responding to a request is a constructive task that requires a rapid reaction. In several experiments (Forgas, 1998b), we investigated the influence of mood on how people react to more or less polite requests directed at them. Once again, a realistic unobtrusive strategy was used. Students entering a library found pictures or text placed on their desks designed to induce good or bad moods. A few minutes later, another student (a confederate) made an unexpected polite or impolite request for several sheets of paper. Subjects' responses were noted, and a short time later a second confederate asked participants to complete a brief questionnaire indicating their perception and recall of the request and the requester. As predicted, we found that people in a negative mood formed a more critical, negative view of the requests and were less inclined to comply than were positive mood participants. In contrast, positive mood resulted in greater compliance and a more generous evaluation of the request and the requester. There is every reason to believe that responses to impromptu requests in real-life personal relationships are likely to be influenced by the very same kinds of mood effects.

Interestingly, mood effects on responses were stronger when the request was impolite and unconventional. Such requests violate expectations and are likely to require more substantive processing. Conventional, polite requests, which can be processed more routinely, were not remembered as accurately later on and were also less influenced by mood. These findings confirm that affective states can have a strong mood-congruent influence not only on the production of requests, but also on how people respond to requests directed at them. As is consistent with the AIM, these results also show that mood effects on communication are mediated by the processing strategies that people employ.

Mood Effects on Bargaining and Negotiation

The results so far discussed suggest that mood has a significant influence on the way people produce and respond to strategic messages such as requests. The same kinds of mood effects may also influence planning and execution of more complex, elaborate encounters in relationships. Such a link between affect and strategic interactions was demonstrated in a series of studies investigating mood effects on bargaining and negotiation (Forgas, 1998a). In these studies, we asked happy, neutral, and sad participants to engage in an informal and in a formal negotiating task. Results showed that participants in a positive mood set higher and more ambitious goals for themselves, formed higher expectations about the forthcoming encounter, and also formulated specific action plans that were more optimistic, cooperative, and integrative than did neutral or negative mood participants. Furthermore, they actually behaved more cooperatively when bargaining and were more willing to seek and find integrative solutions and to offer and reciprocate deals than were those in a negative mood. Surprisingly, positive mood also resulted in more successful actual outcomes. These results illustrate how even slight changes in mood can produce a significant influence on the way strategic encounters are planned and executed in relationships.

In terms of the AIM, thinking about and planning a strategic encounter is by definition a complex, indeterminate, and personally involving cognitive task, in which substantive processing is required. Positive mood should selectively prime more positive thoughts and associations and should ultimately lead to the formulation of more optimistic expectations and more cooperative strategies. In contrast, negative mood should prime more pessimistic, negative thoughts and associations, leading to less cooperative and more acrimonious interactions.

SUMMARY AND CONCLUSIONS

The evidence reviewed here suggests that affect plays an important and largely underestimated role in how people think about their relationships and their partners, how they explain and attribute the causes for their conflicts, and how they communicate with each other. Attribution judgment, decision making, communication, and interaction lie at the very heart of personal relationships. The way we perform these tasks has a fundamental influence on whether our relationships progress or decline. Recent research now clearly shows that affect is an essential influence on adaptive thinking and decision making (Damasio, 1994).

The AIM and supporting evidence presented here strongly suggest that mood states have a subtle and highly context-dependent influence on people's thoughts and behaviors in relationships. This model predicts that affect infusion into judgments and behaviors depends on what kind of processing strategy is used by a person. An important and counterintuitive prediction of the AIM for relationship cognition is that as more extensive and substantive processing is recruited by complex tasks, affect infusion should be enhanced rather than inhibited (Forgas, 1995b). The affect priming hypothesis, in particular (Bower, 1981, 1991), offers a powerful and parsimonious account of many mood-congruent phenomena, including judgmental and communication effects in relationships (Bower & Forgas, 2000).

However, according to the AIM, mood congruence is not necessarily an all-pervasive phenomenon. Affect infusion should be reduced or reversed whenever people adopt a highly targeted, motivated processing strategy that interferes with their open and constructive use of mood-primed thoughts and associations. For example, we found no mood-congruent bias when people made a personally relevant choice and were highly motivated to obtain a specific outcome (Forgas, 1991a). Sometimes, mood congruence may also be a self-correcting process. It appears that most people have effective strategies for limiting the distorting effects of mood on their thoughts and judgments. In recent studies, we found that high self-esteem was positively related to people's ability to limit the effects of negative moods on their thoughts and judgments (Forgas, Johnson, & Ciarrochi, 1998).

Personal relationships represent a subtle combination of affective, cognitive, and motivational processes. While much prior attention has been devoted to analyzing the behavioral and cognitive aspects of relationships, the role of affect in attributions and communication in relationships received less than adequate attention. It now appears that subtle differences in information processing strategies can play a major role in explaining whether moods will influence a particular relationship judgment or behavior. I hope that this discussion will be useful in clarifying the characteristics and conditions conducive to affect infusion into attributions and communication in relationships.

REFERENCES

Argyle, M., & Henderson, M. (1985). *The anatomy of relationships,* Harmionsworth, UK: Penguin.

Berkowitz, L., Jaffee, S., Jo, F., & Troccoli, B. T. (2000). On the correction of feeling-induced judgmental biases. In J. P. Forgas (Ed.), *Feeling and thinking: The role of affect in social cognition* (pp. 131–152). New York: Cambridge University Press.

Bower, G. H. (1981). Mood and memory. *American Psychologist, 36,* 129–148.

Bower, G. H. (1991). Mood congruity of social judgments. In J. P. Forgas (Ed.), *Emotion and social judgments* (pp. 31–53). New York: Pergamon Press.

Bower, G. H., & Forgas, J. P. (2000). Mood and social memory. In J. P. Forgas (Ed.) *The handbook of affect and social cognition.* Mahwah, NJ: Erlbaum.

Bradbury, T., & Fincham, F. (1987). Affect and cognition in close relationships: Towards an integrative model. *Cognition and Emotion, 1,* 59–87.

Bradbury, T., & Fincham, F. (1992). Attributions and behavior in marital interaction. *Journal of Personality and Social Psychology, 63,* 613–628.

Clark, H. H. (1989). Language use and language users. In G. Lindzey & E. Aronson (Eds.), *The handbook of social psychology* (Vol. 2, pp. 179–231). New York: Random House.

Clark, H. H., & Schunk, D. H. (1980). Polite responses to polite requests. *Cognition, 8,* 111–143.

Clore, G. L., & Byrne, D. (1974). The reinforcement model of attraction. In T. L. Huston (Ed.), *Foundations of interpersonal attraction* (pp. 143–170). New York: Academic Press.

Clore, G. L., Schwarz, N., & Conway, M. (1994). Affective causes and consequences of social information processing. In R. S. Wyer & T. K. Srull (Eds.) *Handbook of social cognition* (pp. 323–417). 2nd Ed. Hillsdale, NJ: Erlbaum.

Damasio, A. R. (1994). *Descartes' error.* New York: Grosset Putnam.

Feshbach, S., & Singer, R. D. (1957). The effects of fear arousal and suppression of fear upon social perception. *Journal of Abnormal and Social Psychology, 55,* 283–288.

Fiedler, K. (1991). On the task, the measures, and the mood in research on affect and social cognition. In J. P. Forgas (Ed.), *Emotion and social judgments* (pp. 83–107). Oxford: Pergamon.

Fitness, J., & Strongman, K. (1991). Affect in close relationships. In G. J. O. Fletcher & F. D. Fincham (Eds.), *Cognition in close relationships* (pp. 175–203). Hillsdale, NJ: Erlbaum.

Fletcher, G. J. O., & Fincham, F. (Eds.). (1991). *Cognition in close relationships.* Hillsdale. NJ: Erlbaum.

Fletcher, G. J. O., Fitness, J., & Blampied, N. M. (1990). The link between attribution and happiness in close relationships: The roles of depression and explanatory style. *Journal of Social and Clinical Psychology, 9,* 243–255.

Forgas, J. P. (1979). *Social episodes: The study of interaction routines.* London: Academic Press.

Forgas, J. P. (1985a). *Interpersonal behavior: The psychology of social interaction.* Oxford, UK: Pergamon Press.

Forgas, J. P. (Ed.). (1985b). *Language and social situations.* New York: Springer.

Forgas, J. P. (Ed.) (1991a). *Emotion in social judgments.* Oxford, UK: Pergamon Press.

Forgas, J. P. (1991b). Affective influences on partner choice: The role of mood in social decisions. *Journal of Personality and Social Psychology, 61,* 208–220.

Forgas, J. P. (1991c). Affect and cognition in close relationships. In G. Fletcher & F. D. Fincham (Eds.), *Cognition in close relationships.* Hillsdale, NJ: Erlbaum.

Forgas, J. P. (1992a). Affect in social judgments and decisions: A multiprocess model. In M. Zanna (Ed.) (pp. 154–174). *Advances in experimental social psychology* (Vol. 25, pp. 227–275). New York: Academic Press.

Forgas, J. P. (1992b). On bad mood and peculiar people: Affect and person typicality in impression formation. *Journal of Personality and Social Psychology, 62,* 863–875.

Forgas, J. P. (1993). On making sense of odd couples: Mood effects on the perception of mismatched relationships. *Personality and Social Psychology Bulletin, 19,* 59–71.

Forgas, J. P. (1994). Sad and guilty? Affective influences on the explanation of conflict episodes. *Journal of Personality and Social Psychology, 66,* 56–68.

Forgas, J. P. (1995a). Mood and judgment: The affect infusion model (AIM). *Psychological Bulletin, 117,* 39–66.

Forgas, J. P. (1995b). Strange couples: Mood effects on judgments and memory about prototypical and atypical targets. *Personality and Social Psychology Bulletin, 21,* 747–765.

Forgas, J. P. (1998a). On feeling good and getting your way: Mood effects on negotiation strategies and outcomes. *Journal of Personality and Social Psychology, 74,* 565–577.

Forgas, J. P. (1998b). Asking nicely? Mood effects on responding to more or less polite requests. *Personality and Social Psychology Bulletin, 24,* 173–185.

Forgas, J. P. (1998c). Happy and mistaken? Mood effects on the fundamental attribution error. *Journal of Personality and Social Psychology, 75,* 318–331.

Forgas, J. P. (1999a). On feeling good and being rude: Affective influences on language use and request formulations. *Journal of Personality and Social Psychology, 76,* 928–939

Forgas, J. P. (1999b). Feeling and speaking: Mood effects on verbal communication strategies. *Personality and Social Psychology Bulletin, 25,* 850–863.

Forgas, J. P. (Ed.) (2000). *Feeling and thinking: The role of affect in social cognition.* New York: Cambridge University Press.

Forgas, J. P., & Bower, G. H. (1987). Mood effects on person perception judgments. *Journal of Personality and Social Psychology, 53,* 53–60.

Forgas, J. P., Bower, G. H., & Krantz, S. (1984). The influence of mood on perceptions of social interactions. *Journal of Experimental Social Psychology, 20,* 497–513.

Forgas, J. P., Bower, G. H., & Moylan, S. J. (1990). Praise or blame? Mood effects on attributions for success or failure. *Journal of Personality and Social Psychology, 59,* 809–819.

Forgas, J. P., & Fiedler, K. (1996). Us and them: Mood effects on intergroup discrimination. *Journal of Personality and Social Psychology, 70,* 36–52.

Forgas, J. P., Johnson, R., & Ciarrochi, J. (1998). Affect control and affect infusion: A multi-process account of mood management and personal control. In M. Kofta, G. Weary, & G. Sedek (Eds.), *Personal control in action. Cognitive and motivational mechanisms* (pp. 155–189). New York: Plenum Press.

Forgas, J. P., Levinger, G., & Moylan, S. (1994). Feeling good and feeling close: Mood effects on the perception of intimate relationships. *Personal Relationships, 2,* 165–184.

Frijda, N. H. (1986). *The emotions.* Cambridge, UK: Cambridge University Press.

Gibbs, R. (1985). Situational conventions and requests. In J. P. Forgas (Ed.), *Language and social situations* (pp. 97–113). New York: Springer.

Gottman, J. M. (1979). *Marital interaction: Experimental investigations.* New York: Academic Press.

Gottman, J. M., & Levenson, R. (1986). Assessing the role of emotion in marriage. *Behavioral Assessment, 8,* 31–48.

Griffitt, W. (1970). Environmental effects on interpersonal behavior: Ambient effective temperature and attraction. *Journal of Personality and Social Psychology, 15,* 240–244.

Holmes, J. G. (1991). Trust and the appraisal process in close relationships. In W. H. Jones & D. Perlman (Eds.), *Advances in personal relationships* (Vol. 2, pp. 57–104). London: Jessica Kingsley.

LeDoux, J. E. (1996) *The emotional brain: The mysterious underpinnings of emotional life.* New York: Simon & Schuster.

Mayer, J. D., Gaschke, Y. N., Braverman, D. L., & Evans T. W. (1992). Mood congruent judgment is a general effect. *Journal of Personality and Social Psychology, 63,* 119–132.

Niedenthal, P., & Halberstadt, J. (2000). Emotional categorization. In J. P. Forgas (Ed.). *Feeling and thinking: The role of affect in social cognition and behavior* (pp. 357–387). New York: Cambridge University Press.

Noller, P., & Ruzzene, M. (1991). Communication in marriage: The influence of affect and cognition. In G. J. O. Fletcher & F. D. Fincham (Eds.). *Cognition in close relationships* (pp. 175–203). Hillsdale, NJ: Erlbaum.

Salovey, P., O'Leary, A., Stretton, M., Fishkin, S., & Drake, C. A. (1991). Influence of mood on judgments about health and illness. In J. P. Forgas (Ed.), *Emotion and social judgments* (pp. 241–263). Oxford: Pergamon.

Schachter, S. (1959). *The psychology of affiliation.* Stanford, CA: Stanford University Press.

Schwarz, N., & Clore, G. L. (1988). How do I feel about it? The informative function of affective states. In K. Fiedler & J. P. Forgas (Eds.), *Affect, cognition, and social behavior* (pp. 44–62). Toronto: Hogrefe.

Sedikides, C. (1994). Incongruent effects of sad mood on self-conception valence: It's a matter of time. *European Journal of Social Psychology, 24,* 161–172.

Sedikides, C. (1995). Central and peripheral self-conceptions are differentially influenced by mood: Tests of the differential sensitivity hypothesis. *Journal of Personality and Social Psychology, 69,* 759–777.

Smith, C. A., & Kirby, E. (2000). Appraisal and memory: Toward a process model of emotion-eliciting situations. In J. P. Forgas (Ed.). *Feeling and thinking: The role of affect in social cognition* (pp. 83–108). New York: Cambridge University Press.

Zajonc, R. B. (1980). Feeling and thinking: Preferences need no inferences. *American Psychologist, 35,* 151–175.

CHAPTER TWO

Communication and Attribution

An Exploration of the Effects of Music and Mood on Intimate Couples' Verbal and Nonverbal Conflict Resolution Behaviors

James M. Honeycutt and Michael E. Eidenmuller

Over the past four decades, academic fields, including cultural anthropology, social psychology, sociology, and communication have shown marked interest in the relationships between music and being. More recently, the relationship has been the subject of intensive exploration and theoretical development in the field of music therapy. Music therapy is the prescribed use of music in order to restore, maintain, and improve emotional, physiological, physical, and spiritual well-being. Among its strategies and objectives, and particularly relevant for our purposes, music therapy attempts to induce particular kinds of cognitive and affective mental states in order to enhance communicative and social skills.

This chapter examines attributions made about music and communication in the context of interpersonal interaction. More particularly, we report the results of exploratory research involving multiple data sets and triangulated methods on questions regarding the potential effects of music on mood, as well as attributions made about music and communication while couples are discussing relational issues. Our study begins by examining some of the ways that researchers conceptualize and measure the relationship between music and communication. We then present the results of discrete data sets in which attributions of the effects of music on intimate couples' conflict management skills are made both by the couples themselves and by independent external observers. Finally, we propose a theoretical link between music therapy and interpersonal-intrapersonal communication in the form of self-talk and imagined interactions.

James M. Honeycutt is professor in the communications studies department at Louisiana State University, Baton Rouge, LA, 70803-3923. Michael E. Eidenmuller is assistant professor of speech communication at the University of Texas at Tyler. James Honeycutt can be contacted at *sphone@lsu.edu* or at his Internet relational communication column, *www.batonrougemall.com* at the "Relationships 2000" icon.

MUSIC AND COMMUNICATION

For present purposes, we define communication as the dynamic process of constructing and attributing *meaning* by and among humans, who by nature respond to symbols. Music is a phenomenal presence comprising unique combinations of raw sound and attendant symbolic attributes expressing a determinate form. So conceived, music has long been recognized for its communicative power on the individual and collective personalities of listeners (Barzun, 1958; Chaffee, 1985; Frith, 1981, 1996; Lull, 1985, 1992; Merriam, 1964).

Merritt, McGregot, and Bell (1996) have explained the effect of music vis-à-vis the interaction of cognitive-affective functioning and personality:

> The patterns in the music stimulate emotional patterns on different levels simultaneously. As we hear the tension and release in the music, it reminds us of different physical, emotional, and mental responses that have the same energy pattern. ... Music, always in constant movement, shifts and changes, and we, as resonators, shift and change along with it. (Merritt et al., 1996, p. 116)

A number of studies reflect ties between emotions and music. Fried and Berkowitz (1979), for example, found that individuals listening to "soothing" music showed more helpful behaviors following the listening experience than did individuals exposed to aversive music. Winner (1982) demonstrated how a variety of listeners with different musical preferences such as country, classical, rock, soul, or jazz show high agreement in categorizing music using emotional labels. Research by Trunk (1982) and Slattery (1984) reveals that the labeling of emotional content in music occurs as early as age 5.

Research specifically exploring the nonverbal dimension of music exposure acknowledges that music produces powerful sensory stimulation and tactile sensation through sheer sonic vibration. This, in turn, promotes a variety of nonverbal behaviors that are associated both with the sound vibrations themselves and with the symbolic meaning attributed to them. Thus, McFarland (1984) finds that individuals listening to tension-producing music while interpreting ambiguous pictures reported more anxiety and frustration than those listening to calming music.

INDUCING MOOD IN INDIVIDUALS THROUGH MUSIC

Interest in the relationship between music and mood has produced a substantial body of experimental research, in which music is used to express, evoke, or augment feelings of sadness and happiness, as well as depressed or elated mood states. A number of studies within this literature have been devoted to developing reliable techniques for inducing mood in the laboratory to study potential beneficial outcomes, such as enhancing positive emotions or minimizing depressed mood (Clark, 1983).

One particularly prominent technique, initially developed by Sutherland, Newman, and Rachman (1982), is known as musical mood induction. This technique exposes individuals to "suggestive" music and asks them to use the music as a background for their moods. Clark (1983) reviews a number of studies using the musical induction procedure in which individuals were placed into "depressing" versus "elating" music (treatment) conditions. For example, participants listening to depressing music, such as the *poco allegretto* movement of Brahms' Symphony No. 3, reported higher levels of sadness (Clark, 1983; Sutherland et al., 1982). Participants exposed to depressing music also showed higher levels of anxiety. Participants who were exposed to elating music (e.g., Dvorak's "Romanza" from his Czech Suite) generally indicated less despondency than those in the depressing condition (Clark & Teasdale, 1982). Clark (1983) also reviewed a few studies that found that individuals listening to depressing music preferred isolated and passive activities to social and active activities in contrast to those listening to elating music.

The musical induction procedure has been criticized for eliciting demand characteristics; that is, the music itself will not automatically induce a desired mood state (Clark, 1983). Yet, Pignatiello, Camp, and Rasar (1986) found that music produced affect differences between elated and depressed groups without demand characteristics. Participants were randomly assigned to one of three mood groups (depressed, neutral, and elated) and listened to musical selections that had previously been judged on a 7-point Likert scale ranging from very depressing to very elating. The participants were not told that the music was designed to alter emotional affect. The elated group differed from the depressed group in that they attributed their mood of feeling more positive in conjunction with the valence of the background music.

MUSIC MOOD WHEEL

The music mood wheel, originally introduced by Hevner (1937), is a methodological device used to measure the effects of music on emotion. The mood wheel is a selection of 66 adjectives in eight related groups for attributing emotional expressions of music. Figure 2.1 contains the wheel.

Directions: Please tell us what you thought about the music in the background. Following are some adjectives in various groups. This is known as the mood wheel. If the music did not affect you at all or you did not notice it, then leave all of the adjectives blank. Only circle the adjectives that really reflect how the music made you feel. *Source:* Adapted from Hevner (1937).

6
merry, joyous, happy,
cheerful, bright

7
exhilarated, soaring, triumphant,
dramatic, passionate, sensational,
agitated, exciting, impetuous, restless

5
humorous, playful, whimsical,
fanciful, quaint, sprightly, delicate,
light, graceful

8
vigorous, robust, empathic, martial,
ponderous, majestic, exalting

4
lyrical, leisurely, satisfying, serene,
tranquil, quiet, soothing

1
spiritual, lofty, awe-inspiring, dignified,
sacred, solemn, sober, serious

3
dreamy, yielding, tender, sentimental,
longing, yearning, pleading, plaintive

2
pathetic, doleful, sad, mournful, tragic, melancholy,
frustrated, depressing, gloomy, heavy, dark

Figure 2.1.   Arrangement of Adjectives for Recording the Mood Effect of Music

The eight groups of adjectives are arranged in a counterclockwise direction along a solemn–exalting continuum, such that the adjectives in a group are compatible with each other, and any two adjacent groups have some adjectives in common. Groups at diagonally opposite points in the circle are more dissimilar. Hence, mood transitions between adjacent groups are made without abrupt changes. Participants listen to a musical selection, then check the mood adjective group that they feel most corresponds to the mood of the music. The circle can be used as a continuous scale by instructing participants to circle as few or as many adjectives in any group as they feel symbolize the affective tone of the music. The mood wheel essentially asks listeners to attribute emotional affect in relation to the musical pieces that they are listening to.

ATTRIBUTIONS ABOUT THE FUNCTIONS OF MUSIC IN MUSIC THERAPY

As mentioned previously, music therapy involves the selective prescription of music to ameliorate a variety of psychosocial disorders.

Smeijsters (1995) conducted a study about the functions of music in music therapy. One category of functions was motor movement, such as singing, dancing, or moving to music. Another category was compensatory, such as getting into a better mood, being pepped up, letting off steam, feeling more at ease, feeling less lonely, and filling the silence. A third category of functions included physiological reactions, such as gooseflesh, stomach pains, heart palpitations, and respiratory changes. Smeijsters reports that 65% of his respondents used the compensatory function of music to get into a better mood. He also indicates that only a minority of individuals (25%) reported that music functioned to calm them down. He further reports that music functions to bring relaxation, replenish energy, and serve as an aid to intrapersonal communication.

Formal music therapy is administered by trained therapists who employ music strategically for cognitive and affective purposes, most always with the conscious awareness and agreement of the participant(s). Many individuals, however, implement music consciously in a variety of interpersonal contexts to serve some of the same cognitive and affective needs. Indeed, people seem well aware of what music can do for them and employ it actively in ways that facilitate a variety of communicative purposes (Lull, 1985, 1992). Given this, it is important to investigate the kinds of descriptions of and attributions about music that are offered when intimate couples are induced to communicate about pressing interpersonal issues in the presence of music not chosen by them and where the choice to alter or eliminate the music is beyond their immediate control.

In an effort to explore this question, we observed separately and in an informal environment two heterosexual couples who were prompted to discuss and/or argue about an interpersonal issue deemed important by them to the success of their relationships while music was playing in the background. This was the first investigation of attributions about music by couples communicating about serious issues in their relationship.

The couples were brought into a communication laboratory used for simulating particular types of close-quartered, external communication environments. The laboratory was set up to look like a modestly adorned apartment living room, including a small stereo system with elevated speakers that were 15 feet removed from where the couples were asked to communicate. The experiment was so designed that the music was already playing when the couples came into the room. The volume of the music was loud enough to be audible but not so loud as to be obtrusive. At no time was either couple asked to attend to the music while they were discussing their relational issues. The couples engaged this process for 10 to 15 minutes, after which time they completed a questionnaire. The questionnaire contained the musical mood wheel and items pertaining to present mood state, the relative levels of awareness of and attendance to the music, and whether the music had soothing or aggravating effects on their emotions.

The first couple we observed were in their early 20s. They had known each other for 7 years and were formally engaged. The woman chose to discuss her partner's attitude about having children. She wanted to delay having children for 5 or 6 years after they were married. In contrast, her partner was unable to think of or to initiate a conversation on any problem in their relationship. The second couple had known each other for 4 years and had been married for 18 months. The problematic issue for the wife concerned her husband's failure to disclose his personal feelings on a variety of intimacy matters. For him, the problematic issue was his wife's treatment of his parents, in-laws, and friends. Neither couple had ever participated in communication therapy or music therapy.

The first couple was exposed to Ravel's *Bolero*. The tempo of this piece is relatively moderate. Its most outstanding musical feature is a melodic motif repeated 18 times in succession. With each successive completion of the piece's melodic motif, the instrumental arrangement changes, different instruments or instrument combinations picking up both the motif and the harmonic backing. Although less apparent in the beginning, there is a palpable increase in the piece's intensity and volume with each successive turn of its melodic motif. Using the musical mood wheel, the woman rated the music as somewhat elating. She also circled four adjectives from group 7 of the mood wheel, including triumphant, passionate, agitated, and restless. She checked robust from group 8, soothing from group 4, and happy from group 6. The man checked two adjectives in group 7, impetuous and agitated. He also checked majestic from group 8.

The second couple listened to Stravinsky's *Rite of Spring*. This piece is quite dissonant in comparison with *Bolero*, and its respondents have indicated its propensity to incite restless, agitated, sensational, and passionate moods from group 7 of the mood wheel (Merritt et al., 1996). The husband and wife reported in the debriefing that they noticed it and described it as elating. Their comments reflect how individuals who are aware of their moods may attribute it to the music. This reflects the ultimate attribution bias in which we make external attributions to objects in the environment for describing our own behaviors and moods. We concentrate on events and behaviors that surround us rather than being introspective and concentrating on ourselves. Yet, we attribute others' behaviors to internal causes because our attention tends to center on them to the exclusion of the surrounding environment (Ross, 1977). In both types of attribution, attention is centered externally; yet for oneself, the focus of external attention is the surrounding objects in the environment, whereas the object of attention when observing other people is the people.

The husband reported feelings of passion, exhilaration, triumph, and excitement from group 7 of the mood wheel. He reported vigor from group 8 and satisfaction from group 4. The wife reported similar feelings from group 7, as well as feeling restless from group 7 and feeling majestic from group 8. Hence, the music affected their emotions similarly, with a few slight differences.

This couple's attributions also reflect what Olson (1977) has referred to as the insider's perspective, in which couples report on their affect, motivations, and beliefs about each other's feelings or behavior. The outsider's perspective reflects individuals outside of the relationship who make attributions about the insiders. Knapp and Vangelisti (1992) report how couples may be seen by outsiders or observers as having a special relationship with few problems, but there may be underlying problems that are not known to others. Hence, this is information known to the couple but not to outsiders. From the outsider's perspective, there may be attributions made about the couple that are known to the outsiders but not the couple.

THE ISO PRINCIPLE OF MUSIC THERAPY

According to the ISO principle of music therapy, a person's mood state may be altered on exposure to music that evokes or tends to evoke a similar mood state. The principle first assumes that individuals attend to music selectively that is relatively congruent with their current mood state. At a subconscious level a process of identification occurs to the extent that one's moods may, by degrees, be modified.

Variations in certain musical properties, including tempo and dynamic intensity, encourage or reproduce variations in an individual's mood state. At its most potent, the vectoring power of music is such that mood states may actually vary, not simply by degrees across the same mood state, but also across altogether different mood states, from one affective pole (anger) to its opposite (joy), for instance. Finally, the use of the ISO principle in music therapy suggests that music can be used to energize and facilitate structural order in couples' argumentative patterns, with changes in mood states reflecting a progressive pattern that may be similarly expressed in verbal and nonverbal behavior. For these reasons, *Bolero* was appropriate for our mood-inducing procedure. The piece's instrumental changes and ever-increasing intensity are calculated to move the listener through a series of more or less subtle changes in mood, not at all unlike the kind of transposition in tone, tempo, and intensity we hoped for and to some extent observed in our participants' discursive exchanges.

Empirical evidence does offer support for the ISO principle in music therapy. Behne (1986), for instance, found that angry individuals picked aggressive, fast, and exciting music and thereby attempted to vent their frustrations. Sad individuals wanted music that fit their sadness. More importantly, practices consistent with the ISO principle have an established following among professional music therapists. Merritt et al. (1996) indicate that if one is feeling irritable, hyperactivated, or edgy, the musical therapist starts with music that is not too quiet so that the listener may transfer some of his or her anxiety over to the music. (There is a parallel here known in clinical psychology as the transference effect, in which individuals in therapy often transfer feelings of anger about others to the psychotherapist.) If a person is feeling depressed, then a quiet piece of music would be played at a slow tempo, such as Pachelbel's Canon in D or the second movement from one of Bach's Brandenburg concertos. If he or she is feeling joyful or wants to celebrate, Vivaldi's *The Four Seasons* has been recommended. If a person is feeling angry, Mozart's *Eine Kleine Nachtmusik* or the first or third movement of his Symphony No. 41 in C has been used (see Merritt et al., 1996, for sample pieces of music and accompanying emotional states derived from the musical mood wheel).

ATTRIBUTIONS OF THE EFFECTS OF MUSIC BY OBSERVERS

To help investigate how people make sense of or provide attributions for the effect of music on behavior, we used a pair of graduate students trained in nonverbal behaviors to code the tapes of 18 dating couples listening to positive music while arguing about problems in their relationship. Intercoder reliability averages were above .90 for coding use of self- and object adaptors, gaze, preening behaviors, nonverbal illustrators such as gesturing while speaking, body lean, and posture.

In this trial, we again configured the communication laboratory to reflect a relatively informal communicative environment. This time, however, we introduced contemporary popular songs into the context. We constructed two different cassette tapes, each of which contained 45 minutes worth of continuously playing music. The first tape contained only "positive" or "elating" songs; the second tape contained only "negative" or "doleful" songs. Sample artists included Mariah Carey, Madonna, Celine Dion, UB40, and Cheap Trick. Songs were chosen according to the suggestions of university students and validated externally by a popular local radio disc jockey (at an urban contemporary music station), on whose final judgment we relied for the relative mood-inducing properties of each song as well as for the relative order of their appearance on the tape.

To minimize the likelihood that the atypical consistency in the emotional pattern of the music would draw attention to itself, we asked the disc jockey to provide verbal voiceovers at strategic points on each tape. The content of the disc jockey's voiceovers ranged from articulation of fictional call letters to brief previews of the song set to follow. The two tapes we created were thus designed to simulate a real-time or live instantiation of an adult contemporary music station.

On entering the laboratory, the couples were instructed to discuss a problem with each other and further to discuss how the problem might be resolved. They also filled out a survey asking about imagined interactions during their relationship (Honeycutt, 1989, 1991, 1995; Honeycutt & Wiemann, 1999), as well as about the most problematic issue in their relationship. Music was playing in the background from the onset. They were told that the music helped the research assistants pass the time while waiting for couples to show up. Interestingly, not a single couple asked that the music be turned off. This provides support for the pervasiveness of music, particularly in the lives of young adults, as background, contextual stimuli.

A common observation by the coders was that the communicators would occasionally rock back and forth to the rhythm of the music. Some individuals tapped their fingers to the music. For example, while a Celine Dion song was playing, a man moved closer to his girlfriend while commenting that he liked the song. Another man rocked in his chair when the song, "The Flame," came on. He used nonverbal illustrators when he spoke. The coders noted that some women commented on the "happy, love music" and leaned forward to their boyfriends.

There were a few sex differences in attributions about the effect of music on the couples. The coders noted that the music seemed to have more of a subconscious influence on the women even though a few individuals lip-synced to the lyrics regardless of sex. However, women made more comments about the music than men. These observations are compatible with the popular music and communication research finding that women show stronger preferences than males for mainstream popular music. They are also consistent with the finding that music is more functional for women in managing, producing, and sustaining various mood states (Gantz, Gartenberg, Pearson, & Schiller, 1978; Lull, 1992). Similar research has also revealed that women spend more time interpreting the meaning of the lyrics than men (Roe, 1985). Even though the women appeared to notice the background music, they also were more focused on the conversations. In contrast, the men showed more signs of awareness of their surroundings.

Our coders believed that using instrumental music (or classical type music with no lyrics), which is not as recognizable by the individuals, may be desirable in order to rule out effects of familiarity with the recording artist. For example, three women stated that they did not like Mariah Carey regardless of her lyrics. We believe that instrumental music may be conducive to conflict resolution because the harmonics, rhythm, and intensity involved are such that individuals can mimic these attributes verbally or nonverbally without having consciously or subconsciously to process language in the form of lyrics. The combination of lyrics and music introduces an additional cognitive presence, and hence the possibility of unhelpful cognitive disturbance, into the communicative environment.

On the other hand, popular music is, and has been for some time, designed for "artificial" rhythmic enhancement. Drum kits, drum machines, and other rhythmic devices, when they are not the primary focus of the song, are typically "up-mixed" in proportion to other the other instruments. Their characteristic polyrhythmic and hyperrepetitive patterns are woven into the song's soundscape to facilitate motor mimicry in the body. In the context of interpersonal conflict, however, we believe that the relatively natural rhythmic undulations of instrumental music would of seem more conducive to the kind of normative verbal and nonverbal behavioral responses we desired to elicit from our participants.

OBSERVER ATTRIBUTIONS OF THE EFFECTS OF MUSIC ON RELATIONAL TOPOI AND NONVERBAL COMMUNICATION

Burgoon and Hale (1987) developed an instrument to rate eight themes of relationships that actors and observers attribute to couples and that are essential to defining the relationship. One of these dimensions is immediacy or affection, in which the couple display interest, attraction, and involvement in their interaction. Another theme is similarity–depth, in which the partners make each other try to feel similar and act like good friends. A third theme is receptivity–trust, which communicates sincerity, trust, willingness to listen, and being receptive to each other's communication. A fourth theme is composure, in which the partners are calm, poised, relaxed, and comfortable when talking with each other. A fifth theme is formality, in which communication is perceived as formal, ritualized, or poised. A sixth dimension is dominance, which is concerned with controlling the conversation, trying to persuade the partner, or winning the other's favor. A seventh dimension is equality, which reflects cooperation in the conversation and treating each other as equals. Burgoon and Hale's (1987) final theme is task orientation, in which the partners are work-oriented and are working on the task at hand rather than straying off into social conversation. These dimensions have consistent reliabilities above .95 and have been shown to have predictive validity in terms of differentiating a variety of nonverbal behaviors, such as immediacy behaviors indicative of attraction, eye gaze, pleasant versus hostile voices, dimensions of credibility, and high versus low reward communicators.

The dominance dimension cited in earlier studies by Wish, Deutsch, and Kaplan (1976) is split into equality and dominance. Equality is perceived as different from dominance, and control may entail an implicit notion of mutual respect (Burgoon & Hale, 1987). Composure and formality are likely to form composites with the other themes when the situation mandates a relaxed, nonaroused, or informal style of communication. Yet, as Burgoon and Hale (1987) noted, when composites of arousal, composure, formality, and task orientation are used, they are separate indicators of several distinctive themes.

A sample of 248 students in Speech Communication classes at Louisiana State University viewed one of two tapes involving the

Bolero and *Rite of Spring* couples and used the relational dimension scales to rate the man's and the woman's involvement in the interaction. A stepwise discriminant analysis was used to determine if a linear combination of the relational ratings, in which the ratings for both partners were analyzed as dependent variables, distinguished the two couples. The function yielded an 81% correct classification percentage for predicting the *Rite of Spring* couple by identifying specific themes of interaction.

The function was less accurate in classifying the *Bolero* couple even though it was still statistically significant, with a 66% correct classification rate. The relational dimensions distinguishing the two couples were attributing the man listening to *Bolero* as (1) being less intensely involved in the conversation, and (2) being less task-oriented and more interested in social conversation while concurrently showing more similarity and depth of communication than the husband exposed to the *Rite of Spring*. Conversely, the woman exposed to *Bolero* was rated as showing less similarity and depth, which may result in her fiancé converging toward her in this domain as he attempted to move the conversation to a deeper level.

The student observers also rated a number of nonverbal behaviors that resulted in a classification rate of 89% for both couples. Nonverbal behaviors that were rated including self-adaptors (e.g., scratching oneself) and object adaptors (e.g., playing with jewelry), backward–forward body lean, closed–open body orientation toward each other, negative–positive facial expression, amount of gesturing, number of interruptions, amount of gaze at the partner, and frequency of touching the partner during the conversation. The male participant in the *Bolero* condition had more gaze and self-adaptors than the *Rite of Spring* husband. The woman listening to *Bolero* used fewer gestures and self-adaptors and had a more closed body orientation than the *Rite of Spring* wife. In addition, both partners listening to *Bolero* smiled more than the husband and wife listening to the *Rite of Spring*.

A discriminant analysis was also used in which the musical mood wheel dimensions were the dependent variables for the observers. The observers circled the number of feelings in each category that they believed represented the music. This function yielded a classification rate of 66% for the *Bolero* couple and 84% for the *Rite of Spring* couple. The discriminating mood dimensions were the lofty, awe-inspiring feelings of mood category 1, the tender and sentimental feelings of mood category 3, the serenity and tranquillity ratings of category 4, the humorous and playful ratings of category 5, and the joyous and happy ratings of category 6. The observers rated the *Bolero* music higher in mood categories 1, 3, 4, 5, and 6 as compared with the *Rite of Spring*. The only mood category rated higher for the *Rite of Spring* was category 7, which included feeling triumphant, agitated, impetuous, and restless. These findings show that Stravinsky's *Rite of Spring* is rated by listeners as more agitating and may facilitate arguing, whereas *Bolero* may facilitate resolution because of its repetitiveness and tranquillity. Another interesting finding was that the observers reported that both the man's and the woman's projected mood mirrored the intensity of the music more in the *Rite of Spring* condition as compared with *Bolero.*

These results represent intricate findings on the association of relational themes and ratings of nonverbal involvement as a function of two pieces of symphonic music playing in the background while couples are arguing. It is clear from the reports of the student observers and the relational partners themselves that the music is associated with the behavior. The findings offer some support for the ISO principle.

REPORTS OF IMAGINED INTERACTIONS WHILE ARGUING AND LISTENING TO MUSIC

Another influence of music is on the imagined interactions that people often have with relational partners about arguments, such that conflict is kept alive by recalling old arguments. In numerous studies, Honeycutt (1991, 1995a, 1995b) has evaluated the role of imagined interactions in maintaining relationships and keeping conflict alive. Imagined interactions are a type of daydreaming and intrapersonal communication in which individuals imagine conversations with significant people in their lives, such as romantic partners, friends, family members, individuals in authority, work associates, ex-relational partners, and prospective partners in order to review prior conversations as well as to rehearse for anticipated encounters (Honeycutt, Edwards, & Zagacki, 1989–90; Honeycutt, Zagacki, & Edwards, 1989; Honeycutt & Wiemann, 1999).

The study of imagined interactions in personal relationships explains one reason for recurrent conflict and themes that characterize the encounters between relational partners. Imagined interactions link a series of encounters together as individuals replay what was previously said (e.g., "Last time I said X with poor results, but next time I see him (her) I am going to say Y with alternative results"), as well as anticipating what may be said at the next encounter. Conflict is kept alive by reliving old arguments and imagining the next interaction such that the next encounter may become a self-fulfilling prophecy as the interaction expectancy is enacted.

The study of recurrent imagined interactions in individuals is one way that relational themes are identified. Some individuals have imagined interactions with a variety of people, whereas others have recurrent imagined interactions with the same individuals over selected topics. Imagined interactions may be induced in which individuals relive pleasant or conflictual encounters. For example, research by Klos and Singer (1981) reveals that induced imagined interactions may elicit different kinds of emotions in thinking about parental conflict (Honeycutt, 1991). Klos and Singer (1981) studied the determinants of adolescents' ongoing thought following simulated parental confrontations. They examined the effect of fulfilled versus unresolved situations with parents, mutual nonconflictual parental interaction versus mutual, conflictual interaction, and a simulated interaction in which the parents' attitude was coercive or collaborative. It was proposed that exposure to these conditions through a simulated interaction would affect later recurrence of simulation-relevant thoughts (e.g., thinking about the parent).

The data revealed that anger persisted for a while after a conflictual imagined interaction had been induced between adolescents and their parents. This contrasts with more positive emotional affect conditions in which students imagined discussing an issue with their parent that was resolved. Klos and Singer (1981) surmised that the reawakening of unpleasant past experiences is enough to sustain arousal and recurrent thought even if the conflict was resolved. However, music also awakens arousal and recurrent conflict. Smeijsters (1995) reports that 41% of individuals indicated that music reminds them of things from the past and that they also used music to vent frustration. Individuals sometimes hear songs that remind them of old conflicts and loves. When this occurs, they may have a retroactive imagined interaction in which they replay old conversations in their mind. In fact, a classic song by the old Motown group, the Four Tops, called "It's the Same Old Song," expounds on how the memory of music affects current emotions (e.g., You've gone and left my heart in pain. All you've left is our favorite song, the one we danced too all night long, which brings sweet memories of all the tender love that used to be).

While listening to music in a car, we may have imagined interactions that keep conflict and relationships alive. Indeed, a number of couples may feel that they have "their song," which has particularized meaning for them. Hence, music as a process of creating and reifying certain memory forms, may, as part of that process, take individuals back to former scenes of interaction.

SUMMARY AND CONCLUSIONS

Individuals make attributions routinely about the worth of their relationships based on current emotions or mood states, especially insofar as those states have their relational partners as their object. Conversely, individual attributions concerning the meaning of music appear to vary according to the mood states associated with interpersonal conflict. Our results offer tentative but nonetheless suggestive grounds for examining the relationships between music and mood in the context of interpersonal conflict.

The ISO principle of music therapy posits that music can be used to change mood states incrementally, through a correspondingly incremental change in the music. The rhythm and intensity of the change are gradually altered to affect the listener's mood state. Evidence obtained from informal experimental procedures in which relational partners, who were exposed to music while arguing, exhibited differential patterns in the *kind* and *degree* of verbal and nonverbal behaviors. We believe this finding offers indirect evidence in support of the ISO principle.

These findings further suggest a link between music therapy and communication theory through seeing in the ISO principle a rationale for exploring the possibility that imagined interactions—and the variety of verbal and nonverbal behaviors with which they are associated—may also be subject to incremental changes according to changes in mood-inducing musical arrangements. We further wish to emphasize the idea that in situations in which music is introduced as an unobtrusive aspect of an informal communicative environment, its influence may, nevertheless, be a salient part of the communicative interactions that occur. It is our belief that these exploratory efforts provide heuristically promising grounds for a line of research that synthesizes concepts germane to music therapy and intra- and interpersonal communication. It is our hope that such a line of research might extend our understanding of the ongoing dialectic between the recovery of the *self* and the engagement with the *other* in the face of intransigent human conflict.

REFERENCES

Barzun, J. (1958). *Music in American life.* New York: Doubleday.

Behne, K. E. (1986). *Die Benützung von Musik.* Wilhelmshaven: Florian Noetzel Verlag.

Burgoon, J. K., & Hale, J. L. (1987). Validation and measurement of the fundamental themes of relational communication. *Communication Monographs, 54,* 19–41.

Chaffee, S. (1985). Popular music and communication research: An editorial epilogue. *Communication Research, 12,* 413–424.

Clark, D. M., (1983). On the induction of depressed mood in the laboratory: Evaluation and comparison of the velten and musical procedures. *Advanced Behavioral Research Therapy, 5,* 27–49.

Clark, D. M., & Teasdale, J. D. (1982). Diurnal variation in clinical depression and accessibility of memories of positive and negative experiences. *Journal of Abnormal Psychology, 91,* 87–95.

Fried, R., & Berkowitz, L. (1979). Music hath charms … and can influence helpfulness. *Journal of Applied Social Psychology, 9,* 199–208.

Frith, S. (1981). *Sound effects: Youth, leisure, and the politics of rock and roll.* New York: Pantheon.

Frith, S. (1996). *Performing rites: On the value of popular music.* Oxford U.K.: Oxford University Press.

Gantz, W., Gartenberg, H. M., Pearson, M. L., & Schiller, S. O. (1978). Gratifications and expectations associated with music among adolescents. *Popular Music and Society, 6,* 81–89.

Hevner, K. (1937). An experimental study of the affective value of sounds and poetry. *American Journal of Psychology, 49,* 419–434.

Honeycutt, J. M. (1989). A functional analysis of imagined interaction activity in everyday life. In J. E. Shorr, P. Robin, J. A. Connelia, & M. Wolpin (Eds.), *Imagery: Current perspectives* (pp. 13–25). New York: Plenum Press.

Honeycutt, J. M. (1991). Imagined interactions, imagery and mindfulness/mindlessness. In R. Kunzendorf (Ed.), *Mental imagery* (pp. 121–128). New York: Plenum Press.

Honeycutt, J. M. (1995a). The oral history interview and reports of imagined interactions as marriage therapy. *Journal of Family Psychotherapy, 6,* 63–69.

Honeycutt, J. M. (1995b). Imagined interactions, recurrent conflict and thought about personal relationships: A memory structure approach. In J. Aitken & L. J. Shedletsky (Eds.), *Intrapersonal communication processes* (pp. 138–150). Plymouth, MI: Midnight Oil & Speech Communication Association.

Honeycutt, J. M., Edwards, R., & Zagacki, K. S. (1989–1990). Using imagined interaction features to predict measures of self-awareness: Loneliness, locus of control, self-dominance, and emotional intensity. *Imagination, Cognition, and Personality, 9,* 17–31.

Honeycutt, J. M., & Wiemann, J. M. (1999). Analysis of functions of talk and reports of imagined interactions (IIs) during engagement and marriage. *Human Communication Research, 25,* 399–419.

Honeycutt, J. M., Zagacki, K. S., & Edwards, R. (1989). Intrapersonal communication and imagined interactions. In C. Roberts & K. Watson (Eds.), *Readings in intrapersonal communication* (pp. 167–184). Scottsdale, AZ: Gorsuch Scarisbrick Publishers.

Klos, D. S., & Singer, J. L. (1981). Determinants of the adolescent's ongoing thought following simulated parental confrontations. *Journal of Personality and Social Psychology, 41,* 975–987.

Knapp, M. L., & Vangelisti, A. (1992). *Interpersonal communication and human relationships* (2nd ed.). Boston: Allyn & Bacon.

Lull, J. (1985). On the communicative properties of music. *Communication Research, 12,* 363–372.

Lull, J. (1992). Popular music and communication: An introduction. In J. Lull (Ed.), *Popular music and communication* (2nd ed., pp. 134–151). Newbury Park, CA: Sage.

McFarland, R. A. (1984). Effects of music upon emotional content of TAT stories. *Journal of Psychology, 116,* 227–234.

Merriam, A. P. (1964). *The anthropology of music.* Northwestern University Press.

Merritt, S., McGregor, J., & Bell, J. (1996). *Mind, music, and imagery.* Fairfield, CT: Aslan.

Olson, D. H. (1977). "Insiders" and "outsiders" views of relationships: Research studies. In G. Levinger & H. Raush (Eds.), *Close relationships: Perspectives on the meaning of intimacy* (pp. 115–136). Amherst, MA: University of Massachusetts Press.

Pignatiello, M. F., Camp, C. J., & Rasar, L. A. (1986). Musical mood induction: An alternative to the velten technique. *Journal of Abnormal Psychology, 95,* 295–297.

Roe, K. (1985). Swedish youth and music: Listening patterns and motivations. *Communication Research, 12,* 353–362.

Ross, L. (1977). The intuitive psychologist and his shortcomings: Distortions in the attribution process. In L. Berkowitz (Ed.), *Advances in experimental social psychology* (Vol. 10, pp. 173–220). New York: Academic Press.

Slattery, W. S. (1985). *The effect of music and visuals on mood agreement under cue stimulation and channel interference conditions.* Unpublished doctoral dissertation, Boston University.

Smeijsters, H. (1995). The functions of music in music therapy. In T. Wigram, B. Saperston, & R. West (Eds.), *The art and science of music therapy: A handbook* (pp. 385–394). Chur, Switzerland: Harwood Academic Publishers.

Sutherland, G., Newman, B., & Rachman, S. (1982). Experimental investigations of the relationship between mood and intrusive, unwanted cognitions. *British Medical Journal of Psychology, 55,* 127–138.

Trunk, B. (1982). *Children's perception of the emotional content of music.* Unpublished doctoral dissertation. Ohio State University, Columbus.

Winner, E. (1982). *Invented worlds.* Cambridge, MA: Harvard University Press.

Wish, M., Deutsch, M., & Kaplan, S. J. (1976). Perceived dimensions of interpersonal relations. *Journal of Personality and Social Psychology, 33,* 404–420.

CHAPTER THREE

Making Sense of Hurtful Interactions in Close Relationships

When Hurt Feelings Create Distance

Anita L. Vangelisti

"A while ago, my brother and I were sitting at home watching TV when my dad came charging into the room. He said, 'Why aren't you two helping your mother clean up? You're worthless! All you do is take—you never give anything back!' ... My brother and I just looked at each other. I shrugged, but he looked like he was about to cry. I just figured dad was in a bad mood—but my brother was really upset. He hardly talked to dad for a week after that."

Almost everyone has been hurt by someone he or she loves. Accusations are made, criticism is put forth, sensitive issues are raised, and commitments are broken. In some cases, these hurtful episodes are quickly forgotten. Those who were hurt may excuse their partner's behavior, reasoning that it was unintentional (that, perhaps, their partner was unaware of the impact of what he or she said). In other cases, though, the episodes have lasting effects on individuals' relationships. Even very close relationships can be irreparably damaged by hurtful interactions.

The purpose of this chapter is to address issues related to the perceived causes and effects of hurtful messages. To provide a context for considering how hurt feelings are evoked, the chapter begins with a brief discussion of the social elicitation of emotion. Then, the way people conceptualize and respond to hurt is described. Next, the findings of studies investigating the relevance of attributions of intent to individuals' reactions to hurtful communication are reviewed, and

The author would like to thank Mark Knapp, Valerie Manusov, Denise Solomon, Brant Burleson, and John Harvey for their thoughtful contributions to this chapter. Correspondence for this chapter should be sent to Anita L. Vangelisti, College of Communication, University of Texas at Austin, Austin, TX 78712.

variations among people's explanations for hurt they believe was unintentionally elicited are noted. Finally, a discussion is provided of the explanations and perceptual processes that encourage people to stay close to, or to distance themselves from, someone who hurt them.

THE ELICITATION OF EMOTION

"It amazes me that one little comment like that could make me feel so bad. It happened a long time ago, but I still feel awful when I think about it."

The social and cognitive processes associated with the elicitation of emotion provide a backdrop for understanding how hurt is elicited. Emotions are often closely tied to social behavior (Metts & Bowers, 1994; Planalp, 1998; Weiner, 1986). They can influence the way people communicate as well as the outcomes of social interactions. Individuals' feelings sometimes serve as the topic of their conversations and at other times are the means for understanding the interactive behavior of others (Shaver, Schwartz, Kirson, & O'Connor, 1987).

When people experience an emotion, they do so in part based on an assessment of their social environment (see Forgas, this volume). Appraisal theories suggest that emotions are evoked as a consequence of individuals' evaluations of a particular event or situation (e.g., Scherer, 1984). From this perspective, the elicitation of emotions occurs when people perceive a stimulus event and assess its influence on their well-being. Most who adhere to this view argue that individuals make two different types of appraisal, primary and secondary appraisals (Lazarus, 1991). Primary appraisals involve the degree to which a stimulus event deviates from people's goals and their current patterns of behavior. By contrast, secondary appraisals center on people's ability to deal with the event and its outcomes. Both types of appraisal require individuals to evaluate the link between themselves and their social environment. If, for instance, people encounter a social situation that they feel is contentious, they may assess the extent to which that situation will affect their current behavior and they may think about their own ability to deal with any antagonism that comes their way. The conclusions they reach with regard to these and similar issues will influence the emotions they feel. People's interpretations of their social environment, in short, are associated with their emotional experiences.

Although appraisals provide important information about the way people experience emotions such as hurt, they capture only part of the complex relationships between people's thoughts and their emotions. Those who advocate appraisal theories argue that appraisals determine the nature and the intensity of individuals' responses to emotion. From this perspective, people's immediate evaluations of the relationship between themselves and their social environment are linked directly to the way they feel. Yet, the elicitation of emotion involves a much more interactive, circular process than this. Emotional experiences are embedded in and influenced by ongoing streams of social behavior. People often observe their social environment and make appraisals during the course of interacting with others. They take in new information, talk with others about their feelings, think about their appraisals, and consider how their appraisals and their emotional experiences fit within a dynamic social context. Appraisals and emotions, thus, are in a constant state of flux. Furthermore, as Parkinson (1997) notes, emotions "are not only reactions to interpretations of events but also modes of social action and communication" (p. 75). The elicitation, experience, and expression of emotion are social.

To untangle the complex associations between appraisals and emotion, Parkinson (1997) distinguishes two different levels of connections. One, the *empirical level* of connections, involves the links between actual appraisal processes and emotions. Empirical level connections are consistent with the direct, causal associations between appraisals and emotion that are posited by many appraisal theorists. The other, *conceptual level* of connections, focuses on the associations between the way people talk and think about their emotions and their evaluations of an emotional event. These connections emphasize the interpersonal aspects of emotion. They depict appraisals as having "message value," as being expressed to others in people's emotional responses.

Previous literature reveals more data supporting conceptual connections between appraisals and emotional responses than supporting empirical connections. As Parkinson argues, "there is little direct evidence that a specific cognitive process of appraisal always precedes and determines emotional reactions" (p. 73). This is not to say that appraisals are unimportant but instead that they should be examined as social, rather than strictly cognitive, phenomena. The way people talk about and interpret their appraisals and their emotional experiences provides a great deal of information about the way interpersonal and relational processes affect and are affected by emotions such as hurt.

RESPONDING TO HURT

"I stopped talking to him after that ... I knew how abusive he could be, and I just wanted to end our contact ... He's still my father, but we haven't spoken for many years."

Individuals' appraisals of their social environment are integral to the elicitation of hurt. When people feel hurt, they perceive that they have been emotionally injured or wounded (Folkes, 1982). They have evaluated something that someone else said or did as a transgression (i.e., as an act that inflicted emotional pain). Of course, hurt is not the only emotion people experience when they perceive a transgression has been committed against them. Prior research demonstrates that under similar circumstances, other feelings such as anger and even pity may be elicited (Weiner, 1986; Weiner, Amirkhan, Folkes, & Verette, 1987). What distinguishes hurt from other emotions is a sense of vulnerability; those who feel hurt are open or accessible to being hurt (Kelvin, 1977). To one degree or another, they have appraised their own role in the relevant interaction as victims. They see themselves as unprotected from and vulnerable to emotional injury. Hurt, thus, is what some have termed as an emotion "blend" (Weiner, personal communication). It is a combination of sadness or sorrow (over a felt loss) and fear (evidenced by feelings of vulnerability or threat).

Like all emotions, hurt is associated with a tendency to engage or disengage various aspects of the social environment (Frijda, 1986; Lazarus, 1991). People's responses to hurt feelings reflect a readiness to enact certain behaviors. Because hurt is a relatively aversive emotion (Miller, 1997) and because it involves a sense of vulnerability, the action tendency associated with hurt centers around efforts to avoid further pain. A number of theorists suggest that individuals' responses to emotion can be characterized by their tendency to approach or avoid the source of their feelings (Gray, 1987; Horney, 1945). When a conversational partner hurts them, people may reconstrue their relationship with that individual in a way that decreases their vulnerability. Perhaps the most obvious way to do this is to avoid or distance themselves from the person who hurt them. As described by Helgeson, Shaver, and Dyer (1987), distancing involves "a noticeable rift in an otherwise, or formerly, intimate relationship" (p. 224). Kreilkamp (1981) and de Rivera (1981) similarly note that distancing takes place within the context of intimacy. Individuals who are hurt have a heightened readiness to engage in distancing because it affords them the opportunity to protect themselves from further harm.

A readiness to engage in distancing does not necessarily dictate the way people react to hurt, however. The links between emotions, modes of action readiness, and actual responses to emotion are not that simple (see, e.g., Knobloch & Solomon, in progress). People do not always approach pleasant feelings, and they do not always distance themselves from pain. In fact, many times friends, family members, and lovers experience a great deal of hurt in their relationships and still opt to stay close to each other. Hurt feelings are only weakly correlated with people's tendency to distance themselves from individuals who hurt them (Vangelisti & Young, 1999).

ATTRIBUTIONS OF INTENT

> "She wanted to hurt me so that I would leave her alone and get out of her life … she was trying to get rid of me."

One means of accessing the influence of individuals' emotional experiences on their relationships is to examine people's attributions, that is, their explanations for how and why their emotions are evoked through hurtful communication. These explanations are inherently social. As Parkinson (1997) notes, individuals evaluate their emotional experiences in the context of relationships. The evaluations are expressed—to varying degrees and in various forms—when individuals respond to their emotion. The explanations people generate as they assess their emotional experiences thus become part of their social environment. The way people think about and explain their hurtful experiences affects the way in which they interact with others.

If individuals' explanations for hurtful episodes were uniformly negative, their interpersonal relationships might bear the brunt of this negativity. Indeed, a number of theorists suggest that interpersonal behaviors perceived as negative have detrimental influences on relationships (Levinger, 1976; Thibaut & Kelley, 1959). The results of research examining the association between such negative "costs" and relational quality, however, are mixed. Clark and Grote (1998) argue that one of the reasons why research in this area is inconclusive is that scholars have failed to differentiate negative behaviors that are intentional from those that are unintentional and from those that are motivated by an effort to meet another person's needs.

The cues individuals use in assessing intentionality certainly support the notion that hurtful comments perceived as intentional carry a different relational force than do those viewed as unintentional. Researchers have found that people consider a number of different factors when appraising whether or not a behavior is intentional (Malle & Knobe, 1997; Weiner, 1995). These include knowledge of the behavior's consequences (whether the individual was aware of the outcomes associated with the action), volition (whether the person chose to engage in the behavior), forethought (whether the individual planned the behavior), skill (whether the person was able to perform the behavior), and valence (whether the individual believed that the outcomes of the behavior were desirable). People who perceive that someone hurt them intentionally tend to believe that the individual chose to hurt them, wanted to do so, had the skill to hurt them, and planned the interaction.

Attributions of intent involve more than an explanation of cause. They also include judgments of responsibility. People may explain the causes of a hurtful comment without attributing intent. For example, if a child tells her father that she "hates his guts," the father may see the cause of the hurtful statement as internal and controllable (e.g., the speaker was being obnoxious) without perceiving that the consequences of the utterance (e.g., hurt feelings on the part of the father) were intentional. Weiner (1995) argues that even when the causes of negative behaviors are perceived as internal and controllable, if they are seen as unintentional, "the individual ... is not judged as harshly as when the act and the outcome were intended" (p. 14).

The relative impact of hurtful comments perceived as intentional and as unintentional has been examined in several studies (e.g., Vangelisti, 1994; Vangelisti & Young, 1999). In these investigations, people were asked to describe and evaluate an interaction when someone said something to them that was extremely hurtful and to note whether the individual who hurt them did so intentionally. The findings of these studies indicated that individuals who judged something a conversational partner said as intentionally hurtful reported the interaction had more of a distancing effect on their relationship with the partner than did those who perceived the hurtful comment was unintentional. Individuals who reported that they were hurt intentionally appeared to have heightened emotional responses to what their partners said. Because hurt involves feeling emotionally injured, those who perceived that their partner hurt them purposefully may have felt particularly vulnerable to further harm and opted to protect themselves by distancing themselves from the source of their pain.

HURT FEELINGS AND ATTRIBUTIONS OF INTENT IN CONTEXT

"She really didn't mean to hurt me … I know she loves me. She was upset and she just wasn't thinking at that moment."

Judgments of intent, like other appraisals, are made against a backdrop of relational quality. When people are hurt, their attributions of intent are affected by their past, present, and future associations with the person who hurt their feelings. Those who are hurt in the context of extremely close, satisfying relationships may be less likely to believe that their partner intended to hurt them (e.g., that the partner chose to hurt them, planned to elicit hurt, and wanted to do so) than those who are hurt within relatively distant, unsatisfying partnerships. Studies on marital and romantic relationships support the argument that individuals' interpretations of their partner's behavior are linked to their feelings about their relationship (Noller & Fitzpatrick, 1990). People who perceive their partner's behavior in ways that enhance their relationship tend to be relatively satisfied, whereas those who emphasize the distress-maintaining qualities of their partner's behavior are comparatively dissatisfied (Grigg, Fletcher, & Fitness, 1989; Holtzworth-Munroe & Jacobson, 1985).

While these investigations focus specifically on romantic partnerships, they have ramifications for other interpersonal associations as well. Friends, family members, and even coworkers who are highly satisfied with their relationships probably think they have good reason to believe that their partners would not hurt them purposefully. Indeed, a study that examined the relational satisfaction and closeness of people who said they were hurt by someone else (e.g., a friend, acquaintance, or coworker) suggested that this may be the case (Vangelisti & Young, 1999). People who perceived that their conversational partner hurt them intentionally were less satisfied with their relationship and felt less close to their partner than those who saw their hurt feelings as unintentionally elicited.

The link between relational quality and people's tendency to attribute intent to their partner's hurtful behavior raises an important question about the extent to which attributions of intent, in and of themselves, have an impact on relationships. As previously noted, people who perceive that a conversational partner hurt them intentionally tend to feel that the hurtful interaction created more distance in their relationship than do those who believe their hurt feelings were elicited unintentionally. However, because hurtful interactions take place in the context of existing relationships, it is important to consider whether differences in the amount of relational distancing are due to relational quality rather than to perceptions of intent. It may be that when relational quality is controlled, the impact of perceived intent on feelings of distance will fade.

To examine this possibility, Vangelisti and Young (1999) contrasted the amount of relational distancing reported by people who felt they were hurt intentionally with the amount reported by those who believed they were hurt unintentionally. The results revealed that even when relational satisfaction and closeness were controlled, people who attributed intentionality to their conversational partner's hurtful utterance felt the message had more of a distancing effect on their relationship than did those who saw their hurt as unintentionally evoked.

VARIATIONS IN UNINTENTIONAL HURT

"I don't think he was trying to hurt me ... he's just like that. He always makes smart remarks and he doesn't care who he hurts. He thinks he knows everything..."

Although hurtful comments that are perceived as intentional are associated with more relational distancing and more intense feelings than those seen as unintentional, there are important variations among the comments viewed as unintentional. Because feelings of hurt are characterized by vulnerability, there may be cases in which people respond quite strongly to being hurt in spite of the fact that they perceive their feelings to have been evoked unintentionally. For instance, individuals who come to the conclusion that a relational partner hurt them because the partner is selfish and inconsiderate may end up distancing themselves from their relationship even if they do not believe the partner set out to hurt them intentionally. Even though these individuals perceive that the hurt feelings were elicited unintentionally, the prospect of being repeatedly injured may create as much distance as being hurt intentionally.

To explore the possibility that hurtful comments perceived as unintentional vary in the degree to which they create relational distance, Vangelisti and Young (1999) conducted a study examining the nature of people's explanations or attributions for hurtful communication. The results of this study are the basis for the analysis in this current chapter. A questionnaire that required them to describe an interaction in which someone said something that hurt their feelings was completed by 486 subjects. They were asked to rate the intensity of their hurt feelings, note the degree to which the interaction made them feel more distant from the persons who hurt them, and report whether the other persons hurt them intentionally. Respondents also were required to explain why the other persons said whatever it was that made them feel hurt. The content of the explanations people provided for the other persons' hurtful behavior was examined. As Manusov and Koenig (this volume) argue, the content of attributions can help to uncover the meaning of communication behaviors. The various meanings individuals associate with hurtful messages are of particular interest because they indicate how people interpret the messages and provide information about the influence of hurtful interactions on individuals' relationships.

An inductive analysis of respondents' explanations suggested that people's attributions for others' hurtful comments could be characterized by one of eight different categories (Table 3.1). Some individuals noted that the hurtful message they reported was *expressive*, that it was a reflection of the other person's physical or emotional state. Some noted that it was *strategic*, that the other person used the hurtful comment to achieve an interpersonal goal. A number of people reported that the hurtful message they received was *descriptive*. These individuals believed that their conversational partners said what they did in an effort to describe, or provide an honest response to, a particular situation. Others explained their conversational partners' hurtful behavior as *supportive*. They noted that their partner said something hurtful to them in order to help them or to meet their needs. Hurtful comments explained as *accidental* were those that people felt were inadvertent or spoken without an awareness that they would elicit hurt. Those that were *justified* were messages people believed they themselves had caused. Individuals who explained their partners' behavior in this way felt that their partners hurt them in response to something they initially said or did. Other people reported that their conversational partners hurt them for *self-centered* reasons. These indi-

Table 3.1.   Descriptions and Examples of Content Categories that Characterize Unintentional Attributions Associated with Hurtful Messages

Category Description	Examples
Expressive: The hurtful message was a consequence of the partner's emotional or physical state.	"Because he was hurting…" "She was just upset at that time…"
Strategic: The partner employed the hurtful message as a tactic to achieve an interpersonal goal.	"He was frustrated and tired…" "He wanted to get the upper hand in the argument"
Descriptive: The hurtful message was an accurate description of, or an honest response to, the situation at hand.	"She was trying to make a point" "I asked him a question … he answered it" "Because it was true…"
Supportive: The partner said something hurtful in an effort to help the other or meet the other's needs.	"He was just being honest and up-front…" "…she was concerned about my health" "Because he thought it would help me get out of a rut"
Accidental: The hurtful message was inadvertent; the partner was not aware of the emotional impact the message would have.	"She simply didn't know…" "Because she wasn't thinking…" "He didn't realize what he had said"
Justified: The partner's hurtful utterance was a response to something the other person said or did.	"I hurt him and put him on the defensive" "I deserved it for what I had just said…"
Self-Centered: The hurtful message was employed as a means to fulfill the partner's own wants or needs.	"Because he was thinking of himself" "She is obsessed with our family looking perfect"
Trait-Oriented: The hurtful message was a result of the partner's enduring traits or characteristics.	"He was trying to have 2 girl friends…" "She is extremely, very conservative" "He is insecure about himself" "Because he's a guy…"

Adapted from Vangelisti, A. L., & Young, S. L. (1999).

viduals noted that the hurtful message they described was used by their conversational partners as a way to fulfill their own desires. Finally, a number of people explained the other persons' hurtful behavior as *trait-oriented.* They noted that the behavior reflected enduring characteristics of their partners.

While the content of these attributions alone is interesting, it becomes even more intriguing when examined in conjunction with individuals' reports of the degree to which they distanced themselves from their conversational partners after the hurtful interaction. As a group, hurtful messages perceived as unintentional had less of a distancing effect on people's relationships than did those viewed as intentional. However, there also were variations among the comments deemed as unintentional. In two cases, messages perceived as unintentional had as much of a distancing effect on people's relationships as those that were viewed as intentional. More specifically, individuals who explained their conversational partner's hurtful behavior as self-centered or as trait-oriented felt that the hurtful interactions they described created just as much distance in their relationships as did those persons who felt their partners' behavior was intentional.

What is it about self-centered and trait-oriented explanations that encourages this type of relational distancing? Self-centered and trait-oriented attributions have at least three qualities in common, which together provide an initial response to questions such as this one. First, hurtful comments that are self-centered or trait-oriented demonstrate an explicit disregard for the recipient's thoughts or feelings. When people disregard someone, they fail to consider that the individual may be hurt by what they are about to say; they devalue or ignore the other's feelings in favor of their own. For instance, self-centered explanations suggest that the speaker focused on the self to the exclusion of the other. As one respondent noted, the person who hurt her "didn't care about ... [her] at all ... he was only thinking of himself." Explanations that are trait-oriented similarly imply that some aspect of the speaker's personality enabled him or her to easily set aside concern for others and inflict emotional pain. One participant reported that the individual who hurt him was "too inconsiderate to worry about whether what she said would hurt anyone."

Previous research suggests that rejection or relational devaluation is tied closely to individuals' feelings of hurt (Leary, Springer, Negel, Ansell, & Evans, 1998; Vangelisti, 1994). The current findings further imply that some of the most salient forms of rejection or relational devaluation may be those in which people who are hurt perceive they are of little value to the individual who hurt them. Disregarding another person is a very different act from rejecting that individual. The latter involves negative attention, whereas the former may involve little attention at all. Lomore and Holmes (1999) found that perceived regard predicts how upset people get over a relational partner's transgression. Our data similarly suggest that when individuals perceive they have been disregarded, they are more likely to distance themselves from those who hurt them. Explanations involving an explicit disregard of the recipient or the relationship may have a particularly potent relational force—the lack of attention individuals receive when they are disregarded may close down any opportunity for continued interaction. People may opt to distance themselves from those they feel disregard them in part because being ignored leaves them few alternatives.

A second quality that self-centered and trait-oriented explanations have in common is that both imply that the hurtful behavior is likely to recur. If someone generally is selfish enough to hurt others, he or she may very well do so repeatedly. Likewise, if a person possesses traits that encourage him or her to inflict hurt, that individual will probably be involved in hurtful episodes over and over again. In providing self-centered or trait-oriented explanations for a conversational partner's hurtful comments, people may recognize the likelihood that the individual who hurt them will do so frequently.

The third, and perhaps most important, quality that links self-centered and trait-oriented explanations is that both suggest that there may be little discrepancy between the hurtful behavior and the individual's typical relational behavior. The speaker's hurtful comments, in other words, are perceived as relatively common. When asked to explain why their conversational partner hurt them, respondents noted that their partner was "just that way," was "really insecure," or "never thinks about others." Eliciting hurt is consistent with the behavior of someone who is selfish, insecure, or controlling. When people explain someone's hurtful behavior by noting that it was self-centered or trait-oriented, they acknowledge that the individual may have a general tendency to evoke hurt. And, if the hurtful behavior is typical, there is relatively little hope that it will change. Given this, self-centered and trait-oriented attributions may provide those who feel hurt with a rationale for distancing themselves from the persons who hurt them.

WHY DO PEOPLE STAY CLOSE OR DISTANCE THEMSELVES?

The way people explain a partner's hurtful behavior provides a glimpse of how they have made sense of (i.e., provided attributions for) their hurt feelings. These explanations allow individuals to reconcile their perceptions that someone caused them emotional pain with their subsequent attitudes toward the persons who hurt them. The data described thus far suggest that when people feel hurt, they are less likely to distance themselves from individuals who hurt them if they make an unintentional attribution for the hurtful behavior. By contrast, if individuals perceive that a conversational partner hurt them on purpose—if they believe the partner wanted to inflict emotional pain—they are less likely to stay close to that partner. Similarly, when people see a hurtful behavior as unintentional but self-centered or trait-oriented, they are relatively likely to distance themselves from the source of their pain.

Up to this point, two different situations have been discussed: one in which individuals experience intense hurt feelings and then distance themselves from the person who hurt them (high hurt, high distancing) and one in which people feel intense hurt but do not distance themselves from the individual who elicited their feelings (high hurt, low distancing). These two situations can be viewed as two of the cells in a two-by-two matrix (Figure 3.1). The intensity of people's hurt feelings makes up one axis of the matrix, with the degree to which individuals engage in distancing as the other axis.

In the first cell, people react to hurt as they might to any number of other aversive stimuli, by distancing themselves from the source of their pain. Given that individuals characterized by this first cell dis-

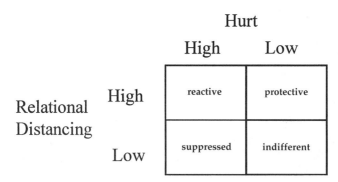

Figure 3.1.   Distancing Response Versus Intensity of Hurt

play a relatively measured, active response to the person who hurt them, their behavior could be termed *reactive*. These individuals react to, or counter, the hurtful stimulus by withdrawing their affection. However, because the stimulus in this case is situated in the context of an interpersonal relationship, the act of distancing is much more complex than it might be otherwise. When people distance themselves from each other, they give up something; by definition, they sacrifice a degree of relational closeness. The act of distancing, thus, is one fraught with varying degrees of tension. The resolution of this tension is evident, in part, in the explanations people provide for hurtful behavior. If people believe the behavior was intentional, self-centered, or trait-oriented, they are more likely to move away emotionally from the person who hurt them. Those who perceive they were hurt for these reasons may very well believe that the costs of distancing themselves from the individual who hurt them are outweighed by the benefits of avoiding further pain.

The second cell in this two-by-two matrix is one in which people experience a great deal of hurt but do not distance themselves from the source of their feelings. Because these individuals control their urge to move away from the person who hurt them, their behavior could be labeled *suppressed*. Although the lack of distancing exhibited here may seem somewhat counterintuitive, there are a variety of circumstances in which people maintain a sense of relational closeness to someone who has hurt them. In some cases, the hurtful interactions may be so infrequent that they are deemed insignificant when compared with the rewards associated with the relationship. In others situations, the hurtful behavior may be a consequence of a temporary condition (e.g., a bad mood) or an external force (e.g., stress in the workplace) that those who are hurt are willing to excuse.

There also may be cases in which people perceive they have few alternatives to being hurt. Some may feel that the relationship they have with the person who hurt them is irreplaceable; they may have a relatively low comparison level for alternatives (Thibaut & Kelley, 1959). For example, prior research suggests that individuals who are hurt by family members may be less likely to distance themselves from the source of their pain than those who are hurt by friends or romantic partners (Vangelisti & Crumley, 1998; Vangelisti & Young, 1999), and this may stem in part from the belief that family relationships are difficult, if not impossible, to replace. Other people may perceive they have few alternatives to hurt because they believe that they "deserve" to be

hurt. The literature on physical and emotional abuse in close relationships underlines the idea that some individuals stay in relationships in
which they are continually hurt because being hurt is the only viable
alternative they see for themselves (Walker, 1979).

Many of the circumstances that characterize the second cell depicted
in Figure 3.1 are reflected in the explanations people provided when
they were asked to account for the behavior of the persons who hurt
them. For example, a number of individuals noted that the hurtful
behavior was *accidental.* Because accidental behavior is usually seen as
atypical, people who perceive that a conversational partner accidentally hurt them probably do not believe they will be hurt repeatedly or
frequently. As a result, these individuals may feel that the rewards they
receive from the relationship outweigh the costs associated with the
hurtful episode and that the costs of distancing themselves from their
conversational partner are too great. By contrast, a number of people
noted that the behavior of the person who hurt them was meant to be
supportive. For instance, one respondent said that his coach was trying
to motivate him to play better when the coach called him a loser and
an idiot in front of his teammates. Another participant reported that a
male friend who said she was "really getting fat" was concerned about
her health. As Clark and Grote (1998) suggest, when individuals
believe a relational partner is acting in their best interest, the negative
consequences typically associated with undesirable behavior often are
tempered or subdued.

Another set of explanations that reflect cases in which people who
are extremely hurt opt not to distance themselves from a partner are
those labeled *justified.* Because these explanations suggest that the
behavior was a legitimate response to something they, themselves, did,
these individuals may suppress any urge to distance themselves from
the person who hurt them. Similarly, those who note that the hurtful
behavior was *descriptive*—that it was an accurate rendition of the circumstances at hand—may not believe they have a rationale for changing their attitudes toward the individual who hurt their feelings.

While both of these two cells (high hurt, high distancing and high
hurt, low distancing) depict situations that involve relatively strong
hurt feelings, it is important to acknowledge that hurt feelings vary in
terms of their intensity. Sometimes people feel so much emotional pain
that they are in anguish; at other times they barely notice the hurt they
feel. The third and fourth cells represent cases in which the intensity of
people's hurt is relatively low. Despite being exposed to interactions

that many would deem hurtful, in these cases individuals do not feel a great deal of emotional pain.

More specifically, the third cell is one in which people do not experience much hurt but still opt to distance themselves from the person who elicited their feelings (low hurt, high distancing). The behavior of these individuals might be called *protective* because it involves what appears to be an effort to shield or protect the self from further pain. Those who respond to less intense hurt by distancing themselves from their conversational partner may have decided that the rewards they could get from maintaining a relatively close relationship are not worth even the small amount of emotional pain they have already experienced. They may opt to protect themselves rather than risk another hurtful interaction. For instance, in the initial stages of a relationship, people may not have enough invested in the relationship to be vulnerable. As a consequence, they may not believe that the benefits of future interactions are worth the risks of being hurt. Individuals in the initial stages of a relationship also may reason if their partners are willing to hurt them early on, when social norms suggest that people should be relatively careful and polite (Berger & Bradac, 1982), the chances for rewarding interactions down the line are fairly bleak.

Another group of individuals who might be characterized by this third cell consists of those who have been exposed to hurtful interactions repeatedly. Zahn-Waxler and Kochanska (1990) proposed a neurophysiological model of "kindling," which suggests that people's responses to certain emotions may become "kindled" or exaggerated over time. This model, originally put forth by Meyersberg and Post (1979), suggests that when organisms are repeatedly exposed to noxious stimuli (e.g., electric shocks), they become extremely sensitized, so that over time smaller doses of the stimuli are necessary to evoke a response (e.g., seizures). Eventually, the organisms may begin to react to the stimuli with little or no exposure. Applied to the elicitation of hurt feelings, the model suggests that people who are repeatedly injured may begin to respond to their feelings in hyper-sensitive, protective ways. People who have an avoidant attachment style (see, e.g., Bartholomew & Horowitz, 1991)—who feel uncomfortable with intimacy and tend to distrust others—may display this sort of a response to hurtful interactions.

An alternative to the notion that individuals in this third cell react in extreme ways to relatively subdued hurt feelings is that they have become habituated to intense feelings of hurt. People who are hurt by someone again and again may become numb to their own feelings. For instance, spouses who are highly dissatisfied with their marital relationships sometimes withdraw emotionally, so that by the time their relationship ends they feel very little pain (Knapp, 1984). Similarly, children who have been raised in abusive environments, who have been repeatedly hurt by family members, sometimes have difficulties experiencing a full range of emotions (Arias & Pape, 1994). Although individuals in situations such as these may have invested quite a bit in their relationships, the emotional calluses they have developed eventually may enable them to evaluate their hurtful interactions in a relatively dispassionate way. These dispassionate assessments, in turn, may provide people with reasons to protect themselves by distancing themselves from the source of their emotional pain.

The fourth cell in Figure 3.1 represents situations in which people feel relatively little hurt and do not distance themselves much from the source of their feelings (low hurt, low distancing). If the hurtful interaction they have experienced is one that most people would see as fairly benign, these individuals, like those in the first cell, may be demonstrating a measured response to the hurtful stimulus. However, if the interaction is one that most people would see as extremely hurtful, something else is going on. Assuming that they have been involved in an exchange that would typically be deemed as hurtful, the people characterized by this fourth cell are displaying subdued affective and behavioral responses to an emotionally painful stimulus. Their reaction, thus, could be termed *indifferent*. Individuals in this situation, like some of those in the third cell, may have been repeatedly hurt and over time may have become habituated to their hurt feelings. Unlike those in the third cell, though, these people may feel that they have few if any alternatives to their current relationship. They may believe they have so much invested that they cannot afford to further distance themselves from their partner, or they may already have distanced so much from their partner that they are no longer hurt by what the partner says.

Another possibility is that individuals in this fourth cell have a tendency to discount or minimize the hurtful comments they receive. If the comments are deemed unimportant, they may not elicit much hurt. This tendency could take one of at least two different forms. First, it could take the form of a trait or disposition. Some individuals may have a general proclivity to discount or disregard most of the hurtful comments or questions they receive. Second, the tendency to minimize hurtful statements or questions could be limited to the utterances of a specific individual so that only the things a certain person says are discounted. In either case, people who have a penchant for discounting hurtful interactions may have learned that minimizing what others say is one way to minimize their own hurt feelings and thus one way to stay close to someone who hurts them.

DISCUSSION

Parkinson (1997) argues that individuals' appraisals of an emotional experience are reflected in the way they think and talk about that experience. When people are hurt, evidence of how and why they feel they were hurt can be found in their attributions. The way individuals explain hurtful interactions shows how they have made sense of the notion that someone else said something that emotionally injured them. These explanations also reflect how people deal with potential discrepancies between another person's negative interpersonal behavior (e.g., a hurtful comment or question) and their subsequent attitudes toward that individual (e.g., their tendency to distance themselves from him or her).

Conceptualizing hurtful behavior as unintentional can provide people with a rationale for staying close to others who hurt their feelings. It can reinforce their want (or their need) to maintain a degree of intimacy with such individuals in spite of the fact that those persons caused them emotional pain. By contrast, conceiving of hurtful behavior as intentional creates a psychosocial context that is ripe for relational distancing. Likewise, describing a hurtful comment or question as unintentional, but self-centered or trait-oriented, sets up an environment that encourages people to separate themselves from the persons who hurt them. When individuals believe someone purposefully injured them or when they perceive someone hurt them out of selfishness or a tendency to be cruel, they may very well opt to protect themselves by moving away from the source of their pain.

Hurt, like any other emotion, can vary in intensity. Examining differences in the degree to which people feel hurt, in conjunction with individuals' tendency to distance themselves from the source of their pain, raises some interesting questions for future research. The two-by-two matrix presented in this chapter provides a framework for discussing some of these issues. For instance, when people's response to hurtful communication is reactive (high hurt, high distancing) or suppressed (high hurt, low distancing), they feel relatively intense emotional pain. Although both types of responses involve a great deal of hurt, those that are suppressed are incongruent with the action tendency typically associated with hurt feelings (i.e., distancing). One factor that seems to enable individuals to override their readiness to distance themselves from the person who hurt them is attributing the person's hurtful behavior to unintentional causes (e.g., "He didn't mean to hurt me"). Attributions of intent, by contrast, reinforce the sense of vulnerability associated with hurt feelings and thus encourage people to move away from the source of their pain.

Perceptions on which explanations are based can have a profound influence on interpersonal relationships. People's perceptions can be as important for future interactions and for the quality of individuals' relationships as what actually happens (Sillars & Scott, 1983). If partners believe they were hurt intentionally, they will respond as if that were the case. Their relationships will show the marks of their attributions. Attributions of intent are like brush strokes made by relational partners on a social palette—they are constructed by individuals through social interaction. While these explanations may or may not match actors' intentions, they create a picture of reality that relational partners believe in and act upon. They can make the difference between hurtful interactions that are forgotten and those that bring relationships to an end.

REFERENCES

Arias, I., & Pape, K. T. (1994). Physical abuse. In L. L'Abate (Ed.), *Handbook of developmental psychology and psychopathology* (pp. 284–308). New York: Wiley.

Bartholomew, K., & Horowitz, L. (1991). Attachment styles among young adults: A test of a four-category model. *Journal of Personality and Social Psychology, 62*, 226–244.

Berger, C. R., & Bradac, J. J. (1982). *Language and social knowledge: Uncertainty in interpersonal relations.* London: Edward Arnold.

Clark, M. S., & Grote, N. K. (1998). Why aren't indices of relationship costs always negatively related to indices of relationship quality? *Personality and Social Psychology Review, 2*, 2–17.

de Rivera, J. (1981). The structure of anger. In J. de Rivera (Ed.), *Conceptual encounter: A method for the exploration of human experience* (pp. 35–81). Washington, DC: University Press of America.

Folkes, V. S. (1982). Communicating the causes of social rejection. *Journal of Experimental Social Psychology 18*, 235–252.

Frijda, N. H. (1986). *The emotions.* Cambridge, UK: Cambridge University Press.

Gray, J. A. (1987). *The psychology of fear and stress* (2nd ed.). New York: Cambridge University Press.

Grigg, F., Fletcher, G. J. O., & Fitness, J. (1989). Spontaneous attributions in happy and unhappy dating relationships. *Journal of Social and Personal Relationships, 6,* 61–68.

Helgeson, V. W., Shaver, P., & Dyer, M. (1987). Prototypes of intimacy and distance in same-sex and opposite-sex relationships. *Journal of Social and Personal Relationships, 4,* 195–233.

Holtzworth-Munroe, A., & Jacobson, N. S. (1985). Causal attributions of married couples: When do they search for causes? What do they conclude when they do? *Journal of Personality and Social Psychology, 48,* 1398–1412.

Horney, K. (1945). *Our inner conflicts: A constructive theory of neurosis.* New York: W. W. Norton.

Kreilkamp, T. (1981). Psychological distance. In J. de Rivera (Ed.), *Conceptual encounter: A method for the exploration of human experience* (pp. 273–341). Washington, DC: University Press of America.

Kelvin, P. (1977). Predictability, power and vulnerability in interpersonal attraction. In S. Duck (Ed.), *Theory and practice in interpersonal attraction* (pp. 355–378). New York: Academic Press.

Knapp, M. L. (1984). *Interpersonal communication and human relationships.* Boston: Allyn & Bacon.

Knobloch, L. K., & Solomon, D. H. *Responses to changes in relational certainty and uncertainty in dating relationships: Emotions and communication strategies.* (Manuscript submitted for publication.)

Lazarus, R. L. (1991). *Emotion and adaptation.* New York: Oxford University Press.

Leary, M. R., Springer, C., Negel, L., Ansell, E., & Evans, K. (1998). The causes, phenomenology, and consequences of hurt feelings. *Journal of Personality and Social Psychology, 74,* 1225–1237.

Levinger, G. (1976). A social psychological perspective on marital dissolution. *Journal of Social Issues, 32,* 21–47.

Lomore, C. D., & Holmes, J. G. (1999). *The buffering effects of positive illusions and feelings of perceived regard on victim's evaluations of transgressions.* Paper presented at the joint meeting of the International Network on Personal Relationships and the International Society for the Study of Personal Relationships, Louisville, KY.

Malle, B. F., & Knobe, J. (1997). The folk concept of intentionality. *Journal of Experimental Social Psychology, 33,* 101–121.

Metts, S. M., & Bowers, J. W. (1994). Emotion in interpersonal communication. In M. L. Knapp & G. R. Miller (Eds.), *Handbook of interpersonal communication* (pp. 508–541). Thousand Oaks, CA: Sage.

Meyersberg, H. A., & Post, R. M. (1979). An holistic developmental view of neural and psychological processes: A neurobiologic-psychoanalytic integration. *British Journal of Psychiatry, 135,* 139–155.

Miller, R. S. (1997). We always hurt the ones we love: Aversive interpersonal interactions in close relationships. In R. M. Kowalski (Ed.), *Aversive interpersonal behaviors* (pp. 11–29). New York: Plenum Press.

Noller, P., & Fitzpatrick, M. A. (1990). Marital communication in the eighties. *Journal of Marriage and the Family, 52,* 832–843.

Parkinson, B. (1997). Untangling the appraisal-emotion connection. *Personality and Social Psychology Review, 1,* 62–79.

Planalp, S. (1998). Communication emotion in everyday life: Cues, channels, and processes. In P. A. Andersen & L. K. Guerrero (Eds.), *Handbook of communication and emotion* (pp. 29–48). San Diego: Academic Press.

Scherer, K. R. (1984). Emotion as a multicomponent process: A model and some cross-cultural data. In P. Shaver (Ed.), *Review of personality and social psychology: Vol. 5. Emotion, relationships, and health* (pp. 37–63). Beverly Hills, CA: Sage.

Shaver, P., Schwartz, J., Kirson, D., & O'Connor, O. (1987). Emotion knowledge: Further exploration of a prototype approach. *Journal of Personality and Social Psychology, 52,* 1061–1086.

Sillars, A. L., & Scott, M. D. (1983). Interpersonal perception between intimates: An integrative review. *Human Communication Research, 10,* 153–176.

Thibaut, J. W., & Kelley, H. H. (1959). *The social psychology of groups.* New York: Wiley.

Vangelisti, A. L. (1994). Messages that hurt. In W. R. Cupach & B. H. Spitzberg (Eds.), *The dark side of interpersonal communication* (pp. 53–82). Hillsdale, NJ: Lawrence Erlbaum.

Vangelisti, A. L., & Crumley, L. P. (1998). Reactions to messages that hurt: The influence of relational contexts. *Communication Monographs, 65,* 173–196.

Vangelisti, A. L., & Young, S. L. (1999). *When words hurt: The effects of perceived intentionality on interpersonal relationships.* Paper presented at the annual meeting of the International Communication Association, San Francisco.

Walker, L. E. (1979). *The battered woman.* New York: Harper & Row.

Weiner, B. (1986). *An attributional theory of motivation and emotion.* New York: Springer-Verlag.

Weiner, B. (1995). *Judgments of responsibility: A foundation for a theory of social conduct.* New York: Guilford.

Weiner, B., Amirkhan, J., Folkes, V. S., & Verette, J. A. (1987). An attributional analysis of excuse giving: Studies of a naive theory of emotion. *Journal of Personality of Social Psychology, 52,* 316–324.

Zahn-Waxler, C., & Kochanska, G. (1990). The origins of guilt. In R. A. Thompson (Ed.), *Nebraska symposium on motivation* (pp. 183–258). Lincoln: University of Nebraska Press.

CHAPTER FOUR

The Association Between Accounts of Relationship Development Events and Relational and Personal Well-Being

Jeanne Flora and Chris Segrin

Owing to their inherently social nature, most human beings possess a strong drive to establish close and intimate connections with others. In fact, some researchers believe that establishing and maintaining relationships with others is the primary motivation behind most human behavior (Sullivan, 1940). The positive effects of close relationships on both mental and physical health are well documented (e.g., Kiecolt-Glaser et al., 1987), as are their ill effects when relationships become distressed or nonexistent (Beach, Jouriles, & O'Leary, 1985). Despite our understanding of the causes, consequences, and risk factors for relational deterioration, however, the majority of close, intimate relationships ultimately fail. Clearly, a great deal of unfinished business remains in the scientific study of relational quality.

One phenomenon that holds great promise for understanding, explaining, and predicting changes in relational quality is the act of offering accounts for relationship development events. An account is a verbal description, written or spoken, of an event or action (Orbuch, 1997; Scott & Lyman, 1968). Accounts are often provided for events that are salient or unusual. When people account for their behavior, or that of another, they generally offer explanations about how and why the behavior came about (Cody & McLaughlin, 1990; Harvey, Weber, & Orbuch, 1990). Accounts thus illustrate the kinds of attributions that people make for events and behaviors that occurred in their lives and relationships (Harvey, Turnquist, & Agostinelli, 1988).

In this chapter we examine evidence indicating that how people think and talk about the events in the development of their close

Correspondence should be sent to Jeanne Flora, Department of Communication, California State University Fullerton, P. O. Box 6868, Fullerton, CA 92834.

relationships can be markers of current and possibly future relational quality. In particular we highlight findings from a series of studies on dating and marital relationships recently conducted in our laboratory. These findings show that people's explanations for how and why their relationship developed as it did are reflective of their satisfaction and commitment to that relationship as well as of their own psychosocial well-being.

ATTRIBUTIONS, ACCOUNTS, AND RELATIONSHIP WELL-BEING

A great deal of research has examined the attributions romantic partners offer for events in their relationships. Research specific to dating couples identifies attributions associated with positive relational well-being. For example, dating partners who report greater satisfaction with their relationships give more responsibility to their partners for positive events (Thompson & Kelly, 1981) and, in general, produce more attributions that enhance relationship quality (Grigg, Fletcher, & Fitness, 1989). Likewise, dating partners who perceive both partners as contributing equally to relational maintenance efforts are happier, more committed, and more in love (Fletcher, Fincham, Cramer, & Heron, 1987).

Research on married couples' attributions is more developed and shows further how judgments that partners make about relational events relate to spouses' global evaluations of the relationship. As compared with nondistressed spouses, distressed spouses often explain the cause of their partner's negative behaviors as stable, global, and internally driven and see the partner's behavior as intentional, selfishly motivated, and blameworthy (Fincham, Bradbury, & Scott, 1990). Distressed spouses make opposite attributions for positive events, often dismissing relationship-enhancing causes or implications. The attributional tendencies associated with distressed relationships are predictive of declines in relational satisfaction over time (Fincham & Bradbury, 1987).

RELATIONSHIP DEVELOPMENT AND RELATIONAL AND PERSONAL WELL-BEING

Personal relationship researchers have studied how people account for relational deescalation and development. For instance, Weiss (1975) examined how people use accounts to make sense of confusing events surrounding marital separation. Harvey, Wells, and Alvarez (1978) studied how newly separated persons explained the loss of a partner through accounts offered in diaries and interviews. The precedents for using accounts to study relational development are minimal; however, the research that does exist is best exemplified by the use of accounts to study turning points (e.g., how well couples survive their "first big fight") and behaviors that affect relational development and relational well-being (Honeycutt, 1995; Siegert & Stamp, 1994).

Our research is focused on attributions, both public and private, that partners offer for events in their relationship development and how attributions relate to current relational and personal well-being. We begin with a general look at how romantic relationships develop. Many models of relationship development (e.g., Knapp, 1984) suggest that couples pass through a series of stages as they grow closer. A certain pattern of behaviors is manifested in each stage, and partners advance in a Guttman progression so that completion of one stage is necessary for progression to the next step. Developmental behaviors include, for example, shared leisure time (a date), nonverbal intimacy, or saying "I love you."

We take a cognitive-behavioral approach to relationship development, which suggests that as couples engage in behaviors along their relational trajectory, they also make cognitive appraisals of their development. For example, these cognitions could include thoughts about their partner, the future of the relationship, or exclusivity in interests, desires, or both. We believe that a cognitive-behavioral approach holds promise for explaining and predicting relational quality. As reflected in our own research, presented in this chapter, we ask members of the relationship to state both what happened in their relationship and how and why they think things occurred the way they did. In so doing, we try to capture how they *experience* their relational development. As Bradbury and Fincham (1991) noted, it is the experience of interaction more than the interaction itself that affects changes in relational quality.

Although it is likely that either behaviors or cognitions could precede the other in relationship development, one of the fundamental assumptions of attribution theory is that attributions influence spousal behavior (Fincham & Bradbury, 1991). For example, the wish fulfillment model (Murray, Holmes, & Griffin, 1996) suggests that if partners have positive beliefs about the attributes of their partner or behavior, they will be motivated to behave in the future in ways that maintain or increase their love. Thus, while cognitions and behaviors in relationship development need not be closely related, in many cases, they are.

A second assumption of attribution theory is that attributions influence overall marital well-being (Fincham & Bradbury, 1991). Under this guide, our program of research examines how cognitive and behavioral factors associated with relationship development work together to influence relational well-being. It is our assumption that we are happier with our developing relationships when we feel they are progressing behaviorally at an appropriate rate and depth and also as we develop positive cognitions about the other and our relationship with him or her. We extend this assumption further to suggest that as our relationships develop behaviorally and cognitively in a positive direction, we also have better personal well-being (i.e., we are healthier in our lives generally). Similarly, our relational and personal well-being is in jeopardy when our relationships take a negative cognitive and behavioral path.

Our relationship development model of relational and personal well-being depicts how (1) cognitive and behavioral aspects of relationship development are associated with each other; (2) cognitive and behavioral aspects of relationship development are associated with relational well-being; (3) relational well-being is associated with personal well-being; and (4) cognitive and behavioral aspects of relationship development are directly associated with personal well-being. Although these relationships are plausibly recursive, in this chapter we explore relationship development factors as a possible stimulus for relational and personal well-being. There is also strong evidence to support the association between relationship well-being and physical well-being (Kiecolt-Glaser et al., 1987); however, our model reflects only those personal well-being variables that we specifically test in our program of research.

ACCOUNTS OF RELATIONSHIP DEVELOPMENT

As noted earlier, most partners appraise their relationship development. These appraisals often come in the form of accounts, developed both individually and collectively, for how they met, why their relationship progressed the way it did, how they overcame obstacles, and so on (Surra, Batchelder, & Hughes, 1995). Embedded within these accounts are attributions. Such accounts are likely to be an amalgamation of what really happened or did not happen with the individuals' and couples' own cognitive processing of that "reality."

We employ the Oral History Interview (OHI) as a mechanism for soliciting information on couples' attributions for relational development. The OHI (Buehlman & Gottman, 1996; Buehlman, Gottman, & Katz, 1992; Krokoff, 1984) is a semistructured interview, which asks couples a series of open-ended questions about pivotal points in their relationships, starting with how they met and got together and continuing with themes such as good and bad times in their relationship, how they got over bad times, and their expectations and philosophy about marriage. The development of the OHI was inspired by the work of sociologist-reporter Studs Terkel (1980), who conducted interviews that allowed respondents to produce a narrative, storylike account in their answers. A strength of the OHI is that it simultaneously taps into both specific relational events and global relational evaluations.

Since the development of the OHI, Buehlman has created a coding system to describe the perceptions couples reveal about how their relationship has progressed (Buehlman & Gottman, 1996; Buehlman et al., 1992). Couples' responses are coded along some of the following dimensions. *Fondness/affection* refers to how much each partner seems to be in love with or fond of each other, as manifested in compliments, positive affect, and reminiscing about romantic times. *Negativity toward the spouse* depicts the extent to which each partner displays negative affect, criticism, and disagreement toward the spouse in the interview. *Expansiveness/withdrawal* refers to how expressive and expansive versus withdrawn a partner is during the interview. *We-ness/separateness* distinguishes how much a partner sees him- or herself as a part of the couple versus as an individual with independence. *Chaos* measures whether couples feel they have control over their lives or are plagued by unexpected problems and hardships in life. *Glorifying the struggle* assesses the extent to which couples have had hard times in their marriage but made it through and even grew closer. *Disappointment/disillusionment* indicates whether partners have given up on or feel defeated by their relationship and do not know what makes a relationship work.

The coding of many of these dimensions reflects the nature of the attributions couples offer for various relational events. For example, the concept of glorifying the struggle is evident in the couples' response to the questions about what the hard times in their relationship were and why they stayed together. To glorify the struggle is to say, "It was hard, but worth it." People who attribute staying together through tough times to things such as finances, children, and family pressures are not glorifying the struggle because their answers are externally driven and do not emphasize the role of the relationship in overcoming the struggle. On the other hand, those who make more internal attributions, at least internal to the relationship, such as "because I knew I could count on her to get us through this," or "because it brought us closer as we worked together to solve the problem" are clearly glorifying the struggle. Other dimensions such as we-ness/separateness, disappointment/disillusionment, and negativity toward the spouse are also clearly tied to the nature of attributions for relational events.

The coded variables from the OHI have proved to be strong predictors of relational quality. For example, Buehlman et al. (1992) found variables such as fondness, negativity, and disappointment exhibit moderate to strong correlations with concurrent satisfaction and with a prospective measure of satisfaction administered 3 years later. The same researchers found similar associations between variables in the OHI and separation and divorce, again measured 3 years later. These findings lead to a very straightforward conclusion: How couple members view their past will predict their future (Buehlman et al., 1992; Gottman, 1994).

We have instituted some modifications to the OHI for several studies presented below. In some cases we were interested in seeing if these variables would be predictive of relational quality in dating relationships. In such cases, we modified some of the questions to make them appropriate to dating rather than married couples; for example, we asked participants to explain how and why they decided to stay in a committed relationship with their partner rather than a marriage. As noted earlier, an account is a spoken or written explanation. For some studies, it was not feasible to interview both members of the relationship face to face (in one case, one participant had recently broken up with the partner, and in the other, the couple was physically separated because of a prison sentence). In such cases, we developed a shortened, written version of the OHI, which allows respondents to write lengthy answers to our open-ended questions.

RESEARCH DESIGN CONSIDERATIONS

The research presented in the upcoming sections was guided by a number of principles that are more generally applicable to the study of close relationships. First, our studies are within the tradition of attempting to explain variance in relational satisfaction with various interpersonal communication and social psychological predictors. The study of satisfaction in close relationships is predicated on the assumption that dissatisfaction is perhaps the best predictor of relational dissolution. At least among married people, lack of satisfaction alone is not an entirely adequate predictor of divorce or separation (e.g., Gottman, 1991). The quality of a relationship is best described with more than just the members' *satisfaction* with that relationship. For that reason we also consider relational *stability* (duration of the relationship) and relational *commitment* (dedication to remaining in the relationship) to be equally important markers of relational quality.

A second assumption inherent in our program of research is that most relationships do not begin on the wedding day. For this reason, the study of premarital dating relationships is an important complement to studies on marital relations (Karney & Bradbury, 1995). Some, if not much, of the architecture for later relational quality is already present premaritally. For example, many of the risk factors for poor marital quality, such as personality, age, length of courtship, and interaction patterns are things that couples transport from their courtship into their marriages (Hill & Peplau, 1998). In this same vein, we assume there is greater change and fluctuation in young couples who have yet to fully establish patterns and routines in their relationships. For this reason, the focal point of many of our studies is young relationships.

Study 1

As a starting point, we designed our first study to examine how dating couples' relational quality is related to their cognitive appraisals of an event in their relationship development (Flora, 1998). We interviewed 117 dating partners, randomly asked them to describe and account for a positive or negative leisure event, and had them complete a postinterview questionnaire about measures of relational and leisure satisfaction. Studying the joint leisure events of dating couples is important because (1) most of their events together are leisure, and (2) leisure events have the potential for positive *and* negative relational consequences (Flora & Segrin, 1998; Reissman, Aron, & Bergen, 1993).

Past research on dating couples has asked participants to account for hypothetical events (Grigg, Fletcher, & Fitness, 1989; Fletcher, Fitness, & Blampied, 1990), to describe their relationship in general (Fletcher et al.,

1987), or to account for negative relationship events (Bradbury & Fincham, 1990; Siegert & Stamp, 1994). Although negative and unexpected behaviors have been found to instigate attributions, "there is a need to study different behaviors in different settings" as a means of testing the external validity of attribution theory (Fincham & Bradbury, 1991, p. 184; e.g., Manusov, Floyd, & Kerssen-Griep, 1997). Fincham and Bradbury also suggest that data containing attributions for specific partner behavior and events is more informative than attributions offered for global relational behaviors (e.g., relational maintenance).

The complete interview was analyzed by the Content Analysis of Verbatim Explanation (CAVE) technique, which rates causal explanations according to three attributional style dimensions: internal–external, stable–unstable, and global–specific (Peterson, Luborsky, & Seligman, 1983). For this study, relationship members were used as the focal point for rating internal–external causes. However, with regard to relationships, the focus of attributions becomes potentially unclear, particularly when considering internal–external dimensions (see Fletcher et al., 1987). Thus, each interview was rated again to distinguish among causal references attributed to the self, partner, or couple.

Results of this investigation illustrated that in accounts for both positive *and* negative leisure events, relational and leisure satisfaction are related to global–specific attributions. The greater the relational and leisure satisfaction, the more participants made global attributions for positive events and specific attributions for negative events. The following excerpt from one participant illustrates global attributions for a positive event: "She asked me out to a Run-DMC concert last semester at Granada. We talked a lot during the concert ... and that had a big impact. We talked about should we just split up since she graduates in December, or should we keep it going.... Pretty much it turned out for the best, so things were completely different." An excerpt from another participant depicts specific attributions for a negative event: "I remember sitting on the hill and just yelling. I mean it was negative at that point in time ... because I was really upset with the way he was thinking. But I think overall, it was OK in the long run because it helped us understand where we were both coming from." Interaction effects found in this study are consistent with other attribution research, which suggests that nondistressed spouses are more likely to see the cause of positive events as global, compared with distressed spouses, who see the cause of negative events as global (e.g., Fincham, Bradbury, & Scott, 1990).

By pinpointing the locus of control in the self, partner, or couple, we also found that in general participants attributed negative events to the self or partner and positive events to the couple. This attributional pattern lifted up the relationship and may have acted as a face-saving mechanism for the relationship's public image. On one hand, participants offered attributions that were arguably at the public level if they considered the interviewer as a public audience member. Since they have fewer barriers to dissolution than married couples, dating couples may be especially motivated to present a positive public image for the relationship as a means of justifying their commitment to the relationship.

Results from this study were encouraging because they replicated some attributional patterns found in past research on dating couples but in a new context. However, this initial study had some limitations, and we launched our research program toward addressing them. First, we needed to incorporate cognitive and behavioral indices together as a means of simultaneously assessing events in relationship development and what partners think about those events. Second, we sought to remedy the lack of variance in relational satisfaction that was inherent in this study as in many other studies that tap into a dating population, because the data were skewed toward including primarily very satisfied participants.

Study 2

In the second study, we expanded our approach to assess the attributions dating partners offer when they account for a collection of relationship development events (Flora & Segrin, 1999a). As a counterpart to studying how partners' cognitive appraisals of relationship development are associated with relational well-being, we also measured how the path of actual relationship trajectory behaviors is associated with relational well-being. In addition, we began to explore the idea that cognitive appraisals and relationship trajectories are related to personal well-being as well as to relational well-being.

The second study involved 200 participants who were required either (1) to be in a romantic relationship that had existed for at least 4 months (intact group), or (2) to have broken up within the last 4 months from a romantic relationship that had been in existence for at least 4 months (broken-up group). Participants completed a questionnaire that assessed cognitive appraisals of their relationship development and their trajectory of relationship development, as well as relational and personal well-being. Relational well-being was operationalized as satisfaction, commitment, and stability, and personal well-being was operationalized as loneliness and social adjustment.

Participants completed the written version of the OHI. Responses were coded for we-ness versus separateness, glorifying the struggle, and relational disappointment. A measure developed by Flora and Segrin (1999a) was used to assess the trajectory of relationship development. This 19-item instrument asks respondents to indicate whether they have ever experienced certain behaviors, feelings, or thoughts indicative of relational intimacy, and if so, how much time, if any, elapsed between the first date and these experiences. Each respondent was assigned a total score that was an amalgamation of the number of items endorsed, weighted by the speed with which the phenomenon was experienced. This amalgamation reflects the depth and speed of relationship development.

Unlike close relationships with spouses, family members, or coworkers, there are few barriers to the dissolution of dating relationships. Once terminated, people whose relationships have dissolved are effectively excluded from investigations of dating relationships. This exclusion has led to a large body of literature on dating relationships that includes mostly very satisfied participants. Yet many people are not entirely satisfied with the quality of their dating relationships, and in fact some are quite dissatisfied. In an effort to elude this shortcoming of many past investigations of dating dyads, this study sampled equal numbers of intact and broken-up dating relationships. The rationale behind the inclusion of recently broken-up relationships is that the people involved are or were likely to be dissatisfied with their dating relationships, yet they still represent a prevalent and significant reality among people who are in dating relationships.

Results indicated that relationship trajectories *and* cognitive appraisals of the relationship trajectory are related to relational well-being and in some cases to personal well-being. Specifically, we found that persons who appraise their relationship development events with more we-ness versus separateness and less relational disappointment are more satisfied with (and in the latter case, more committed to) their relationships. The following statement from a participant shows high we-ness and low relational disappointment: "In the beginning, my time with John was precious. We spent almost every day together, and we've taken several road trips camping…. For the most part, we have similar beliefs and values. We believe in each other.... There are many little things that I didn't know about John, but for the most part, I would say we continue to have great times together."

The findings in Study 2 are compatible with those of Buehlman et al. (1992), who explain that greater we-ness characterizes relationships with more connection and intimacy, and less relational disappointment characterizes relationships with more fulfillment, hope, and pleasure. The results of Study 2 also demonstrated that dating partners who glorify their struggle to a greater extent are more stable and committed but not necessarily more satisfied. The idea is that glorifiers acknowledge having hard and even dissatisfying times, but they view their glorifying as an expression of how committed they are in the midst of tough times. For example, the following remarks show how one participant glorified struggles that affected the relationship: "A little while ago I was having a lot of troubles with my family, and they were troubles I couldn't tell anyone else, and so I was just trying to deal with those.... She started thinking that I wasn't interested in her and she was worried I was going to try to find someone else. I finally decided to tell her what was going on because I didn't want to lose her.... We were honest with each other, and now we have a pretty good system worked out so that we just know how to make it work when we have something wrong."

As for relational trajectories, when participants reported that their trajectories moved both faster and deeper, they also reported more satisfaction and commitment but not more stability. When relationships develop along an extremely slow and surface-level path, partners are less satisfied, probably because the relationship is not meeting their expectations for intimate relationships, and partners are also less committed, probably because they have not invested the behaviors, cognitions, and emotions that make for commitment.

We also found that when people appraised their relationship development events as disappointing, they reported being more lonely in their lives in general and exhibited poor social adjustment. This effect stood even after controlling for general relational outcomes, such as satisfaction, commitment, and stability. Satisfaction was the only general relational outcome significantly correlated with loneliness, $r = .21$, $p < .01$, and social adjustment, $r = .20$, $p < .01$; however, satisfaction, along with the other relational outcomes, was not found to make a significant contribution to personal well-being above the impact of these relational development variables. Thus, the impact of negative cognitive appraisals on personal well-being is particularly striking. Disappointment with the relationship's development seems to spill over to general feelings of loneliness even in one's larger social network. The link between relational disappointment and poor social adjustment works the same way. A disappointing relationship coincides with being poorly adjusted to social and leisure life in general. The way we view our relationship past is related to our present personal well-being.

Study 3

We conducted our third study in order to collect data from both partners of the relational dyad and to hear from both dating and married couples (Flora & Segrin, 1999b). Given the success of the written form of the OHI, we also wondered what more we could find from conducting the full OHI. Finally, we wanted to begin to explore possible causal relationships between relationship development and relational well-being and to explore further the relational correlates of personal well-being.

The third study included 65 married and 66 seriously dating dyads. On arrival of the couple at the laboratory, an interviewer conducted the full OHI with them together, and then the partners separately completed a survey with questions about their relational and personal well-being and relational trajectory. Trained coders rated the videotaped interviews along the following dimensions: fondness–affection, negativity toward spouse, we-ness–separateness, expansiveness–withdrawal, chaos, glorifying the struggle, and disappointment–disillusionment. Six months later, the participants were contacted by phone for time 2 follow-up measures of relational satisfaction and stability.

The general results were similar to those of study 2, indicating that both the path of couples' relational trajectory and their cognitive appraisals of the path are related to relational well-being and in some cases to personal well-being. Specifically, the findings on relational trajectory in study 3 suggest that couples who progress both more quickly and to deeper levels are more satisfied and, especially, more committed. On one hand, the results further support the idea that couples are happier when their relationships progress with speed and depth. Relationships that progress at a slow, surface pace may contain "omissions" (e.g., what the self or partner is not doing, such as not meeting parents, not talking about future plans as a couple, not getting married) (Honeycutt, 1995, p. 12).

Another possible interpretation of these findings suggests that participants develop positive evaluations, for example, reporting high relational satisfaction and commitment, as a result of or perhaps to justify a fast trajectory. According to Bem's (1967) Self-Perception Theory, "Individuals come to know their own attitudes, emotions, and other internal states partially from inferring them from observations of their own overt behavior and/or circumstances in which this behavior occurs" (Bem, 1972, p. 2). Certain behaviors such as "became sexually intimate and involved with this person," and "done something with this person that you have never done with a past friend, family member, boyfriend, or girlfriend" were reported by 83 to 94% of all dating respondents.

Among this same group, however, various cognitions and emotional states such as "decided that you want to spend the rest of your life with this person" and "felt like you knew this person better than anyone else does" were endorsed by only 55 to 79% of these respondents. The pattern of means also suggested that these particular behaviors (i.e., becoming sexually intimate and engaging in new behaviors with a partner) preceded these cognitions (thinking about spending your life with a partner and feeling as if you know a partner better than anyone else). Consequently, participants may have inferred a sense of satisfaction in their relationship based simply on the fact that they were engaging in many of the behaviors in which satisfied couples engage.

As for cognitive appraisals in the OHI, we found evidence to suggest that one partner's cognitive appraisals of the relationship path are associated with *both* partners' relational well-being. The more positively women viewed their relationship past, the more satisfied and committed they and their partners were. When men viewed their relationship past positively, they and their partners were more concurrently satisfied but not more committed. We also found that some cognitive appraisals, such as men's low negativity toward the partner and high we-ness, were related to greater female satisfaction but had no association with their own satisfaction. For both men and women, relational disappointment and low expansiveness displayed a consistent relationship with loneliness. Women were also more lonely when they appraised the relationship with less fondness, more negativity, and more chaos. In addition, their level of loneliness was high when they had partners who were highly disappointed with the relationship and negative toward them.

We were also able to predict some changes in longitudinal satisfaction and stability. For example, both partners, and especially women, were more satisfied at time 2 when they reported a faster and deeper relational trajectory at time 1. On the basis of their track record, partners who were in slow-moving, surface relationships at time 1 may not have experienced much more development in their trajectories – an unfulfilling, dissatisfying state to be in 6 months later in a relationship.

Relational trajectories that lacked speed and depth at time 1 were also predictive of relationship dissolution. Partners apparently gave up on relationships that demonstrated little previous developmental progress. In addition, couples were at greater risk for relationship dissolution when women's cognitive appraisals were characterized by high negativity toward their partners in the OHI. A large body of evidence supports this idea that women's negativity, in general, is more consequential for relationships than men's. For example, Pasch and Bradbury (1998) found strong evidence that wives' negative behavior when offering support is predictive of later distress. Similarly, Fincham and Bradbury (1987) found that negative attributions made by women have a longer-lasting association with relational outcomes over time than men's.

Study 4

While marriage provides some protection against the experience of loneliness (Stack, 1998), a substantial percentage of married people still experience loneliness (Tornstam, 1992). Because it is so deviant from expectations, the experience of loneliness within the context of a marriage can be particularly devastating (Rokach & Brock, 1997).

We are currently conducting a study of relational histories and loneliness among married prison inmates (Segrin, Flora, & Givertz, 1999). The relational separation imposed by court-ordered incarceration creates a situation in which loneliness is very probable. We hypothesized that married prisoners' accounts of their relationship development would be associated with their experience of loneliness while incarcerated. Because loneliness is a cognitive-affective phenomenon, we expected that those who were are still able to describe their marriage in positive terms would be protected to some extent from the experience of loneliness. As in our past studies, we also expected the accounts to be significantly related to relationship satisfaction and commitment. Thus far, we have data from 36 married inmates (20 men, 16 women) in medium or maximum security facilities. These inmates are serving sentences that range from 4 months to life. The typical participant in this study has served on average 3 years in prison or jail since being married to his or her current spouse, but some have spent over 10 years apart from their spouses.

The method of this study was very similar to that of study 2. Prison inmates completed a questionnaire that began with our written adaptation of the OHI (Buehlman & Gottman, 1996). They then completed measures of loneliness, relational satisfaction, commitment, and several other scales not immediately relevant to the hypotheses presented here. Responses to the OHI questions were coded for chaos, we-ness versus separateness, glorifying the struggle, and relational disappointment.

Preliminary results indicate that the dimensions of chaos and relational disappointment were significantly related to inmates' feelings of loneliness. That is, the more chaotic inmates' marriages were and the more they expressed disappointment in their marriages, the more lonely they felt. There were also strong associations between all of the OHI dimensions and inmates' marital satisfaction and commitment. Those who expressed less chaos and relational disappointment also reported being more satisfied and committed to their marriage. The more their responses reflected we-ness versus separateness and the more they tended to glorify the struggle (something that a prison inmate has a vast opportunity to engage in), the more satisfied and committed they were to their relationships.

For example, the deterioration of a marriage is evident through the chaos, separateness, and disappointment in the following remarks from the responses of one participant. When asked how and why he decided to get married, the participant indicated, "Me and my wife been together for about 2 years when she got pregnant and with her family being religious we decided to get married so our baby wouldn't be born [out of] wedlock. Plus I loved her for all that she had been threw [*sic*] with me and with that I found it easy to say yes when we got married, plus I wanted my lil' boy to have my last name." When asked why they stayed together he stated, "Because she wanted a family more than anything." When asked how his marriage is different now from when they first got together, he stated, "Now she doesn't want to be here for me while I'm locked up this time unlike all the other times. I know that ... she won't always be here for me and I never thought that would happen."

Similar themes are evident in the responses of another inmate. When asked what moments stand out as the really hard times he indicated, "When I got locked up. This might be the end of our marriage. She will not write or let me call or come see me." When asked how the marriage is different now, he stated "She don't care no more since she can't be with me. She has given up on me. She don't think I getting out of prison. I did not know that she wouldn't stay with me in bad times."

Preliminary results from this investigation indicate that prisoners' accounts of their relational histories are indicative of their concurrent satisfaction with and commitment to their marriage. In addition, the themes expressed in these accounts are associated with their experience of loneliness. Prisoners who described their marriages in terms that express disappointment and chaos expressed more loneliness. It is interesting to note that prisoners' experience of loneliness appeared unrelated to the total length of their sentence, to the total amount of time in their lives that they have spent in prison or jail, or to the time that they have spent in prison since being married. These results highlight the fact that loneliness is not the result of mere separation but is influenced by the perceived quality of the marital relationship.

CONCLUSION

When people offer attributions or accounts for relationship development events, they reveal something about the quality of that relationship as well as something about their own personal well-being. Consistently, we have found that people who are satisfied with their close relationship will talk about relational events in ways that attribute positive qualities to their partner and to the relationship as a whole. They do this through such mechanisms as glorifying past struggles, conveying a sense of smoothness and order in their developmental trajectory, expressing events in terms that reflect we-ness, thus taking relational as opposed to personal responsibility for events and phenomena that affect the relationship, expressing minimal disappointment with the relationship, and attributing certain positive events to the couple as opposed to its individuals.

The themes that are evident in couples' discourse proved to be good barometers of their relationship satisfaction and commitment. In addition, we found that partners were more prone to be satisfied and especially committed when they reported a relational trajectory that developed with relative speed and depth. An important goal for future research involves determining the extent to which relationship quality drives cognitive-behavioral tendencies or to which people perceive high quality in their relationship because they hold this cognitive-behavioral style, as in the case of a self-fulfilling prophecy. Presently, there is some evidence to support both of these possibilities.

It is also apparent that people's accounts for relationship development events reveal something about their own psychosocial well-being. We have presented several instances in which people's loneliness and social adjustment appeared to seep into their account and attribution making. Negative themes were associated consistently with greater loneliness and less social adjustment. The quality of the relationship may be a factor that intervenes between the cognitions reflected in the account or attribution and the psychosocial well-being, but, again, other avenues of causality should be considered. As people seek out and develop close, intimate connections with others, they perform and elicit interpersonal behaviors and develop and maintain cognitions about those behaviors. The quality of such relationships is closely associated not just with the behaviors but also with the way that we experience and express those behaviors and events both in our own minds and to other people.

REFERENCES

Beach, S. R. H., Jouriles, E. N., & O'Leary, K. D. (1985). Extramarital sex: Impact on depression and commitment in couples seeking marital therapy. *Journal of Sex and Marital Therapy, 11*, 99–108.

Bem, D. J. (1967). Self-perception: An alternative interpretation of cognitive dissonance phenomena. *Psychological Review, 74*, 183–200.

Bem, D. J. (1972). Self-perception theory. In L. Berkowitz (Ed.), *Advances in experimental social psychology* (Vol. 6, pp. 1–62). New York: Academic Press.

Bradbury, T. N. (Ed.). (1998). *The developmental course of marital dysfunction.* New York: Cambridge University Press.

Bradbury, T. N., & Fincham, F. D. (1990). Attributions in marriage: Review and critique. *Psychological Bulletin, 107*, 3–33.

Bradbury, T. N., & Fincham, F. D. (1991). A contextual model of advancing the study of marital interaction. In G. J. O. Fletcher & F. D. Fincham (Eds.), *Cognition in close relationships* (pp. 127–147). Hillsdale, NJ: Lawrence Erlbaum.

Buehlman, K., & Gottman, J. M. (1996). *The oral history interview and the oral history coding system.* Mahwah, NJ: Lawrence Erlbaum.

Buehlman, K. T., Gottman, J. M., & Katz, L. F. (1992). How a couple view their past predicts their future: Predicting divorce from an oral history interview. *Journal of Family Psychology, 5,* 295–318.

Cody, M. J., & McLaughlin, M. L. (1990). Interpersonal accounting. In H. Giles & W. P. Robinson (Eds.), *Handbook of language and social psychology* (pp. 227–255). Chichester, UK: John Wiley & Sons.

Fincham, F. D., & Bradbury, T. N. (1987). The impact of attributions in marriage: A longitudinal analysis. *Journal of Personality and Social Psychology, 53,* 510–517.

Fincham, F. D., & Bradbury, T. N. (1991). Cognition in marriage: A program of research on attributions. In W. H. Jones & D. Perlman (Eds.), *Advances in personal relationships* (Vol. 2, pp. 159–203). London: Jessica Kingsley.

Fincham, F. D., Bradbury, T. N., & Scott, C. K. (1990). Cognition in marriage. In F. D. Fincham & T. N. Bradbury (Eds.), *The psychology of marriage* (pp. 118–149). New York: Guilford.

Fletcher, G. J. O., Fincham, F. D., Cramer, L., & Heron, H. (1987). The role of attribution in the development of dating relationships. *Journal of Social Psychology, 53,* 481–489.

Fletcher, G. J. O., Fitness, J., & Blampied, N. M. (1990). The link between attributions and happiness in close relationships: The roles of depression and explanatory style. *Journal of Social and Clinical Psychology, 9,* 243–255.

Flora, J. (1998, August). *Attributions, social skills, and the maintenance of romantic relationships in joint leisure time.* Paper presented at the annual meeting of the American Psychological Association, San Francisco.

Flora, J., & Segrin, C. (1998). Joint leisure time in friend and romantic relationships. *Journal of Social and Personal Relationships, 15,* 711–718.

Flora, J., & Segrin, C. (2000a). Relational development in dating couples: Implications for satisfaction and loneliness. *Journal of Social and Personal Relationships,* in press.

Flora, J., & Segrin, C. (2000b). Relational well-being and perceptions of relational history in married and dating couples. *Submitted for Publication.*

Gottman, J. M. (1991). Predicting the longitudinal course of marriages. *Journal of Marital and Family Therapy, 17,* 3–7.

Gottman, J. M. (1994). *What predicts divorce: The relationship between marital processes and marital outcomes.* Hillsdale, NJ: Lawrence Erlbaum.

Grigg, F., Fletcher, G. J. O., & Fitness, J. (1989). Spontaneous attributions in happy and unhappy dating relationships. *Journal of Social and Personal Relationships, 6,* 61–68.

Harvey, J. H., Turnquist, D. C., & Agostinelli, G. (1988). Identifying attributions in oral and written explanations. In C. Antaki (Ed.), *Analyzing everyday explanation.* Beverly Hills: Sage.

Harvey, J. H., Weber, A. L., & Orbuch, T. L. (1990). *Interpersonal accounts: A social psychological perspective.* Cambridge, MA: Basil Blackwell.

Harvey, J. H., Wells, G. L., & Alvarez, M. D. (1978). Attribution in the context of conflict and separation in close relationships. *New directions in attribution research* (Vol. 2, pp. 235–260). Hillsdale, NJ: Erlbaum.

Hill, C. T., & Peplau, L. A. (1998). Premarital predictors of relationship outcomes: A 15-year follow-up of the Boston couples study. In T. N. Bradbury

(Eds.), *The developmental course of marital dysfunction* (pp. 237–278). Cambridge, MA: Cambridge University Press.

Honeycutt, J. M. (1995). Predicting relational trajectory beliefs as a consequence of typicality and necessity ratings of relationship behaviors. *Communication Research Reports, 12,* 3–14.

Karney, B. R., & Bradbury, T. N. (1995). The longitudinal course of marital quality and stability: A review of theory, method, and research. *Psychological Bulletin, 118,* 3–34.

Kiecolt-Glaser, J. K., Fisher, B. S., Ogrocki, P., Stout, J. C., Speicher, C. E., & Glaser, R. (1987). Marital quality, marital disruption, and immune function. *Psychosomatic Medicine, 49,* 13–33.

Knapp, M. L. (1984). *Interpersonal communication and human relationships.* Boston: Allyn & Bacon.

Krokoff, L. (1984). The anatomy of blue-collar marriages (Doctoral dissertation, University of Illinois at Urbana-Champaign, 1984). *Dissertation Abstracts International.*

Manusov, V., Floyd, K., & Kerssen-Griep, J. (1997). Yours, mine, and ours: Mutual attributions for nonverbal behaviors in couples' interactions. *Communication Research, 24,* 234–260.

Murray, S. L., Holmes, J. G., & Griffin, D. W. (1996). The benefits of positive illusions: Idealization and the construction of satisfaction in close relationships. *Journal of Personality and Social Psychology, 70,* 79–98.

Orbuch, T. (1997). People's accounts count: The sociology of accounts. *Annual Review of Sociology, 23,* 455–478.

Peterson, C., Luborsky, L., & Seligman, M. E. P. (1983). Attributions and depressive mood shifts: A case study using symptom context method. *Journal of Abnormal Psychology, 92,* 96–103.

Reissman, C., Aron, A., & Bergen, M. R. (1993). Shared activities and marital satisfaction: Causal direction and self-expansion versus boredom. *Journal of Social and Personal Relationships, 10,* 243–254.

Rokach, A., & Brock, H (1997). Loneliness and the effects of life changes. *The Journal of Psychology, 131,* 284–298.

Scott, M. B., & Lyman, S. (1967). Accounts. *American Sociological Review, 33,* 46–62.

Segrin, C., & Fitzpatrick, M. A. (1992). Depression and verbal aggressiveness in different marital couple types. *Communication Studies, 43,* 79–91.

Segrin, C., Flora, J., & Givertz, M. (1999). *Relationship development and loneliness among prison inmates.* Manuscript in preparation.

Siegert, J. R., & Stamp, G. H. (1994). "Our first big fight" as a milestone in the development of close relationships. *Communication Monographs, 61,* 345–360.

Stack, S. (1998). Marriage, family and loneliness: A cross: National study. *Sociological Perspectives, 41,* 415–432.

Sullivan, H. S. (1953). *Conceptions of modern psychiatry.* New York: Norton.

Surra, C. A., Batchelder, M. L., & Hughes, D. K. (1995). Accounts and the demystification of courtship. In M. A. Fitzpatrick & A. L. Vangelisti (Eds.), *Explaining family interaction* (pp. 112–141). Thousand Oaks, CA: Sage.

Terkel, S. (1980). *American dreams lost and found.* New York: Ballantine.

Thompson, S. C., & Kelly, H. H. (1981). Judgements of responsibility for activities in close relationships. *Journal of Personality and Social Psychology, 41,* 469–477.

Tornstam, L. (1992). Loneliness in marriage. *Journal of Social and Personal Relationships, 9,* 197–217.

Weiss, R. S. (1975). *Marital separation.* New York: Basic Books.

Affect, Attribution, and Communication

Uniting Interaction Episodes and Global Relationship Judgments

Denise Haunani Solomon

It is notable that a collection of essays gathered together under the title *Attribution, Communication Behavior, and Close Relationships* should begin with a section addressing the role of affect. As noted most clearly in the chapter by Forgas, an explicit discussion of mood and emotion is a relatively recent addition to work on attribution processes. The scholarly process of theory development presumes that explanatory frameworks are constructed in a rational, logical, and affectively neutral manner; perhaps social scientists as a group have fallen victim to the common error of projecting those same qualities onto the human processes we seek to explain (Rubenstein, Laughlin, & McManus, 1984). The collection of essays in this section reminds us that human behavior is subject to an intricate web of subtle influences, of which affect is a pervasive part.

Nowhere is the interplay among affect, attributions, and communication more important than in the context of close relationships. Research on attributions in ongoing relationships consistently reveals an association between the explanations that partners construct for each other's behavior and their relationship satisfaction (e.g., Camper, Jacobson, Holtzworth-Munroe, & Schmaling, 1988; Holtzworth-Munroe & Jacobson, 1985; Jacobson, McDonald, Follette, & Berley, 1985). In short, this body of research suggests that attributions for positive and negative relationship events both arise from and serve to reinforce relationship satisfaction or dissatisfaction (see Fletcher & Fincham, 1991). In much the same way, the affective tone of a relationship shapes and is perpetuated by the valence of particular interactions (Alberts, 1988; Christensen & Shenk, 1991; Gottman, 1979; Rands, Levinger, & Mellinger, 1981; Scott, Fuhrman, & Wyer, 1991; Sillars, Pike, Jones, & Redmon, 1983).

Despite the important insights gained from research that differentiates the affective, attributional, and communicative patterns of satisfied and dissatisfied partners, the process by which particular interaction episodes become part of a more global judgment of relationship quality remains unclear. Researchers have alternately focused on how satisfaction influences perceptions or behaviors (e.g., Camper et al., 1988; Hendrick & Hendrick, 1988; Jacobson et al., 1985) or on the effects of perceptions and behaviors on satisfaction (e.g., Canary & Spitzberg, 1989; Fincham & Bradbury, 1987; Metts & Cupach, 1990; Rusbult, Johnson, & Morrow, 1986; Seligman, Fazio, & Zanna, 1980). The most consistently advocated causal model in this body of research specifies that relationship satisfaction, perceptions, and communication behaviors have a mutually or cyclically causal relationship.

This reciprocal causal model accommodates extant empirical findings; however, the prevailing view fails to explain how interaction experiences might result in polar changes in relational attitudes. In particular, the role of specific episodes in the deterioration of satisfaction within satisfying relationships remains unclear. More generally, the model described falls short of identifying the process by which particular interactions have an impact on relational judgments. Although it is axiomatic to say that communication defines relationships (Watzlawick, Beavin, & Jackson, 1967), we know surprisingly little about how this is accomplished in the context of ongoing relationships.

The chapters by Forgas and by Honeycutt and Eidenmuller examine how affect influences attribution, communication, or both within particular interaction episodes; Vangelisti and Flora and Segrin focus our attention on the correspondence between affect, attribution, and relationship quality. Taken together, these efforts suggest that affective and attributional processes can clarify the link between interaction episodes and global relationship judgments. Building on these essays, the pages that follow examine affect, attribution, and communication as mechanisms that unite specific interactions with global perceptions of relationships. First, I review relevant qualities of affect and attributions. From this foundation, I explicate associations among affect, attribution, and communication to clarify how these processes can unify the diversity of interaction experiences people have with close relationship partners. In my view, the impact of specific interaction events on subsequent encounters provides a mechanism by which communication experiences ultimately shape global relationship judgments. In an application of this framework, I speculate on the processes linking conflict episodes to the foundations of dissatisfaction with close relationships.

QUALITIES OF AFFECT AND ATTRIBUTION

Affect and attributions are parts of the general sensorimotor complex that guides an organism's interaction with its environment. Researchers in many different fields have argued that this system is the product of evolutionary forces, such that affect and sense making guide behavior in a manner that enhanced the survival and reproductive success of our ancestors (Dillard, 1998; Izard, 1993; Tooby & Cosmides, 1990).

Attribution refers generally to the process of constructing explanations for events. Although these explanations can be characterized in a variety of ways (see Flora and Segrin), attribution theorists have historically focused on the locus and stability of causes as fundamental qualities (Kelley, 1967; Jones & Davis, 1965). The locus of cause refers to whether the forces causing an event are seen as internal or external to the actor; the stability dimension references whether the causal forces are of a short-term or lasting nature. Importantly, attributions that locate the cause of events in external and unstable forces imply a temporary condition in the environment; internal and stable attributions for events suggest a state of affairs with relevance beyond the particular situation.

In a somewhat parallel fashion, affect has both temporally limited and dispositional or stable qualities (Dillard, 1998). The phasic aspect of affect is embodied in emotions. Emotions are assumed to arise in response to specific changes in an organism's environment (Frijda, 1986; Lazarus, 1991); in other words, emotions depend on the interplay between the organism and the environment. Emotional experience is differentiated into particular emotions that correspond with unique triggering conditions (Scherer, 1984) and have distinct action tendencies (Frijda, 1986). As such, emotions represent fluid and immediate changes in an organism's affective state that guide responses to equally fluid changes within the environment.

The tonic side of affect captures the baseline state that pervades an episode, as exemplified by (but not limited to) an individual's mood. Although tonic states might arise from particular experiences (e.g., exposure to films or music in the Forgas or Honeycutt and Eidenmuller studies), their duration transcends the more momentary changes in a situation. Moreover, Guerrero, Andersen, and Trost (1998) have suggested that moods lack the specific target object that defines emotional experiences (see also Schwarz & Clore, 1983). In this sense, a tonic state constitutes a comparatively stable characteristic that the individual brings to the environment in which interaction occurs.

Dillard (1998) suggested that tonic states are as important as emotions in coordinating an organism's successful interaction with the environment. Whereas emotions direct particular actions, tonic states provide information about the store of resources available to enact various responses. For example, a sad mood might signal depleted resources, whereas a happy mood indicates that energy is available to undertake more demanding actions. Notably, this resource availability interpretation of mood is not inconsistent with the evidence reported by Forgas concerning the impact of mood on perceptions of relationships, attributions for success and failure, and strategic communication.

The most explicit conceptualization of the tonic side of affect in the preceding chapters focuses on the effects of mood on attribution, communication, and relationship perceptions (Forgas; Honeycutt & Eidenmuller). These chapters offer compelling evidence that moods induced by exposure to incidental features of the environment influence a broad range of communicative and attributional activities. In the context of close relationships, however, the dispositional quality of the relationship (i.e., whether it is satisfying or dissatisfying) is highlighted as an additional tonic influence on communication and attribution. Vangelisti reports that relational quality is associated both with attributions about whether hurtful behavior was intentional and with the intensity of hurt feelings. Similarly, Flora and Segrin find that relational well-being is correlated with the valence of accounts for relationship events. Although Flora and Segrin interpret relationship quality as an outcome of the accounts individuals construct for relationship events, the likelihood that relationship quality has a tonic effect on recall for those events is equally plausible.

The phasic and tonic aspects of affect become entwined within particular episodes. On the one hand, tonic affective states influence the propensity to experience particular emotions (Zillman, 1996; Zillman, deWied, King-Jablonski, & Jenzowsky, 1996). For example, a good mood can predispose an individual to respond to expectancy violations with elation, whereas a bad mood would promote a more negative emotional reaction. Alternatively, the emotional residue from a particular episode may have implications for more persistent moods.

As evidence of this, emotions that are not correctly attributed to sources have an ongoing impact on communication processes (Schwarz & Clore, 1983; Schwarz et al., 1991; Sinclair, Mark, & Clore, 1994). Thus, although emotions are evoked in response to more momentary changes in the environment, they can contribute to a tonic affective state.

The phasic and tonic qualities of interaction with the environment are developed more clearly with respect to affective processes; however, I noted previously that attribution has similar temporary and stable implications. In particular, attributions can locate cause in transient characteristics of the situation or forces that transcend the particular episode. In the language of affect, some attributions have phasic qualities, such that they help individuals make sense of momentary conditions in the environment. Other attributions exert a tonic or persistent effect on the individual's interaction with the environment; not unlike moods, perceptions of enduring causal forces inform and constrain the range of behavioral options by defining the parameters of the situation (cf. Chen & Chaiken, 1999). Further, as with emotions, tonic attributional states should increase the propensity to make particular attributions for specific events, whereas phasic attributions should inform more persistent accounts that become part of an individual's enduring reality.

To summarize, affect and attributions are defined as complementary systems that govern an organism's interaction with the environment. Although these systems manage distinct inputs and outputs, I have suggested that both affect and attributions have transient and lasting aspects. At the phasic level, emotions and attributions address the immediate and momentary changes in the environment to which organisms must attend and respond. At the same time, affect and attributions exert a tonic impact that generally structures interaction with the environment. Although phasic processes are tied to particular episodes, they can influence tonic states. Moreover, tonic states transcend the moment and have relevance to subsequent interactions with the environment. In the following section, I explore how the phasic and tonic qualities of affect and attribution can unify communication episodes within close relationships.

AFFECT, ATTRIBUTION, AND COMMUNICATION

As exemplified so poignantly in Vangelisti's program of research, communication with close relationship partners frequently evokes emotions and attributional activity. Certainly, the communication behaviors of others are among the most salient and dynamic features of the environments social creatures inhabit; as such, they constitute a primary target of affective and cognitive processing. In fact, prominence of interaction partners in the perceptual field may lie at the root of both attributional and emotional processing biases. It is well established that individuals tend to explain the behavior of others in terms of internal, rather than external, causes (for recent reviews see Gilbert & Malone, 1995; Trope & Higgins, 1993). In the same way, moods induced by incidental stimuli (e.g., music and films) are more likely to be associated with interaction partners when people misattribute the affective state (Schwarz & Clore, 1983). For these reasons, communication events in close relationships become the focal point of emotional and attributional experiences.

On the other hand, communication is an important subset of the behaviors under the directive influence of emotions and attributions. Scholars have suggested that the action tendencies associated with specific emotions can be generally characterized in terms of approach or avoidance (e.g., Frijda, 1986). In the same way, attributions for the behaviors of others define exchanges in ways that inform and constrain communicative responses (e.g., Sillars, 1998). Although physical withdrawal or engagement may be the most explicit way to accomplish approach or avoidance, flight or physical engagement has limited utility in ongoing close relationships. In this context, communication provides a less radical way to effect approach or avoidance. Thus, within ongoing relationships, communication may be a primary mechanism by which affective and attributional states are manifested.

Affect and attributions also influence communication behavior in more subtle ways. As Honeycutt and Eidenmuller suggest, the affect induced by exposure to music does not produce specific actions targeting the source of the music but rather is insinuated in behaviors directed toward interaction partners. In other words, tonic states are inherently manifested in communication behaviors. Nowhere is this more clearly explicated than in Forgas's Affect Infusion Model. In a similar fashion, attributions that support inferences about stable or dispositional qualities have implications for interaction with partners beyond the particular episode. For example, the attributions married partners make for the spouse's problematic behavior are associated with the negativity of behavior during subsequent interactions (Fincham & Bradbury, 1988; Fincham, Bradbury, & Scott, 1990). More generally, Sillars (1998) suggested that because people take attributions as veridical experience, they have a profound impact on communication in relationships.

A consideration of the phasic and tonic aspects of affective and attributional systems provides insight into how particular interactions can ultimately impact global evaluations of relationships. As we have seen, communication with close relationship partners is likely to evoke emotions and instigate sense-making activities. Although these reactions generally function to guide communication behavior within a particular episode, the affect and attributions generated during an interaction have the potential to transcend the boundaries of that exchange. To the extent that tonic affective states and persistent attributional accounts arise from an interaction, that interaction is implicitly relevant to subsequent communication events. More specifically, tonic states shape subsequent interaction, including the specific emotions and attributions generated during the otherwise unrelated episode. In this manner, discrete and diverse interactions between relationship partners can become unified and ultimately support a global judgment about the relationship.

FROM CONFLICT EPISODES TO GLOBAL RELATIONSHIP JUDGMENTS

Although any communication exchange can participate in the process I have outlined, a partner's negative and unexpected behaviors are particularly likely to evoke strong emotion and sense-making efforts (Weiner, 1986). Conflict, for example, is pervasive in both satisfying and dissatisfying close interpersonal relationships (Argyle & Furnham, 1983; Kirchler, 1988; Lloyd, 1990; Roloff, 1987). Although conflict occurs within both distressed and nondistressed relationships, relationship satisfaction *is* distinguished by perceptions of relational difficulties (e.g., Camper et al., 1988; Holtzworth-Munroe & Jacobson, 1985; Jacobson et al., 1985) and the interaction behaviors of partners discussing those problems (e.g., Alberts, 1988; Christensen & Shenk, 1991; Gottman, 1979; Rands et al., 1981; Rusbult, Zembrodt, & Gunn, 1982; Sillars et al., 1983). As noted in the opening to this chapter, these empirical observations address the perpetuation of prevailing relationship attitudes but fall short of explaining how particular interactions causally impact global judgments about relationships.

I propose that conflict episodes influence satisfaction within close relationships when the affect and attributions associated with these interactions are manifested in otherwise unrelated communication events. To the extent that conflict interactions prompt persistent negative moods and unflattering attributions, subsequent interactions between partners will be compromised. More specifically, a negative tonic state arising from conflict could lead relationship partners to be less supportive of each other, less accommodating of requests, less cooperative about coordinating instrumental activities, etc. In other words, the myriad of every day encounters that are the essence of relationship maintenance are vulnerable to the impact of tonic states that transcend the boundaries of conflict interactions. It is the deterioration in the quality of communication between partners across these diverse environments that results in a general decrease in relationship satisfaction. Thus, the specific conflict episode, through transfer to other communication environments, causally influences global assessments of relationship quality.

Of course, not all conflicts pervade communication between relationship partners. The processes outlined previously suggest that the manifestation of conflict in later interactions depends on whether the conflict produces affective and attributional states that persist beyond the conflict episode, rather than phasic emotions or attributions. For example, situational attributions for conflict locate the cause of relational difficulties outside the partner; therefore, the particular conflict has no implications for communication with the partner in different situations. In contrast, attributing conflict to a partner's stable personality traits implies characteristics that are relevant to all interaction with that individual. In other words, dispositional attributions associated with specific conflicts become a lens through which the partner is viewed, even within nonconflicted domains of the relationship. In the same manner, emotions that are tied to particular events during a conflict exchange should run their course as the interaction comes to a close. When the emotions evoked by a conflict persist beyond the interaction, they exert a more pervasive impact on personal and relational well-being. And more specifically, those emotions create moods that (to borrow a term from Forgas) infuse subsequent and otherwise unrelated interaction.

Understanding the genesis of dissatisfaction within nondistressed relationships requires clarifying the process by which particular conflict experiences influence global relationship judgments. The explanation offered here is that conflict interactions can produce residual affective and attributional states that are manifested in otherwise unrelated communication with partners. Thus, judgments of relationship satisfaction are influenced by both particular conflict experiences and perceptions of communication in nonconflicted relational domains. In this manner, affect and attributional systems unify distinct communication episodes to provide a foundation for general conclusions about the relationship.

CONCLUSION

The process by which particular interactions support conclusions about the state of the relationship is an elusive one, of ongoing interest to communication scholars. Theories of relational information processing variously emphasize schemas (Planalp, 1995), the relational meanings inherent in communication (Burgoon & Hale, 1984), or information processing frames (Dillard, Solomon, & Palmer, 1999; Dillard, Solomon, & Samp, 1996) as mechanisms underlying relationship inferences. As a complement to these efforts, this chapter suggests that affective and attributional systems unify discrete interaction episodes, which in turn support global evaluations of relationship quality.

Although I have taken liberties with the ideas put forward in the preceding chapters, the essays by Forgas, Honeycutt and Eidenmuller, Vangelisti, and Flora and Segrin are important exemplars of the diverse implications of affect and attributions in close relationships. The program of research summarized by Forgas clearly establishes the transcendent impact of affect on attribution and communication. Similarly, Honeycutt and Eidenmuller remind us that incidental features of the environment induce affective states that can have a dramatic effect on communication behavior. The persistence of emotional experiences and their impact on relationship quality is exemplified in Vangelisti's work on hurtful interactions; importantly, Vangelisti also points to how attributions of intent can render those hurtful episodes more or less relevant within an ongoing relationship. Finally, Flora and Segrin demonstrate that accounts for particular relationship events correspond with both perceptions of relationship quality and personal well-being.

By emphasizing the phasic and tonic aspects of an organism's interaction with the environment, I have tried to provide a framework to organize the interplay among affect, attribution, and communication. Although phasic states are integral to managing particular interactions, I have suggested that the tonic by-products of communication episodes influence both subsequent interactions and global evaluations of ongoing relationships. Thus, communication is a product of affect and attribution in the moment, which may both reflect previous interaction episodes and elicit tonic states that shape future exchanges.

REFERENCES

Alberts, J. K. (1988). An analysis of couples' conversational complaints. *Communication Monographs, 55,* 184–197.

Argyle, M., & Furnham, A. (1983). Sources of satisfaction and conflict in long-term relationships. *Journal of Marriage and the Family, 45,* 481–493.

Burgoon, J. K., & Hale, J. L. (1984). The fundamental topoi of relational communication. *Communication Monographs, 51,* 193–214.

Camper, P. M., Jacobson, N. S., Holtzworth-Munroe, A., & Schmaling, K. B. (1988). Causal attributions for interactional behaviors in married couples. *Cognitive Therapy and Research, 12,* 195–209.

Canary, D. J., & Spitzberg, B. H. (1989). A model of the perceived competence of conflict strategies. *Human Communication Research, 15,* 630–649.

Chen, S., & Chaiken, S. (1999). The heuristic-systematic model in its broader context. In S. Chaiken & Y. Trope (Eds.), *Dual-process theories in social psychology* (pp. 73–96). New York: Guilford Press.

Christensen, A., & Shenk, J. L. (1991). Communication, conflict, and psychological distance in nondistressed, clinic, and divorcing couples. *Journal of Consulting and Clinical Psychology, 59,* 458–463.

Dillard, J. P. (1998). Forward: The role of affect in communication, biology, and social relationships. In P. A. Andersen & L. K. Guerrero (Eds.) *Handbook of communication and emotion* (pp. xvii–xxxii). San Diego: Academic Press.

Dillard, J. P., Solomon, D. H., & Palmer, M. T. (1999). Structuring the concept of relational communication. *Communication Monographs, 66,* 49–65.

Dillard, J. P., Solomon, D. H., & Samp, J. A. (1996). Framing social reality: The relevance of relational judgments. *Communication Research, 23,* 703–723.

Fincham, F. D., & Bradbury, T. N. (1987). The impact of attributions in marriage: A longitudinal analysis. *Journal of Personality and Social Psychology, 52,* 739–748.

Fincham, F. D., & Bradbury, T. N. (1988). The impact of attributions in marriage: An experimental analysis. *Journal of Social and Clinical Psychology, 7,* 147–162.

Fincham, F. D., Bradbury, T. N., & Scott, C. K. (1990). Cognition in marriage. In F. D. Fincham & T. N. Bradbury (Eds.), *The psychology of marriage* (pp. 118–149). New York: Guilford Press.

Fletcher, G. J. O., & Fincham, F. D. (1991). Attribution processes in close relationships. In G. J. O. Fletcher & F. D. Fincham (Eds.), *Cognition in close relationships* (pp. 7–35). Hillsdale, NJ: Lawrence Erlbaum.

Frijda, N. H. (1986). *The emotions.* Cambridge, UK: Cambridge University Press.

Gilbert, D. T., & Malone, P. S. (1995). The correspondent bias: The what, when, how and why of unwarranted dispositional inference. *Psychological Bulletin, 117,* 21–38.

Gottman, J. M. (1979). *Marital interaction: Experimental investigations.* New York: Academic Press.

Guerrero, L. K., Andersen, P. A., & Trost, M. R. (1998). Communication and emotion: Basic concepts and approaches. In P. A. Andersen & L. K. Guerrero (Eds.), *Handbook of communication and emotion* (pp. 3–27). San Diego: Academic Press.

Hendrick, C., & Hendrick, S. S. (1988). Lovers wear rose colored glasses. *Journal of Social and Personal Relationships, 5,* 161–183.

Holtzworth-Munroe, A., & Jacobson, N. S. (1985). Causal attributions of married couples: When do they search for causes? What do they conclude when they do? *Journal of Personality and Social Psychology, 48,* 1398–1412.

Izard, C. E. (1993). Four systems of emotion activation: Cognitive and noncognitive processes. *Psychological Bulletin, 100,* 68–90.

Jacobson, N. S., McDonald, D. W., Follette, W. C., & Berley, R. A. (1985). Attributional processes in distressed and nondistressed married couples. *Cognitive Therapy and Research, 9,* 35–50.

Jones, E., & Davis, K. (1965). From acts to dispositions: The attribution process in person perception. In L. Berkowitz (Ed.), *Advances in experimental social psychology* (Vol. 2, pp. 219–266). New York: Academic Press.

Kelley, H. H. (1967). Attribution theory in social psychology. In D. Levine (Ed.), *Nebraska symposium on motivation* (Vol. 14, pp. 192–240). Lincoln, NE: University of Nebraska Press.

Kirchler, E. (1988). Marital happiness and interaction in everyday surroundings: A time-sample diary approach for couples. *Journal of Social and Personal Relationships, 5,* 375–382.

Lazarus, R. S. (1991). *Emotion and adaptation.* New York: Oxford University Press.

Lloyd, S. A. (1990). Conflict types and strategies in violent marriages. *Journal of Family Violence, 5,* 269–284.

Metts, S., & Cupach, W. R. (1990). The influence of relationship beliefs and problem-solving responses on satisfaction in romantic relationships. *Human Communication Research, 17,* 170–185.

Planalp, S. (1985). Relational schemata: A test of alternative forms of relational knowledge as guides to communication. *Human Communication Research, 12,* 3–30.

Rands, M., Levinger, G., & Mellinger, G. D. (1981). Patterns of conflict resolution and marital satisfaction. *Journal of Family Issues, 2,* 297–321.

Roloff, M. E. (1987). Communication and conflict. In C. R. Berger & S. H. Chaffee (Eds.), *Handbook of communication science* (pp. 484–534). Newbury Park, CA: Sage.

Rubenstein, R. A., Laughlin, C. D., & McManus, J. (1984). *Science as cognitive process: Toward an empirical philosophy of science.* Philadelphia: University of Pennsylvania Press.

Rusbult, C. E., Johnson, D. J., & Morrow, G. D. (1986). Impact of couple patterns of problem solving on distress and nondistress in dating relationships. *Journal of Personality and Social Psychology, 50,* 744–753.

Rusbult, C. E., Zembrodt, I. M., & Gunn, L. K. (1982). Exit, voice, loyalty, and neglect: Responses to dissatisfaction in romantic involvements. *Journal of Personality and Social Psychology, 43,* 1230–1242.

Scherer, K. R. (1984). On the nature and function of emotion: A component process approach. In K. R. Scherer & P. Ekman (Eds.), *Approaches to emotion* (pp. 293–317). Hillsdale, NJ: Lawrence Erlbaum.

Schwarz, N., Bless, H., Strack, F., Klumpp, G., Rittenauer-Schatka, H., & Simons, A. (1991). Ease of retrieval as information: Another look at the availability heuristic. *Journal of Personality and Social Psychology, 61,* 195–202.

Schwarz, N., & Clore, G. L. (1983). Mood, misattribution, and judgments of well-being: Informative and directive functions of mood states. *Journal of Personality and Social Psychology, 45,* 513–523.

Scott, C. K., Fuhrman, R. W., & Wyer, R. S. (1991). Information processing in close relationships. In G. J. O. Fletcher & F. D. Fincham (Eds.), *Cognition in close relationships* (pp. 37–67). Hillsdale, NJ: Lawrence Erlbaum.

Seligman, C., Fazio, R. H., & Zanna, M. P. (1980). Effects of salience of extrinsic rewards on liking and loving. *Journal of Personality and Social Psychology, 38,* 453–460.

Sillars, A. L. (1998). (Mis)understanding. In B. H. Spitzberg & W. R. Cupach (Eds.), *The dark side of relationships* (pp. 73–102). Mahwah, NJ: Lawrence Erlbaum.

Sillars, A. L., Pike, G. R., Jones, T. S., & Redmon, K. (1983). Communication and conflict in marriage. In R. N. Bostrom (Ed.), *Communication Yearbook 7* (pp. 414–429). Beverly Hills, CA: Sage.

Sinclair, R. C., Mark, M. M., & Clore, G. L. (1994). Mood-related persuasion depends on misattributions. *Social Cognition, 12,* 309–326.

Tooby, J., & Cosmides, L. (1990). The past explains the present: Emotional adaptations and the structure of ancestral environments. *Ethology and Sociobiology, 11,* 375–424.

Trope, Y., & Higgins, E. T. (1993). The what, how, and when of dispositional inference: New questions and answers. *Personality and Social Psychology Bulletin, 19,* 493–500.

Watzlawick, P., Beavin, J. H., & Jackson, D. D. (1967). *Pragmatics of human communication.* New York: Norton.

Weiner, B. (1986). *An attributional theory of motivation and emotion.* New York: Springer-Verlag.

Zillman, D. (1996). Sequential dependencies in emotional experience and behavior. In R. D. Kavanaugh, B. Zimmerberg, & S. Fein (Eds.), *Emotion: Interdisciplinary perspectives* (pp. 243–272). Mahwah, NJ: Lawrence Erlbaum.

Zillman, D., deWied, M., King-Jablonski, C., & Jenzowsky, S. (1996). Drama-induced affect and pain sensitivity. *Psychosomatic Medicine, 58,* 333–341.

PART TWO

ATTRIBUTIONS AND COMMUNICATION IN DATING AND MARITAL RELATIONSHIPS

CHAPTER FIVE

Attributions, Communication, and the Development of a Marital Identity

Catherine A. Surra and Denise S. Bartell

One of the key tasks that individuals face in premarital relationships is the construction of an identity about their relationship. For some, the construction of an identity involves questions about marriage. Those individuals who do eventually wed must form a marital identity, or an understanding of the self, the partner, and the relationship as a marital unit (Berger & Kellner, 1964/1970; Veroff, Sutherland, Chadiha, & Ortega, 1993). Many dating partners struggle at some point in their relationship with questions involving the development of a marital identity. This chapter concerns the evolution of the marital identity among premarital dating partners.

Marital and other identities are socially constructed: They emerge over time out of face-to-face interactions that partners have with one another and in some cases with other people (Berger & Kellner, 1964/1970; Berger & Luckmann, 1966; Knudson-Martin & Mahoney, 1998). The language exchanged during conversations provides individuals with knowledge from which they construct the meaning of their relationship. The emergence and integration of these meanings constitutes the marital identity of a particular individual. In this chapter we use this social constructionist perspective to analyze partners' accounts of commitment to marriage to each other.

Preparation of this chapter was supported by a grant to the first author from The National Institute of Mental Health (R01 MH47975). We would like to thank Chalandra Bryant, Karin Samii, and others who so diligently assisted with coding of the accounts contained in nearly 2,000 transcripts. Address correspondence to Catherine A. Surra, Department of Human Ecology, Gearing Hall, University of Texas at Austin, Austin, TX 78712.

CAUSAL ACCOUNTS AND THE MARITAL IDENTITY

Causal accounts are one mechanism through which individuals make meaning of their relationship. In their accounts, individuals attempt to explain why events occur in their relationships. Accounts consist of groups of reasons – or attributions – that partners give in order to explain relationship events. However, accounts are more than just packages of attributions (Harvey, Orbuch, & Weber, 1992). The attributions in accounts are grouped into organized pieces of information, which serve to provide the individual with a meaningful explanation for the event (Harvey et al., 1992; Surra & Bohman, 1991). Accounts are storylike in nature, and so they have a plot line and are coherent representations of the causes of events in a relationship from the individual's perspective. These representations are stored in memory, are tied together in cognitive space, and can be called on when needed to provide individuals with explanatory information about the relationship (Surra, Batchelder, & Hughes, 1995). Accounts can therefore be viewed as verbal expressions of partners' social constructions of why events happen as they do.

The accounts we have studied and that we report on here consist of premarital partners' own explanations for why they became more or less committed to marrying one another over time. Each separate explanation given by the partner is considered to be a *reason* for the changes in commitment to their relationship. The accounts reveal, in part, whether partners believe they have successfully forged a marital identity because they contain the meanings that partners attach to their relationship and information about how those meanings are derived.

THE FORMATION OF A MARITAL IDENTITY

In their classic paper, Berger and Kellner (1970) argued that developing a marital identity requires that partners construct a well-defined, cohesive, and stable definition of reality. Furthermore, they maintained that coupled partners enter marriage with a shared or consensual identity. The process by which partners arrive at such a neat identity package is one in which "ambivalences are converted into certainties" (Berger & Kellner, 1964/1970, p. 64). This process may be filled with fits and starts, tensions and conflicts. Although partners do apprehend the more pressing confusions and struggles they face, they are not conscious of the fact that they are forming a marital identity.

Berger and Kellner acknowledged that this view of the marital identity as consensual, stable, and well integrated is an idealized picture of what typically happens. Even though Berger and Kellner recognized the difficulties inherent in the process, their view oversimplifies what the experience is like for many partners. Research on accounts has shown that partners develop a marital identity in a variety of ways (Surra, Batchelder, & Hughes, 1995); the data suggest that there is no one typical marital identity or means by which it develops. The data from accounts also refute the supposition that a common or scripted process characterizes courtship. Most importantly, the view that partners enter marriage with a homogeneous reality that is shared by partners within and across couples is untenable (cf. Surra et al., 1995). Our research suggests, instead, that some individuals never develop a definitive marital identity. Some partners maintain fairly long relationships or may even wed despite the fact that they are filled with doubts about involvement, conflict, and unstable beliefs about their relationships (Surra, 1998; Surra, Arizzi, & Asmussen, 1988; Surra & Hughes, 1997).

Part of the reason why some partners may have difficulty constructing a marital identity is that it is not unidimensional. In order for partners to have a well understood marital identity, several subidentities need to be constructed.

SUBIDENTITIES OF THE MARITAL IDENTITY

Our ideas about the subidentities inherent in the development of a marital identity come from coding partners' accounts of why their commitment to wed changes over time. Over the years, we have coded the reasons for changes in commitment in accounts obtained from four different samples of couples, two of which were newlyweds (e.g., Surra, 1987; Surra et al., 1988) and two of which were dating partners (e.g., Surra, 1998; Surra & Hughes, 1997). In all, we have coded about 3,300 transcripts of accounts (for the most recent coding scheme, see Surra, 1995). The content of the subcategories of our coding scheme suggests that in order for partners to form a marital identity, they must resolve and reconcile at least four subidentities.

The Marriage Identity

The first subidentity is the construction of the partnership as a marriageable relationship, or what we call the marriage identity. To construct this subidentity, partners reconcile the reality of their relationship with their previously held beliefs about the institution of marriage. This subidentity also involves evaluative meanings about the desirability of marriage or dating, given previously held beliefs about these institutions that are rooted in normative and social prescriptions about dating and marriage. Individuals need to work out issues pertaining to both their readiness for and the desirability of marriage. Thus, for example, some individuals begin to view the self as a marriagable person in terms of readiness to assume the role of husband or wife, readiness with respect to life circumstances, or the readiness of their personal qualities for the responsibilities, demands, and perceived restrictions of married life. Individuals must also juxtapose qualities of their partners and of their relationships against their normative beliefs in order to derive the meanings of the marriage identity.

In coding accounts of commitment, we call explanations that pertain to the marriage identity *intrapersonal-normative reasons,* which are statements in which some characteristic of the self, the partner, or the relationship is evaluated against socialized beliefs about dating and marriage. The four subcategories of intrapersonal-normative reasons are defined in Table 5.1. Two of the four reasons, standards met and positive predisposition to wed, provide evidence that the relationship is viewed as marriageable and that individuals are ready to wed, whereas the remaining two, standards unmet and negative predisposition to wed, are evidence of a disinclination toward the institution of marriage.

The Relational Identity

The second subidentity is the forging of a relational identity. This task also concerns constructing a body of knowledge about the relationship, but this knowledge has more to do with what is satisfying and sustainable than with what is normatively prescribed. As a relationship develops, individuals come to understand their attitudes toward and beliefs about their relationship, the way they typically interact with their partners, the implications of such patterns for their relationships, and what their partners are like (Surra & Bohman, 1991). They must also develop a sense of the partners' positive and negative qualities and whether the relationship is a good one. Especially salient to individuals in the development of the relational identity are questions about whether certain attributes, such as companionship, compatibility, enjoyment, respect, trust, love, and comfort, characterize their rela-

Table 5.1. Definitions and Examples of Reasons Central to the Marital Identity

Reasons and Marital Subidentities	Reference to	Example
The marriage identity		
Positive predisposition to wed	Inclination toward the features of a serious relationship or marriage	"I figured someday not too far in the future I'd be getting married."
Negative predisposition to wed	Disinclination toward the features of a serious relationship or marriage	"I didn't want the responsibility of some woman depending on me."
Standards for partnership met	Positive evaluation of partner or relationship against standards for what is ideal	"We liked all of the same things. It's important to have common interests for a good relationship."
Standards for partnership unmet	Negative evaluation of partner or relationship against standards for what is ideal	"I didn't think I was feeling what I should be feeling if I were in love."
The relational identity		
Positive dyadic attribution	Positive beliefs about the other or the relationship	"We had similar interests."
Negative dyadic attribution	Negative beliefs about the other or the relationship	"He was acting like a jerk."
The couple identity		
Positive self-attribution	A positive attribution about the self	"I just matured a lot during that time."
Negative self-attribution	A negative attribution about the self	"I went a little bit crazy."
The social identity		
Separate network interaction	Interaction or activities between one's partner and third parties	"My friends kept telling me that Sue was bad for me."
Joint network interaction	Interaction or activities between both partners and third parties	"She met my whole family."
Positive network attribution	Positive beliefs involving third parties	"I fit right in with his family."
Negative network attribution	Negative beliefs involving third parties	"Her dad just hated me."

tionships. In addition, individuals face questions of how close or intimate they are and whether they are seriously dating, dating exclusively, or engaged to wed.

We do not mean to imply that partners' relational identities are exclusively positive. On the contrary, our data suggest that some individuals' relational identities have many negative elements; for example, they may see their partners as possessing negative qualities and their relationships as conflict-ridden and unreliable (see Surra et al., 1995). Our data also suggest that the negative beliefs about relationships are interspersed with positive beliefs for some partners. Partners may have relatively stable views of the relationship as possessing both positive and negative qualities, or they may see the relationship as positive on one occasion and negative on another, without a well integrated understanding of their relationships as mostly one or the other (cf., Holmes & Rempel, 1989; Surra, 1998). Regardless of the positivity or stability of partners' understandings, the meanings that partners attach to their relationship constitute the relational identity. In this chapter, we use data from two subcategories of dyadic reasons, positive and negative dyadic attributions, to characterize the extent to which the relational identity is seen as having positive and negative content (see Table 5.1).

The Couple Identity

The third subidentity of the marital identity is the couple identity. The emphasis here is on the development of new ideas about the self and perceptions of the couple as a unit. The construction of new ideas about the self means that individuals must begin to understand the self as part of a couple. According to Johnson (1991), this process involves incorporating the couple identity into one's self-concept. For example, a dating partner would need to begin to view the self as a husband or a wife. The process of identifying the self with the couple is part of what Acitelli (1988, 1992a, 1992b) calls *relationship awareness*. A large component of relationship awareness is the extent to which the self is compared with or contrasted with the partner. Viewing the self as like or unlike the partner and incorporating that view into an understanding of one's self-concept are components of a couple identity. Similarly, Aron and Aron (1986) discuss self-expansion in close relationships, a process by which one's self-concept is expanded to include knowledge and resources held by the other.

The development of a couple identity involves a second dimension, seeing the relationship itself as an entity rather than seeing only two individuals. This process concerns acquiring a sense of we-ness and shedding the sense of "me and him" or "me and her." Thoughts about the relationship are focused on the couple as a unit rather than on the individuals in it (cf., Acitelli, 1988, 1992a, 1992b; Burnett, 1987; Cate, Koval, Lloyd, & Wilson, 1995).

In this chapter, we rely on data from three categories of reasons (individual behaviors and positive and negative self-attributions, defined in Table 5.1) to operationalize references to the couple identity. These subcategories relate to the tendency to speak about the causes of commitment in individual terms and in terms of the self. The more individuals make reference to these subcategories in their accounts, the less well formed is their couple identity. The first category, individual behaviors, includes any references to the separate behaviors of the self or of the partner (e.g., statements about what "I did" or statements about what "she did"). The latter two categories of reasons measure the extent to which the causes of commitment focus on either positive or negative attributions about one's own characteristics.

The Social Identity

The fourth subidentity of the marital identity deals with the couple as a social unit. We refer to this as the social identity. This involves the construction of integrated views about the couple as a bounded unit within one's other social relationships. The construction of this identity has several subprocesses. One of these processes involves forming a reality in which each partner is a part of and a participant in the other's social group, where social group is defined in terms of those who are psychologically close (cf. Surra & Milardo, 1988). The reality of social integration concerns the extent to which one's coupleness is socially defined and accepted. Over time, beliefs about coupleness may shift to beliefs about whether social others view the relationship as marriageable or as a marriage.

Data from four categories of reasons are used to characterize the social identity: joint, or couple, interaction with the social network; either partner's separate interaction with the network; and positive and negative attributions involving the network (see Table 5.1). References to joint interaction with the network indicate that the social identity contains elements of social integration, whereas references to separate interaction with the network indicate elements of the couple's lack of social integration. Positive network attributions are beliefs about a good fit with the network and acceptance by and of the network, whereas negative network attributions suggest the opposite.

METHOD

The data used in this chapter are taken from a larger study of the development of commitment in premarital relationships. The sample was obtained by means of random digit dialing of households in greater Austin, Texas. Individuals who were dating someone of the opposite sex and who agreed to participate were asked to provide the name and address of the dating partner. This procedure yielded a sample of 464 respondents (232 couples), all of whom were between 19 and 35 years of age, had never been married, and were currently dating someone of the opposite sex. The sample was diverse with respect to income, education, socioeconomic status, ethnicity, and race (for details, see Jacquet & Surra, 1998). The mean length of relationship was 27 months at the start of the study; 8% of the sample were casually dating; 48%, seriously dating; and 44%, privately or publicly engaged.

Procedure

Participants completed up to nine interviews once per month for approximately 9 months. The longitudinal study had three phases: phase 1 consisted of an initial long interview, phase 2 was a series of seven short monthly interviews, and phase 3 was a replication of the first long interview. Most phase 3 interviews were conducted 1 month after the previous phase 2 interview; however, to interview as many respondents as possible at phase 3, we allowed them up to 3 months after their previous interview to complete the phase 3 interview. Respondents were paid $20 for each phase 1 and phase 3 interview they completed and $5 for each phase 2 interview completed.

In the phase 1 interview, respondents answered questions about their personal and social backgrounds and completed questionnaires to assess other individual characteristics. Then they graphed from memory changes in the chance of marriage to their partners from the date the relationship began until the date of the interview. Respondents were shown a blank graph, with "Chance of Marriage," ranging from 0 to 100%, along the vertical axis and time in months, broken down into weekly increments, along the horizontal axis. The chance of marriage was defined for the respondents as the chance that they and their dating partners would marry. Respondents were instructed to take into account both their own ideas and their dating partners' ideas when estimating the chance of marriage.

The chance of marriage at the date of the interview was marked on the graph first, as was the chance of marriage on the day the relationship began. The respondent was asked to tell (1) when the chance of marriage had first changed from its initial value, (2) what the chance of marriage value was at that time, and (3) the shape of the line connecting these two points on the graph. The period of time between the two points was called a *turning point*. After the line was drawn, the respondent was asked, "In as specific terms as possible, what happened that made the chance of marriage go (*up/down* ___%)?" Then respondents were asked, "Is there anything else that happened that made the chance of marriage go (*up/down* ___%)?" until they replied "No." This procedure was repeated for each subsequent turning point until the respondent had graphed the relationship up to the date of the interview.

During either the first or second short interview in phase 2, respondents were given a set of diaries in which to record how many times in a day they did various leisure, task, and relational activities alone, with their dating partners, with their dating partners and another person or persons, or with others but not with their dating partners. They also indicated how often they did romantic activities with their dating partners and how often they did them with another person. In this chapter, we use the diary data for the eight relational activities that concerned talking about some topic, including, for example, plans to do something; politics, famous people, or events in the news; the events of the day or night; and work or school. We had usable diary data (i.e., at least one day of diary data) for 403 respondents.

Measurement

Reasons for Commitment

The accounts of commitment gathered during the graphing procedure of the phase 1 interview were transcribed from audiotapes and coded according to a 29-category coding scheme (Surra, 1995). Coders identified separate reasons for changes in commitment within the accounts and coded them into one of the categories. Cohen's kappa averaged 81% between independent coders for the half of the phase 1 transcripts that were checked for reliability. All transcripts were consensus coded to resolve disagreements. The *proportion of reasons* in each category was calculated by dividing, for each respondent, the frequency of reasons in the category by the total number of reasons reported over the course of the entire phase 1 graph. The reasons codes used in this chapter as evidence of the marital identity are defined in Table 5.1.

Rates of Communication in Different Social Contexts

We used the diaries to create measures of rates of talk in three social contexts: with the partner, with the joint network (talk with the partner and others), and with the separate network (talk with others without the partner). We first summed the frequency of talk activities across all days for which we had data separately for talk in each of the three social contexts. Then we calculated three rates of talk by dividing this sum by the number of days for which we had diary data. The coefficient alpha for frequency of talk across all items for phase 1 was .83 for talk with the partner, .84 for talk with the partner and others, and .90 for talk with others without the partner.

Perceptions of Communication

Our measure of perceptions of communication comes from two of the reasons categories, positive and negative self-disclosure. These are the proportions of statements in the accounts that refer to episodes during which information with specific positive or negative content was communicated to the partner.

RESULTS

Interrelationships Among the Subidentities of the Marital Identity

It is possible for an individual to construct a strong subidentity in one arena but not another. Such disparities can give rise to tension and doubts within the individual, as well as conflicts between partners. An individual, for example, may have a strong, positive relational identity but a weak marriage identity. In this case, the individual will have a sense that the relationship is good and satisfying but will lack direction or waffle about whether marriage is in the picture.

To examine how the subidentities are interrelated, we intercorrelated the proportions of reasons associated with each of the subidentities (see Table 5.2 for women and Table 5.3 for men). For both men and women, the relational identity and the social identity were tied most strongly to one another; however, the indicators of the relational and social identities were inversely correlated. These findings speak to the construction of meanings that concern both social integration and boundary setting. Attributions of positive qualities to the relationship increased as references to the social network decreased for both sexes. This was true for all network reasons, regardless of whether they involved joint or separate interaction with the network or positive or negative network attributions. These findings reinforce Lewis's (1972) idea that the construction of the social identity involves boundary setting, which has to do with pulling inward and separating outward. The findings further suggest, however, that construction of the boundary between the couple and the network is facilitated to the extent that the relational identity is viewed positively.

Other findings for the relational and social subidentities speak to the meaning of social integration. The more women and men attributed negative qualities to their partnership, the less they reported joint interaction with the network and positive network attributions. It may be that the more partners see their relationship in negative terms, the more difficulty they have seeing themselves as participants in a joint social group and as accepted by and accepting of members of the group. The reverse could also be true: Perceptions of a lack of social integration might affect perceptions of the partnership negatively. Either way, the data suggest that seeing the relational identity more negatively and having difficulty with social integration are tied together.

The development of a marriage identity is tied to both the relational and the social identity. The more partners attributed negative qualities to their relationship, the more they believed that their standards for a partnership were unmet ($p < .06$ for women). Partners may be less likely to see the partnership as marriageable when they have more negative ideas about the relationship. Likewise, predispositions toward the institution of marriage are connected to the social identity. For men, negative predispositions to wed were inversely correlated with both joint interaction with the network and positive network attributions. For women, negative predispositions to wed were positively correlated with negative network attributions. Apparently, a lack of readiness for marriage hinders the construction of a social identity.

Table 5.2. Intercorrelations Among the Subidentities of the Marital Identity for Women (N = 220)

| | Relational Identity | | Couple Identity | | | Social Identity | | | |
| | Dyadic Attribution | | | Self-attribution | | Network Interaction | | Network Attribution | |
	Positive	Negative	Individual Behavior	Positive	Negative	P	P-O	Positive	Negative
Marriage identity									
Predispositions to wed									
Positive	-.06	-.09	-.00	-.06	-.09	-.10	-.01	.08	.10
Negative	-.06	.02	-.12†	.01	-.02	-.10	-.08	.02	.22**
Standards									
Met	.01	-.02	-.15*	.00	-.05	-.11	-.07	.10	-.12†
Not met	-.10	.13†	-.02	.27***	-.08	.05	-.01	-.03	-.01
Relational identity									
Dyadic attributions									
Positive	—	—	-.31***	-.14*	-.13†	-.19**	-.20**	-.18**	-.20**
Negative	—	—	.08	.08	.08	-.03	-.15*	-.14*	.00
Couple identity									
Individual behavior			—	—	—	.21**	-.06	-.03	-.01
Self-attributions									
Positive			—	—	—	-.00	.05	.02	.08
Negative			—	—	—	-.04	-.00	-.07	.03

P, person; O, others.
†p<.10. *p<.05. **p<.01. ***p<.001.

Table 5.3. Intercorrelations Among the Subidentities of the Marital Identity for Men (N = 220)

	Relational Identity		Couple Identity			Social Identity			
	Dyadic Attribution			Self-attribution		Network Interaction		Network Attribution	
	Positive	Negative	Individual Behavior	Positive	Negative	P	P-O	Positive	Negative
Marriage identity									
Predispositions to wed									
Positive	−.06	−.06	−.06	−.02	−.07	−.04	−.12†	−.06	.05
Negative	.01	−.03	−.03	.02	−.05	−.02	−.15*	−.14*	.07
Standards									
Met	.09	−.06	−.06	.01	−.02	−.04	−.08	−.03	−.03
Not met	−.08	.31***	−.05	.10	−.03	.06	−.11	−.12†	.01
Relational identity									
Dyadic attributions									
Positive	—	—	−.30***	−.08	−.07	−.27***	−.18**	−.08	−.28***
Negative	—	—	.15*	.11	−.02	.07	−.16*	−.19**	.06
Couple identity									
Individual behavior			—	—	—	.09	−.20**	−.13†	.11
Self-attributions									
Positive				—	—	−.03	−.10	−.13†	.01
Negative					—	−.01	−.07	−.03	.09

P, person; O, other.
†p<.10. *p<.05. **p<.01. ***p<.001.

The formation of a couple identity is tied to the formation of a relational identity. The more partners attributed positive qualities to their relationship, the less they attributed changes in commitment to individualistic reasons. For women, positive dyadic attributions were inversely correlated with references to individual behaviors, to positive self-attributions, and to negative self-attributions ($p < .07$ for the latter). For men, more positive dyadic attributions were associated with fewer references to individual behaviors, and more negative dyadic attributions were associated with more references to individual behaviors. Partners may have difficulty incorporating the self into the couple when the relationship is seen more negatively and less positively. Alternatively, seeing commitment individualistically may hamper the formation of a relationship with positive qualities.

The couple identity was also connected to the social identity, especially to perceptions of social integration. References to individual behaviors correlated positively with separate network interaction for women, whereas for men they correlated negatively with joint network interaction. Thus, the more individuals see themselves as separate from their partners, the more they see the couple as separate from a common social group. For men, a more individualistic reality is also weakly associated with less positive and more negative network attributions. The couple identity was connected to the marriage identity for women, but not at all for men. The more women made positive self-attributions, the more often they reported that their standards for a partnership were not met. The more references women made to individual behaviors, the less they reported that their standards were met and the more they said they were negatively predisposed to wed ($p < .08$ in the latter case). Seeing the relationship as marriageable and being inclined toward the institution of marriage are tied to a sense of we-ness for women, perhaps because for women coupleness more often implies marriage.

Communication and the Development of a Marital Identity

The marital identity is believed to emerge primarily from the meanings that partners derive from communicating with one another (Berger & Kellner, 1964/1970). Conversations should be of paramount importance in the development of a marital identity, simply because of the opportunities they provide for internally shaping and externally communicating the powerful and sometimes confusing thoughts, emotions, and intentions surrounding relationships. In some situations, individuals seek out third parties to help them define the marital identity (Berger & Kellner, 1964/1970).

In order to examine the connections between communication and the marital identity, we correlated the rates of talk in three different social contexts (with the partner, with the joint network, and with the separate network) with the subidentities evidenced in different reasons for commitment. We found that the rate of talk with the dating partner was correlated with reasons that pertain to the marital identity for women only. For women, rate of talk with the dating partner increased as perceptions that standards were not met increased, $r = .19; p < .01$, as positive attributions to the self increased, $r = .19; p < .05$, and as negative attributions about the network increased, $r = .15; p < .05$. Thus, higher rates of talk with the partner were correlated with more difficulty in the formation of the marriage, couple, and social subidentities. Higher rates of talk with the partner may result from efforts to form, clarify, or work out a marital identity in situations where the positive features of such an identity are not in place. We found no significant correlations between rates of talk with the social network and reasons pertaining to the marital identity.

Perceptions of Communication and the Development of a Marital Identity

Rate of talk with the partner was not associated with our measures of the marital identity for men but was connected to three of the four marital subidentities for women. This finding suggests that something in addition to the sheer amount of communication with the partner influences the development of the marital identity. It is important to keep in mind that the rate of talk is a measure of amount of talk per day about a variety of issues, many of them more mundane, daily occurrences. It may be that the marital identity is formed more on the basis of specific episodes of communication, during which information with specific content or special meaning is conveyed. Although we have no behavioral measures of such communication, we do have measures of perceptions of positive and negative self-disclosures, which are two of our codes for the reasons why commitment changed in the graphs. If self-disclosure of specific content is important in the formation of the relational and other subidentities, then perceptions of self-disclosures should be correlated with the indicators of these identities.

We found evidence that perceived disclosures are related to the relational identity in ways we would expect (see Table 5.4). The more men and women reported positive self-disclosures, the less they reported negative dyadic attributions. The more men and women reported neg-

Table 5.4. Correlations Between Perceptions of Communication and the Subidentities of the Marital Identity

	Women (*N* = 220)		Men (*N* = 222)	
	Positive Self-disclosure	Negative Self-disclosure	Positive Self-disclosure	Negative Self-disclosure
Marriage identity				
Positive pre-disposition to wed	−.01	−.06	.11†	−.05
Negative pre-disposition to wed	−.11	−.16*	.15*	.22**
Standards for partnership met	−.13†	−.15*	−.05	−.08
Standards for partnership not met	−.08	.20**	−.05	.19**
Relational identity				
Positive dyadic attribution	−.05	−.24***	−.12*	−.19**
Negative dyadic attribution	−.29***	.18**	−.20**	.16*
Couple identity				
Individual behavior	−.15*	.10	−.09	−.10
Positive self-attribution	−.08	−.01	−.10	−.05
Negative self-attribution	−.12†	−.03	−.06	−.05
Social identity				
P network interaction	−.11	.11	.04	.18**
P-O network interaction	.16*	−.04	−.02	−.08
Positive network attribution	−.04	−.07	.05	−.11†
Negative network attribution	−.19**	.04	−.08	.06

P, person; O, other.
†*p*<.10. **p*<.05. ***p*< .01. ***p*<.001.

ative self-disclosures, the less they reported positive dyadic attributions but the more they reported negative dyadic attributions. Thus, communicating messages with specific positive content may contribute to the formation of a positive relational identity, but communicating messages with specific negative content may foster the development of a negative relational identity. These data support the social constructionist view that identities emerge from the meanings partners make of conversations that occur between them. One finding that is opposite to this pattern is the weak correlation between positive dyadic attributions and positive self-disclosures for men.

Aspects of the social identity were also associated with perceived disclosures. For both sexes, perceptions of positive disclosures seem to promote the formation of the social identity, and perceptions of negative disclosures hamper its formation. For women, this pattern is seen in results for positive self-disclosures and both joint interaction with network and negative network attributions. For men, the pattern is found in the results for negative self-disclosures and partners' separate network interaction and positive network attributions. Perceptions of self-disclosures were associated with the couple identity for women but not for men. The more women referred to positive self-disclosures, the less individualistic were their views of the couple identity (i.e., individual behavior and negative self-attributions).

The results for the marriage identity are mixed. In some cases self-disclosures were associated with a more positive orientation toward marriage in the way one would expect, but in other cases the reverse was true. The results for negative self-disclosures are almost entirely consistent with the expectation that more negative views of marriageability are associated with perceptions of negative communications. References to negative self-disclosures increased with negative predispositions to wed (for men), increased with perceptions that standards are not met (for men and for women), and decreased with perceptions that standards are met (for women). These findings indicate that perceptions of negative self-disclosures are more closely linked to the marriage identity than are perceptions of positive disclosures. As theories of social construction would predict, the development of a marital identity may be hampered by the communication of negative messages, negative expectations about marriage, or uncertainty about the marriageability of the relationship.

The results for some variables suggest a more complicated connection between perceptions of marriageability and the positive or negative content of self-disclosures. Perceptions that the partnership is a good candidate for marriage (i.e., standards for partnership met) were associated with fewer positive and negative self-disclosures for women ($p < .06$ for positive self-disclosure). In addition, being negatively predisposed towards marriage was associated with fewer negative self-disclosures for women. For men, references to negative predispositions to wed increased with references to both positive and negative self-disclosures. It may be that, for women, strong positive *or* negative beliefs in the marriageability of the partnership decrease the amount of attention they pay to self-disclosure. For men, a negative orientation toward marriage seems to have the opposite effect, whereby self-disclosure takes on greater importance in the formation of a marital identity.

CONCLUSIONS

In this chapter, we have defined four subidentities of the marital identity: the relational identity, the social identity, the couple identity, and the marriage identity. We used social construction theory to guide analyses of linkages among the development of the subidentities themselves, communication, and perceived communication.

Identities and Their Meanings

The results indicate that the relational and social subidentities are most strongly tied to one another and point to two mechanisms that may be at work. First, perceptions that the partnership possesses positive attributes may foster perceptions of the couple as a bounded, separate social unit. Beliefs that the relationship has many positive qualities, in particular, are linked to fewer references to the social network, regardless of whether the references to the network indicate a stronger social identity (e.g., joint or couple network interaction, positive attributions about the network) or a weaker one (e.g., partners' separate interaction with the network, negative network attributions). Second, perceptions that the relationship has negative qualities are tied to a less well developed social identity, perhaps because individuals who have a more negative relational identity lack motivation to develop a social identity or because individuals who lack a social identity have difficulty developing a positive relational identity.

We argued earlier that the characterization of the marital identity as stable, narrow, and positive is an oversimplification (cf. Berger &

Kellner, 1964/1970). The findings underscore the difficulties some individuals have in developing a cohesive marital identity across subidentities. The data show evidence of associations between negative elements in one arena and uncertainties in another arena. This was true for the relational and couple identities, the relational and social identities, and the marriage and social identities. Under conditions of a more negative relational identity, for example, perceptions that standards for marriage are not met increase.

Our data do not speak to the causal directions by which the subidentities affect one another. In order to ferret out the causal interplay among the identities, one would need to make a study with frequent observations of identities and analyze their causal sequence.

The Role of Communication in the Development of a Marital Identity

Communication plays a dual role in the development of a marital identity. Both roles are captured by the theory of social construction. The first role concerns the idea that individuals derive the meaning of identities from face-to-face conversations. This role emphasizes the emergence of meaning from communication. The second function of communication is to work out, clarify, or repair conflicting or ambiguous meanings. Although the second role is acknowledged by the theory, it has been given somewhat less attention.

We measured communication in two ways: (1) rates of communication with the partner and with the network obtained from behavioral self-reports and (2) perceptions of self-disclosures with positive or negative content obtained from accounts. The results for rate of talk entirely support the repair and clarifying function of communication in the development of a marital identity. In all cases in which communication with the partner is associated with elements of the marital identity, a higher rate of talk with the partner is associated with more negative aspects of the identity. This is true for women only and for aspects of the marriage, couple, and social identities but not for the relational identity. Some of the results for perceived communication also provide evidence that communication is used to repair or negotiate an ill-defined marital identity; for men, a more negative orientation toward marriage is associated with more reports of both positive and negative self-disclosures.

Other findings point to the role of perceived communication in the emergence of meaning from conversations. Nowhere is this function more evident than in the results for the relational identity and perceptions of self-disclosure. For both men and women, perceptions of positive self-disclosures are associated with more references to positive relationship qualities and fewer references to negative relationship qualities, whereas perceptions of negative self-disclosures are associated with fewer references to positive relationship qualities and more references to negative relationship qualities. Results for the social, marriage, and couple identities are also consistent with the role of communication in the provision of meaning. The disclosure of specific or important positive and negative messages may define the marital identity, as social constructionism suggests.

The findings for this study may be due, in part, to the methods we employed. Our measure of self-disclosure was perceived, rather than real, and it was obtained from the same accounts as were the measures of the subidentities themselves. Future research should examine the role of actual self-disclosures in the formation of the marital identity. In addition, it is important to verify our results with longer longitudinal designs in which the linkages between communication and identities can be better traced over time. In part, the finding that rate of talk is implicated primarily in communication-as-repair may be a function of the timing of our observations. People who had weak identities already in place may have communicated more later on in an attempt to clarify their identities.

It is important to keep in mind that our respondents were dating, and only a subset of them will eventually marry one another. Individuals who do wed may be those who construct a marital identity with relative ease, whereas those who do not wed may never construct the sort of well-defined marital identity that Berger and Kellner (1964/1970) had in mind. As we noted above, however, other data strongly suggest that some individuals wed without a well-formed marital identity in place. The results presented here give some insight into how difficult it is for some individuals to convert their ambiguities into a definitive marital identity.

REFERENCES

Acitelli, L. K. (1988). When spouses talk to each other about their relationship. *Journal of Social and Personal Relationships, 5,* 185–199.
Acitelli, L. K. (1992a). Gender differences in relationship awareness and marital satisfaction among young married couples. *Personality and Social Psychology Bulletin, 18,* 102–110.

Acitelli, L. K. (1992b). Reflecting on relationships: The role of thoughts and memories. In W. Jones & D. Perlman (Eds.), *Advances in personal relationships* (Vol. 4, pp. 71–100). London: Jessica Kingsley.

Aron, A., & Aron, E. N. (1986). *Love and the expansion of self: Understanding attraction and satisfaction.* New York: Hemisphere Publishing Corp.

Berger, P., & Kellner, H. (1970). Marriage and the construction of reality. In H. P. Dreitzel (Ed.), *Recent sociology No. 2* (pp. 50–73). New York: Macmillan. (Reprinted from *Diogenes, 46,* 1964, 1–25.)

Berger, P. L., & Luckmann, T. (1966). *The social construction of reality: A treatise in the sociology of knowledge.* New York: Doubleday.

Burnett, R. (1987). Reflection in personal relationships. In R. Burnett, P. McGhee, & D. D. Clarke (Eds.), *Accounting for relationships: Explanation, representation, and knowledge* (pp. 74–93). London: Methuen.

Cate, R. M., Koval, J. E., Lloyd, S. A. & Wilson, G. (1995). The assessment of relational thinking in dating relationships. *Personal Relationships, 2,* 77–95.

Harvey, J. H., Orbuch, T. L., & Weber, A. L. (1992). Introduction: Convergence of the attribution and accounts concepts in the study of close relationships. In J. L. Harvey, T. L. Orbuch, & A. L. Weber (Eds.), *Attributions, accounts, and close relationships* (pp. 1–18). New York: Springer-Verlag.

Holmes, J. G., & Rempel, J. K. (1989). Trust in close relationships. In C. Hendrick (Ed.), *Review of personality and social psychology* (Vol. 10, pp. 187–220). Newbury Park, CA: Sage.

Jacquet, S. E., & Surra, C. A. (2000). *Parental divorce and premarital couples: Commitment and other relationship characteristics.* Manuscript submitted for publication.

Johnson, M. P. (1991). Commitment to personal relationships. In W. H. Jones & D. Perlman (Eds.), *Advances in personal relationships* (Vol. 3, pp. 117–143). London: Jessica Kingsley.

Knudson-Martin, C., & Mahoney, A. R. (1998). Language and processes in the construction of equality in marriage. *Family Process, 47,* 81–91.

Lewis, R. A. (1972). A developmental framework for the analysis of premarital dyadic formation. *Family Process, 11,* 17–48.

Surra, C. A. (1987). Reasons for changes in commitment: Variations by courtship type. *Journal of Social and Personal Relationships, 4,* 17–33.

Surra, C. A. (1995). *Reasons coding manual IV: Rules and definitions.* Unpublished manuscript, University of Texas at Austin.

Surra, C. A. (1998, June). *Processes and outcomes in the development of commitment to marriage.* Paper presented at conference on the Ties that Bind: Perspectives on Marriage and Cohabitation. National Institute of Health and Human Development, Washington, D. C.

Surra, C. A., Arizzi, P., & Asmussen, L. (1988). The association between reasons for commitment and the development and outcome of marital relationships. *Journal of Social and Personal Relationships, 5,* 47–63.

Surra, C. A., Batchelder, M., & Hughes, D. K. (1995). Accounts and the demystification of courtship. In M. A. Fitzpatrick & A. L. Vangelisti (Eds.), *Explaining family interactions* (pp. 112–141). Thousand Oaks, CA: Sage.

Surra, C. A., & Bohman, T. (1991). The development of close relationships: A cognitive perspective. In G. J. O. Fletcher & F. D. Fincham (Eds.), *Cognition in close relationships* (pp. 281–305). Hillsdale, NJ: Erlbaum.

Surra, C. A., & Hughes, D. K. (1997). Commitment processes accounts of the development of premarital relationships. *Journal of Marriage and the Family, 59*, 5–21.

Surra, C. A., & Milardo, R. M. (1991). In W. H. Jones & D. Perlman (Eds.), *Advances in personal relationships* (Vol. 3, pp. 1–36). London: Jessica Kingsley.

Veroff, J., Sutherland, L., Chadiha, L. A., & Ortega, R. M. (1993). Predicting marital quality with narrative assessments of marital experience. *Journal of Marriage and the Family, 55*, 326–337.

CHAPTER SIX

Causal Attributions of Relationship Quality

Ellen Berscheid, Jason Lopes, Hilary Ammazzalorso, and Nora Langenfeld

The causal attributions people make about their close relationships are exceedingly important and justify the considerable effort scholars have made to understand these attribution processes and outcomes. Relationship attribution theory and research have focused primarily on the causal attributions marital partners make for events that have occurred within their marriage. The type of relationship event studied most frequently has been a specific behavior performed by the attributor's partner, often a behavior the attributor believes to be undesirable or injurious to the relationship or a chronic problem in the relationship. (For a review of this body of research, see Bradbury & Fincham, 1990.)

In addition to the causes people give for their partners' behaviors, also important are the attributions people make for the general quality of the relationship: the reasons why they believe their relationship is the happy and satisfying relationship it is or why it has deteriorated into an unhappy and unsatisfying one. If an individual wishes to maintain the quality of a satisfying relationship, then that person's beliefs about the causes of the relationship's present quality will guide his or her maintenance strategies. If the relationship is in trouble, an analysis of the cause of the relationship's poor quality necessarily will precede the individual's remedial efforts. The success of those remedial efforts – whether initiated by the partners themselves, by a relationship therapist, or by well-intentioned friends and relatives – depends on identification of the causal conditions that are adversely affecting the relationship.

Correspondence concerning this chapter should be addressed to Ellen Berscheid, University of Minnesota, Department of Psychology, N309 Elliott Hall, 75 East River Road, Minneapolis, Minnesota 55455. Electronic mail may be sent via Internet to bersc001@tc.umn.edu. The authors would like to thank Lynelle Mattson and Syana Mukadam for the hundreds of hours that they spent coding the data.

Accurate causal diagnoses of the source of the problems troubling a relationship are often difficult to make, because the relatively stable factors that influence the partners' established patterns of interaction and thus the quality of the relationship are potentially numerous. Moreover, one or more, or even all, of these conditions may interact with each other to produce the unsatisfactory outcomes observed. Despite the difficulty, and although little is known about the attributions people make for the relationship as a unit as opposed to attributions for specific behaviors by the partners (see Fletcher, Fincham, Cramer, & Heron, 1987 for discussion), people doubtless make spontaneous attributions about the causes of the quality of their relationship, especially when the relationship has become unsatisfying (see, e.g., Weiner, 1985), and subsequently act on these attributions to try to improve the relationship.

THE CAUSAL POSSIBILITIES FOR RELATIONSHIP QUALITY

Kelley et al. (1983) classify the causal conditions that may affect interpersonal relationships into two types, personal and environmental. Personal causal conditions include the personal properties of each of the partners, P (person) and O (other), such as each partner's personality traits (e.g., extraversion or neuroticism), physical characteristics (e.g., physical attractiveness), abilities (e.g., communication skills), and beliefs (e.g., religious beliefs). One partner's personal properties also may interact with the other partner's properties to influence interaction patterns. These P × O causal conditions, such as the partners' similarity of attitudes and interests (e.g., both partners liking to dance), are located in neither P nor O but rather represent their conjunction.

Environmental causal conditions influencing the relationship may include the social environmental (E_{soc}) conditions in which the relationship is embedded, such as the partners' network of family and friends, and its physical environment (E_{phys}), such as a crowded neighborhood or living quarters that afford little privacy. Again, each type of causal condition may interact with one or more other types of causal conditions to influence the partners' interaction and the quality of the relationship. Of the several types of conditions, P and O causal conditions most frequently have been the focus of relationship attribution research, just as they have been in other realms of relationship research (see Berscheid, 1999; Sarason, Sarason, & Pierce, 1995).

THE EMPHASIS ON PERSONAL CAUSAL CONDITIONS IN ATTRIBUTIONS FOR RELATIONSHIP DYNAMICS AND EVENTS

The emphasis on personal causal conditions in relationship attribution research and the relative neglect of environmental causal conditions are perhaps not surprising, for relationship scholars have been deeply influenced by basic attribution theory and research in their approaches to relationship attribution. Although it may not be surprising, it does seem ironic that the relationship attribution literature, with only a few exceptions (e.g., Fletcher et al., 1987; Lloyd & Cate, 1985), has maintained its individualistic cast.

The individualistic perspective is reflected in at least two ways. First, it is reflected in the tendency for the attributional target to be a specific behavior by one of the partners as opposed to a property of the relationship itself, such as its quality or its longevity. For example, the Relationship Attribution Measure developed by Fincham and Bradbury (1992) focuses exclusively on specific behaviors the respondent is to imagine that the spouse has performed. The partner's behavior no doubt plays an important causal role in people's satisfaction with their relationships, but it is questionable whether people would assign the entire cause of a relationship's quality, even if the relationship is unsatisfactory, to actions performed by their partners.

Second, and as we have noted, the individualistic perspective is reflected in the tendency to emphasize P and O conditions among the causal possibilities presented to respondents in structured questionnaires; that is, the P × O causal alternative usually is excluded. Even when evaluating the cause of the partner's behavior as opposed to a feature of the relationship itself, respondents are not allowed to express the causal possibility that the partner's behavior was a function of a property of the partner interacting with one or more of their own properties. In addition to the exclusion of P × O causes, the environmental causal alternatives included usually are vague and undifferentiated, often represented by the single word *situation*.

The individualistic orientation of much relationship attribution research also may be the result of the fact that one of the most highlighted findings of basic research on attribution processes has been the tendency for laypersons, like psychologists, to take an individualistic perspective when explaining other people's behavior. The preference for dispositional as opposed to environmental (or situational) attributions for another's behavior – the "fundamental attribution error," as it has been termed (Ross, 1977) – is well documented, at least among respondents acculturated in Western societies (see Morris & Peng, 1994). However, the fundamental attribution error has been demonstrated largely within a single methodological paradigm. In that paradigm, the individual making the causal attribution usually is *not* in a relationship with the person whose behavior is the target of the causal attribution. Rather, the other whose behavior is the attributional focus usually is a stranger to the individual or even a hypothetical other.

Because the attributor and the other have never interacted, two causal possibilities that are always present in relationships simply do not exist: the possibility that the other's behavior was caused by the attributor and the possibility that the other's behavior was caused by an interaction between the attributor's properties and the other's properties. Although these two causal alternatives are always viable in relationships, adaptations of the traditional attribution research paradigm to investigations of relationship attribution frequently have restricted the respondents' causal alternatives to those typically included in the traditional attribution paradigm. Occasionally, the causal response alternatives are expanded to include the properties of the individual attributor (a P causal condition) but very rarely is the $P \times O$ alternative included. Moreover, when the partner's behavior is the attributional focus, as it usually is in relationship attribution research, the measurement scales used sometimes provide two causal alternatives, other's dispositions and other's situation, an either-or choice for the attributor (see Bradbury & Fincham, 1990).

One example of the truncation of causal alternatives in relationship attribution studies is provided by a recent relationship attribution study by Robins, Spranca, and Mendelsohn (1996). Although the attributor and the other were initially strangers to one another, as they are in most traditional attribution studies, this study had the virtue that the participants actually interacted with the person about whose behavior they later were asked to make causal attributions. The respondents in this study, in fact, were asked to make causal attributions not only for their partner's interaction behavior but also for their own interaction behavior. On a structured questionnaire, the attributors were asked to rate the extent to which their partner's behavior or their own behavior was caused by (1) the partner's mood or when rating themselves, their own mood; (2) the partner's personality or when rating themselves, their own personality; (3) themselves or, when rating themselves, the partner; and (4) the situation. Thus, as in much relationship attribution research, the participants' causal possibilities were restricted to P and O causal conditions (i.e., specified as mood, personality, and undifferentiated) and an undifferentiated E causal condition (the situation).

In summary, even when a specific behavior performed by another is the attributional focus, when the other is a relationship partner as opposed to a stranger, the causal possibilities are more numerous than reflected by the causal alternatives that many relationship attribution researchers provide their respondents. When the individual attributor is in a relationship with another, the possible causes of the other's behavior are expanded to the full array outlined by Kelley et al. (1983). Thus, and ironically, what participants in many relationship attribution studies are not allowed to express directly are relational causes.

RELATIONAL CAUSAL CONDITIONS

Among the array of causal conditions outlined by Kelley et al. (1983), it is the P × O causal condition that is truly relational; the locus of cause is neither P nor O alone but rather the combination of the partners' properties. Relationship counselors typically recognize this causal source of a couple's problems even if attribution researchers usually do not. To illustrate to their clients that it is the blend of P's and O's properties that is problematical and thus that neither partner can be assigned sole causal responsibility for the unsatisfying outcomes they are experiencing, some counselors use a color analogy (e.g., "You are blue and he is yellow and so your relationship is green, whereas your relationship would be different if you were paired with a red"). Similarity or dissimilarity of P and O along certain dimensions is perhaps the most prominent example of a P × O causal condition known to strongly influence relationship dynamics. The P × O causal condition is usually viewed as a combination of a relatively stable property each partner has brought to the relationship, that is, their possession of the property predates the relationship. To differentiate this type of relational causal condition from other relational causal conditions, we shall term it a *relational property* condition (Rel_{prop}).

Other types of P × O, or relational, causal conditions neither predate the relationship nor represent the manner in which the partners' stable properties combine; rather, they represent causal conditions that emerge from the participants' interaction with each other. As Kelley et al. (1983) outline, norms, agreements, and understandings that develop within the partners' interaction and that often serve to regulate their subsequent interactions are of this nature.

One important type of relational, or $P \times O$, causal condition was not explicitly discussed by Kelley et al. (1983) but has been highlighted by Newman (1981) (see also Newman & Langer, 1988). In addition to recognizing the traditional dispositional/internal – situational/external attributional dichotomy, Newman describes a third attributional category, which she regards as essentially "communicative" in nature and which she terms "interpersonal" attributions. Although Newman and Langer (1988) do not provide empirical data to support their contention that people commonly use this attributional category, they theorize that it is

...relevant to intimate relating over time. It takes into account those developing interactive patterns of communication that are jointly perceived to exist *between* the two relationship partners. By interpersonal attributions, we mean those explanations pointing, for the most part, to how the self is in regard to the other and how the other is in regard to the self (e.g., She wants to dominate me; He is always competing with me; I was trying to please him; We communicate well); thus, they consider features of the communicative relationship, as created and sustained by *both* partners interactively. (p. 149)

This type of relational causal attribution refers to features of the couple's actual interaction pattern rather than to how the partners' personal properties meld, and rather than predating the relationship, this causal condition – as would norms, agreements, and understandings – emerges from the partners' interactions with each other. To differentiate emergent relational causal conditions from Rel_{prop} conditions (which are also interpersonal in nature), we shall term these conditions *relational interaction* attributions (Rel_{intr}).

ENVIRONMENTAL CAUSAL ATTRIBUTIONS

Whether relationship partners commonly make relational attributions is an empirical question, which has yet to be answered definitively. One purpose of the study we shortly shall describe was to examine the types of attributions relationship partners make when their causal alternatives are unrestricted. In addition to examining the extent to which people refer to relational causal conditions when answering relationship causal questions, however, we also were interested in learning the extent to which relationship partners spontaneously make environmental attributions. The list of causal alternatives typically presented respondents in relationship attribution studies includes an environmental alternative, which is frequently identified as situation or as outside circumstance or sometimes as external circumstance. Whether respondents spontaneously mention the environmental causal possibility, as opposed to being reminded that such a causal alternative exists by its inclusion in the list of alternatives presented to them, might better reflect the extent to which people are aware that the environment in which their relationship is embedded influences their relationship outcomes.

One might expect fewer mentions of environmental causal conditions under spontaneous response conditions. Much research conducted within the traditional attribution methodological paradigm indicates that, at least when another's behavior is the attributional focus, people prefer to attribute the other's behavior to his or her dispositions rather than to environmental forces, as we have noted. The tendency to prefer dispositional attributions when the partner's behavior is undesirable was evident in the earliest relationship attribution research (e.g., Braiker & Kelley, 1979). Subsequent research, however, has shown that the general tendency to prefer dispositional to environmental attributions for the partner's behavior is due to an interaction between the individual's satisfaction with the relationship and whether the partner's behavior is regarded by the attributor as desirable or undesirable (see Bradbury & Fincham, 1990). As contrasted to attributions for the partner's behavior, we hoped to examine the extent to which people make environmental causal attributions for such properties of the relationship as its overall quality.

There is theoretical reason to believe that the general tendency to make dispositional rather than situational attributions when the attributional focus is another's behavior might be heightened when making attributions of the cause of a relationship's quality. Heider (1958) predicted that researchers would find what has been termed the fundamental attribution error because "Behavior ... tends to engulf the total field, rather than be confined to its proper position as a local stimulus whose interpretation requires the additional data of a surrounding field–the situation in social perception" (p. 54). A partner's behavior should be even more likely than a stranger's to engulf the field because the individual is usually dependent on the partner for many outcomes. Because the partner and his or her behavior are usually motivationally and emotionally important to the individual, the partner should be especially salient to the individual, and as a consequence, the environmental ground should be even less salient than it is with a stranger. Thus, it might be predicted that the partner's dispositions will be especially prominent in causal explanations of relationship quality.

People's tendency to emphasize causally the properties of their partner as responsible for their feelings toward that other and toward the relationship was observed in early interpersonal attraction research. When people were asked to tell why they liked another person, their answers often referred to such dispositional properties as the other's honesty, sense of humor, and physical attractiveness (see Berscheid & Walster, 1969). The fact that people's feelings toward another actually more often reflect an interaction between their own and the other's properties—that the "eye of the beholder" is causally important in accounting for an individual's attraction to another—is seldom reflected in people's causal explanations for their attraction to or disaffection for another, however. Thus, it also may be the case that the quality of a relationship with another tends to be causally attributed to the partner's properties.

On the other hand, because the individual is an integral part of the relationship, there is some, although perhaps less, theoretical reason to suspect that, in contrast to their attributions for another's behavior, people may be more likely to cite environmental causal factors as responsible for the quality of their relationship. Basic attribution research suggests that people often prefer to attribute their own behavior to their environmental situation rather than to their own dispositions (Jones & Nisbett, 1972; Watson, 1982). When thinking about a relationship of which they are an essential part, people may tend to give environmental explanations more frequently—at least more frequently than when causally evaluating either their partner's or a stranger's behavior.

To date, relationship scholars have relatively ignored the influence of the relationship's environment on relationship dynamics and outcomes, including such outcomes as the partners' satisfaction with the relationship and its stability (see Berscheid, 1998, 1999; Karney & Bradbury, 1995). It is not entirely clear why the influence of environmental factors on the relationship has been neglected although it has been has been commented on by many, including Levinger (1994) and Berardo (1980). The latter's review of trends and directions in family research, for example, called for researchers in the 1980s to refocus their efforts and investigate "the macroenvironment and how it impacts on the ... [relationship's] microenvironment" (p. 727) or the partners' interactions. Such a refocus did not occur.

The individualistic orientation may be one reason for the relative neglect of environmental conditions and the emphasis on personal causal conditions. Another reason why the effects of environmental conditions on relationships may have been neglected is that, as Bradbury, Cohan, and Karney (1998) discuss, much relationship research has been aimed at developing intervention strategies for troubled relationships. Traditionally, many scholars and marital and family therapists have regarded the environment in which the relationship is embedded as "immutable" at worst, and difficult to change at best. Relationship partners, too, may believe that the environmental surround of their relationship is immutable. If so, people may disregard environmental factors in their causal analyses of the properties of their relationship because they believe there is nothing they can do to maintain or change the relationship's environment should they find it causally responsible for the relationship's quality or for its other features.

Whether the relationship's environmental surround is more difficult to change than an individual partner's dispositions is questionable. But difficult to change or not, it is clear that features of the relationship's environment do influence internal relationship dynamics as well as important outcomes for the partners, such as the relationship's stability. For example, aspects of the relationship's social environment, such as whether people in the partner's social network approve of the relationship (e.g., Sprecher & Felmlee, 1992) or whether attractive alternatives to the relationship partner are present (e.g., South & Lloyd, 1995; Udry, 1981), have been shown to influence the stability of a relationship.

METHODS

To examine people's spontaneous and unconstrained causal attributions for various features of their relationship, we asked college students to identify an ongoing relationship. Each respondent identified one of the following relationships: a family relationship, a friend relationship, a coworker relationship, or a romantic relationship. For that one relationship, we asked the students to evaluate the quality of the relationship on a scale ranging from 1 (low quality) to 9 (high quality). We then asked them to tell us, in a written, open-ended response format, why the relationship was of its present quality. Later, respondents completed Hendrick's (1988) Relationship Assessment Scale, a measure of satisfaction. We discuss our findings with respect to romantic relationships primarily ($N = 59$, 35 female and 24 male). The average length of our respondents' romantic relationships was 2.5 years, and their satisfaction with these relationships was high ($M = 28.01$, SD = 5.13; for all relationships, $M = 27.98$, SD = 5.09; minimum possible score = 7.00 and maximum possible score = 35.00), as was the quality of the relationship as measured by the single item ($M = 7.14$, SD = 1.81; for all relationships $M = 7.16$, SD = 1.58).

Our coding scheme for the causal attributions present in their answers reflected the array of causal conditions outlined by Kelley et al. (1983). After preliminary examination of our respondents' answers to why their relationship was of its present quality, however, we gained renewed respect for Newman and Langer's (1988) theorizing and, as a consequence, we partitioned the P × O relational category into Rel_{prop} and Rel_{intr} attributions, as previously discussed. Causal attributions thus were classified into six causal categories: personal (P, O), relational (Rel_{prop}, Rel_{intr}), and environmental (E_{soc}, E_{phys}). The mean concordance for the two coders across all the respondents who evaluated their romantic relationships was .78 (and .77 across all four types of relationships).

The coders were instructed to parse each respondent's answer into elements, each element containing a single thought (often reflected by a single verb). If a compound sentence, or two separate sentences, had more meaning when coded as one element than as separate elements, they were treated as one element (e.g., "I am good at English, and she is good at math"). If a respondent provided a list of reasons (e.g., "He is tall, dark, and handsome"), each reason was treated as a separate element.

Responses that referred to either Ps' or Os' dispositions or properties were classified into the P and O causal categories, respectively. Responses that referred to the joint combination of each partner's dispositions or other properties were coded in the Rel_{prop} category (e.g., "I am five years older than she is"; "I'm shy, and he's gregarious"). The Rel_{intr} category included responses that referred to a specific interaction or interaction pattern between the partners (e.g., "We always argue about who is going to do the dishes") or to a combination of dispositions that emerged from the relationship (e.g., "We trust each other"). Also included in the Rel_{intr} category were elements that referred to the length of the relationship (e.g., "We have been dating for two years") and to the amount of time the partners spend with each other (e.g., "We only spend 1 hour a week with each other"). The E_{soc} category included responses that referred to alternative partners, social norms, the influence of other people such as family members and friends, children produced by the relationship, and joint legal and financial obligations. Coded into the E_{phys} category were references to physical proximity, including sharing the same residence; other references to physical surroundings; and physical aids to communication (e.g., "E-mail makes it easy for us to talk").

After coding the causal elements of each respondent's answer to the question of why their relationship was of the quality it was into each of the six causal attribution categories, for each respondent we calculated the total number of causal elements mentioned and the proportion of the total represented by each of the six attributional categories. This procedure was necessary because some respondents' answers were brief, whereas other respondents' answers approached novella length. We then averaged these category proportions across respondents. The mean proportion of elements mentioned by each respondent that were deemed uncodable for romantic relationships was 3% ($M = 4\%$ across all relationship types).

RESULTS AND DISCUSSION

The results of this study were clear and unequivocal. Although we suspected that respondents might cite the dispositions of their partner as an important cause of the quality of their relationship, they did not. Only 5% of our respondents' attributions, on average, were to their partners' dispositional or other properties (across all relationship types, $M = 7\%$). Nor did the respondents frequently cite their own properties (P attribution, $M = 5\%$; across all relationship types, $M = 7\%$). Thus, personal causal conditions constituted only a small percentage ($M = 10\%$) of the causal attributions made by our respondents for the quality of their romantic relationships. Moreover, our respondents seldom cited environmental causal conditions as being responsible for the quality of their romantic relationships ($M = 5\%$). Environmental causal citations divided almost equally between E_{soc} conditions ($M = 3\%$) and E_{phys} conditions ($M = 2\%$).

When asked to make causal attributions for the quality of their romantic relationships, then, people overwhelmingly cited relational conditions ($M = 81\%$; across all relationship types, $M = 77\%$). Of these relational conditions, relatively few were of the Rel$_{prop}$ variety, or references to the blend of their own and their partner's dispositions and other properties ($M = 13\%$). However, this type of relational condition was mentioned, on average, about as often as were personal causal conditions, $t(58) = .52$, ns (across all relationship types, $t[144] = 1.63$, $p = .11$), and significantly more often than were environmental causal conditions, $t(58) = 2.38$, $p = .02$ (across all relationship types, $t[144] = 3.33$, $p = .001$). Thus, an overwhelming proportion of the relational conditions cited were of the Rel$_{intr}$ variety ($M = 68\%$; across all relationship types, $M = 66\%$), or causal references to the nature of their interactions with their partner. It is clear, then, that when thinking about the properties of their relationship, at least its present quality, people simply point to the nature of their interactions with each other, just as Newman (1981), and Newman and Langer (1988) theorize.

In the view of many relationship scholars, however, those interactions *are* the relationship, its essence and vital tissue (see Berscheid & Reis, 1998). Thus, our respondents' answers seem tautological; that is, when asked why the relationship (i.e., their pattern of interaction) is of the quality it is, they simply describe selective interactions. Perhaps when unconstrained by a structured causal alternative checklist, people commonly confuse description with causation, just as relationship scholars sometimes do (see Kelley, 1992). In any event, our respondents' answers appear to be akin to those given by the person who, when asked why his friend is a wife beater, responded "Because he beats his wife."

Being largely descriptive, our respondents' causal answers can be viewed as proximal in the extreme. If one considers causal references falling in all the other categories–references to their own dispositions, to their partner's dispositions, to the interaction of these (Rel$_{prop}$) conditions, and to the environmental context of their relationship–on average only about one-fifth of our respondents' attributions can be considered even minimally "distal," or in the strict sense (as viewed by a scientist) as potentially causative of their relationship interaction pattern. Their answers to the causal question put to them resemble, in fact, the responses obtained by Fletcher et al. (1987), who did not ask their respondents a causal question about their dating relationships but rather simply instructed their respondents as follows: "Describe your relationship in your own words. Write down any thoughts or feelings you have about you or your dating partner. Write down whatever comes to mind. Take as much time as you need." (p. 483). (It should be noted that, like our respondents, those of Fletcher et al. [1987] were happy with their romantic relationships, although their relationships had lasted for a shorter time [approximately 1.3 years, SD = 71.5 weeks] than those of our respondents [2.5 years]).

Fletcher et al. (1987) coded their respondents' descriptive responses into four categories. The first two, *actor descriptions* and *partner descriptions*, were analogous to our P and O categories, respectively. Their third category was termed *interpersonal descriptions*, and it appears to be roughly parallel to our relational categories. Finally, Fletcher et al. included an external description category, which "included any item not directed at the relationship" (p. 483). It is difficult to know if this category was analogous to our environmental categories, but their findings certainly were similar to our own: Fletcher et al. report that they received so few external descriptions that they dropped this category from their analyses. Finally, and of greatest interest here, Fletcher et al. combed their respondents' descriptions for evidence of causal attributions. They found very few ($M = 0.9$, SD = 1.3).

Because Fletcher et al. (1987) focused on associations between type of description, stage of relationship, and happiness, satisfaction, and other issues, they do not report the frequency with which their respondents' descriptions fell in their P, O, and relational categories. Our guess is that their relational category was frequently used, for our results suggest that what is causally salient to people when thinking about their relationship, at least about its quality, is not the partner's behavior or their own behavior. Contrary to the results of much basic attribution research and the focus on the partner's behavior in many relationship attribution studies, it is not the partner's behavior that "engulfs the field." The field–the environment in which the relationship is embedded–*is* engulfed, but it is engulfed by the partners' interactions. It appears that when one is in an ongoing relationship, especially a satisfying relationship, it is difficult to see the causal relationship forest in which the relationship tree is located because of the overwhelming salience of the interactions internal to the relationship.

It is difficult to know if our results are reliable and representative of people's spontaneous causal thinking about features of their relationships given the absence of comparable studies. One of the first studies to examine open-ended attributions was reported by Orvis, Kelley, and Butler (1976), who recruited both members of romantic couples and separately asked each member to identify up to five ongoing or specific behaviors by the participant and up to five ongoing or specific behaviors by his or her partner for which each partner in the couple had different explanations.

The participant was asked to describe the behavior identified, the participant's own explanation for the behavior, and, finally, the partner's explanation for the behavior. The explanations were coded into 32 specific categories within 13 broader classes. Six of these classes referred to characteristics of the person practicing the behavior in question: *actor's state, actor's characteristics, actor's preference or belief, actor's concern, actor's intention to influence partner,* and *actor's negative attitude toward partner.* Three more classes referred to characteristics of the behavior: *"activity is desirable," "activity is undesirable,"* and *"activity has desirable indirect consequences."* The other categories referred to characteristics of the actor's partner ("Partner is responsible") or to environmental factors (circumstance or environment, people or objects) or they were deemed uncodable.

As did we in our study, Orvis et al. (1976) found that environmental attributions were rare (11.8%). Most of the attributions pertain to characteristics of the actor (58.4%). Of the remaining attributions, 21.1% pertained to the behavior, 6.1% concerned the partner of the actor, and 2.7% were uncodable. The investigators were surprised that they did not find many attributions similar to those that we have termed relational, not even enough to justify creating a category for such attributions. They speculated that the lack of relational attributions

...may be due to our asking for instances in which the behavior of *one person* was the subject of explanatory conflict. If we had asked for joint events or experiences of the couple (for example, joint success or failure, miserable times they had gone through), it seems reasonable that we might have found more explanations of this sort. (p. 362, emphasis in original)

Our results suggest that the traditional person–dispositional–internal versus environmental–situation–external causal dichotomy, adequate for capturing people's causal reasoning about an individual's behavior, does not sufficiently capture people's causal reasoning about the quality of their relationship. However, our respondents were mostly satisfied with their relationships. It may be that the reasons why their relationships were of their present high quality was not a matter to which they previously had given much thought; perhaps people do not look relationship gift horses in their causal mouths. If so, it seems unlikely that people in satisfied relationships typically have deliberate and conscious "maintenance" strategies to ensure the continued high quality of their relationships.

If our respondents had been dissatisfied with their relationships, perhaps we would have observed a broadening of their causal analyses from mere descriptions of their interactions to naming of the causal conditions responsible for the nature of those interactions. Then again, maybe we would not have. Perhaps people are truly as causally unaware as they appear to be here. At the least, our participants' free-response causal answers do not seem to substantiate their "attributor-as-scientist" reputation among basic attribution researchers. Perhaps people simply are unaware of the extent to which personal and environmental conditions influence relationship dynamics and outcomes. If so, counselors – and relationship scholars – have their work cut out for them and a valuable service to perform when the relationship turns sour and the partners are motivated to change the nature of their interactions, for chances are that their causal diagnoses will not extend very far beyond the specific interactions they find unsatisfactory.

More recently, another study that allowed the respondents unfettered opportunity to make whatever causal attributions about their relationship occurred to them spontaneously was conducted by Lloyd and Cate (1985). Again, however, their study is not entirely comparable with our own because the causal attribution task differed, the nature of the relationship that respondents evaluated differed, and the coding categories differed. Lloyd and Cate's respondents were asked to provide reasons for the change in the chance of marriage in the development of one of their previous (now dissolved) romantic relationships. The respondents' answers were coded into *individual* attributions (e.g., fear and attraction dispositions, beliefs), *network* attributions (e.g., "reasons that result from interaction with others," p. 425), *circumstantial* attributions (e.g., "factors which affected the chance of marriage but over which the partners had little or no control ... [including] events related to jobs, health, accidents or any factor that is external to the partners and to their relationship," p. 425), and, finally, *dyadic* attributions ("reasons rooted in the interaction of the partners," p. 425).

If one is willing to regard Lloyd and Cate's (1985) network and circumstantial attributional categories as roughly comparable with our combined environmental categories, their individual category comparable with our combined person categories, and their dyadic category as comparable with our relational categories, then their results do not correspond to our own in several respects. Lloyd and Cate (1985) examined their four types of attributions for a turning point in the relationship as a function of the stage of the relationship (casual, couple, committed, uncertain of marriage, and certain of marriage) and report as follows:

> Generally, dyadic attributions decreased over the history of the relationship (from casually dating to certain of a breakup). Individual attributions were stable to the stage of commitment and then increased markedly during the "uncertain" and "certain" stages. Network and circumstantial attributions remained relatively stable across relationship stage. (p. 427)

Lloyd and Cate express surprise that "nearly 50 percent of the attributions were nondyadic ones" at the casual, couple, and committed stages. These stages presumably were characteristic of most of our respondents' ongoing romantic relationships but we, of course, found that less than one-fifth of our respondents' attributions were nondyadic or nonrelational. However, our respondents' romantic relationships were ongoing as contrasted to the dissolved and retrospectively viewed romantic relationships of Lloyd and Cate's respondents. Our data clearly indicate that when actually *in* an ongoing romantic relationship, the attributions tend to be relational (or dyadic) rather than nonrelational.

With respect to our unexpected results, we spent some time wondering if we had asked our respondents the right causal question. We initially thought that the question of why their relationship was of its present quality was general enough and unstructured enough that we would minimally influence our respondents' answers – that we would capture, untainted, in this wide net whatever causal reasoning they had done about this important property of their relationship. Although our later ruminations on the issue of whether we asked the right question did not produce any special insights into what a better causal question might be, it should be noted that in our next study we structured our causal questions about the quality of the relationship somewhat differently (Berscheid, Ammazzalorso, Langenfeld, Lopes, & Heller, 1999).

In addition, we also structured our respondents' causal response alternatives. Specifically, we asked our respondents to identify for us the factors that were presently "enhancing" the quality of their ongoing romantic relationship – that is, keeping its quality as high as it was – and the factors presently "reducing" the relationship's quality from what it otherwise would be. Respondents were given a large number of possible causal alternatives, each printed on a card, representing each of our six attributional categories.

Mindful that presenting an array of causal alternatives in a structured manner might lead respondents to think about or recognize the role of causal conditions they would not think about spontaneously, we suspected that we might see a different attributional pattern than we did in the free-response study. We did not. Again, relational causal conditions were overwhelmingly cited and personal and environmental conditions were infrequently chosen from the array of causal alternatives. Thus, our respondents' causal emphasis on relational causal conditions was replicated when a slightly different causal attribution task, a different procedure, and a somewhat different dependent measure were used.

CONCLUSION

Our finding that the features of a relationship are viewed as having relational causes probably should not have come as a surprise to us and may not be regarded as surprising by others. However, to those of us steeped in the traditional person–situation dichotomy typical of traditional attribution theory and research, the relative disuse of person and environmental causal alternatives was unexpected. At the least, our results suggest that the causal tasks and dependent measures typical of many attribution studies, both basic and relationship attribution studies, may not provide a true picture of the causal reasoning people engage in (or, perhaps more accurately, seem *not* to engage in) about their relationships in naturalistic settings.

REFERENCES

Berardo, F. M. (1980). Decade preview: Some trends and directions for family research and theory in the 1980s. *Journal of Marriage and the Family, 42,* 723–728.

Berscheid, E. (1998). A social psychological view of marital dysfunction and stability. In T. N. Bradbury (Ed.) *The developmental course of marital dysfunction* (pp. 441–459). New York: Cambridge University Press.

Berscheid, E. (1999). The greening of relationship science. *American Psychologist, 54,* 260–266.

Berscheid, E., Ammazzalorso, H., Langenfeld, N., Lopes, J., & Heller, M. (1999). *An unstructured examination of attributions for relationship quality.* Manuscript in preparation.

Berscheid, E. & Reis, H. T. (1998). Attraction and close relationships. In D. T. Gilbert, S. T. Fiske, & G. Lindzey (Eds.) *The handbook of social psychology* (4th ed., Vol. 2, pp. 193–281). Boston: McGraw-Hill.

Berscheid, E., & Walster, E. H. (1969). *Interpersonal attraction.* Reading, MA: Addison-Wesley.

Bradbury, T. N., Cohan, C. L., & Karney, B. R. (1998). Optimizing longitudinal research for understanding and preventing marital dysfunction. In T. N. Bradbury (Ed.), *The developmental course of marital dysfunction.* New York: Cambridge University Press.

Bradbury, T. N., & Fincham, F. D. (1990). Assessing attributions in marriage: The Relationship Attribution Measure. *Journal of Personality and Social Psychology, 62,* 457–468.

Braiker, H. B., & Kelley, H. H. (1979). Conflict in the development of close relationships. In R. L. Burgess & T. L. Huston (Eds.), *Social exchange in developing relationships* (pp. 135–168). New York: Academic Press.

Fincham, F. D., & Bradbury, T. D. (1992). Attributions and behavior in marital interaction. *Journal of Personality and Social Psychology, 63,* 613–628.

Fletcher, G. J. O., Fincham, F. D., Cramer, L., & Heron, N. (1987). The role of attributions in the development of dating relationships. *Journal of Personality and Social Psychology, 53,* 481–489.

Heider, F. (1958). *The psychology of interpersonal relations.* Hillsdale, NJ: Lawrence Erlbaum.

Hendrick, S. S. (1988). A generic measure of relationship satisfaction. *Journal of Marriage and the Family, 50,* 93–98.

Jones, E. E., & Nisbett, R. E. (1972). The actor and the observer: Divergent perceptions of the causes of behavior. In E. E. Jones, D. E. Kanouse, H. H. Kelley, R. E. Nisbett, S. Valins, & B. Weiner (Eds.), *Attribution: Perceiving the causes of behavior* (pp. 79–94). Morristown, NJ: General Learning Press.

Karney, B. R., & Bradbury, T. N. (1995). The longitudinal course of marital quality and stability: A review of theory, methods, and research. *Psychological Bulletin, 118,* 3–34.

Kelley, H. H. (1992). Common sense psychology and scientific psychology. *Annual Review of Psychology, 43,* 1–23.

Kelley, H. H., Berscheid, E., Christensen, A., Harvey, J. H., Huston, T. L., Levinger, G., McClintock, E., Peplau, L. A., & Peterson, D. R. (1983). Analyzing close relationships. In Kelley, H. H., Berscheid, E., Christensen, A., Harvey, J. H., Huston, T. L., Levinger, G., McClintock, E., Peplau, L. A., & Peterson, D. R. (Eds.), *Close relationships* (pp. 20–67). New York: Freeman.

Levinger, G. (1994). Figure versus ground: Micro and macroperspectives on the social psychology of personal relationships. In R. Erber & R. Gilmour (Eds.), *Theoretical frameworks for personal relationships* (pp. 1–28). Hillsdale, NJ: Erlbaum.

Lloyd, S. A., & Cate, R. M. (1985). Attributions associated with turning points in premarital relationship development and dissolution. *Journal of Social and Personal Relationships, 2,* 419–436.

Morris, M. W., & Peng, K. (1994). Culture and cause: American and Chinese attributions for social and physical events. *Journal of Personality and Social Psychology, 67,* 949–971.

Newman, H. (1981). Communication within ongoing intimate relationships: An attributional perspective. *Personality and Social Psychology Bulletin, 7,* 59–70.

Newman, H., & Langer, E. J. (1988). Investigating the development and courses of intimate relationships: A cognitive model. In L. Y. Abramson (Ed.), *Social-personal inference in clinical psychology* (pp. 148–173). New York: Guilford.

Orvis, B. R., Kelley, H. H., & Butler, D. (1976). Attributional conflict in young couples. In J. H. Harvey, W. J. Ickes, & R. F. Kidd (Eds.) *New directions in attribution research* (Vol. 1, pp. 353–386). Hillsdale, NJ: Erlbaum.

Robins, R. W., Spranca, M. D., & Mendelsohn, G. A. (1996). The actor-observer effect revisited: Effects of individual differences and repeated social interactions on actor and observer attributions. *Journal of Personality and Social Psychology, 71,* 375–389.

Ross, L. (1977). The intuitive psychologist and his shortcomings: Distortions in the attribution process. *Advances in Experimental Social Psychology, 10,* 173–220.

Sarason, I. G., Sarason, B. R., & Pierce, G. R. (1995). Social and personal relationships: Current issues, future directions. *Journal of Social and Personal Relationships, 12,* 613–619.

South, S. J., & Lloyd, K. M. (1995). Spousal alternatives and marital dissolution. *American Sociological Review, 60,* 21–35.

Sprecher, S., & Felmlee, D. (1992). The influence of parents and friends on the quality and stability of romantic relationships: A three wave longitudinal investigation. *Journal of Marriage and the Family, 54,* 888–900.

Udry, J. R. (1981). Marital alternatives and marital disruption. *Journal of Marriage and the Family, 43,* 889–897.

Watson, D. (1982). The actor and the observer: How are their perceptions of causality divergent? *Psychological Bulletin, 92,* 682–700.

Weiner, B. (1985). Spontaneous causal thinking. *Psychological Bulletin, 97,* 74–84.

CHAPTER SEVEN

The Content of Attributions in Couples' Communication

Valerie Manusov and Jody Koenig

Our attempts to try to find the causes of our own and others' actions reflect a general human tendency toward sense making. Private attributions can be viewed as part of an overall propensity to understand or create meaning for the things that people do. Similarly, communication is the primary way in which we attempt to share messages with others and, through interaction, interpret the events in our lives. The joint concern with meaning is one of the most important links between attributions and communication.

Attributions also are made *for* communication behavior (Seibold & Spitzberg, 1982; Sillars, 1982) and can be part of the meaning ascribed to communication cues. That is, in any given interaction, people may try to figure out why their partners said what they did or acted as they did by making attributions for their partners' behaviors. These attributions necessarily result in different interpretations of what was communicated. Once an attribution has been made, certain meanings are no longer available to an attributor because they are inconsistent with the cause provided for an action. For example, an internal attribution can result in a belief that another's words or actions were meant to show kindness, but the attribution would be inconsistent with a view that the communication behaviors revealed pressure to conform to norms. According to Manusov (1990), different types of attributions start people down particular meaning "trajectories" and lead them away from other possible messages that the behavior may have had.

Correspondence should be addressed to Valerie Manusov in the Department of Speech Communication at the University of Washington, Box 353415, Seattle, WA 98195. The authors thank April Trees, Anna Liotta, and Tom Cochran for help in data collection for this chapter and John Harvey for feedback on a previous version. These data were collected with the support of a University of Washington Royalty Research Fund grant.

Importantly, however, attributions are not only a means to an end (i.e., they do not just lead people toward certain meanings); they may also *be the meaning* for the communication event (see Sillars, Roberts, Dun, & Leonard, this volume). When the primary function of communication behaviors is to reveal what another is thinking or feeling, the message may take the form of a causal or responsibility attribution. For instance, a person may apologize for being late and explain that the traffic was bad. The meaning that the person was trying to convey, that her lateness was due to the traffic, is also the attribution for her behavior. Similarly, a husband may accuse his wife of "trying to hurt me" (see Vangelisti, this volume), and the accusation reflects his belief about, and his meaning for, the cause of his wife's behavior.

The direct tie between the attribution and the meaning also occurs for nonverbal communication but in a somewhat different way. For example, forward lean, brief touches, and a quiet vocal tone can be caused by and communicate feelings of intimacy. Intimacy in this situation is both the cause and the meaning ascribed to the cues (i.e., the behaviors were caused by feelings of intimacy and they also communicated the message of intimacy). Indeed, the idea that causal attributions may actually be the meaning given to behavior is particularly important for understanding nonverbal communication, as behaviors that are part of the nonverbal system (e.g., gaze, movements, facial expressions) have the potential for ambiguity, which often requires interpretation of why the cues occurred (Manusov, 1990, 1995).

Links between attributions and communication have been explored to some degree within personal relationships. Thus far, most research has examined these ties rather broadly, following a path similar to attribution research that studies marital behavior in general. In their review of work on attributions and marriage, Bradbury and Fincham (1990) argue that scholarship on marital attributions focuses largely on the nature of those attributions and their tie to relational outcomes such as satisfaction. The nature of attribution processes refers to the dimensions on which attributions may differ (e.g., locus, stability, control, or responsibility). For example, if a person believes her partner brought her a gift because he is a thoughtful person, she has made an attribution whose nature is internal and stable. This attribution is of a different nature – and meaning – from one that places the cause outside the partner (e.g., "He bought the gift because people are supposed to do that on birthdays").

The most common finding in marital research is that couples can be contrasted in their attributions according to whether they make relationship-enhancing or distress-maintaining attributions (Holtzworth-Munroe & Jacobson, 1985). These attribution types are differentiated on the basis of the dimensions they reflect (e.g., relationship-enhancing attributions tend to be more internal than external and more stable than unstable when interpreting positive events). Discovering the dimensions of attributions, such as those tied to marital satisfaction, is particularly useful for understanding how attributions move people down particular meaning trajectories.

Besides the nature of attributions, however, there also is specific *content* provided in the attributions people ascribe for an event. The content of attributions "refers to the attribution itself" (Bradbury & Fincham, 1990, p. 4) and allows a glimpse into the particular causes spouses provide for behavior (e.g., "He acted that way, because he's afraid of what I'd say."). The content of attributions provides a detailed framework for assessing how people make sense of behaviors. It is also capable of revealing the range of meanings that can be given to actions. Yet, despite its potential to illustrate more fully the attributions people make in their relationships – particularly to show how attributions can be the actual meaning given to a communicative act – content has been the subject of few investigations (see Pretzer, Fleming, & Epstein, 1983, cited in Epstein, Pretzer, & Fleming, 1987, who focus on attributional content, and Reivich, 1995, who discusses content analysis of explanatory styles).

There are at least two reasons why people interested in attributions and communication in close relationships should look more at the content of the attributions themselves. First, assessing content may reveal more about the *nature* of attributions for communication behaviors. For example, other sources or types of attributions have been put forward as likely in close relationships, for example, attributions that reference the relationship, the other spouse, and the interaction (e.g., Berscheid, Lopes, Ammazzalorso, & Langenfeld, this volume; Newman, 1981; Vangelisti, Corbin, Lucchetti, & Sprague, 1999). These go beyond the dimensions that currently guide research on the nature of attributions and seem particularly important for attributions made in close relationships. Yet these types of attributions are only beginning to be explicated or applied to any significant degree. Seeing what relational and interactional attributions look like (i.e., identifying their content) could help to incorporate them more fully into studies focusing on the nature or dimensions of attributions.

Second, descriptive assessments of content may allow for a better understanding of what it means for an attribution to be relationship-enhancing or distress-maintaining. Although we know that the former attributions tend to include internal, stable, and controllable causes for positive but not negative behavior and that the latter usually involve more external, unstable, and uncontrollable causes for positive but not negative actions, we are less aware what specific information people cite when they use them. Examining the content could illuminate more fully the characteristics of both types of attributions that guide much of the research in close relationships.

In this chapter, we discuss these two possibilities further, using data from an investigation of couples' attributions for their partners' nonverbal behavior. We do this with the goal of arguing that content-based attribution studies can enhance, not replace, dimension-based research. This elaboration follows a discussion of the difference between attributional content and related constructs (e.g., stories, narratives, and accounts) and a brief overview of the study in which the data to which we refer were generated.

DIFFERENTIATING THE CONTENT OF ATTRIBUTIONS FROM ACCOUNTS, STORIES, AND NARRATIVES

Along with attributions, other cognitive and communicative forms are connected with explanation and sense making. To understand the value of studying the content of attributions, it is important to distinguish them from related forms of explanations. Specifically, accounts, stories, and narratives are all ways in which people report their explanations for events. A number of scholars have studied the nature of and the processes associated with account making, story telling, and narrative construction. More importantly, the research into these communication activities often focuses specifically on the content of the explanations people make for the events in their lives. Each of these explanation types will be discussed, with the goal of showing how looking at the content of attributions complements and extends research into accounts, stories, and narratives.

The term *account* has been defined in multiple ways. Many scholars conceptualize accounts as public presentations of self, intended to meet goals, excuse behavior, and/or avoid blame (e.g. Cody & McLaughlin, 1985; Read, 1992; Scott & Lyman, 1968). The foundational work in this area has defined an account as "a statement made by a social actor to explain unanticipated or untoward behavior – whether that behavior is his own or that of others, and whether the proximate cause for the statement arises from the actor himself or from someone else" (Scott & Lyman, 1990, p. 220). This definition highlights the socially constructed nature of accounts by stressing the importance of explaining one's negative behavior to another person.

Others view accounts as storylike constructions that feature elements such as plot and character development, time-ordered events, or expressions of emotion and attributions (Harvey, Orbuch, & Weber, 1992; Weber, Harvey, & Stanley, 1987; Weiss, 1975). From this perspective, accounts serve as detailed reconstructions of significant events in close relationships, and, as Weiss (1975) deduced from his examination of divorce accounts, such reconstructions help people make sense of the events they describe. For example, accounts for the end of romantic relationships have been linked to adjustment, emotional purging, establishing a sense of control, obtaining a sense of closure, and understanding (Koenig, 1999; Weber et al., 1987).

Research on storytelling and narratives parallel in many ways this second conceptualization of accounts. Gergen and Gergen (1987) discuss storytelling as a means of rendering accounts and refer to these story accounts as narratives. These scholars assert that the accuracy or truth value that others have associated with accounts is less important in narratives; instead, the description of events becomes the focus of narrative study. They also outline elements of a well-formed narrative (i.e., one that arranges events in chronological order, establishes a goal state, selects events relevant to the goal state, establishes causal linkages, and employs demarcation signs), indicating that narratives reflect a plot structure and a more detailed process of sense making than accounts might provide.

In general, accounts, stories, and narratives produce rich portraits of peoples' perceptions and understandings of the events in their lives and in their relationships (Orbuch, 1997). They not only allow people to explain or justify their behavior to others, they also provide a means for constructing often detailed and organized descriptions thus facilitating the sense-making process for a wide variety of important experiences in their lives. Although accounts and narratives contain attributions, such as attributions of responsibility for marital distress, their breadth and detail allow people to impose a greater organizational structure on relational events, which further assists them in dealing with the outcomes of those relationships (Weiss, 1975). Conversely, attributions are seen as very specific forms of sense-making. Harvey et al. (1992) define attributions as explanations for the causes of behavior.

Attributions apply naïve psychology (Heider, 1958) to explain some type of behavior, perceive causes of success and failure (for a review of such studies see Weiner, 1985), and assign responsibility for actions. As such, they reflect a particular, focused type of explanation making.

While little research connects attributions to stories or narratives, attributions have been linked to accounts in a number of studies. For example, some researchers argue that accounts contain attributions, such as attributions of responsibility for marital distress, and can be studied for their causal structure (Dickson, Manusov, Cody, & McLaughlin, 1996; Folkes, Koletsky, & Graham, 1987; Manusov, Trees, Reddick, Carrillo Rowe, & Easley, 1998; Weiner, Figueroa-Munoz, & Kakihara, 1991). This view of attributions and accounts often has as its goal an understanding of how different attributional dimensions imbedded in accounts may be more or less impression-managing for their tellers (e.g., presenting an external cause for a failure event may be more face-saving than accepting an internal one).

Harvey et al. (1992) and Orbuch (1997) also discuss the examination of attributions in terms of accounts and have referred to accounts as "packages of attributions" (Orbuch, 1997, p. 464). Their work indicates that the larger framework of accounts allows for the investigation of multiple attributions and various themes in one relational event, such as the dissolution of a relationship. In addition, they assert that accounts often serve as the basis for attributions.

Although there are a variety of ways to conceptualize attributions, accounts, narratives, and stories, the most notable difference between the content of attributions and account making or related constructs is in the level of focus. While accounts and narratives explore the larger frameworks used to describe and explain events in personal relationships, the content of attributions is linked with particular behaviors. Further, as Orbuch (1997) notes, "[a]ttributions concentrate more strongly on the cognitive aspects of judgment and responsibility than on the social processing of these statements [as accounts do]" (p. 464).

This "restricted" analysis reflects a far greater level of specificity than do the explanations elicited typically by accounts, stories, or narratives and may thus provide insight not revealed as fully in other forms. In addition, linking attributional content to specific behaviors increases our ability to connect explanations more closely with actual communicative behavior, a practice neglected in some attribution research (see Spitzberg, this volume). Simultaneously, however, attribution research has been criticized for failing to capture the richness of explanations for interpersonal processes in the same way that storylike constructions do (Fincham, 1992; Harvey et al., 1992). Looking at the content of the attributions allows for this expansion. The present line of research parallels the investigation of self-reported detail captured by accounts, stories, and narratives by examining the explanations that people make for and the meanings they assign to others' behaviors. This perspective advocates not only the study of the elements involved in people's attributions for events in close relationships but also the study of the richness associated with these elements themselves.

STUDY

The data we are using to examine the content of attributions came from a study by Manusov, Trees, Liotta, Koenig, and Cochran (1999). Our primary concern in that investigation was the ways in which married couples' expectancies for their partners' behaviors influence the patterns of nonverbal cues that emerge in the interaction. Data were also collected for the meanings assigned to the partners' nonverbal cues; these open-ended responses provided the data for the content of attributions reported here.

The study participants were 51 couples recruited from community postings, from the newspaper, and by word of mouth. Each couple was paid $20 for their participation. The couples had been married for an average of 4.86 years (range 2 months to 40 years, SD = 7.39); 16 of the couples had children (mean number of children 1.81, SD = .98); and the spouses varied in age from 21 to 63 years (mean age 31.22, SD = 9.02). Of the couple members, 77 identified themselves as White or Caucasian, 9 as Hispanic, 8 as Asian or Asian-American, and 4 as of mixed ethnicity. The remaining 4 did not indicate their ethnic group. The couples were generally quite satisfied in their marriages; the mean rating was 31.25, SD = 3.37, with a range of 22 to 35 on Hendrick's (1988) scale, which ranges from 7 to 35. No attempt was made to diversify the satisfaction level of the sample.

When the couples arrived at the study, either the wife or husband was selected and assigned to the role of confederate by random selection that was counterbalanced by sex. The confederate was asked to pick three topics for discussion: one that was neutral, one that was positive for the couple, and one that was negative for them. They were given a list of possible topics (e.g., what was happening at work, something current in their relationship, what their children were doing, money and finances, and sports) but could choose anything to discuss that they wished. The confederates were also asked to "show nonverbally" the affect that they had about each topic when they talked to their partners (e.g., anger or sadness with the negative topic, happiness or enjoyment with the positive topic).

Each topic was discussed on videotape for 5 minutes, so the final conversation with all three topics lasted 15 minutes. Following the taping, the nonconfederates were asked to review 2 minutes of each topic period on the videotape. After each 2-minute segment, they rated the importance, valence, and emotional significance of the topic. The participants were also asked, "What nonverbal behaviors (e.g., eye behavior, facial expressions, movements, sounds or silences) do you remember noticing (even very slightly) that your spouse used at this time in the interaction?" They were encouraged to write "none" if they had not noticed any.

Those who did write down behaviors (this included 50 of 51 nonconfederates) were then asked:

Did those behaviors have some meaning to you (i.e., did your spouse communicate something to you with those behaviors)? If so, what message did they send? If different behaviors that you noticed had different meanings, please note which behaviors had which meanings. Briefly explain why they had those meanings to you.

The order of the positive and negative topics was randomly assigned and counter-balanced to be sure that the order did not affect the likelihood of writing down the behaviors and their meanings.

After data collection, we reviewed the open-ended responses for reflections of (1) a variety of "interpersonal" attributions; (2) examples of distress-maintaining and relationship-enhancing attributions for both positive and negative behaviors; and (3) suggestions of other variables that may be important to attribution making in marriage. The results of this inquiry are discussed in the following sections.

Investigation of Attributional Content

Expanding Attributional Dimensions

As noted, previous research has identified a number of fairly reliable dimensions representing differences in attributions (e.g., locus, stability, controllability, and responsibility). This research has been particularly fruitful in showing the variety inherent in causal and responsibility attributions by pointing toward the range of forms attributions can take. These dimensions refer specifically to situational influences or dispositional qualities of the person engaging in the behaviors in question. Other dimensions have been identified but not researched as extensively, however. Of particular interest to relationship researchers is what Newman (1981) called the interpersonal dimension of attributions.

For Newman (1981), "interpersonal attributions differ from ordinary situational or dispositional attributions by virtue of an interactive focus" (p. 63). That is, the relationship between people may be seen as part of the cause for behaviors. Vangelisti et al. (1999) recently expanded Newman's (1981) discussion by asserting that romantic partners' cognitions about each other's communicative behavior tend to fall into one of six types: (1) self, where the attributor is the focus; (2) partner, where qualities of the other are emphasized; (3) third party, where another person is seen as the behavior's cause; (4) relationship, where some characteristic of the relationship itself is identified; (5) interpersonal, where the interaction between the partners is the focus; and (6) miscellaneous (see Cate, Koval, Lloyd, & Wilson [1995] for another typology of relationship cognitions).

Our data provided some support for "traditional" attributional dimensions (e.g., to the partner-internal locus or to the environment-external locus) but were more pronounced in their illustration of the interpersonal dimensions like those discussed in Newman (1981) and in Vangelisti et al.'s (1999) research. There was also, however, an additional dimension, a specific focus on the nature of communicative behavior as a source or type of attributions. Because of their importance to close relationships, relationship, interpersonal, and communication attributions, which represent an extension of Vangelisti et al.'s typology, will now be discussed, with illustrative examples.

Relationship

Despite our assumption that they would be quite common in interaction between partners, particular references to the relationship itself, without mention of the participants in it, occurred infrequently. In the instances that they did occur, they tended to tie directly to the topic being discussed. For instance, one husband said that his wife's giggle (a vocalic cue) "confirmed the fact that she is happy with our current living situation" (the topic chosen by the wife). Another husband noted that his wife's smile and eye behavior "indicated that she enjoyed her memory of our vacation." Finally, in a discussion of their marriage, one husband noted "she held the cards to her heart to show that our relationship is important and sacred to her." Few other overt references to the relationship itself were found in our data. In these data, attributions to the relationship itself focused on talk about relational events or the relationship specifically and occurred infrequently.

Interpersonal

Although there were few relational attributions and they occurred only within the constraints of talk about the relationship, there was a large number of attributions for nonverbal behaviors that referenced the attributor and his or her influence on the partner explicitly. In most of these cases, the meanings referred specifically to the attributor as a part of the interaction. Participants explained their partners' behaviors in terms of how their own presence influenced or reflected those behaviors. These interpersonal attributions tended to take one of two forms: attributions that reflected nonverbal feedback or comments and attributions that provided interpretation for the content of the talk.

The first type, feedback, refers to seeing the cause of nonverbal cues as based in their use as devices for showing interest or its lack and involvement or its lack. This feedback-as-cause is reflected in the following examples. One wife attributed the fact that her husband "kept the same look most of the time" to her belief that "he wanted [her] to think he was really listening and understanding me." One husband attributed his wife's smiles to "anticipating my replys (sic) and answers," and another wife stated that her husband's eye behavior, nodding, and smiling "seemed to be responding to me, but also felt happy about the topic itself." A different husband said his wife's head tilt was caused by her "inviting, enticing me." In a less positive interpretation, a wife said her husband's yawn showed "he wasn't interested in my interpretation."

All the above examples reflect attributions that the behaviors were the result of intended or unintended responses to the attributor. A few interpersonal attributions referenced the topic more explicitly or some combination of feedback and topic. For instance, one husband said that his wife's facial expression was due to her concern for him (empathic feedback) and his happiness at work (the topic they were discussing). Similarly, a wife noted that her husband's smile "meant sarcasm. Because he knows that I really don't approve of some of his friends." In these examples, the interpersonal cause was based on a direct response to both the partner and the topic the two were discussing.

Occasionally, there was more explicit reference to general feelings about the partner, although these occurred most often when people were also talking about their relationships or an activity they did together. For example, one wife said her husband's open arms, gestures, and smile were because "He loves me. He accepts me" as they discussed a weekend they recently spent together. A husband attributed his wife's eye contact to his belief that "she really cares about me" when talking about an otherwise negative topic, their tendency to disagree. Another wife commented that "when he gave me a lot of eye contact, he was letting me know that he was serious about loving me" (the topic he had chosen was how much he loves his wife). As before, there was a strong connection between the attributions given and the process or topic of communication.

In all of these cases, the attributors referenced themselves as involved in the cause of their spouses' behavior by virtue of their engaging in the specific interaction. This occurred for behaviors that were both negatively and positively valenced. The nature of these interpersonal attributions varied, however, to include references to feedback, to the topic, or more specifically to feelings for the partner.

Communication

Although people often referenced themselves in their attributions for their partners' nonverbal cues, of particular note for scholars interested in the link between attributions and communication in relationships is the number of very specific references to the interaction offered by our participants. These frequent references provide insight into the attributors' perceptions of how interaction and communication work, particularly the ways in which nonverbal cues support language. Commonly occurring attributions indicated that the nonverbal cues were used specifically to keep the conversation going, to encourage discussion, to show agreement, to underscore what was said verbally, and to help explain what was being said. For example, one wife said that the other's gestures were used "to emphasize" what he was discussing; another said that her husband's head nodding was used "to let me know he hears and understands, agrees." A husband attributed his wife's forward lean and lack of movement as indicative of her desire to "interject."

Other frequently used attributions referred to nonverbal behaviors caused by a partner's degree of attentiveness or by his or her feelings about the topic. Examples of the former are from a wife who said her husband "lifts his eyebrows to show he is involved in the conversation," and another's attribution that her husband's lack of movement was due to his "interest in and concentration on what I was saying." Conversely, one wife noted her husband's hand holding up his head and attributed this to the belief that "he was bored, not really present," and another husband said his wife's "looking around is usually a sign of not being 'into' the conversation."

Instances of the latter, topic-based attributions included attribution of one spouse's hushed vocal tone and rocking to the fact that the spouse "found the issue to be distressing" and the comment by another that his wife used an open body position and shifted because "she got very interested in the first baseman conversation." Another's reference to "picking fingers" meant, for the attributor, that it was a stressful topic for the partner. For one wife, her husband's arm scratching was indicative of her belief that "he is not comfortable with the topic and feels threatened." In all cases, the attributions reflected a very specific understanding of how nonverbal cues function in interaction. Although they appear similar to the interpersonal attributions, the primary distinction is that in interpersonal attributions the attributor is mentioned explicitly along with interaction and topic, whereas in communication attributions, the partner is not mentioned as the cause.

Summary

There was a range of content identified in our data, but overwhelmingly the content appeared to reflect attributions that were strongly behavior- and interaction-specific. We provided the participants with an opportunity to provide any "meaning" that they had given to the behaviors, and the participants themselves chose what that meaning was. The fact that they often referenced themselves, made very focused, communication-based attributions, or both reveals the potential domains of attributions not commonly discussed in previous research.

Investigating the Content of Relationship-Enhancing and Distress-Maintaining Attributions

As noted previously, most studies on marital attributions link attributional activity with marital satisfaction (Bradbury & Fincham, 1990, 1992). Much of this research compares and contrasts the attributions made by satisfied partners and dissatisfied partners for both positive and negative behaviors. Results indicate that attributions are most common when actions are highly salient, negative, or unexpected (Manusov, Floyd, & Kerssen-Griep, 1997; Wong & Weiner, 1981).

Researchers further distinguish positive and negative behavioral attributions by rating the attributions people make for their partner's behaviors according to the dimensions identified previously (e.g. locus, stability, controllability, responsibility). This type of rating compares people's marital satisfaction and their attributions for the positive and negative behaviors of their partners. Research indicates that satisfied couples make relationship-enhancing attributions, which explain their partner's positive behavior as internal, controllable, stable, and global. On the other hand, people dissatisfied with their marriages make distress-maintaining attributions for their partners' negative behaviors by identifying these behaviors as internal, controllable, stable, and global. Although several studies have replicated these results (for a review see Bradbury & Fincham, 1990) and these types of dimensions continue to guide attribution research in the marital context, little is known about what these types of attributions look like.

A number of interesting themes emerged within this example. First, distress-maintaining attributions may also have some relationship-enhancing elements. For example, a husband presented the following description of his wife's behaviors during their discussion on the division of household labor: "picking fingers – a stressful topic; looking down – not wanting to be responsible for what she's saying; shrunken shoulders – resignation about what she's talking about." He described her as "want[ing] me to feel sympathy for her and change my position." Although overall this type of attribution for what the husband viewed as negative behavior represents a distress-maintaining attribution, it also attributed some of her negative behavior to the topic (a characteristic of a relationship-enhancing attribution). In other words, his attribution does not just categorize her negative behaviors as based in internal causes such as not wanting to be responsible for what she's saying (a distress-maintaining attribution). It also supplements his overall attribution with external causes, such as the stressfulness of the topic (a relationship–enhancing attribution).

Examples of what might be considered relationship-enhancing attributions also revealed potentially distress-maintaining characteristics. One wife described her husband's behaviors in response to a conversation about her mother-in-law in the following way: "He is uncomfortable talking about his mom. I think that's why he fidgets more. His mom has always been a touchy subject and she is the bain (sic) of many a communication 'episode.'" Although she seems to describe his behaviors somewhat negatively, her explanation of his goals revealed a much more relationship-enhancing attribution: "[He was] trying to set me a little at ease. Common ground for the two of us – so we approach the conversation with 'solidarity' instead of as an insider (him) and an 'other.'"

These data seem to indicate that a clear distinction between relationship-enhancing and distress-maintaining attributions does not always exist. Instead, the process through which people make sense of and assign meaning to behavior can contain mixed messages and may reveal a muddier picture of the attribution process than is currently conveyed in the literature.

Our study included relatively satisfied couples overall, and not surprisingly, participants provided more relationship-enhancing than distress-maintaining attributions to explain their spouses' behaviors. At the same time that it was not always easy to distinguish the two types of attributions when examining their content, we also found that relationship-enhancing attributions as a category contained a wide variety of messages. These included attributing behavior to more general purposes, such as "to be kind" or "keeping the conversation going," to situational and relational objectives, such as showing support of the partner (e.g. "eye contact used to show support for what I was saying"), and to more global aspects of the overall relationship and the individual (e.g., "when he gave me a lot of eye contact, he was letting me know that he was serious about loving me. He shook his chest because he likes to make jokes and make people laugh. He likes to have fun. All of his nonverbal communication tells me that he loves me. He is listening to me, he cares, he is always there for me.")

People not only made these types of global relationship-enhancing attributions for relational topics (the subject in the above example was "how much my husband loves me"), but they also provided them for the more mundane, everyday conversations in which couples engaged. One wife made attributions for her husband's behavior (opened arms, hand to chin, smiles a lot) surrounding a conversation on "how was the weekend trip" in the following way: "He loves me, he accepts me, he's happy, some kind of energy thing because he's uncovering his heart area; to encourage me."

An analysis of the content also reveals that people seem to attach value to nonverbal behaviors and in turn, to give worth to the meaning associated with those behaviors in both relationship-enhancing and distress-maintaining attributions. For example, one wife's distress-maintaining attribution stated: "rubbing face – he is not being direct in his conversation; squirming – he is not being responsible for how things are; scratching arms, etc. – he is not comfortable with the topic and feels threatened; [overall] he is passing the buck for raising the children. Complaining and not really being a partner." Conversely, in a relationship-enhancing attribution, a wife described her appreciation of her husband's nonverbal behaviors by saying "He didn't seem as emotional about the topic as I did, although he did appear very understanding. I liked that he really looked as though he was listening to me." It seems, then, that both relationship-enhancing and distress-maintaining attributions express rich detail and assign value to the explanations for behavior.

In summary, looking at the content of attributions helped reveal that relationship-enhancing and distress-maintaining attributions often include characteristics that might be ascribed to the other category, that they include a variety of different kinds of interpretations, and that they reflect underlying beliefs about the importance of nonverbal communication as part of reflecting relationships, feelings, etc.

Discussion and Conclusion

Our analysis of the content of attributions for spouses' nonverbal behavior revealed a number of dimensions and characteristics of attributional activity currently underdeveloped in the literature on close relationships. As noted, the data suggest that dimensions referencing the partner and the communicative interaction emerge consistently in marital partners' explanations for each other's actions. In addition, the attributions themselves are more specific, complex, valenced, and amorphous than those characterized by the typologies used in most attribution research. Future research will benefit from examining these complexities further.

Not surprisingly, our data showed that attributions made for nonverbal behaviors and the meanings assigned to those behaviors often made specific reference to the communication in the interaction. This helps reveal the importance that *task* plays on the type of attributional activity in which couples engage. The complexities that may be inherent to attributions in close personal relationships often reference the communicative behavior that prevails during one or a series of interactions. Our assertion that sense making links attributions and communication suggests that research ought to explore further the relationship between attributional activity and communication processes.

The idea that the task given to participants, namely, commenting on the meaning of their partners' behaviors, influenced the content of the attributions is an important outcome of this research and also reflects a limitation. Our methodology encouraged participants to become very aware of their partners' nonverbal cues, and this may have encouraged more, and different, attributional activity than the couples may perform in their lives outside the laboratory. Also, we purposefully asked participants to provide meanings rather than attributions. Our belief was that this request was more in line with how people think about nonverbal cues (and potentially other situations in which attributions are likely, such as conflict or support settings). Nonetheless, we based our analysis on the belief that such meanings were the content of attributions (i.e., that a particular meaning ["showing concern"] was also what caused the partner to act as he or she did). This methodological choice may have overemphasized how much attributional activity occurred.

Finally, the taped nature of these discussions and the participants' knowledge that the investigators would be reviewing the written meanings given to the partners' behaviors, may have encouraged more self-presentation than would be likely in the communication behaviors and their attributions for naturally occurring interactions (see Arkin, Gabrenya, Appelman, & Cochran, 1979; Orbuch, 1997 for more discussion on the role of self-presentation in communicated explanations). It may be, for example, that the reason people had "mixed" attributions (e.g., some relationship enhancement even in largely distress-maintaining attributions) was due, at least in part, to the participants' knowledge that their thoughts and actions would be analyzed. Other methodologies that discourage artificial self-presentation concerns would help further in investigating the actual content of most attributions.

Despite these limitations, we believe that investigating the "stuff" of attributions has allowed for some useful extensions of the attributional domain, specifically as applied to communicative behaviors in marital relationships. Although most of our analysis focused on how investigation of content may expand previous conceptions of the nature and type of attributions found in previous research on causal sense making in relationships, we also wanted to use our data to see if it suggested variables – other than satisfaction – that may be usefully linked to attributions. Previous research has suggested the importance of similarity to marital partners, and investigating the content of attributions may be one way to explore such similarity. Particularly, while some work has looked at the degree to which couples provide the same attributional dimensions to communication (Manusov et al., 1997), little comparison has been made of the more specific meanings couples provide. While our current data do not reveal similarity in that we asked for attributions from only one spouse, the detailed nature of the attributions, as well as the sureness with which couples provided these meanings, suggests an important area for future research.

Frequent reference to the relationship and the interaction in the content of attributions may also suggest a need to focus on the relational, patterned, dyadic sequence of attribution making. For example, if people do make specific, on-line attributions for their partners' communication behavior, it seems particularly likely that the attributions they make during the process of an interaction will influence their own communicative behavior. These behaviors may reflect or become part of an ongoing pattern of communication between the partners across their interactions. Thus, specific content may lead to particular behavioral patterns and may play a role in the "success" or "failure" of a communicative exchange. In this way, attributions become a dyadic level variable reflective of relationship processes.

REFERENCES

Arkin, R. M., Gabrenya, W. K., Appelman, A. S., & Cochran, S. T. (1979). Self-presentation, self-monitoring, and the self-serving bias in causal attribution. *Personality and Social Psychology Bulletin, 5,* 73–76.
Bradbury, T. N., & Fincham, F. D. (1990). Attributions in marriage: Review and critique. *Psychological Bulletin, 107,* 3–33.
Bradbury, T. N., & Fincham, F. D. (1992). Attributions and behavior in marital interaction. *Journal of Personality and Social Psychology, 63,* 613–628.
Cate, R. M., Koval, J., Lloyd, S. A., & Wilson, G. (1995). Assessment of relationship thinking in dating relationships. *Personal Relationships, 2,* 77–95.
Cody, M. J., & McLaughlin, M. L. (1985). Models for the sequential construction of accounting episodes: Situational and interactional constraints on message selection and evaluation. In R. L. Street & J. N. Cappella (Eds.), *Sequence and pattern in communicative behaviour* (pp. 50–69). London: Edward Arnold.
Dickson, R. E., Manusov, V., Cody, M. J., & McLaughlin, M. L. (1996). When hearing's not believing: Perceived differences between public and private explanations for two compliance failures. *Journal of Language and Social Psychology, 15,* 27–39.

Epstein, N., Pretzer, J. L., & Fleming, B. (1987). The role of cognitive appraisal in self-reports of marital communication. *Behavior Therapy, 18,* 51–69.

Fincham, F. D. (1992). Richness and rigor: Advancing the study of attributions and accounts in close relationships. In J. H. Harvey, T. L. Orbuch, & A. L. Weber (Eds.) *Attributions, accounts, and close relationships* (pp. 1–18). New York: Springer-Verlag.

Folkes, V. S., Koletsky, S., & Graham, J. L. (1987). A field study of causal inferences and consumer reaction: The view from the airport. *Journal of Consumer Research, 13,* 534–539.

Gergen, K, J., & Gergen, M. M. (1987). Narratives of relationships. In R. Burnett, P. McGhee, & D. Clarke (Eds.) *Accounting for relationships* (pp. 269–288). London: Methuen.

Harvey, J. H., Orbuch, T. L., & Weber, A. L. (1992). Introduction: Convergence of the attribution and accounts concepts in the study of close relationships. In J. H. Harvey, T. L. Orbuch, & A. L. Weber (Eds.) *Attributions, accounts, and close relationships* (pp. 1–18). New York: Springer-Verlag.

Heider, F. (1958). *The psychology of interpersonal relations.* New York: John Wiley.

Hendrick, S. S. (1988). A generic measure of relationship satisfaction. *Journal of Marriage and the Family, 50,* 93–98.

Holtzworth-Munroe, A., & Jacobson, N. S. (1985). Causal attributions of married couples: When do they search for causes? What do they find when they do? *Journal of Personality and Social Psychology, 48,* 696–703.

Koenig, J. (1999). *The influence of post-relational narrative completeness on tellers' emotional adjustment.* Unpublished masters thesis, University of Washington, Seattle, WA.

Manusov, V. (1990). An application of attribution principles to nonverbal messages in romantic dyads. *Communication Monographs, 57,* 104–118.

Manusov, V. (1995). Intentionality attributions for naturally-occurring nonverbal behaviors in intimate relationships. In J. Aitken & L. J. Shedletsky (Eds.), *Reader in intrapersonal communication* (pp. 339–350). Plymouth, MI: Midnight Oil & Speech Communication Association.

Manusov, V., Floyd, K., & Kerssen-Griep, J. (1997). Yours, mine, and ours: Mutual attributions for nonverbal behaviors in couples' interactions. *Communication Research, 24,* 234–260.

Manusov, V., Trees, A. R., Liotta, A., Koenig, J., & Cochran, A. T. (1999, May). *I think therefore I act: Interaction expectations and nonverbal adaptation in couples' conversations.* Paper presented to the Interpersonal Division of the International Communication Association, San Francisco.

Manusov, V., Trees, A. R., Reddick, L. A., Carrillo Rowe, A. M., & Easley, J. M. (1998). Explanations and impressions: Investigating attributions and their effects on judgments of friends and strangers. *Communication Studies, 49,* 209–223.

Newman, H. (1981). Communication within ongoing relationships: An attributional perspective. *Personality and Social Psychology Bulletin, 7,* 59–70.

Orbuch, T. L. (1997). Peoples' accounts count: The sociology of accounts. *The Annual Review of Psychology, 23,* 455–478.

Read, S. J. (1992). Constructing accounts: The role of explanatory coherence. In M. L. McLaughlin, M. J. Cody, & S. J. Read (Eds.), *Explaining one's self to others: Reason-giving in a social context* (pp. 3–20). Hillsdale, NJ: Lawrence Erlbaum.

Reivich, K. (1995). The measurement of explanatory style. In B. G. McClellan & M. E. P. Seligman (Eds.), *Explanatory style* (pp. 21–47). Hillsdale, NJ: Lawrence Erlbaum.

Scott, M. B., & Lyman, S. M. (1968). Accounts. *American Sociological Review, 33,* 46–62.

Scott, M. B., & Lyman, S. (1990). Accounts. In D. Brisset & C. Edgley (Eds.) *Life as theater: A dramaturgical sourcebook* (pp. 219–242). New York: Aldine De Gruyter.

Seibold, D. R., & Spitzberg, B. H. (1982). Attribution theory and research: Review and implications for communication. In B. J. Dervin & M. J. Voight (Eds.), *Progress in communication sciences* (Vol. 3, pp. 85–125). Norwood, NJ: Ablex.

Sillars, A. (1982). Attribution and communication: Are people naïve scientists or just naïve? In M. E. Roloff & C. R. Berger (Eds.), *Social cognition and communication* (pp. 73–106). Beverly Hills, CA: Sage.

Vangelisti, A. L., Corbin, S. D., Lucchetti, A. E., & Sprague, R. J. (1999). Couples' concurrent cognitions: The influence of relational satisfaction on the thoughts couples have as they converse. *Human Communication Research, 25,* 370–398.

Weber, A. L., Harvey, J. H., & Stanley, M. A. (1987). The nature and motivations of accounts for failed relationships. In R. Burnett, P. McGhee, & D. D. Clarke (Eds.) *Accounting for personal relationships: Explanation, representation and knowledge* (pp. 11–133). London: Methuen.

Weiner, B. (1985). An attributional theory of achievement motivation and emotion. *Psychological Review, 92,* 548–573.

Weiner, B., Figueroa-Munoz, A., & Kakihara, C. (1991). The goals of excuses and communication strategies related to causal perceptions. *Personality and Social Psychology Bulletin, 17,* 4–13.

Weiss, R. S. (1975). *Marital separation.* New York: Basic Books, Inc.

Wong, P. T. P., & Weiner, B. (1981). When people ask "why" questions, and the heuristics of the attributional search. *Journal of Personality and Social Psychology, 40,* 650–663.

CHAPTER EIGHT

Handling Pressures for Change in Marriage

Making Attributions for Relational Dialectics

Patricia Noller, Judith A. Feeney,
and Anita Blakeley-Smith

The dialectical contradictions inherent in social interaction provide pressures for change and promote vitality in close relationships. According to Montgomery (1993), relationship partners must adjust constantly to the presence of opposing relational forces. Baxter (1988) claims that personal relationships involve needs for both autonomy and connection, both openness and closedness, both novelty and predictability, and that couples have to work out ways to manage these contradictions in their relationships. In this way, the dialectical perspective focuses on change resulting from the interaction of relational forces.

According to Baxter and Montgomery (1997), a core presumption of dialectical perspectives on change is that change is driven by the nature of the contradiction, which assumes that some aspect of the opposition is always lacking. In other words, it is not a case of partners finding the "right balance" between the two poles of the contradiction. Rather, the interplay between the poles fluctuates, and the contradictions have to be addressed and negotiated time after time. Adjusting to the presence of opposing forces leads to continuous change, and pressure towards change is seen as the "natural path for all relationships" (Baxter & Simon, 1993, p. 226). For this reason, it is important to understand how couples see these pressures and the attributions they make for changes that occur on these dimensions.

The interplay between opposing relational forces may surface as interpersonal conflict between parties (Giddens, 1979). In particular, conflict is likely to arise if the partners are "out of sync" in their experi-

Please address correspondence to Patricia Noller, Department of Psychology, University of Queensland, Brisbane, Queensland 4072, Australia.

ence of a contradiction at a given point in time, such that one person aligns his or her interests with one pole (e.g., autonomy) and the other person aligns his or her interests with the other pole (e.g., connectedness). As is consistent with the notion that dialectical tension has the potential to create conflict, Spitzberg (1993) argues that relational competence can be seen as the negotiation of dialectics. He argues that the hallmark of relational competence is "the capacity to select from among tactical options those tactics that accommodate often opposing or incompatible goals" (p. 140).

PRIMARY RELATIONSHIP CONTRADICTIONS

Autonomy–connection has been described as the primary exigency of relating (Baxter, 1988; Baxter & Simon, 1993). This contradiction has been called the "me–we pull," because it reflects individuals' desire to be with their partner while at the same time being their own persons (Baxter, 1990). According to dialectical researchers, relationship satisfaction is maintained through the process of managing these conflicting desires. Problems with autonomy needs tend to surface in such reasons for relationship breakup as a desire for freedom and independence and a sense of entrapment. Inability to fulfill connection demands surfaces in such expressed reasons for breakup as insufficient time together, lack of commitment and fidelity, and discrepant relationship definitions and goals (Baxter & Simon, 1993).

The *openness–closedness* contradiction reflects the tension experienced between the partners in what to say and what not to say to one another. That is, both candor and discretion are required in interaction with intimate partners. The development of intimacy requires disclosure of thoughts, feelings, and needs. However, disclosure also involves the risks that the partner may have difficulty in responding appropriately to needs that are shared, may respond in a rejecting manner, or may use the disclosure in a hurtful way. This contradiction is prevalent in self-reports of dilemmas about how much to share needs and desires with partners (Baxter, 1988).

The *novelty–predictability* contradiction arises because relational well-being is based on conflicting demands for both certainty and novelty (or for both stability and change). Uncertainty reduction theory suggests that predictability and certainty are important aspects of relationships. However, excessive certainty can produce emotional deadening for the relational parties, which tends to undermine romantic love. Boredom has emerged as a frequently reported fear about entering relationships and is often given as a reason for the breakup of romantic and marital relationships (Baxter & Montgomery, 1996).

THE NATURE AND FORM OF CHANGE

There may be changes in how dialectical tensions are manifested across the course of relationships. For example, Goldsmith (1990) argues that the experience of tension between the needs for autonomy and connection changes with relationship development. Specifically, in the early stages of relationships these tensions seem to be reflected in concerns about getting involved with the partner, whereas in later stages they may be manifested in concerns about tradeoffs between involvement in the relationship and other activities. These qualitatively different tensions produce gradual change in the connection between partners.

The importance of change processes in relationships highlights the need to study attributions for change. For example, little is known about spouses' perceptions of each partner's role in pressuring for change and whether such pressure is seen as driven by sex differences with respect to relational dimensions. A further issue concerns the extent to which couples see relational change as driven by forces that are internal or external to their relationship. These issues are an important focus of the studies reported here.

THE PRESENT RESEARCH PROGRAM

In this chapter, we present two studies exploring married couples' experiences of relationship change and their attributions for that change. Study 1 focused on semistructured accounts of relational tensions. This method provided rich data by allowing the participants to express their feelings and thoughts freely and enabled us to use the couples as experts to provide information about how such issues were handled in their relationships. We then built on the important themes emerging from this study to develop a questionnaire study (Study 2).

Study 1

The first study included 84 couples, who had been married from a few months to 27 years ($M = 9.16$ years). Educational level varied from tertiary (52% of husbands and 45% of wives) to less than grade 10 (1% of husbands and 2% of wives). Occupational status varied widely, with 64% of husbands and 36% of wives holding professional or managerial positions and the remainder spread fairly evenly across clerical and manual occupations. We recruited the participants from among introductory psychology students, although typically only one member of the couple was a student.

In addition to providing the semistructured accounts (detailed in a later section), the couples completed standardized questionnaires. Relationship satisfaction was measured by the Dyadic Adjustment Scale (Spanier, 1976). Spouses with scores above 120 are generally considered highly satisfied with their relationships, whereas those with scores below 100 are considered low in satisfaction (the highest possible score is 151). In the present sample, marital satisfaction varied from 74 to 143 for men and from 60 to 147 for women. We also included the Marital Communication Inventory (Noller & Feeney, 1998), which explores couples' perceptions of their communication across 6 different dimensions and 12 topic areas. The dimensions assessed are frequency of discussion, frequency of initiation (assessed for both self and partner), recognition (self and partner), disclosure (self and partner), communication satisfaction (self and partner), and conflict. All dimensions were rated on 4-point scales. The topics covered include "likes, dislikes and interests," "feelings about our relationship," "plans for the future," and "things that lead to anger or depression."

Interaction Tasks

Couples came into the laboratory and completed the questionnaires described above. They then engaged in three interaction tasks in which they were asked to discuss, for approximately 10 minutes, the extent to which a particular contradiction was (or had been) an issue in their relationship. They were also asked to discuss how they dealt with that issue. The order in which the contradictions were discussed was counterbalanced so that a similar number of couples completed the task in each possible order. Before each interaction, spouses completed a short questionnaire assessing the extent to which they and their partner differed on the particular contradiction (ranging from 1 = not at all to 6 = a great deal), as well as the direction of that difference (e.g., whether the respondent or the partner desired more autonomy or more connectedness). The interactions were videotaped and later transcribed for coding. Two coders worked through the transcripts and answered the

---

Table 8.1. Questions Answered by Coders from Videotaped Interactions

---

Are they reporting change over time?
What is the specific nature of this change?
What factors seem to have caused this change?
Who initiates moves for change?
What are the roles each partner generally plays in pressuring for resolution of this issue?
   Role of wife?
   Role of husband?

Note: All questions were answered twice, once according to what the wife seemed to be saying and the other according to what the husband seemed to be saying.

---

questions set out in Table 8.1. The two coders worked independently and then discussed and resolved any discrepancies.

Extent of Difference Between Spouses

Subjects reported moderate levels of difference between self and spouse for all three contradictions. For autonomy–connectedness, the mean level of difference was 3.34 for husbands (SD = .96) and 3.08 for wives (SD = .89) on a 6-point scale. For openness-closedness, mean levels were 3.28 for husbands (SD = .88) and 3.79 for wives (SD = .83). For novelty–predictability, mean levels were 3.45 for husbands (SD = .99) and 3.48 for wives (SD = 1.01). The following comment by a wife in this study illustrates the tensions that can be created by differences between spouses on the openness–closedness dimension:

I always want to know more, and you don't want to tell me more. I hear you talking to other people, and you tell them things you haven't told me. And I get upset about that. I think that in that way, you're being private, and I want to know more. And you know, I always say to you things like "You can remember that in 1954, someone played footy and wore a hankie in his trousers and that was the day that he cut his toenails." And yet if I ask you something personal, you can't even remember.

Links with Relationship Functioning

Given this type of comment, we were interested in whether the extent of difference on the three contradictions was related to the quality of couples' relationships. In terms of the communication between the spouses, we found that those who reported a larger difference generally reported fewer interactions, less recognition to both self and partner in interactions, less disclosure by self and partner, less satisfaction for both self and partner, and more conflict. As can be seen from Table 8.2, there were more significant links for husbands than for wives, particularly for the autonomy–connectedness contradiction.

Marital satisfaction was negatively related to the extent of difference on autonomy–connection and openness–closedness. Differences on novelty–predictability were linked to lower marital satisfaction for husbands only.

Change Over Time

Participants' accounts were coded for references to change in their relationships with regard to the contradictions. Issues coded included the extent of change over time, the nature of the change, and attributions for the change (in terms of who was seen as pressuring for change, who was seen as responsible for actively initiating change, and what causal factors were seen as leading to change).

Extent of Change. Around half the couples spontaneously referred to change on each of the relational contradictions. That is, these couples reported substantial change over time in either their own or the partner's relational needs or in the balance between the needs of the two spouses.

Table 8.2. Significant Relations Between Extent of Difference on the Contradictions and Communication Quality (Study 1)

Communication Variable	Autonomy–Connectedness	Openness–Closedness	Novelty–Predictability
Frequency	Husbands	Husbands	No effects
Recognition for self	Husbands	Both	Husbands
Recognition for partner	Wives	Wives	No effects
Disclosure by self	Husbands	Both	Wives
Disclosure by partner	Husbands	Wives	Husbands
Satisfaction for self	Husbands	Both	Husbands
Satisfaction for partner	Husbands	Husbands	Both
Conflict	Husbands	Husbands	Wives

Note: each cell entry indicates whether the relation was significant for husbands, wives, both, or neither. All associations are negative except for those with conflict. For example, husbands who reported a large difference in spouses' needs for autonomy-connectedness tended to report less frequent communication.

However, fewer couples reported change for openness–closedness (32 husbands, 36 wives) than for other contradictions (49 husbands and 50 wives for autonomy–connection and 41 husbands and 52 wives for novelty–predictability). It is possible that differences in openness–closedness are just accepted in stable relationships because they are generally in line with sex role stereotypes that portray men as wanting more independence and less closeness than women (Aries, 1996).

Nature of Change. Overall, moves for change tended to be in the direction of more autonomy, openness, and predictability. For example, 36% of the couples reported that either one or both partners had moved toward more autonomy, whereas only 13% reported moving toward more connectedness, with a further 19% reporting change to a compromise position. The pattern of change toward one particular pole was even more marked for the other two contradictions, with only a small percentage of the couples reporting that there had been moves toward more closedness (4%) or toward more novelty (7%). These results are not surprising, given that moves toward closedness are likely to have negative implications for the future of the relationship. Further, moves toward novelty would be difficult, given the very busy lives that most of these couples reported, with work, study, and children's activities imposing a need for organization and structure.

Responsibility Attributions. We were interested in the question of which partner was seen as responsible for bringing about change on the contradictions. This question was investigated from two angles: which partner was seen as generally pressuring for change and which partner actively initiated moves for change. Husbands were more likely to be seen by both spouses as pressuring for autonomy rather than for connectedness, whereas wives were more likely to be seen as pressuring for connectedness rather than for autonomy. As is consistent with this finding, husbands were likely to see autonomy as the more important pole, whereas wives were likely to see connectedness as more important. For openness–closedness, both spouses were generally seen as pressuring for openness, but this effect was much stronger for wives than for husbands. A similar number of husbands and wives saw openness as more important than closedness, but more husbands than wives saw closedness as more important than openness. There were no clear patterns with regard to spouses' desires for novelty–predictability.

In summary, the clearest gender differences with regard to pressures for change were for autonomy–connectedness, with wives tending to pressure for connectedness and husbands for autonomy. This finding is in line with a large literature on gender differences, which shows that women tend to be socialized for connection and affiliation and for acting as the caretakers of relationships (Surra & Longstreth, 1990). Women were seen as the main initiators of change for all three contradictions, but they tended to give themselves more credit for change than husbands gave them. On the other hand, change initiated by husbands and mutually initiated change were reported at similarly low levels. It is important to note that many spouses seemed to see change as "just happening," except for openness–closedness (for which there was less change overall). Participants generally reported that attempts to initiate change on the contradictions met with relatively positive responses from their partners (either acceptance or negotiation). However, for novelty–predictability, spouses were as likely to reject the attempt as to be willing to negotiate. This latter finding may reflect the perception that with the increasing demands of work and family life, a focus on novelty is simply unrealistic.

Causal Attributions. Husbands and wives were generally fairly similar in their reports of the factors leading to change on the relational dimensions (Table 8.3). If participants reported more than one reason for change in a particular contradiction, only the most important factor is included in the table. For all three contradictions, a considerable

Table 8.3. Frequency of Causal Attributions for Each Contradiction (Study 1)

Factor	Autonomy–Connection		Openness–Closedness		Novelty–Predictability	
	Husband Report	Wife Report	Husband Report	Wife Report	Husband Report	Wife Report
Changed needs	10	8	14	13	13	8
Maturity	14	10	2	3	6	4
Time together	7	6	13	8	5	5
Children	7	4	1	1	10	5
Her work/study	9	13	0	0	7	7
His work/study	6	5	0	0	4	4
Money	0	0	0	0	5	7
Problems	0	0	4	4	0	0
None	30	37	49	54	33	43

number of participants reported no reason for change, because they did not mention significant patterns of change.

For autonomy–connection, changes were attributed to spouses' increased maturity, changes in needs, her work and study, time together, having children, and his work and study. It is interesting to recall that the nature of reported change was the most varied for this particular contradiction. It is easy to understand that changing patterns of work and study, for example, can be associated with either more autonomy or more connection, depending on whether work and study commitments increase or decrease. More generally, the reports of changes in autonomy–connection tended to focus on the delicate balance between each partner's autonomy levels. One husband noted that, throughout the child-rearing years, his wife had been "the glue that holds the family together," while he had had a lot of autonomy:

And now I've sort of scaled back, I guess, and you're doing your own study. I guess that one of the things I've wondered is whether you took Indonesian because it was something totally separate to anything I would have done.

The importance of establishing a balance between each partner's autonomy levels is also clear in the following comment from a wife who perceives a serious imbalance between herself and her husband in this area:

Well it's a bigger issue than it used to be, because in the past I had my own work and I had my own study, and I was busy and you were busy, and we didn't have a lot of time for each other. But that didn't really bother us, because we both had interesting things outside our relationship. But at the moment, you've got work and you've got study, and you've got swimming, and you've got, you've got all the, you've got the car. And I'm stuck at home with two kids, sick and pregnant again. And so it probably is a problem at the moment, because I feel like you've got autonomy and I haven't.

For openness–closedness, change was attributed primarily to changes in needs, time together, and relationship problems. In terms of change toward more openness, several extracts focused on couples' ongoing relationships helping partners from nondisclosing backgrounds to talk about issues more openly. This was the only contradiction in which change was attributed to relationship problems. Some couples mentioned that having problems in their relationship forced them to be more open with each other; in fact, the need to talk openly had emerged as the only way of dealing with crises and traumas that beset the family. Opening up to one another seemed essential to resolving the situation and brought the partners closer together. For example, one husband noted:

> I came up through a family with two boys and a mother, and you didn't – nothing was disclosed. Like, self-disclosure was a thing you never did. You never gave. You never expressed your feelings. And it was only at recent times, when we've had enormous trauma in our lives, and not between you and me, but with our children, that we've really been, our relationship has strengthened in every way. And you know, you've seen me cry – well I wouldn't have ten years ago. That was against all regimental principles that I grew up with, and my era grew up with. But you know there's nothing I don't reveal.

On the other hand, some respondents reported change toward more closeness, resulting either from attempts to manage the couple relationship (narrowing down to the "safe" topics) or from the presence of children and the associated pressures. The following exchange between husband and wife illustrates the issue of safe topics:

> H: It's not that we might want to keep things private from each other. It's just that we avoid discussing them, because sometimes when you discuss these matters, it leads to disagreement or embarrassment. So um – sometimes it's best just left alone. Nothing secretive or sinister or anything.
>
> W: Yes, I think over the years, we've learned what we can talk about and what we can't talk about to each other, so that's led to the more privacy sort of business, so it's not a purposeful privacy.

Similarly, the following exchange between husband and wife illustrates the pressure that children can place on open communication and interaction:

> H: Whereas it was very easy to go out to dinner before, it's much more difficult now. Because either there's no one to look after the kids, or the kids want to come.
>
> W: Certainly it's frustrating. Our sex life is in tatters, isn't it? Because we have to sort of work around the children. It puts a terrible stress. These young couples that are coming in [doing this research] don't know how easy they've got it, do they?

For novelty–predictability, change was attributed to changing needs, having children, the wife's work and study, money, maturity, and time together. As we noted before, change in this contradiction was almost always reported in the direction of more predictability. This change was sometimes attributed to the couple's familiarity with one another ("When you've known each other for 30 years, it's a bit hard to be novel, isn't it?")

For other couples, time constraints were seen as reducing the opportunities for novelty ("I guess it's like at the moment, I don't have time for novelty"; and "We were forced into predictability by time routines. We have to be at certain places at certain times, on the dot."). Time constraints, in turn, were attributed to the demands of work, study, children, and home life generally. For example, consider the following exchange:

H: The way life is at the moment, the spontaneous side is sort of getting chucked away to one side, isn't it?
W: Yes, it's inconvenient probably, more than anything.
H: Like before, we didn't have a dog and a bird. We could just get up and go. And now we can't.
W: That's probably a big problem. If we did, it's only more or less overnight. With a cage and a dog!

In summary, change on the relational dimensions was generally attributed to changing needs of the individuals or to the experience of married life. Specifically, factors such as maturity, time together, children, and study were frequently mentioned. Relationship problems were suggested as a cause of change only for openness–closedness.

Methodological Issues

Because of the way this study was designed, with the emphasis on spouses' general reports of their relationship experiences, there was only a limited possibility of picking up short-term change. Van Lear (1991) studied the conversations of unacquainted student pairs over a 4-week interval and also conducted a 10-week diary study in which individuals rated the extent of openness–closedness in their conversations with friends and romantic partners. His studies showed cyclical patterns of openness and closedness, both within and across conversations. For this reason, we were interested in asking couples in the later study about short-term as well as long-term change.

More generally, in Study 1 our focus was on insiders' conversations about their differences on the contradictions. With such semistructured accounts, participants can only discuss the factors that come to mind.

Hence, we could not be sure that asking participants to rate the nature and extent of change in their relationships directly would produce similar responses. For this reason, in Study 2 we sought to investigate these issues by asking each couple about change in their relationship more directly, using the knowledge gained from Study 1. It was expected that priming participants in this way would ensure that they considered each specific question and might therefore give a more complete picture of the relevant issues. Despite the potential limitations of the data obtained from semistructured accounts, many couples reported enjoying the opportunity to talk about the issues raised in Study 1.

Study 2

There were 80 couples in the second study, with one member of each couple again being an undergraduate student who participated in the study for course credit. The couples had been married between a few months and 41 years, with a mean length of marriage of 10.41 years. The mean age for husbands was 35.6 years, and the mean age for wives was 33.6 years. Highest education achieved varied from tertiary (68.8% of husbands and 67.5% of wives) to less than grade 10 (3.75% of husbands and 2.5% of wives). The number of children in the families varied from 1 to 9, with a mean of 1.54. The characteristics of this sample were very similar to those of the sample used in Study 1.

The questionnaire for this study focused primarily on change in the relational contradictions over the course of couples' relationships and particularly on the attributions (both responsibility and causal) couples made for those changes. Because the novelty–predictability contradiction generally produced fairly weak results in the first study, only the autonomy–connectedness and openness–closedness contradictions were addressed in this one. All items on the questionnaire were rated on 6-point scales. Couples were first provided with a description of the two contradictions and were asked whether differences on these contradictions characterized their relationship. They were then asked whether there had been change over the period of their relationship with regard to the balance between the poles. If they thought that there had been change, they were asked to indicate the type of change from a list of six possible types derived from the earlier study. That is, for each contradiction, they were asked which spouse had changed (husband, wife, or the husband and wife as a couple) and which pole of the contradiction they had moved toward (e.g., autonomy or connectedness). Spouses were also asked to rate the extent to which their own and their spouse's needs for autonomy–connection and openness–closedness fluctuated from day to day.

In terms of attributions, couples were asked who was responsible for change, both in terms of pressuring for change and in terms of actively initiating change. In addition, the major factors that were found to have caused a change in the balance on the relational contradictions in the earlier study were listed in the questionnaire, and spouses were asked to rate each factor in terms of its importance for them. The seven factors were maturing as individuals, maturing as a couple, length of time spent together, having children, changing individual needs, husbands' work and study, and wives' work and study. In addition to the questions dealing with the two contradictions, couples also completed the Dyadic Adjustment Scale (Spanier, 1976), which has been described earlier in this chapter.

Extent of Difference

Participants tended to report a moderate amount of difference both in their needs for autonomy versus connection (for husbands $M = 3.81$, $SD = 1.58$; for wives $M = 3.66$, $SD = 1.73$) and in their needs for openness versus closedness (for husbands $M = 3.15$, $SD = 1.84$; for wives $M = 3.09$, $SD = 1.83$). Marital satisfaction was negatively related to the extent to which the marriage was characterized by conflicting desires for autonomy–connectedness ($r = -.54$ for husbands and $-.43$ for wives, $p < .01$ in each case) and for openness–closedness ($r = -.55$ for husbands and $-.46$ for wives, $p < .01$ in each case). All of these results are similar to those found in study 1, with happy couples reporting less difference on these basic dimensions of relationships.

Change over Time

Participants were asked to rate the extent to which they believed that the balance in each contradiction had changed over the period of the relationship. They were also asked about such issues as the extent of daily change, pressures for change, which spouse initiated change, and the factors causing change.

Extent of Change over Time. Participants tended to report a moderate amount of change over time in both contradictions. The mean level of change in the balance between autonomy and connection was 3.53 for husbands (SD = 1.65), and 3.58 for wives (SD = 1.60). Similarly, the mean level of change in the balance between openness and closedness was 3.91 for husbands (SD = 1.82), and 3.80 for wives (SD = 1.88). In the previous study, between one half and one third of the sample reported change over time, with a tendency for less change to be reported on openness–closedness than on autonomy–connectedness. More change was reported in study 2 when participants were asked directly about the extent of change over the duration of their relationship. Perhaps with semistructured accounts, current and recent issues rather than broad patterns of change are particularly salient for many respondents.

Reports of Daily Change. For both contradictions, spouses also reported moderate levels of day-to-day fluctuations in both partners' needs (mean scores ranged from 3.12 to 3.62 on the 6-point scale). Further, for both contradictions, husbands and wives generally agreed in their perceptions of the extent of daily change. However on average, daily change in husbands' own needs for openness and closedness was seen as greater by husbands than by wives. The fact that wives tended to be less willing to acknowledge their husbands' fluctuating needs for openness, as well as closedness, fits with stereotyped perceptions of males as being generally inexpressive (Balswick, 1986). This apparent failure on the part of the wife to acknowledge her husband's changing needs may be problematic, particularly if she tends to demand responses at times when he is feeling uncommunicative (Christensen & Heavey, 1990).

To explore whether day-to-day fluctuations were problematic for the relationship, we correlated reports of the extent of daily change with marital satisfaction. Few significant results were obtained. Specifically, for autonomy–connectedness, there was no relation between daily change and satisfaction; for wives only, the belief that their own needs for openness and closedness changed on a daily basis was associated with lower satisfaction ($r = -.25$, $p < .05$). Perhaps husbands find it difficult to respond appropriately to wives' fluctuating needs for openness and closedness, which results in these wives being less satisfied with their relationships.

Nature of Change. In order to understand the nature of the change that couples had experienced over the course of their relationships, repeated-measures multivariate analyses of variance (MANOVAs) were conducted on the ratings of change over time for each contradiction. These analyses assessed the effects of three variables: sex of reporter, which spouse's needs have changed (husband, wife, both), and direction of the change (toward pole 1, toward pole 2).

For autonomy–connection, there was a main effect for which spouse's needs had changed, and there were two interaction effects (which spouse's needs had changed by direction of change; and sex of reporter by direction of change). Overall, participants were more likely to report that they had both come to want the same pole than that they had wanted different poles. When both partners wanted change in the same direction, they tended to want more connectedness; in contrast, when they differed in their needs, they were equally likely to want more autonomy as to want more connectedness. The different perspectives of husbands and wives on these issues is illustrated by the finding that husbands were more likely to report change toward connection than toward autonomy (for either spouse or for the couple as a whole), whereas wives were equally likely to report change in either direction. Perhaps husbands' perceptions of change toward connectedness reflect their greater initial emphasis on autonomy, in line with traditional sex roles.

For openness–closedness, there were main effects for which partner's needs had changed and for direction of change, together with an interaction between these two variables. Again, spouses overall were more likely to report that they had both come to want the same pole, in this instance, openness. Further, couples were more likely to report that they had both come to want more openness than that they had come to want more closedness; in contrast, when only one spouse wanted change, both directions of change were equally likely. As with autonomy–connectedness, it is clear that in this group of generally stable couples, spouses' needs on the relational dimensions tended to converge over time.

Responsibility Attributions. We also explored the question of what happens when change is desired. This question was addressed by using repeated-measures MANOVAs, with the three variables being sex of reporter, attributions of who was pressuring for change (husband, wife), and attributions for the direction of the pressure (toward pole 1, pole 2, or more balance).

For autonomy–connection, there was a main effect of direction and an interaction between who was pressuring for change and the direction of the pressure. Spouses generally reported more pressures for balance than for autonomy. Both sexes were equally likely to be seen as pressuring for more balance, but husbands were more likely than wives to be seen as pushing for autonomy and less likely to be seen as pushing for connection. Both husbands and wives saw husbands as more likely to push for autonomy than for connection.

For openness–closedness, there was again a main effect of direction, together with two interaction effects (sex of reporter by who was pressuring for change and who was pressuring for change by direction of pressure). Overall, participants reported more pressures for openness and balance than for closedness, with husbands rating their own pressure for change as particularly high. Husbands were more likely than wives to be seen as pressuring for closedness and less likely to be seen as pressuring for openness (again, both sexes were equally likely to be seen as pressuring for more balance). The apparent importance of balance is consistent with the idea that there is a dynamic tension between the two poles of a given contradiction. Also, given the overall emphasis on balance, it is not surprising that relational events (both day-to-day and major) tend to bring about change on the dimensions as couples seek to redress any resulting imbalances. As noted earlier, however, there is no single point of balance, but rather, there are continuing fluctuations between the two poles.

The question of responsibility attributions was also investigated by using frequency comparisons relating sex of reporter to which partner initiates change. This analysis was significant for each contradiction. In each case, wives were approximately twice as likely as husbands to be seen (by both spouses) as the initiators of change. These findings are similar to those from the first study and fit with the argument that women tend to be the caretakers of relationships (Surra & Longstreth, 1990). Researchers have also shown that women tend to be somewhat less satisfied than men with the state of their relationships, and hence the initiation of change may emanate from their lower satisfaction.

Participants were also asked to provide open-ended reports of how the moves for change were initiated. Almost all of the responses placed the emphasis on communication between spouses. Responses varied, however, in terms of the extent to which the communication was open and honest and the extent to which it was mutually constructive or involved challenges and arguments. Quoting directly from the reports, participants described their initiation of change as including "direct" and "honest" communication, "bargaining," "pillow talk," "arguments," "suggesting a goal with a time," "mutual agreement," "challenging one another," and "blurting it out." These responses generally fit with Rusbult's (1987) concept of *voice* (or engaging in discussion of the issue), which she describes as the most constructive response to dissatisfactions in relationships.

Causal Attributions. To look at the kinds of attributions spouses were making for change in their relationships, reports of what caused the change were analyzed by MANOVAs. Our interest was in the reported causes of change (maturing as individuals, maturing as a couple, time spent together, having children, individuals' changing needs, husbands' work and study, wives' work and study) and in whether husbands and wives attributed the change to similar or to different factors. For both contradictions, the only significant effect was for cause (see Table 8.4); there were no sex differences in attributions. For both husbands and wives, the factors seen as most responsible for change on autonomy–connection and openness–closedness were maturing as a couple, maturing as individuals, and time together. In contrast, husbands' work and study, wives' work and study, and having children were endorsed less strongly.

Many participants saw a complex of factors as responsible for change in the contradictions. This pattern is further illustrated by participants' open-ended reports of the causes of change. For *autonomy–connectedness,* reports of the causes of change were equally likely to focus on factors internal to the individual partners or the relationship as on factors external to it. In terms of internal factors, several participants talked about the effects of the moods and emotions of either self or spouse (including anger, jealousy, insecurity, and depression, and "own individual interests and attitudes"). With regard to factors internal to the relationship, participants generally focused on the effects of relationship conflict (disagreements and quarrels) and perceptions of the overall state of the relationship ("the way our relationship is going"). It seemed that both distance and connection could be tolerated to a certain point, but then

Table 8.4. Mean Ratings of Factors Causing Change (Study 2)

Causal Factor	Autonomy–Connectedness	Openness–Closedness
Matured as individuals	4.02 (1.08)	3.76 (1.33)
Matured as a couple	4.23 (1.11)	3.93 (1.34)
Time together	3.86 (1.07)	3.76 (1.25)
Having children	3.23 (1.76)	2.87 (1.74)
Changing needs	3.68 (1.28)	3.19 (1.39)
Husband's work/study	3.14 (1.34)	2.61 (1.36)
Wife's work/study	3.35 (1.44)	2.69 (1.44)

change would be precipitated by conflict over such issues as time together and time apart.

For openness–closedness, fewer participants were able to articulate factors causing change from one pole to the other. Again, several respondents talked about factors internal to the individuals or their relationship. These factors included changes in emotion (anger and resentment were seen as sometimes "getting in the way" of openness) and in general well-being (e.g., being "fatigued" versus being "refreshed"). In addition, in terms of change toward openness, some participants mentioned the need for partners to be "ready or wanting to open up" on issues. Conversely, in terms of moves toward closedness, others noted the effect of "tiredness of talking about something for long periods" or, alternatively, of resolving the issue and not needing to discuss it further. One wife, who was concerned about the effect of their noisy children on her introverted husband (who "craved solitude"), talked about how she would organize privacy for him or, in her words, "create space for him to be alone for a while." This report illustrates how spouses who are sensitive to each other's state of mind ("he gets frantic") can minimize the potentially negative effects of differing needs on their relationship.

GENERAL DISCUSSION AND CONCLUSIONS

These two studies help us to understand the dynamics of couple relationships in a number of ways. For example, they help us to understand how dynamic tensions between needs for autonomy–connectedness and openness–closedness contribute to change in some couples' relationships. In both studies, couples reported having moved toward more openness despite the fact that husbands were likely to be seen as pushing for closedness. Change with regard to autonomy–connectedness was more complex. In Study 1, change was in the direction of more autonomy, but this pressure was attributed mainly to husbands. In Study 2, obtaining a balance between the two poles seemed important for both contradictions. Couples in that study also reported substantial daily fluctuations in their needs on the dimensions being studied, which suggests that both short-term and long-term changes are occurring in these relationships. Short-term changes may occur in response to mood, fatigue, or other states of the individual. However, over time, increased awareness of these patterns of daily change may also contribute to the kinds of long-term change reported by the couples in this study.

With regard to participants' causal attributions for change, maturity and length of time together were seen as important factors in both studies. This finding also highlights the dynamic nature of couple bonds, with partners recognizing that although the contradictions are never fully resolved, their perceptions of the issues change as they mature as a couple. Given the results concerning pressures for change, one consequence of this increasing maturity seems to be an acceptance of the need to find a balance between the poles of the contradictions, whether autonomy–connectedness or openness–closedness.

Although overall, the factors linked to change were similar for both contradictions and across both studies, couples in study 2 placed less emphasis on changes in individual needs than did those in study 1. It is possible that, because participants were supplied with a list of potential contributing factors in study 2, other factors, and particularly relationship-based factors, became more salient. This proposition is consistent with the finding that relationship partners tend to overlook interactional causes of behavior, especially in emotionally charged situations (Sillars & Scott, 1983).

More research is needed to explore further the concepts of stability and change in established relationships. For example, little is known about the ways in which married couples' needs for openness and closedness fluctuate from conversation to conversation and from day to day. It is important for researchers to gain a better understanding of the factors linked to such short-term changes and how these changes are organized into larger patterns of stability, change, or both. In terms of responsibility attributions, questions remain concerning how these attributions develop and the extent to which they reflect actual differences in behavior, as opposed to sex role stereotypes. A further issue concerns whether the perception of one partner as more actively involved in promoting relationship change is linked to communication patterns and to relationship functioning. In terms of causal attributions, it is important to examine whether attributing change to internal versus external factors is linked to perceptions of relational competence and relationship satisfaction. Resolving these issues would enhance our understanding of the many facets of attributions in marriage.

REFERENCES

Aries, E. (1996). *Men and women in interaction: Reconsidering the differences.* New York: Oxford University Press.

Balswick, J. (1986). *The inexpressive male.* Lexington, MA:Lexington Books.

Baxter, L. A. (1988). A dialectical perspective on communication strategies in relationship development. In S. W. Duck (Ed.), *Handbook of personal relationships* (pp. 257–273). New York: Wiley.

Baxter, L. A. (1990). Dialectical contradictions in relationship development. *Journal of Social and Personal Relationships, 7*, 187–208.

Baxter, L. A., & Montgomery, B. M. (1996). *Relating: Dialogues and dialectics.* New York: Guilford Press.

Baxter, L. A., & Montgomery, B. M. (1997). Rethinking communication in personal relationships from a dialectical perspective. In S. W. Duck (Ed.), *Handbook of personal relationships: Theory, research and interventions* (pp. 325–349). Chichester, UK: John Wiley & Sons.

Baxter, L. A., & Simon, E. P. (1993). Relationship maintenance strategies and dialectical contradiction in personal relationships. *Journal of Social and Personal Relationships, 10*, 225–242.

Christensen, A., & Heavey, C. L. (1990). Gender, power, and marital conflict. *Journal of Personality and Social Psychology, 59*, 73–85.

Giddens, A. (1979) *Central problems in social theory: Action, structure and contradiction in social analysis.* Berkeley: University of California Press.

Goldsmith, D. (1990). A dialectical perspective on the expression of autonomy and connection in romantic relationships. *Western Journal of Speech Communication, 54*, 537–556.

Montgomery, B. M. (1993). Relationship maintenance versus relationship change: A dialectical dilemma. *Journal of Social and Personal Relationships, 10*, 205–223.

Noller, P., & Feeney, J. A. (1998). Communication in early marriage: Responses to conflict, nonverbal accuracy and conversational patterns. In T. N. Bradbury (Ed.), *The developmental course of marital dysfunction* (pp. 11–43). New York: Cambridge University Press.

Rusbult, C. E. (1987). Responses to dissatisfaction in close relationships: The exit-voice-loyalty-neglect model. In D. Perlman & S. Duck (Eds.) *Intimate relationships: Development, dynamics, and deterioration.* (pp. 209–237). Newbury Park, CA: Sage.

Sillars, A. L., & Scott, M. D. (1983). Interpersonal perception between intimates: An integrative review. *Human Communication Research, 10*, 153–176.

Spanier, G. B. (1976). Measuring dyadic adjustment: New scales for assessing the quality of marriage and similar dyads. *Journal of Marriage and the Family, 38*, 15–28.

Spitzberg, B. (1993). The dialectics of (in)competence. *Journal of Social and Personal Relationships, 10*, 137–158.

Surra, C. A., & Longstreth, M. (1990). Similarity of outcome, interdependence, and conflict in dating relationships. *Journal of Personality and Social Psychology, 59*, 501–516.

Van Lear, C. A. (1991). Testing a cyclical model of communicative openness in relationship development: Two longitudinal studies. *Communication Monographs, 58*, 337–361.

CHAPTER NINE

The Role of Marital Behavior in the Longitudinal Association Between Attributions and Marital Quality

Matthew D. Johnson, Benjamin R. Karney, Ronald Rogge, and Thomas N. Bradbury

The fundamental premise of the cognitive model of psychopathology is that cognition precedes affect and behavior (Beck, 1976; Ellis, 1962). Likewise, the addition of cognitive variables to the behavioral model of marriage presumes that cognition leads to emotionally expressive dyadic behaviors, which determine marital satisfaction. The reasoning behind both the psychopathology model and the behavioral model of marriage thus rests on the idea that cognition shapes behavior. Importantly, however, this causal order has not yet received empirical validation.

For researchers whose interest lies in a desire to prevent dysfunctional relationships (i.e., to find an early point of intervention allowing the subsequent problems to be avoided), it is imperative to know the causal order of cognition and behavior, including communication behavior such as conflict. Examining the "placement" of cognition in marriage is also a necessary first step toward a deeper understanding of the origin of maladaptive behavior. While cognitive variables and particularly attributions have received extensive attention (see Fincham, 1994), both in relation to marital satisfaction (e.g., Fincham & Bradbury, 1987) and marital interaction (Bradbury & Fincham, 1992), the central premise of the cognitive-behavioral model – the assumption that attributions precede dyadic behavior – has yet to be tested.

This chapter was supported by National Institute of Mental Health grant #R29 48674 awarded to Thomas N. Bradbury and by a grant from the Fahs-Beck Fund for Research and Experimentation awarded to Matthew D. Johnson. Preparation of the chapter was also facilitated by a grant from the John Templeton Foundation. Correspondence should be sent to Matthew Johnson, Department of Psychology, State University of New York at Binghamton, Binghamton, New York 13902-6000.

In an effort to understand the best way to utilize the preliminary findings supporting the cognitive-behavioral model of marriage, psychologists have developed treatments based on the model (e.g., Baucom & Epstein, 1990). There is some evidence that these interventions have incremental advantages over traditional behavioral marital therapy (for review, see Baucom, Epstein, & Rankin, 1995). However, if the focus on intervention is to become more prophylactic, a better understanding of the development of discord in marriage is necessary to create more efficacious primary interventions. This paper attempts to provide this understanding.

BRIEF REVIEW OF BEHAVIORAL LITERATURE

Serious study of the behavioral model of marriage began in the late 1970s. Most of the early studies of behaviors were cross-sectional, which enabled researchers to distinguish dissatisfied and satisfied couples using indices such as rate of negativity, reciprocity of negative behaviors, and avoidance. Subsequent longitudinal studies examining the relationship of behavior to change in marital satisfaction have consistently presented a more complicated picture. Generally, it has been found that negativity and reciprocation of negativity predict lower satisfaction longitudinally (e.g., Huston & Chorost, 1994).

Karney and Bradbury's (1995b) meta-analysis of the longitudinal effects of behavior on marriage supported the idea of negativity having a detrimental effect on the marriage. However, the meta-effects of behavior were relatively small, and the findings of individual studies "varied substantially in direction and magnitude" (Karney & Bradbury, 1995b, p. 22). The variation in the direction of findings resulted from some evidence that negative behavior is inversely associated with concurrent marital satisfaction but has a positive impact on change in satisfaction over time. For example, Karney and Bradbury (1997) found that wives' negative behavior had a positive impact on change in husbands and wives' satisfaction over time. Similarly, Heavey, Layne, and Christensen (1993) noted that husbands' negativity and demandingness predicted wives' satisfaction. These surprising and contradictory results suggest that the role of behavior in marriage is more complicated than first believed.

One plausible explanation for these inconclusive findings is that intrapersonal factors might mediate or moderate the effect of behavior on marital quality. Following the cognitive-behavioral model, it is proposed that individual spouses' expectations, beliefs, interpretations, perceptions, and attitudes influence the longitudinal association between behavior and marital quality. The findings from behavioral research on marriage suggest that behavior influences marital outcome. In the rest of this chapter, literature and data will be presented suggesting that cognition is also influential in predicting satisfaction and that cognition and behaviors are integrated in a specific manner to predict marital quality.

BRIEF REVIEW OF COGNITIVE LITERATURE

In the 1980s there was an eruption of research on the role of cognition in marriage. Because others have reviewed this literature (e.g., Baucom & Epstein, 1990; Bradbury & Fincham, 1990; Fincham, 1994; Fincham, Bradbury, & Scott, 1990), this section discusses only the prospective research on cognition. Furthermore, the focus will be on attributions, the cognitive variable that has been studied the most in the marital domain. However, the principles described here may also describe the role that other cognitive variables may play in marriage (cf. Bradbury & Fincham, 1993).

A large research literature has developed that examines the attributions, or explanations, that spouses make for events in their marriage. Models of attributions in marriage propose that distressed spouses accentuate the impact of problematic events in a marriage and minimize the impact of positive events (see Bradbury & Fincham, 1990). This theory has been supported by the meta-analytic findings of the effects of maladaptive attributions on change in marital satisfaction (effect–size $r = -.26$ for wives and $-.21$ for husbands; Karney & Bradbury, 1995b). Individual studies have also confirmed that the attributional model is supported when attributions are classified into causal and responsibility attributions. Causal attributions focus on who or what caused an event or condition, whereas responsibility attributions concern who "is accountable, and therefore liable to sanction" (Fincham, 1994, p. 187) for the event or condition. Both dimensions of attributions were found to be significantly correlated with concurrent marital satisfaction (correlations ranged from $-.40$ to $-.44$, $p < .001$; Fincham & Bradbury, 1992).

These data are important in that they establish that there is a relationship between attributions and satisfaction and while not conclusive, suggest a direction of causality with attributions predicting marital satisfaction. The findings also led Fincham (1994) to ask three questions: (1) Do attributions lead to marital distress? (2) Do attributions cause changes in marital behavior? (3) What conclusions may be drawn from the relationship of attributions, behavior, and satisfaction? This chapter will attempt to answer these questions by reviewing the literature, commenting on ongoing studies, and proposing future directions of research.

DO ATTRIBUTIONS LEAD TO MARITAL DISTRESS?

Correlational data on the relationship between attributions and marital satisfaction make it clear that unhappy spouses, as compared with happy spouses, tend to make more negative attributions. Yet, the measurement of thought is a difficult matter, and attributions are not an exception. The problem of measurement has been addressed in a systematic way by testing the Relationship Attribution Measure (RAM; Fincham & Bradbury, 1992) across three different studies and examining its reliability and validity. The RAM is a brief self-report measure that asks couples to imagine their partner exhibiting a certain behavior, and then it requires the participant to answer six questions about each situation on a 6-point Likert-type scale. Three of the items for each situation assess causal attributions, and three assess responsibility attributions. Reliability was determined by examining internal consistency and test–retest correlations, both of which were well within the acceptable range. The validity of the RAM was determined by examining associations of the RAM with satisfaction, attributions for actual marital events, and affect (reported and observed) about marital events.

Causal and responsibility attribution scores were correlated with marital satisfaction, attributions for actual marital difficulties, and attributions for actual partner behaviors. In addition, responsibility attribution scores were correlated with reported anger in response to the descriptions on the RAM (Fincham & Bradbury, 1992). In a subsequent problem-solving interaction, responsibility attribution scores were also correlated with the amount of displayed anger by wives and with whining by both spouses. Although there is still no way of verifying the presence of a thought, the systematic analysis of the internal and external validity of the RAM by Fincham and Bradbury (1992) provides researchers with a better understanding of measurement error when assessing attributions and presents further support for the association of attributions and marital satisfaction.

The association of maladaptive attributions and marital distress has led to the plausible hypothesis that attributions influence satisfaction. The temporal nature of this hypothesis (i.e., attributions lead to satisfaction) reveals an assumption that has become part of larger theories of relationship development (e.g., Bradbury & Fincham, 1991) and has been incorporated in treatments designed to diminish or prevent marital distress (e.g., Baucom & Epstein, 1990; Markman, Stanley, & Blumberg, 1994). These theories contend that spouses make attributions and that those attributions are informally catalogued as part of their dyadic exchange (see Thibaut & Kelley, 1959). From those attributions, an understanding of their relationship and their satisfaction with that relationship (i.e., a schema for the relationship) develops. This causal order differs from the traditional social psychological view of the relationship between schema and attributions, which notes that "a schema may be defined as a cognitive structure that represents knowledge about a concept or type of stimulus, including its attributes and the relations among those attributes" (Fiske & Taylor, 1991, p. 98). The traditional social psychological model and the sentiment override model suggest a top-down approach, in which satisfaction (i.e., schema) determines attributional structures. The clinical view, however, takes a more bottom-up approach.

Longitudinal Studies

To better understand the influence of attributions and their role in the development of discord, there has been a move toward the use of longitudinal designs in close relationship research studying attributions. Fincham and Bradbury (1987) conducted the first longitudinal study of the effects of attributions in marriage. They demonstrated that maladaptive causal and responsibility attributions for partner behavior and negative events in the marriage predicted negative changes in wives' satisfaction over a 12-month period. The finding did not hold for husbands' satisfaction.

The study also tested whether attributions change as a function of initial satisfaction and concluded that this was not the case (for similar findings involving relationship beliefs, see Fincham & Bradbury, 1987). These results were replicated for husbands and wives in a larger subsequent study by Fincham and Bradbury (1993). In that study, depression was also ruled out as a possible confound; this is important because of the view that depression is associated with a generally maladaptive attributional style (Abramson, Seligman, & Teasdale, 1978). In a third study, nonviolent newlywed husbands' maladaptive responsibility attributions predicted declines in marital satisfaction 1 year later, but initial satisfaction did not predict changes in attributional styles (Fincham, Bradbury, Arias, Byrne, & Karney, 1997). Overall, the results of these studies provide evidence to support the assumption that maladaptive attributions exert a causal influence on marital satisfaction over time.

Stability and Causality of Attributions

According to Karney and Bradbury (in press), theory and research to date suggest that attributions are assumed to represent the cognitive products of enduring characteristics that each spouse contributes to the relationship. This assumption is a product of the attributional theory of depression (Seligman, Abramson, Semel, & von Baeyer, 1979), which presumes that some people possess a maladaptive attributional style which is stable over time and situations (e.g., Horneffer & Fincham, 1996). The literature provides support for the view that the general attributional style of an individual plays a causal role in the development of marital distress, an assumption underlying the longitudinal studies discussed in the preceding section (e.g., Fincham & Bradbury, 1987).

The combination of these two assumptions, one as yet untested and one partially supported, has led to the conclusion that the tendency to make maladaptive attributions represents an enduring vulnerability that places couples at risk for marital discord. Yet, if attributions are found to be a reflection of the current state of a spouse and not an enduring trait, this would call into question the conclusions of the attributional literature and would suggest that some of the interventions that focus on attributions may be targeting an indicator of distress, personal or marital, rather than a predictor of developing marital discord.

To address the questions of stability and causality of attributions in marriage, Karney and Bradbury (in press) conducted a longitudinal study of newlywed marriage, using multiple waves of data that were quantified by growth curve analysis. Sixty couples married less than 6 months at the start of the study were assessed at 6-month intervals over 4 years, yielding eight waves of data. Individual indicators of attributions were collected at each time point by use of the RAM.

Marital satisfaction was assessed by a standard instrument, the Marital Adjustment Test (MAT) (Locke & Wallace, 1959), and marital dissolution was assessed at each wave of data collection. In addition, to answer questions about the effects of attributions independently of neuroticism (i.e., depressive symptoms) the neuroticism subscale of the Eysenck Personality Questionnaire (Eysenck & Eysenck, 1978) was administered at the first and second assessments.

Growth curve analysis is a method of assessing change derived from hierarchical linear modeling (Bryk & Raudenbush, 1987), which plots all of the data points (e.g., marital satisfaction) collected from an individual over time and regresses a line to fit those data. The slope of that line is then considered the measure of change for that individual. This method of analysis was chosen because it is more sensitive to change than other methods that have been used in the literature, many of which rely on just two waves of data to assess marital change (Karney & Bradbury, 1995a).

To test the first assumption, that attributional style is constant over time and situations, a model of linear change in attributions was compared with a model of stable attributions. The model of linear change was a better fit of the data than the model hypothesizing that attributions vary around a stable mean, which suggests that attributions tend to develop over time and are not a fixed or innate characteristic. This finding is consistent with cross-sectional findings in the depression literature, which also call into question the stability of maladaptive attributions across situations (e.g., Cutrona, Russell, & Jones, 1984).

With regard to the second assumption, that attributions play a causal role in the development of marital discord, the finding that attributions are not traitlike does not preclude causation. Attributions may be a reaction to current relationship functioning, but changes in attributional tendencies following changes in marital satisfaction may have implications for future satisfaction. For example, if a spouse becomes dissatisfied with marriage, this may lead to change in the attributional style that spouse exhibits, and the degree and direction of the attributional shift may in turn predict further changes in marital satisfaction. To test this hypothesis, Karney and Bradbury (in press) examined the direction of causality between attributions and marital satisfaction.

Previously, research examining attributions and satisfaction has suggested that attributions are more stable than satisfaction. To determine if attributions are stable or vary in a manner similar to that of marital satisfaction, the within-spouse cross-sectional covariance of attributions and satisfaction over time was examined (i.e., do changes in satisfaction covary with changes in attributions?). To answer this question, two sets of analyses were conducted. First, changes in attributions (i.e., attribution trajectories) were examined for the extent to which they were associated with deviations from the trajectory of satisfaction. Second, the variables were reversed testing for the association of changes in satisfaction with deviations from the trajectories of attributions. In both analyses, the within-spouse attribution–satisfaction association was of similar magnitude, significant, and negative. That is, increased husband satisfaction was associated with decreases in husbands' maladaptive attributions and vice versa (decreases in maladaptive attributions were associated with increases in satisfaction). The results were the same for wives. These results do not support the assumption that attributional styles are more stable than satisfaction and suggest that the influence is bidirectional.

Controlling for the covariance between attributions and satisfaction over time (the association discussed in the preceding paragraph), we examined the following two associations: (1) the association between initial attributional (time 1) styles and changes in satisfaction over 4 years (time 1 to time 8), controlling for changes in attributional styles over the 4 years; (2) the association between time 1 marital satisfaction and changes in attributional styles from time 1 to time 8, controlling for changes in marital satisfaction over the 4 years. The analyses indicated that, while controlling for the covariance of attributions and satisfaction over time, the attributions partners make early in the marriage have an impact on subsequent marital satisfaction. Specifically, early maladaptive responsibility attributions predict steeper declines in satisfaction for wives, and maladaptive causal attributions predict steeper declines for both spouses. When initial marital satisfaction was used to predict changes in attributions, no significant results were found for husbands or wives for either type of attribution (causal or responsibility).

These findings suggest that attributions have more power to predict changes in marital satisfaction than satisfaction has to predict changes in attributions. The findings also further the understanding of previous longitudinal studies by demonstrating that the reciprocal effect of satisfaction and attributions happens only at the cross-sectional level, but initial attributional styles have more power to predict changes in marital satisfaction than initial satisfaction has to predict changes in attributions. The conclusions are strengthened by using hierarchical linear modeling, which simultaneously analyzes all data points, increasing the confidence that initial levels of attributions are not confounded with the association of changes in attributions and changes in satisfaction.

Summary

The longitudinal findings reviewed in this section present a reasonably strong argument that attributions play a significant role in the development of marital distress. However, the findings should be viewed as a rejection of the hypothesis that attributions are stable, consistent, enduring, and traitlike. Given that behavioral marital interventions have developed to include cognitive components, the findings on the reciprocal nature of attributions and satisfaction provide insight that may be used to develop or refine interventions. However, the relationship of attributions and satisfaction provides only part of the information necessary for better understanding of the cognitive-behavioral model of marriage. To examine the model more systematically, marital researchers need to examine the interplay of behavior, attributions, and satisfaction. In the following sections all three variables are considered together.

DO ATTRIBUTIONS CAUSE CHANGES IN MARITAL BEHAVIOR?

The study of cognition in marriage was largely a reaction to the rigorously behavioral theories of marriage that characterized early empirical work on marriage (e.g., Stuart, 1969). As the field moved away from a straightforward and easily testable behavioral theory of marriage to more complicated cognitive theories of marriage, the term *cognitive-behavioral* became a label for a group of theories of how marriages develop (e.g., Baucom & Epstein, 1990). Yet, the interaction of cognition and behavior has not been fully articulated or tested. As noted below, the studies that have examined the association of cognition and behavior in marriage have been cross-sectional, thereby neglecting the longitudinal impact of the interaction of behavior and cognition on marriage. Nevertheless, the findings give some insight into associations among behavior, attributions, and satisfaction at a fixed point in time and thus will be briefly reviewed here.

Brief Review of Association of Attributions and Behavior

In addition to being associated with longitudinal declines in relationship functioning, cognition was associated with concurrent behavior displayed in communicative, problem-solving interactions. Bradbury and Fincham (1993), for example, found that wives' dysfunctional beliefs (e.g., that disagreements are destructive to a relationship), as assessed by the Relationship Belief Inventory (Eidelson & Epstein, 1982), were associated with lower rates of avoidant behavior and higher rates of negative behavior. For husbands, more dysfunctional beliefs were associated with spouses' tendencies to reciprocate negative communication in discussions. This is the only known study that examined the association of beliefs and behavior in marriage.

In contrast, four studies have examined the relationship of attributions and behavior. Bradbury and Fincham (1992) examined this relationship in two studies comparable to their studies relating beliefs and behavior. In their first study, 47 established couples were recruited through media advertisements. During the session they were asked to rate their attributions for a significant problem in their marriage and then discuss the problem while working toward a resolution. The discussion was then observed and evaluated for problem-solving skills by independent raters. Maladaptive attributions were associated with less effective problem-solving behaviors, even when controlling for the effect of marital satisfaction. The effects were more pronounced with wives.

In Bradbury and Fincham's (1992) second study, 40 couples were recruited through advertisements and through a clinic. In a procedure similar to that of the first study, couples rated their attributions about a problem in their marriage and discussed the problem, and their discussion was observationally coded (with a different system than in study 1). Maladaptive attributions were associated with more negative discussion behaviors for both spouses even when controlling for marital satisfaction (the range of partial correlations for husbands was .27 to .45, and that for wives was .59 to .62). For wives, maladaptive attributions were also negatively associated with positive behaviors (partial correlations ranged from −.44 to −.55) and positively correlated with reciprocation of negative behavior (range .41 to .59).

Interestingly, in their second study, Bradbury and Fincham (1992) also examined the moderating effect of marital satisfaction on the association of maladaptive attributions and behaviors in problem-solving discussions. They found that the association between attributions and behavior was stronger for distressed couples than for nondistressed couples. Specifically, the combination of lower marital satisfaction and more maladaptive attributions was associated with less avoidance and less reciprocity of wife avoidance by husbands and fewer positive behaviors and more negative reciprocity by wives. These were the first two studies to draw the link clearly between attributions and dyadic behaviors in marriage.

Miller and Bradbury (1995) replicated and refined the Bradbury and Fincham (1992) findings by (1) examining behaviors in supportive interactions, in which each spouse discussed a problem not involving their marriage in separate interactions; (2) asking that attributions be made about specific marital events, assessed with the RAM, not the topic to be discussed in the subsequent interaction (cf. Bradbury & Fincham, 1992); and (3) sampling newlywed rather than established couples. Miller and Bradbury found that wives' maladaptive attributions were associated with less functional problem-solving and supportive behaviors. Spouses with lower concurrent satisfaction tended to have stronger associations between attributions and behavior.

Bradbury and Fincham (1992) and Miller and Bradbury (1995) present a compelling case that there is a strong association between attributions and behavior. However, because depressive symptoms have been found to covary with attributions (e.g., Fincham & Bradbury, 1993) and with marital interaction behavior (Beach, Whisman, & O'Leary, 1994), it may be possible to explain the attribution–behavior association with the confounding variable of depression. In an effort to understand the influence of depression on the relationship of attributions and behavior, Bradbury, Beach, Fincham, and Nelson (1996) compared the attribution–behavior association among three groups: both spouses satisfied and not depressed, both spouses dissatisfied and wife not depressed, and both spouses dissatisfied and wife depressed. They replicated the findings of previous studies, even replicating stronger associations for wives than husbands. Not only were behavior and attributions associated for distressed couples, but (in contrast to Miller & Bradbury, 1995) nondistressed couples also showed a strong association between behavior and attributions, which suggests a more pervasive role of attributions. The moderating effect of wives' depression on the association of attributions and behavior was also tested with no significant results (Bradbury et al., 1996). These findings suggest that the association of attributions and behavior for wives is pervasive and substantial.

The results of these studies are consistent with cognitive-behavioral formulations of marriage (e.g., the contextual model of Bradbury & Fincham, 1991), but as yet there is little evidence for the key assumption that the association between attributions and marital satisfaction is mediated by behavior. In addition, there are no data addressing an alternate hypothesis that the effect of observable marital behavior on longitudinal change in marital functioning is moderated by maladaptive attributions (i.e., that the interaction of attributions and behavior predicts changes in satisfaction). In the absence of data supporting the hypothesis of causality and explicitly addressing the joint effects of behavior and attributions on marital quality, the cognitive-behavioral view of marriage is significantly weakened. To better understand the developmental impact of the cognitive-behavioral association, two models are presented in the following section, with preliminary data supporting one model over the other.

What Conclusions May be Drawn from the Relationship of Attributions, Behavior, and Satisfaction?

The integration of cognition and behavior in marriage has been described with both a mediating model (e.g., Bradbury & Fincham, 1990) and a moderating model (e.g., Gottman, Notarius, Gonso, & Markman, 1976), yet neither has been fully tested. Newlyweds represent the best opportunity for understanding the development of marital discord, because most couples are relatively happy around their wedding date. Moreover, 40% of the couples who get divorced do so within the first 4 years of their marriage (Cherlin, 1992). In addition, in order to best understand how changes in behaviors, attributions, and satisfaction are associated, it would be best to obtain multiple assessments of each over time. Data from two studies that meet these criteria were used to test for mediation and moderation effects and are presented in the following sections. (For a theoretical and methodological review of mediation and moderation, see Baron & Kenny, 1986.)

Behavioral Mediation of Attributions and Change in Satisfaction

In the mediating model, behavior is hypothesized to account for the relationship between attributions and changes in marital satisfaction (see Figure 9.1). In other words, attributions predict marital satisfaction because they first predict particular behaviors, which in turn predict changes in satisfaction. Johnson, Karney, and Bradbury (1999) tested this model using the 60-couple sample reported in the Karney and Bradbury (in press) study, with the RAM data being used to predict observed problem-solving behaviors, which were then used to

Figure 9.1. Mediating model.

predict change in marital satisfaction over 4 years. Marital satisfaction was measured by administering the MAT (Locke & Wallace, 1959) to both spouses individually at time 1 (i.e., when the attribution data were collected) and 4 years later. Change in marital satisfaction was calculated by subtracting time 1 satisfaction scores from the follow-up satisfaction scores. To assess behavior, at time 1 couples were asked to discuss a problem in their marriage and to work toward a resolution to that problem, for 15 minutes. These interactions were subsequently coded with the Specific Affect Coding System (SPAFF) (Gottman & Krokoff, 1989). Mediation was not present when tested by procedures outlined by Baron and Kenny (1986; for specific results see Johnson et al., 1999).

To increase the power to detect a mediating relationship between the variables, the same analysis was run in another data set. The second data set was larger (N = 172 couples at time 1) but again sampled newlyweds in the first 6 months of their marriage. Attributions and marital satisfaction were assessed with the same instruments as in the first study, the RAM and the MAT. However, in this study two communicative behavior samples were collected, with one topic picked by each spouse. This was done to avoid the potential confound of gender effects in picking the topic. The behavioral data were again coded by the SPAFF system; however, this time a Behavioral Affect Rating System (BARS) (Johnson, Johns, Kitahara, Ono, & Bradbury, 1998) was also used as a validity check of the SPAFF. Both the SPAFF codes and the BARS ratings were used in the analyses. In a replication of the results of the first sample, a mediating pattern of findings was not obtained (Johnson et al., 1999). Although null findings cannot be considered conclusive, these two studies provide some evidence that the hypothesis that attributions predict behavior, leading to changes in marital satisfaction, is not an appropriate developmental model of marriage. Rather, it may be the case that the association of attributions and marital satisfaction is moderated by interaction behaviors.

Behavioral Moderation of Attributions and Change in Satisfaction

A mediator is a variable that explains why one variable predicts another variable, whereas in a moderating model the predictor and moderator variables are at the same conceptual level. In other words, in the moderating model attributions and dyadic behaviors are both considered to directly predict change in marital satisfaction, yet an interaction of the two constructs is also hypothesized to account for change above that predicted by attributions and behaviors independently. To test for moderation, the same two data sets outlined above were examined by regressing change in marital satisfaction onto attributions and behaviors and then adding the interaction term hierarchically, allowing the influence of the main effects of attributions and behavior to be fully accounted for prior to testing the interaction term (for methodological review, see Cohen & Cohen, 1983).

Eight behavioral affect codes (humor, affection, excitement, anger, contempt, whining, sadness, and anxiety) were examined in conjunction with causal and responsibility attributions. No differences were obtained between responsibility and causal attributions. Of all of the specific behaviors, anxiety and sadness were the two specific behaviors that had a consistent and significant moderating (i.e., interaction) effect on change in marital satisfaction (see Table 9.1). The interaction of anxiety and attributions predicted negative changes in marital satisfaction in both of the data sets, whereas the moderation of sadness was found only in the larger data set. In other words, the combination of maladaptive attributions with anxious behaviors and sad behaviors predicted changes in marital satisfaction beyond the changes predicted by the behaviors and attributions independently. Both anxiety and sadness moderated the association of attributions and satisfaction across differing methods of assessing behaviors (rating and coding) and assessing change in satisfaction (difference scores and residualized change scores). The moderating effect appears to be stronger for husbands than for wives, which represents a departure from the current literature on marital behavior and attributions (e.g., Miller & Bradbury, 1995).

Verbal aggression (i.e., anger), humor, and frustration also moderated the predictive power of attributions, such that the combination of these communication behaviors and attributions predicted negative changes in marital satisfaction. These behaviors did not predict as consistently across methods of assessment. Therefore, there is a need to replicate these findings, perhaps with use of a more sensitive measure

Table 9.1.   Results of Hierarchical Multiple Regression of Change in Marital Satisfaction on Attributions, Behaviors, and Attributions X Behaviors

	Husbands' Attributions and Marital Satisfaction					
	Behavior		Attribution		Behavior X Attribution	
Behavior	R^2change	Fchange	R^2change	Fchange	R^2change	Fchange
Anxiety						
Study 1, causal attributions[a]	.00	<1	.00	<1	.13	4.82*
Study 1, responsibility attributions[a]	.00	<1	.01	<1	.17	6.95*
Study 1, causal attributions[b]	.00	<1	.01	<1	.10	4.71*
Study 1, responsibility attributions[b]	.00	<1	.00	<1	.11	5.68*
Study 2, causal attributions[a]	.06	3.82†	.01	<1	.01	<1
Study 2, responsibility attributions[a]	.06	3.82†	.00	<1	.02	1.13
Study 2, causal attributions[b]	.02	<1	.07	4.79*	.00	<1
Study 2, responsibility attributions[b]	.02	1.31	.00	<1	.00	<1
Sadness						
Study 2, causal attributions[a]	.01	<1	.00	<1	.12	3.12†
Study 2, responsibility attributions[a]	.01	<1	.05	1.34	.14	3.96†
Study 2, causal attributions[b]	.01	<1	.05	1.17	.14	3.75†
Study 2, responsibility attributions[b]	.01	<1	.00	<1	.13	3.26†

(continued)

Table 9.1 (continued)

Behavior	Wives' Attributions and Marital Satisfaction					
	Behavior		Attribution		Behavior X Attribution	
	R²change	Fchange	R²change	Fchange	R²change	Fchange
Anxiety						
Study 1, causal attributions[a]	.04	<1	.03	<1	.01	<1
Study 1, responsibility attributions[a]	.03	<1	.01	<1	.00	<1
Study 1, causal attributions[b]	.11	4.95*	.08	3.79†	.00	<1
Study 1, responsibility attributions[b]	.09	4.00†	.04	2.07	.01	<1
Study 2, causal attributions[a]	.01	<1	.01	<1	.00	<1
Study 2, responsibility attributions[a]	.01	<1	.03	1.96	.06	4.13*
Study 2, causal attributions[b]	.00	<1	.02	1.80	.01	<1
Study 2, responsibility attributions[b]	.00	<1	.05	4.26*	.03	2.92†
Sadness						
Study 2, causal attributions[a]	.01	<1	.00	<1	.14	4.62*
Study 2, responsibility attributions[a]	.01	<1	.01	<1	.12	3.78†
Study 2, causal attributions[b]	.03	<1	.00	<1	.21	7.32*
Study 2, responsibility attributions[b]	.03	<1	.04	<1	.07	2.08

Notes. For study 1, dfs = 1,35 for step 1 (behavior); 1,34 for step 2 (appraisals); 1,33 for step 3 (behavior); For study 2, dfs = 1,63 for step 1 (behavior); 1,62 for step 2 (appraisals); 1,61 for step 3 (behavior x appraisals). Behavior codes in Study 1 are based on one spouse's behavior, matching husbands' behaviors with husbands' attributions and wives' behavior and wives' attributions. Behavior codes in study 2 combine husbands' and wives' behavior. In study 2 anxiety codes were assessed with (SPAFF), and sadness codes were assessed with BARS. [a]Change in satisfaction is measured with difference scores. [b]Change in satisfaction is measured with residualized change scores.
† p < .10. *p < .05. **p < .01. ***p < .001.

of change (e.g., growth curve analysis). Be that as it may, it appears that for at least two behaviors, a moderating model of attributions and behaviors predicting change in marital satisfaction is clearly supported over the mediating model.

These data represent the first study that has examined the longitudinal impact of behavior and attributions in marriage. Given the correlational design of these studies and the considerations that go with such a design, these data should be interpreted with caution; however, the data shed light on important questions. It appears that the interaction of attributions and behaviors leads to changes in satisfaction. In other words, attributions matter when negativity is exhibited. If marital interactions are all sweetness and light, it does not matter what kinds of attributions are made for behaviors in as much as there are no negative behaviors to explain. Attributions only seem to matter if negative behaviors (e.g., sadness and anxiety) are present. When there are negative behaviors that need to be understood, those who make maladaptive attributions will suffer negative changes in their relationship. These findings are all the more interesting in two newlywed samples with levels of negative behavior that were very low relative to those of established couples. Taken together with the results of Karney and Bradbury (in press), the results of Johnson et al. (1999) represent a clarification of the cognitive-behavioral model of marriage, which to this point has not been specified.

CONCLUSION

Over the last 25 years the psychological study of marriage has changed from an operant conditioning–behavioral model to a cognitive-behavioral model. Despite the wide acceptance of this model, its basic premise, namely, that cognition and behavior are related and influence the development of marital discord, has not been tested. This lack of testing and theory development has come at a cost to our understanding of marriage in general and the best point of intervention in relationships. Jacobson (1999) recently noted that "perhaps [marital] treatments don't work as well as they could because in implementing a matching to sample strategy – trying to make distressed couples look like non-distressed couples – we have mistaken barometers of marital happiness for causes of marital happiness" (p. 1).

This confusion is partly due to the tendency of marital researchers to examine behavior and cognition independently, preventing an understanding of how they covary and combine to influence changes in marriage. Most studies that have combined the two constructs have employed cross-sectional designs disallowing an understanding of the predictive power of the constructs. This chapter has highlighted the differences between predictors and barometers of marital discord as posited by cognitive-behavioral theory. Existing literature on the role and function of behavior and cognition was reviewed and two models that combined them were then presented and tested. There was no evidence to suggest that there is a mediating relationship between attributions and behavior, in which attributions only influence marital satisfaction via dyadic behavior. Rather, a moderating relationship was supported, which indicates that it is the interaction of maladaptive attributions and negative behavior that has the strongest influence on marital satisfaction. The data indicated that maladaptive attributions are most powerful when there is negative behavior displayed by the spouses and that maladaptive attributions do not seem to matter when there are no negative behaviors to explain. Therefore, using only behavior or cognition to predict marital outcomes dilutes the predictive power of the cognitive-behavioral model.

REFERENCES

Abramson, L. Y., Seligman, M. E. P., & Teasdale, J. F. (1978). Learned helplessness in humans: Critique and reformulation. *Journal of Abnormal Psychology, 87*, 49–74.

Baron, R. M., & Kenny, D. A. (1986). The moderator-mediator variable distinction in social psychological research: Conceptual, strategic, and statistical considerations. *Journal of Personality and Social Psychology, 51*, 1173–1182.

Baucom, D. H., & Epstein, N. (1990). *Cognitive-behavioral marital therapy.* New York: Brunner/Mazel.

Baucom, D. H., Epstein, N., & Rankin, L. A. (1995). Cognitive aspects of cognitive-behavioral marital therapy. In N. S. Jacobson & A. S. Gurman (Eds.), *Clinical handbook of couple therapy* (pp. 65–90). New York: Guilford.

Beach, S. R. H., Whisman, M. A., & O'Leary, K. D. (1994). Marital therapy for depression: Theoretical foundation, current status, and future directions. *Behavior Therapy, 25*, 345–371.

Beck, A. (1976). *Cognitive therapy and emotional disorders.* New York: International Universities Press.

Bradbury, T. N., Beach, S. R. H., Fincham, F. D., & Nelson, G. M. (1996). Attributions and behavior in functional and dysfunctional marriages. *Journal of Consulting and Clinical Psychology, 64*, 569–576.

Bradbury, T. N., & Fincham, F. D. (1990). Attributions in marriage: Review and critique. *Psychological Bulletin, 107*, 3–33.

Bradbury, T. N., & Fincham, F. D. (1991). A contextual model for advancing the study of marriage. In G. J. O. Fletcher & F. D. Fincham (Eds.), *Cognition in close relationships* (pp. 127–147). Hillsdale, NJ: Erlbaum.

Bradbury, T. N., & Fincham, F. D. (1992). Attributions and behavior in marital interaction. *Journal of Personality and Social Psychology, 63,* 613–628.

Bradbury, T. N., & Fincham, F. D. (1993). Assessing dysfunctional cognition in marriage: A reconsideration of the Relationship Belief Inventory. *Psychological Assessment, 5,* 92–101.

Bryk, A. S., & Raudenbush, S. W. (1987). Application of hierarchical linear models to assessing change. *Psychological Bulletin, 101,* 147–158.

Cherlin, A. J. (1992). *Marriage, divorce, remarriage.* Cambridge, MA: Harvard University Press.

Cohen, J., & Cohen, P. (1983). *Applied multiple regression/correlation analysis for the behavioral sciences* (2nd ed.). Hillsdale, NJ: Erlbaum.

Cutrona, C. E., Russell, D., & Jones, R. D. (1984). Cross-situational consistency in causal attributions: Does attributional style exist? *Journal of Personality and Social Psychology, 47,* 1043–1058.

Eidelson, R. J., & Epstein, N. (1982). Cognition and relationship maladjustment: Development of a measure of dysfunctional relationship beliefs. *Journal of Consulting and Clinical Psychology, 50,* 715–720.

Ellis, A. (1962). *Reason and emotion in psychotherapy.* New York: Lyle Stuart.

Eysenck, H. J., & Eysenck, S. B. G. (1978). *Manual for the Eysenck Personality Questionnaire.* Kent, England: Hodder & Stoughton.

Fincham, F. D. (1994). Cognition in marriage: Current status and future challenges. *Applied and Preventive Psychology, 3,* 185–198.

Fincham, F. D., & Bradbury, T. N. (1987). The impact of attributions in marriage: A longitudinal analysis. *Journal of Personality and Social Psychology, 53,* 481–489.

Fincham, F. D., & Bradbury, T. N. (1992). Assessing attributions in marriage: The Relationship Attribution Measure. *Journal of Personality and Social Psychology, 62,* 457–468.

Fincham, F. D., & Bradbury, T. N. (1993). Marital satisfaction, depression, and attributions. *Journal of Personality and Social Psychology, 64,* 442–452.

Fincham, F. D., Bradbury, T. N., Arias, I., Byrne, C. A., & Karney, B. R. (1997). Marital violence, marital distress, and attributions. *Journal of Family Psychology, 11,* 367–372.

Fincham, F. D., Bradbury, T. N., & Scott, C. K. (1990). Cognition in marriage. In F. D. Fincham & T. N. Bradbury (Eds.), *The psychology of marriage: Basic issues and applications* (pp. 118–149). New York: Guilford.

Fiske, S. T., & Taylor, S. E. (1991). *Social cognition* (2nd ed.). New York: McGraw-Hill.

Gottman, J. M., & Krokoff, L. J. (1989). Marital interaction and satisfaction: A longitudinal view. *Journal of Consulting and Clinical Psychology, 57,* 47–52.

Gottman, J. M., Notarius, C. I., Gonso, J., & Markman, H. J. (1976). *A couple's guide to communication.* Champaign, IL: Research Press.

Heavey, C. L., Layne, C., & Christensen, A. (1993). Gender and conflict structure in marital interaction: A replication and extension. *Journal of Consulting and Clinical Psychology, 61,* 16–27.

Horneffer, K. J., & Fincham, F. D. (1996). Attributional models of depression and marital distress. *Personality and Social Psychology Bulletin, 22,* 678–689.

Huston, T. L., & Chorost, A. F. (1994). Behavioral buffers on the effect of negativity on marital satisfaction: A longitudinal study. *Personal Relationships, 1,* 223–239.

Jacobson, N. S. (1999). Theory in marital research. *AABT Couple Interest Group listserve.* Available: http://www.psy.sunysb.edu/aabt/listserv.htm

Johnson, M. D., Johns, A., Kitahara, J., Ono, M., & Bradbury, T. N. (1998). *Behavioral Affective Rating System (BARS).* Unpublished manual, University of California, Los Angeles.

Johnson, M. D., Karney, B. R., & Bradbury, T. N. (2000). *Attributions, interaction behavior, and marital satisfaction: Mediation or moderation?* Manuscript in preparation, State University of New York at Binghamton.

Karney, B. R., & Bradbury, T. N. (1995a). Assessing longitudinal change in marriage: An introduction to the analysis of growth curves. *Journal of Marriage and the Family, 57,* 1091–1108.

Karney, B. R., & Bradbury, T. N. (1995b). The longitudinal course of marital quality and stability: A review of theory, method, and research. *Psychological Bulletin, 118,* 3–34.

Karney, B. R., & Bradbury, T. N. (1997). Neuroticism, marital interaction, and the trajectory of marital satisfaction. *Journal of Personality and Social Psychology, 72,* 1075–1092.

Karney, B. R., & Bradbury, T. N. (2000). Attributions in marriage: State or trait? *Journal of Personality and Social Psychology, 78,* 295–309.

Locke, H. J., & Wallace, K. M. (1959). Short marital-adjustment and prediction tests: Their reliability and validity. *Journal of Marriage and Family Living, 21,* 251–255.

Markman, H. J., Stanley, S., & Blumberg, S. L. (1994). *Fighting for your marriage.* San Francisco: Jossey-Bass.

Miller, G. E., & Bradbury, T. N. (1995). Refining the association between attributions and behavior in marital interaction. *Journal of Family Psychology, 9,* 196–208.

Seligman, M. E., Abramson, L. Y., Semel, A., & von Baeyer, C. (1979). Depressive attributional style. *Journal of Abnormal Psychology, 88,* 242–247.

Stuart, R. B. (1969). Operant-interpersonal treatment for marital discord. *Journal of Consulting and Clinical Psychology, 33,* 675–682.

Thibaut, J. W., & Kelley, H. H. (1959). *The social psychology of groups.* New York: Wiley.

CHAPTER TEN

Stepping Into the Stream of Thought
Cognition During Marital Conflict

Alan Sillars, Linda J. Roberts, Tim Dun,
and Kenneth Leonard

Accounts of interpersonal and intimate conflict are profoundly selective. Conflicts are nearly always seen differently from the perspectives of different parties, more so in intense, emotional disputes. While this much is clear, suppose that we could read the thoughts of other people at the very time that conflict is manifest. What sort of process should we expect to observe? We might expect to find that two people have different ideas about who or what is at fault but also, what events feed into the conflict, what constitutes the real issue, and even, what is going on in the immediate interaction. As conflicts become more severe, we are increasingly likely to find that people attend to different potential objects of perception within the interaction, resulting in idiosyncratic and incompatible interpretations of communication. Thus, we propose that selective perception is a fundamental dynamic in interpersonal conflict, particularly insofar as selectivity is manifested in differential monitoring of communication. Further, selective attention to and interpretation of communication helps drive escalation and entrenchment of conflict generally and marital disputes in particular.

There is considerable precedent for studying insider perspectives on intimate and marital conflict, although the level of analysis typically varies from that adopted here. Differences in perspective (i.e., actor versus partner or insider versus outsider) have been a basic concern of attribution research (Bradbury & Fincham, 1990; Fletcher & Fincham,

This research was supported by National Institute on Alcohol Abuse and Alcoholism Grant R01-AA08128. We wish to thank coders Jennifer Brodsky, Michele Crepeau, Shannon Marr, and Karissa Reinke, project directors Maria Testa and Tanya Bowen, and experimenters Rachel Ley, Tom Daniels, Daria Papalia, Jennifer Livingston, John Sabino, and Bill Zywiak. We would also like to acknowledge Richard E. Heyman and Robert L. Weiss for their input and advice on the implementation of the video-assisted recall protocol.

1991) and are the impetus for cognitively oriented models of marital communication (Berscheid, 1994). Cognitive models emphasize the role of spouses' cognitive and affective processing of communicative events during the interaction, explicitly acknowledging the potential for differing meanings and perspectives for each partner. Attribution research clearly documents an association between attributions and marital satisfaction (see Bradbury & Fincham, 1990). In comparison with nondistressed spouses, distressed spouses are more likely to see the cause of negative marital events as stable, global, and located in the partner and to see the partner's behavior as selfishly motivated and blameworthy. However, the types of attributions assessed most often have been global judgments about past or hypothetical events. There has been less exploration of covert attributions that may occur spontaneously in the context of ongoing interactions, despite the theoretical significance afforded to the "proximal processing" of interaction behavior (Fincham, Bradbury, & Scott, 1990).

In this chapter, we consider the type of attribution process that occurs *during* interaction. We describe and analyze the content of the stream of thought occurring concurrently with overt interactional behavior. What interactional events do partners attend to? What behaviors and feelings do they monitor? What covert evaluative appraisals and attributions do they make? While it may not be possible to directly know what people are thinking as they interact, researchers may simulate the in vivo character of these thought processes through video-assisted recall methods (Halford & Sanders, 1990; Waldron & Cegala, 1992). In this approach, individuals first hold a discussion and then reconstruct their earlier thoughts and feelings while viewing a videotape of the interaction. In our subsequent comments, we draw on video-assisted recall data from a major study of marital interaction. We are especially concerned here with the way spouses develop different perspectives on the same interaction and how divergent perspectives affect the course of marital conflict.

By way of background, it is useful to consider how participation in communication may affect cognition. Sillars (1998) and Sillars, Roberts, Leonard, and Dun (in press) suggest that several inherent properties and demands of communication shape the cognitive environment of live interaction, the following points being most germane here. First, participation in communication imposes significant demands and constraints on cognition, given the need to interpret ambiguous verbal and nonverbal signals, integrate multiple and often conflicting items of information, plan and adapt complex behavioral sequences, reconcile conflicting goals, and respond in real time (Waldron & Cegala, 1992). Second, communication necessarily involves a drastic selection process, since there are many potential objects of perception. Thus, the individuals engaged in communication are frequently, if not routinely, thinking about different aspects of the interaction or background context. Third, participation in interaction requires numerous concrete inferences about communication. In particular, individuals have a need to understand the stream of communication in terms of pragmatic intentions (e.g., inferences about whether the partner is requesting information, criticizing, changing the topic, or apologizing). Although relatively concrete, these pragmatic interpretations represent ambiguous inferences, which are made quite subjectively. Fourth, given the need to keep pace with interaction, most inferences are necessarily snap judgments that go unquestioned. Pragmatic interpretations, in particular, are made so routinely and automatically throughout interaction that they are mostly experienced as unmediated observations. In sum, we might expect cognition during interaction to reflect a high degree of selectivity and great variability in focus of attention, to show considerable mindfulness about the process of communication, and to be framed with subjective certainty in spite of the ambiguity and difficulty of communication.

STUDY OVERVIEW

Our observations are based on 118 couples from the Buffalo Marital Interaction Project (BMIP; see Leonard & Roberts, 1998), which combined direct observation of marital interactions with video-assisted recall of interaction. Although the larger aims of the BMIP involved linkages between marital interaction, husband-to-wife aggression, and alcohol effects, our primary aim here is to integrate formal analyses of the cognitive recall data with informal, qualitative observations in order to identify descriptive and theoretical properties of interaction-based cognition. More details about the formal analyses are provided by Sillars et al. (in press).

The couples visited a family research laboratory, where they discussed an issue that represented the greatest current disagreement in the marriage. The discussions took place in a room equipped for video recording, which was set up to resemble a living room–dining room combination. Immediately after the discussion, each spouse went to a separate room to view a videotape of the interaction. They were both asked to imagine going through the interaction again and to attempt to reexperience how they felt and what they were thinking during the discussion. Individuals were left alone while the videotape played. Every 20 seconds the tape paused automatically and the subjects reported (by speaking into a microphone) what they remembered thinking or feeling at that time. Although individuals heard the full audio recording of the interaction, the videotape only showed the spouse, thus modeling the visual perspective that individuals had during the interaction. The thoughts were audiotaped and later transcribed for analysis.

THE TOPOGRAPHY OF INTERACTION-BASED COGNITION

A Descriptive Typology

We developed a set of categories for coding the participants' articulated thoughts and feelings by inductively analyzing a portion of the recall data. The final coding system (the Interaction Cognition Coding Scheme) contains 50 codes. Although the codes collapse into five summary categories, we retained a large number of specific codes for descriptive purposes. Five coders used the system to classify nearly 19,000 thought units. A complete description of the coding categories is given by Sillars et al. (in press).

The first summary category refers to *emotions* (e.g., "I felt good." "He's getting aggravated."). Reported emotions were fairly easy to distinguish and clustered within a few types. Another cluster of thoughts involved *issue appraisal*, that is, analysis of the ostensible topic, ideas, and opinions in the discussion. Issue appraisal codes were generally concerned with the content level of conflict (i.e., perceptions about the nature of the situation, what to do, how to allocate resources, and other objectifiable issues). A third category, *person appraisal*, consisted of personal evaluations and perceptions of the partner, the self, or the relationship. These codes reflect classic attribution concerns, such as trait attribution and analysis of blame and responsibility for conflicts.

A fourth summary category referred to thoughts about the interaction *process*. Process codes included inferences about pragmatic intentions and communicative strategies (e.g., inferences to the effect that the partner was exaggerating, criticizing, or changing the topic), as well as general evaluations of communication. Many of the process codes fell into three intermediate categories–constructive engagement, avoidance-detachment, and confrontation–which closely parallel a familiar trilogy in the literature on communicative strategies and tactics in conflict, namely, the distinction between collaboration, avoidance, and competition (Hocker & Wilmot, 1991). Other process codes (termed *process appraisal*) provided a broader appraisal of the nature of the discussion and how it was proceeding, for example, whether the subject felt understood by the partner and thought that the discussion was moving toward resolution or impasse.

The process codes reveal the subjective nature of pragmatic inference. In general, the verbalizations characterizing these codes lacked behavioral specificity but were framed with subjective certainty. While a few codes describe moderately specific communicative acts (e.g., changing the topic or speaking with a negative tone of voice), most references to communication strategy were stated in terms of broad intentions (e.g., "I'm trying to make a point." "He's attacking me."). Even the most descriptive examples (e.g., "He's interrupting.") involve subjective interpretations of pragmatic intent (e.g., an inference about who holds legitimate possession of the floor and who is trying to take it). Yet, much more extreme attributions about communication (e.g., "He wants to change the topic because he knows I'm right." "She's backed into a corner and just wants to push the blame off on me.") were typically made without any hedging, qualification, or other self-conscious attention to the possibility of error.

The remainder of the codes were considered uncodable or off topic and were used only to determine how easily people were able to remember their thoughts and stay with the task. Finally, we also coded the *actor* for each emotion and strategy code (i.e., whether the emotion or strategy was attributed to self, partner, or both persons), and we coded each thought as either a *direct perspective* (the subject's own perspective) or a *meta perspective* (a perspective attributed to the partner).

Overall Trends

Several patterns in the overall distribution of codes are of interest, including the extent to which people focused on message content versus implicit relationship issues, pragmatic interpretation versus abstract attributions, individuals versus relationships, and direct versus meta perspectives.

Content Versus Relationship Issues

The extent to which spouses focused on message content versus implicit relationship issues is suggested by the comparison of issue appraisal, person appraisal, and process codes. The issue appraisal codes show awareness of objectifiable content issues in marital conflicts. These codes were common but were still overshadowed by other types of thoughts. About one-fifth (19%) of the reported thoughts revealed issue appraisal. By comparison, the person appraisal and process categories combined accounted for about three-fifths (58%) of the reported thoughts. These latter categories primarily reflect implicit relationship issues associated with the way the conflict is discussed and acted out. The results lend support to a common observation that interpersonal conflicts are more concerned with underlying relationship issues (perceptions related to power, affect, blame, respect, etc.) rather than with surface content (e.g., how much money to budget for food) (see Hocker & Wilmot, 1991).

Pragmatic Interpretation Versus Abstract Attributions

It is evident from the process codes that spouses were quite mindful of the communication process. About one-third (34%) of the reported thoughts were process codes.[1] It is interesting to compare these thoughts about the communication process with person appraisal, as these general categories reflect different levels of attribution. Attributions about communication are concerned with an immediate stimulus within the discussion situation, whereas the person appraisal codes provide a more abstract assessment of person and relationship characteristics that transcend the here and now. Overall, about one-fourth (25%) of the thoughts were instances of person appraisal. However, the codes that most clearly reflect abstract attributional analysis of causes and justifications for behavior (i.e., admission, denial and justification, and hostile attribution categories) collectively comprised 6% of the thoughts reported. Although these examples of direct attributional analysis seemed significant to the tone and direction of the interactions, they did not comprise a large percentage of the thoughts reported. The conscious thoughts of subjects were more often directed toward immediate inferences concerned with pragmatic intentions and communicative outcomes.

---

[1] These figures vary slightly from those reported by Sillars (1998), since the earlier report was based on a preliminary analysis of 73 couples.

Individuals Versus Relationships

A further observation about the person appraisal codes is that most of these codes were about the partner, the greatest number of which being complaints and other negative thoughts. Very few of the person appraisal codes were concerned with the relationship. A similar trend occurred within the emotion and process codes. Although many of the emotion and process codes could apply to both persons (e.g., "We're getting more and more irritated." "We're both acting stubborn."), very few of the codes were framed in this manner. All instances of relationship-level thinking (the combination of emotion, process, and person appraisal codes that focused on the relationship) collectively accounted for only 3% of the codable thoughts. The lack of relationship-level thinking and the complaining tone of many thoughts suggests a tendency to overlook interdependent causes of behavior and to blame the partner for conflicts.

Direct Versus Meta Perspectives

A final issue addressed by the overall distribution of codes is the degree of perspective taking reflected in spontaneous thought. In general, we found very little indication of spontaneous perspective taking. Explicit meta-perspectives (i.e., thoughts about how the partner was interpreting the situation) comprised only 5% of the codable thoughts. Further, in the few explicit meta-perspectives that we did find, the perspectives attributed to the partner were often undifferentiated and simplistic (e.g., "He knows that's a lie." "She knows I'm sick of talking about this."). Thus, individuals only occasionally considered the partner's perspective, and when they did, it was often in a manner that was likely to inflame dissatisfaction and anger.

HIS AND HER CONFLICTS

We suggested previously that attention to the different elements in interpersonal or marital conflicts is highly selective and somewhat idiosyncratic, particularly in more intense conflicts. Our analysis of the coded thought data suggests that selective attention in marital conflict is partly a function of gender. Wives showed evidence of being more other-directed and relationship-sensitive overall, whereas husbands focused more on message content and their own role in the conversations. Husbands, in comparison with wives, focused more on issue appraisal, thought more often about self and less often about the partner, and had fewer meta-perspectives. Thus, the husbands had a somewhat greater tendency to track the discussion topic in a literal manner rather than analyzing implicit relationship issues (as reflected in the emotion, person, and process domains). In an interesting reversal, husbands thought about themselves more than they thought about their partners, whereas wives thought about their partners more than themselves. Each of these trends is consistent with the conclusion that women show greater vigilance of relationship issues than men (Acitelli & Young, 1996; Roberts & Krokoff, 1990; Scott, Fuhrman, & Wyers, 1991).

These trends underlie a phenomenon that we believe is fairly common in marital conflicts. That is, one person tracks communication primarily in terms of the ostensible topic of discussion (money, housework, etc.), whereas the other party focuses intently on the process of interaction and the implicit relationship messages contained therein, that is, how people see themselves in relation to their partners (Watzlawick, Beavin, & Jackson, 1967). For example, in one discussion about spending time together, the husband thinks about how his band can only practice on Tuesdays and Fridays, while at the same moment the wife thinks that he does not listen to her. This phenomenon leads to a type of process-content confusion, in which one person assigns (often poignant) relationship-level meaning to messages of which the other person is not aware. The pattern is not inherently gender-based, but most examples we have isolated involve a husband who is content-oriented and a wife who analyzes and reacts to his messages in terms of implicit relationship level meaning. For example, a wife and husband reported the following thoughts while discussing his commitment to the marriage. The husband's thoughts narrate and elaborate on the same ideas he expressed in the discussion, whereas the wife interprets his comments as symbolic of his insensitivity and evasiveness. The wife's process-oriented thoughts are indicated in bold print.

She Thinks…	*He Thinks…*
I felt hurt because **he wasn't really listening to what I said** about my feelings.	I was just trying to explain to Penny here that uh, in my mind, she is always first to me, even though sometimes it seems like I try harder to do other things.

Now I think **he was trying to avoid the real issues,** so I was getting upset and mad again.	Well, Penny is starting to talk about when she was sick in the hospital and she doesn't think I contributed enough at that time or that … and I thought I did.
Now I was angry **'cause he was trying to avoid the issue.**	Well, Penny was on morphine when she was in the hospital, and she doesn't remember half of the time when I was there.
Now **I wanted him to just understand what I was saying** so I was aggravated that **he was just kind of smirking and not listening.**	Well, this is what I get all the time at home, I think … I don't go out all that often, I just go out when … when I have something to do, which ain't all that often.

Characteristically, the person who intently analyzes the process of interaction reacts more strongly to the discussion. Further, the content-oriented spouse often fails to anticipate or compensate for the strong reactions of the partner. This reflects the fact that the spouses are not tracking the discussion at the same level of analysis and cognitive shifts to a concerted effort at perspective taking are rare. In some cases, including the preceding example, the husband may simply fail to register the wife's reaction. In another instance, the husband eventually realizes that his wife has taken offense; however, he is at a loss to explain her reaction. The discussion in this case is about work inside and outside the home. He believes that she must work outside the home if she wants money and that housework is also "her job." She finds his comments to be condescending, domineering, and "stupid." Eventually, she becomes upset and stops talking. At that point he thinks, "I don't know why she got mad. I didn't say nothin' for her to get mad, not that I can remember. I guess she's a very sensitive person."

Constructive management of conflict probably requires balanced attention to content and relationship levels of meaning. Sensitivity to relationship meaning is necessary in order to sense impending difficulties, track areas of probable misunderstanding, and make adjustments in communication. However, an exaggerated state of relationship vigilance may lead to strong, idiosyncratic inferences about communicative intent and escalate relationship conflicts. Overall, the men in our sample showed a tendency to err in the direction of insensitivity to the partner's reactions. This is suggested both by the greater emphasis on self-perception versus partner perception among husbands and also by the fact that wives were significantly more likely than husbands to express a variety of thoughts that center on the imperviousness of the partner (e.g., the partner withdraws, is insincere, changes the topic, and will not give in).

ACTOR–PARTNER PHENOMENA

Actor–Partner Differences

One of the most familiar conclusions of attribution research is that people make attributions for their behavior on the basis of their perspective as either actor or observer (Jones & Nisbett, 1971). Further, actor–observer effects carry over to personal relationships, where one is both actor and observer simultaneously. For example, dissatisfied spouses tend to make self-enhancing and partner-effacing attributions about marital interactions (Bradbury & Fincham, 1990). Watzlawick et al. (1967) discuss much the same phenomena but from the standpoint of how people frame immediate perceptions of the communication sequence. That is, individual spouses mentally "punctuate" communication into simple cause–effect sequences in which they both see themselves as merely reacting to and not determining the other's behavior. This description suggests that actor–partner attributional phenomena exist at a proximal level concerned with the immediate sequence of communication, as well as at a more global and distal level that is concerned with interpretation of the event as a whole. Presumably, there is feedback in both directions between proximal and distal levels of attribution. That is, immediate perceptions of communication contribute to and are in turn partly cued by broader inferences about the relationship.

At a proximal level of inference, spouses are rather self-serving in the way they identify communication strategies during conflicts. In the present study, both husbands and wives attributed constructive engagement more often to themselves than to their partners, and they attributed confrontation more often to the partners than to themselves. Similarly, there was a lack of congruence between the strategies attributed to the partner and the partner's self-attributed strategies. Each spouse attributed less constructive engagement and more confrontation to the partner than the partner attributed to self. This can be seen in Figure 10.1, which shows the percentage of self and partner strategies identified by husbands and wives. The only symmetrical pattern in Figure 10.1 involves wives'

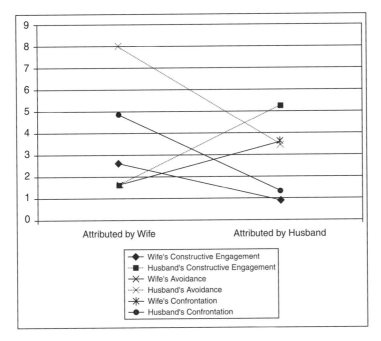

Figure 10.1.   Percentage of strategies attributed to self and partner by each spouse.

avoidance. Husbands and wives attributed avoidance to wives at nearly the same rate. On the other hand, avoidance attributed to husbands was well out of sync, with wives attributing avoidance to husbands at much higher rates than husbands acknowledged it to themselves.

Actor–partner differences in attributions that occur at a proximal level seem to reflect broader differences in each individual's construction of the event. At a more global or distal level of inference, spouses may construct quite different stories about conflicts. These internal narratives define, from the perspective of each individual, what the conflict is about and what role is played by each of the parties.

The construction of incompatible narratives seems to underlie some cases of escalating conflict avoidance and confrontation. For example, in one case in which the couple discussed the husband's drinking, the wife had a series of related thoughts: the husband knows he has a problem but he will not accept it; until he accepts it, they cannot work it out; he never wants to talk about it; he is always changing the topic and making it into a joke; he needs to wake up; he won't look at her because he knows she is right; she is sick of his tactics and may move out to make him understand. At the same time, the husband constructs a different scene: he drinks because he wants to, not as an escape; he loves her, even though she is overly critical, insensitive, and needs to relax; he does not want to get into a deep argument and thinks that bickering is a waste of breath; she is getting offended for little reason and is trying to upset and intimidate him; she resorts to name calling because she knows that he is right.

There are three notable features in this example that typify the thought data we have analyzed here. First, each person's thoughts reflect a coherent narrative, that is, a connected chain of events leading toward a particular outcome. Second, each person falsely assumes that the partner shares the same bedrock perceptions of reality (e.g., "she knows I am right"). There is a notable lack of hedging or complex perspective taking. Third, each person's internal narrative provides a frame for interpreting and responding to the partner's communication. The wife's narrative provides a frame for assimilating and reacting to specific cues linked to the husband's withdrawal (e.g., the meaning of his jokes and topic shifts), whereas the husband's narrative likewise furnishes an interpretive frame for the wife's assertive behavior, which he construes as manipulative and extreme. The result is a mutually escalatory demand–withdraw sequence, which is likely to reinforce the original attributions of each person.

Subjective Narratives as Frames of Reference

Because subjective narratives provide a frame of reference for interpreting the other's communication, it follows that irreconcilable narratives promote incompatible attributions about communication. It seems apparent from a number of anecdotes that spouses interpret the partner's communication as tangential, evasive, distorted, or dishonest primarily when their subjective accounts of the conflict are out of sync. For example, spouses attribute topic shifts to the partner when the partner's comments do not mesh with the subject's own account of the conflict. This happens frequently when spouses define the core issues of a conflict differently, for example, he thinks that the conflict is about spending money responsibly, she thinks that the conflict is about respect and autonomy. Thus, each person finds a lack of relevance in the other's comments.

On the other hand, more extreme attributions about communication seem to occur when subjective narratives clash directly. For example, one couple quarreled about cleaning. From the wife's perspective, the husband rarely helps with the housework and treats her like a "slave." From the husband's perspective, the wife is lazy and expects him to do everything, although she won't admit it. She also refuses to discipline their child for leaving his toys everywhere. These different subjective constructions of the conflict lead to contrasting attributions about communication. The wife sees the husband as making excuses, complaining, changing the subject, and acting in a domineering manner in order to avoid helping with housework. The husband sees the wife as lying, ignoring his concerns, and verbally attacking him in order to get out of the housework herself. These attributions about communication are highlighted in the following account of the husband's and wife's thoughts during the same segment of interaction.

She Thinks…

As far as most of the work goes, when I do ask for help, he refuses. Oh it's "Yeah, I'll help you in a few minutes," but then he's too busy playing his Nintendo or supergraphics, listening to the radio, calling in for a contest…

I feel that if I have to clean up he really should help, workin' or not. Many men do help their wives and they don't complain, but **he always seems to find a complaint.**

Here **he uses the excuse** that the child walks all over me, when in fact, the only reason the child does anything when he's there is because he's afraid of him.

Here **he acts as if he is the boss with me,** and I have no bosses as far as I'm concerned and I don't see any reason why … I have to do what he wants and **he just comes right out of the blue with it.**

He Thinks…

There **she's trying to lie** to get out of doing house cleaning because this is the way I was feelin' … that she doesn't want to do it. She's too lazy. She'd rather just lay around and watch TV all day and all night, and that's it … do nothing else.

Here she's makin me angry because after I had done the attic she goes and redoes it and makes it worse … It's just too much sometimes for me to handle. She expects me to handle everything.

…**she's just saying this so she don't have to listen to it so she can ignore it** so it don't bother her and she knows it's bothering me.

There I was feelin' like I never do something for her and how **she's throwing stuff up in my face,** and it was hurtin' me. It hurts and makes me angry because **she says one thing and she totally does another.**

THOUGHT PROCESSES IN TROUBLED MARRIAGES

While reading and analyzing thought transcripts, we were struck by the sense of frustration and despair that characterized the thoughts of some individuals and couples. These thought patterns characteristically reveal frustration and dissatisfaction with the partner in combination with low expectations for positive change through communication. To investigate further, we created measures of negative sentiment from the thought codes and correlated these scores with marital satisfaction. The results of this analysis revealed that dissatisfied couples expressed more *anger and frustration* (e.g., "I was really aggravated." "I'm still frustrated and tense.") and *blame* (e.g., "She is never on time." "She just totally stays away from my family on purpose." "I hate it when she does that." "Some of it's his blame too."). Dissatisfied couples also had a tendency to express a sense of *pessimism* about the discussion, that is, they thought that the partner did not understand their perspective, that the interaction was repetitious or foreboding and leading toward impasse rather than resolution. On the other hand, satisfied couples had a greater focus on content issues in the discussion (i.e., issue appraisal).

Particularly striking was the sense of inertia that some spouses attributed to their discussions versus the futility expressed by others. In the latter case, feelings of frustration typically alternated with the perception of being stuck in a highly predictable and futile sequence and being misunderstood by an aloof or impervious partner. For example, one couple discussed a conflict about sex. As they separately view the videotape, they report a remarkably parallel series of thoughts. Each person thinks that the partner is impervious to any influence and regards the discussion as so highly predictable that he or she already knows what the other is going to say (as revealed in the thoughts highlighted in bold in the following transcripts).

She Thinks…	*He Thinks…*
Well, I thought I was feeling that **he was just kind of letting me talk** and **I was saying the same thing that I said a million times** and I was wondering if he was going to respond any differently this time.	At this point I felt kind of uh … frustrated, because **it's the same thing we said over and over again.**

I felt that he was, when he said that **he always turns it back to me every time** I say well, you know you turned me down this morning, he turned it back to me, and said uh, you've done that to me a million times, **it's just his excuse for everything,** well you've done it.

I was thinking, well **she says the same thing over and over again. You know it's like the same conversation repeated over word for word over and over again.** So it's uh, **I was thinking it's kind of futile.**

I was thinking that **once again he didn't listen to a word I said,** because he wants to make a chart and he's making a big joke out of it, and **he doesn't care what my feelings are** and **I try to share my feelings and he doesn't care…**

I was thinking about how frustrating it is, because **it's all she has said before like dozens and dozens of times. Nothing ever changes.**

Oh I was thinking that uh, I thought the same way, **we do it over and over again, and nothing ever happens, pointless.**

This time I was thinking **how futile this is 'cause it's the same things repeated over and over again.**

Raush, Barry, Hertel, and Swain (1974) note that spouses may develop rigid, absorbing schemata for marital conflict that short-circuit the search for new information or in-depth processing of the other's messages. The anxiety provoked by marital conflicts and repetitiousness of marital interactions encourages the tendency to fit the other's comments within existing schemata rather than to listen for new information (Raush et al., 1974; Sillars, 1998). In the above exchange and many others like it, the spouses show acute sensitivity to and frustration about the partner's imperviousness and lack of movement in the discussion. Ironically, two spouses may engage in parallel tendencies simultaneously, which further drives and escalates conflict. It is not uncommon for one person to show rigidity in processing or attending to the other's message (e.g., "There he goes again." "She's like a broken record.") and, at the same time, express despair at the partner's lack of responsiveness.

In contrast, other couples demonstrate a capacity to learn from the discussion in spite of sharp disagreements. For example, one couple discussed the equity of their work situations and their respective feelings of being unappreciated by the other (he works outside the home, and she takes care of their two small children, an infant and toddler).

Whereas the husband thinks that his job is more difficult than "sitting home," the wife thinks that her husband doesn't realize the work involved in housework and child care. Although the discussion escalates initially, the husband eventually acknowledges to himself that she has "got a good point" and that he is "understanding more of what she's talking about." This leads to a shift in the discussion. The wife then thinks to herself, "We try to understand one another" and "We never stay mad for long." This anecdote confirms an observation by Raush et al. (1974) that the flexibility of schemata for marital conflict sets limits on the capacity for constructive communication. As Raush et al. (1974, pp. 48–49) state:

...the more flexible and differentiated the [cognitive] system, the less threatening is newness in the other, the more appropriate is the affect, and the more able the person is to learn from the interaction. On the other hand, the more rigid and undifferentiated the system, the more necessary it is that the other conform to it, the more likely it is that rigid pigeonholing will occur, the more threatening otherness or newness is, and therefore the less likely it is that learning and creative resolution of interpersonal conflict will take place.

CONCLUSIONS

Within the context of a conflictual interaction, spouses make and act upon numerous snap judgments, many of which are concerned with pragmatic intentions and the process of communication. There is tremendous selectivity to the inferences made during the course of an interaction, and the extent to which individuals construct similar or dissimilar scenarios may establish limits on the potential for constructive conflict. Some differences in perspectives during conflict are inevitable and probably generic to marital conflict. Overall, there were few indications of conscious perspective taking during interaction, and individuals showed little self-reflexive attention to the possibility of inferential bias. These tendencies may be encouraged by the inherent demands of communication, especially the need to keep pace with interaction. Spouses also saw their own communication in more favorable terms than the partner's communication. While these trends are fairly general, we can also draw inferences from our research about the thought patterns that tend to distinguish constructive versus destructive conflict and compatible relationships versus distressed marriages. The following conjectures are suggested by our analyses.

First, in constructive conflict, issues and events tend to be seen more similarly, and as a consequence, communication is more focused and concerned with negotiating details of the conflict. In escalating conflicts, perspectives are increasingly difficult to reconcile and may depict entirely different issues and events from the point of view of either party. Attributions about the conflict as a whole (i.e., the important issues and the respective roles played by either party) provide a context for pragmatic interpretation; for example, the partner's communication is seen as evasive or distorted when the partner's comments do not mesh with a person's own account of the conflict. In such cases, communication is apt to lose focus and to contain frequent relational digressions (Sabourin & Stamp, 1995).

Second, in constructive conflict the individuals are mindful of the interaction process without being obsessed by it. Both individuals show balanced attention to the process and content of communication. Third, the individuals within constructive conflicts exhibit a degree of flexibility in thought. For example, they show more optimism than pessimism about the prospects of communication and remain attentive to new information. In contrast, escalating conflict is fueled by a high degree of certainty attached to existing perceptions, the belief that communication is repetitious and futile, and an attribution that the partner is impervious to influence. Fourth, constructive conflict is characterized by a mutual focus on the other more than on oneself. This focus is accompanied by effort at understanding the partner in terms that are differentiated and realistic.

REFERENCES

Acitelli, L. K., & Young, A. M. (1996). Gender and thought in relationships. In G. J. Fletcher & J. Fitness (Eds.), *Knowledge structures in close relationships: A social psychological approach* (pp. 147–168). Mahwah, NJ: Lawrence Erlbaum Associates.

Berscheid, E. (1994). Interpersonal relationships. *Annual Review of Psychology, 45*, 79–130.

Bradbury, T. N., & Fincham, F. D. (1990). Attributions in marriage: Review and critique. *Psychological Bulletin, 107*, 3–33.

Fincham, F. D., Bradbury, T. N., & Scott, C. K. (1990). Cognition in marriage. In F. D. Fincham & T. N. Bradbury (Eds.), *The psychology of marriage: Basic issues and applications* (pp. 118–149). New York: Guilford.

Fletcher, G. J. O., & Fincham, F. D. (1991). Attribution process in close relationships. In G. J. O. Fletcher & F. D. Fincham (Eds.), *Cognition in close relationships* (pp. 7–35). Hillsdale, NJ: Lawrence Erlbaum Associates.

Halford, W. K., & Sanders, M. R. (1990). The relationship of cognition and behavior during marital interaction. *Journal of Social and Clinical Psychology, 9*, 489–510.

Hocker, J. L., & Wilmot, W. W. (1991). *Interpersonal conflict* (3rd. ed.). Dubuque, IA: William C. Brown.

Jones, E. E., & Nisbett, R. E. (1971). *The actor and the observer: Divergent perceptions of the causes of behavior.* Morristown, NJ: General Learning Press.

Leonard, K. E., & Roberts, L. J. (1998). The effects of alcohol on the marital interactions of aggressive and nonaggressive husbands and their wives. *Journal of Abnormal Psychology, 107*, 602–615.

Raush, H. L., Barry, W. A., Hertel, R. K., & Swain, M. A. (1974). *Communication, conflict and marriage.* San Francisco: Jossey-Bass.

Roberts, L. J., & Krokoff, L. J. (1990). A time-series analysis of withdrawal, hostility, and displeasure in satisfied and dissatisfied marriages. *Journal of Marriage and the Family, 52*, 95–105.

Sabourin, T. C., & Stamp, G. H. (1995). Communication and the experience of dialectical tensions in family life: An examination of abusive and nonabusive families. *Communication Monographs, 62*, 213–242.

Scott, C. K., Fuhrman, R. W., & Wyers, R. S. (1991). Information processing in close relationships. In G. J. O. Fletcher & F. D. Fincham (Eds.), *Cognition in close relationships* (pp. 37–67). Hillsdale, NJ: Lawrence Erlbaum Associates.

Sillars, A., (1998). (Mis)understanding. In B. H. Spitzberg & W. R. Cupach (Eds.), *The dark side of close relationships* (pp. 73–102). Mahwah, NJ: Lawrence Erlbaum Associates.

Sillars, A., Roberts, L. J., Leonard, K. E., & Dun, T. (in press). Cognition during marital conflict: The relationship of thought and talk. *Journal of Social and Personal Relationships.*

Waldron, V. R., & Cegala, D. J. (1992). Assessing conversational cognition: Levels of cognitive theory and associated methodological requirements. *Human Communication Research, 18*, 599–622.

Watzlawick, P., Beavin, J., & Jackson, D. D. (1967). *Pragmatics of human communication: A study of interactional patterns, pathologies, and paradoxes.* New York: Norton.

Thanks for the Curry

Advancing Boldly into A New Millennium of Relationship Attribution Research

Frank D. Fincham

Research on attributions in close relationships has come of age, and as the field enters adulthood, there is the opportunity to fashion its identity in new ways. In seizing this opportunity, the current set of chapters add spice to a staple diet of attribution studies that have documented some of the most robust phenomena in the close relationships literature (for a review see Fincham, in press). By questioning, both explicitly and implicitly, basic assumptions of attribution research in close relationships, these chapters do yeoman service to the field and provide flavorful food for thought. The purpose of this commentary is to highlight some of the challenges posed by this intellectual meal, and the commentary is structured to reflect its two main components, curry and rice. New and relatively neglected directions for attribution research provide the curry, and the challenge of building on almost 25 years of experience constitutes the rice on which it is served.

NEW AND RELATIVELY NEGLECTED DIRECTIONS FOR ATTRIBUTION RESEARCH

In this section I highlight some themes that unite the chapters and pose challenges for future research. In doing so, I offer them as destinations that are distinct from the current locus of research efforts. This is merely a heuristic device to emphasize their contribution. It in no way implies that we should discontinue or deemphasize current research efforts.

The preparation of this manuscript was supported by a grant from the Templeton Foundation. Correspondence concerning this chapter should be addressed to Frank Fincham, Department of Psychology, Park Hall, State University of New York at Buffalo, Buffalo, NY 14260-4110 (e-mail: fincham@buffalo.edu).

From Individuals to Relationships

Like much relationship research, the study of attributions has focused on the individual. The focus on individuals' attributions for partner behavior and relationship problems has been productive, as illustrated in Johnson, Karney, Rogge, and Bradbury's chapter, but it is necessarily incomplete. The need for a broader attributional canvas is a theme echoed in several chapters. This is most evident in regard to expanding the attributional dimensions studied, as well as the phenomena for which attributions are made.

In regard to attribution dimensions, Berscheid, Lopes, Ammazzalorso, and Langenfeld and Manusov and Koenig offer useful conceptual analyses that explore the implications of relationships for the very nature of attributions. As research on attributions in relationships evolved, Newman's (1981) important analysis of interpersonal attributions decreased in impact, and it is gratifying to see these authors build on it. The analyses may well presage an important empirical advance, for as Heider (1958) noted, "...each definite advance in science requires a theoretical analysis and conceptual clarification of the problem" (p. 4). However, these authors move beyond conceptual analysis and offer data to document the utility of studying attributions that reflect interpersonal and relationships properties, a task in which they are joined by Surra and Bartell.

An important future task in this endeavor is to achieve some consensus (ideally based on a combination of logical analysis and empirical inquiry) on the number and precise nature of attribution dimensions needed to capture relationship-based explanations. The widespread acceptance of a few key dimensions underlying causal attributions in basic research, notwithstanding problems with the person–situation distinction (see Malle, 1999), has been an important element in the field's success. Noller, Feeney, and Blakely Smith join with the authors whom we have just mentioned in expanding the phenomena for which attributions are made to include relationship phenomena. Their data pertaining to attributions for different relationship contradictions demonstrates the importance of what is explained for understanding attributions.

One might expect dramatically different findings when different types of phenomena are explained (e.g., a partner behavior, versus relationship state), which is consistent with the assumed similarity between cause and effect (see Harvey, Ickes, & Kidd, 1978). Thus, the preponderance of relationship causes in the data of Berscheid et al. might reflect, among other things, the fact that the authors requested attributions for a relationship state. This does not in any way detract from the findings but suggests that their work, like the basic and relationship attribution research they criticize, may provide only a piece in the jigsaw puzzle that constitutes what Berscheid et al. call "a true picture of the causal reasoning people do." In any event, investigation of explanations across different types of phenomena in relationships is long overdue, and these chapters go some way toward redressing this omission.

Perhaps the greatest challenge posed by a relationship perspective is to transcend completely the individual level of analysis. This may take at least two forms that remain unexplored in attribution research. First, there is the patterning provided by the conjunction of each partner's attributions. The utility of considering the conjunction of partner explanations is suggested by Orvis, Kelley, and Butler's (1976) original study of attributional conflict, in which each partner had a different attribution for the same behavior. But that study did not investigate attributions as an emergent relationship property in the manner that is being suggested. Second, one could analyze *the couple* as attributor. Here the precedent offered by the study of transactive memory in relationships may prove instructive. Is there a specialization of function when couples explain events, and if so, does it mirror the performance ecology of the relationship, so that dimensions such as importance and self-relevance define areas of expertise? The importance of this level of analysis is emphasized by the fact that relationship interdependence exists at many levels, including attitudes and personal characteristics.

From Insider to Outsider Perspectives

Most of what we know about attributions in close relationships comes from questionnaire data and so reflects a single perspective, that of the relationship participant. However, the perspective of the scientist (outsider) provides a useful complement to the insider perspective in the study of attributions, and in a recent analysis of the field I called for greater attention to this perspective (Fincham, in press). Several of the chapters have risen to this challenge and provide valuable data on attributions coded by trained observers. This is no small achievement, as the difficulty of developing a reliable coding system and the labor-intensive nature of coding attributions are reasons why early efforts to code attributions (e.g., Holtzworth-Munroe & Jacobson, 1988) did not give rise to a literature on attributions analyzed from an outsider perspective.

However, the complexities of coding attributions are not as apparent in the chapters as they might be. Consider for example, the old but unresolved problem raised by Ross (1977, p. 176; see Malle, 1999 for a suggested resolution). Ross contrasted two explanations; "Jill bought the house because she wanted privacy," typically classified as a person attribution, and "Jack bought the house because it was secluded," usually classified as a situational attribution. The problem is that classification of the attributions is based on subtle linguistic differences, not on fundamental differences in the underlying causal structure. One could, for example, as easily view Jack's action as reflecting the fact that he is a person who values seclusion (a person attribution). It is easy to translate this problem into its interpersonal analogue ("Jill complimented me because she wanted to be nice," "Jack complimented me because I looked good"), and just how such subtleties are resolved vis-a-vis partner, self, interpersonal, and relationship attributions is no trivial matter in developing a cumulative body of literature on coded attributions.

The development and adoption of a system for coding attributions in relationships would open up new research vistas. It could, for example, allow study of archival data on relationships (e.g., personal diaries), examination of relationships in different historical periods (e.g., through analysis of historical texts), attributions in different contexts (e.g., family therapy, family reunions, dating), and would allow for comparison of attributions that are made spontaneously with those that occur more deliberately (Berscheid & Reis, 1998). As noted, developing a database of coded attributions in relationships poses numerous challenges. These were discussed more fully some time ago, and that discussion remains pertinent (see Bradbury & Fincham, 1988). Finally, it should be noted that this task does not have to be approached from scratch, as there is a system that has been used to code attributions in families for over a decade. The Leeds Attribution Coding System has recently been published (Munton, Silvester, Stratton, & Hanks, 1999), which may now result in it being used outside of the laboratory in which it was developed. This system does not include the relationship-based attributions discussed earlier, but it may nonetheless provide a useful starting point for relationship researchers.

From General Attributions to Attributions in Action

One driving force in the study of attributions in relationships concerns their presumed influence on relationship satisfaction and behavior. Johnson et al. provide a timely review of the literature relating to this influence, and their data provide an important advance in this line of inquiry. The astute observer, however, will note that research that relates attributions to behavior combines two different levels of analysis. General attributions, rather than attributions for specific behaviors exchanged in an observed interaction, are examined in relation to observed behavior exchanges. Implicit is the assumption that these general attributions guide attributional responses in interactions, which then presumably influence subsequent behavior. What this makes apparent is the need to study on-line attributions.

Two of the chapters, those by Sillars et al. and by Manusov and Koenig, examine attributions for "live" interactive behavior. Both illustrate the value of a communication perspective in studying attributions, a perspective that has been underexploited in the literature to date. The analysis of specific nonverbal communication behaviors (Manusov and Koenig) provides an example of the earlier mentioned broadening of phenomena explained in relationships, whereas the documentation of gender-linked differences in the phenomena requiring explanation in an interaction (specific conflict content vs. relationship implication of content, Sillars et al.) points to the importance of viewing the explained-attribution link as a unit of analysis. Phenomena may vary on a variety of dimensions (e.g., availability of normative explanations, aforementioned individual vs. relationship focus) that can potentially influence attributions, and it is therefore important to ensure that attributional phenomena do not simply reflect differences in what is explained.

The study of on-line attributions emphasizes the need to build bridges to the social cognition literature. This is a task that challenges the study of relationships more generally (see Reis & Downey, 1999), but it is particularly acute in the present context because the rapidly unfolding nature of interaction means that live attributions are likely to reflect automatic rather than controlled cognitive processes. This again opens up new areas of inquiry (see Fincham & Beach, in press), including the study of primed material on attributional processes and the role of goals in understanding relationships. The latter is particularly intriguing, as disruption of goal pursuit (rather than event

valence or unexpectedness) may be the underlying process that insti-
gates attributional processing. If correct, this goal-thwarting hypothesis has considerable integrative potential because it is cut from the
same cloth as Berscheid's (1983) theory of emotion in close relationships, in which interrupted goal pursuit gives rise to emotion. Goals
may be a vehicle for minting the coin that displays affect and cognition on each side. In any event, a step has been taken in this direction
by applying a goal-theoretic framework to conflict, the topic that
stimulated attribution research in close relationships (Fincham &
Beach, 1999).

From Attributional to Attribution Research

Some time ago, Kelley (Harvey et al., 1978; see also Kelley & Michela,
1980) distinguished between two sets of phenomena both of which had
attracted the label "attribution." He argued that attributional theory,
which referred to attribution-based theory dealing primarily with the
outcomes of attributions, was quite different from attribution theory or
theory about the casual attribution process ("the theory about data,
rules, inferences, and the cognitive-inferential part of the process" Harvey et al., 1978, p. 375). At the time, he noted that most research was
attributional, an observation that applies with even greater force to the
contemporary attribution literature.

Perhaps its origin in applied problems (marital conflict) ensured
that attribution research in close relationships would focus almost
exclusively on attributional theory. In contrast to their (assumed and
empirically documented) sequelae, we know very little about
the processes that lead to and influence attributions in close relationships. This is perhaps surprising in view of Kelley's initiation
of attribution research in relationships at a time when he was
emphasizing that partner interdependence was not limited to the
behavioral level (see Harvey et al., 1978). How does interdependence at the attitudinal and personal characteristic levels influence
attribution-making processes? We certainly know that relationship
quality is correlated with the nature of attributions made, but
how do relationship characteristics and dynamics influence attribution processes?

The present chapters do not answer such questions nor do they set
out to redress the imbalance between attributional and attribution theory in close relationships explicitly. Yet, they represent a first step

toward doing so. Broadening the area of inquiry to span explanations for phenomena ranging from specific nonverbal communication behaviors through the quality of the relationship to changes in commitment to the relationship leads naturally to questions about possible differences in the way these explanations are causally processed. Once this type of inquiry is embraced, a variety of new lines of investigation suggest themselves. These range from applying elements of Heider's (1958) work neglected in the attribution literature (e.g., his analysis relating attributions and power) to mainstream ideas in social cognition, such as the influence of activated knowledge structures on attribution processes in close relationships.

From Isolation to Integration

Attribution research in close relationships has been somewhat egocentric, a characteristic that has served it well in focusing energy on establishing replicable phenomena, ruling out artifactual explanations for the phenomena, documenting their relevance, and so on. One unfortunate side effect has been an even greater balkanization than is found in the parent relationship literature. Thus, for example, substantial literatures exist on attributions in parent–child relationships and in marital relationships but "thus far there has been little attempt to integrate findings from the two literatures" (Miller, 1995, p. 1579). With its credentials well established, the field now needs to work toward integration at multiple levels.

At the most basic level, there is the need to integrate different existing strands of attribution research. Johnson et al.'s chapter is exemplary in this regard. It integrates research linking attributions to marital quality with research on the association between attribution and marital behavior to provide a more complete attributional analysis in the marital literature. At a slightly different level of integration, Manusov and Koenig outline the relation between attributions and accounts and narratives in close relationships. Moving to integration with broader frameworks, Noller et al. link attributions to a dialectical perspective of relationships, Surra and Bartell place the study of attributions within the context of work on marital identity, and Berscheid et al. provide a much needed and overdue integration of attribution with the interdependence framework offered by Kelley et al. (1983). What is particularly pleasing about these integrative efforts is the ease with which disciplinary barriers are negotiated. The current chapters do not exhaust the types of integration needed in attribution research in close relationship; however, they constitute a stellar contribution to efforts to provide a more integrated literature (see Fincham, in press).

THE CHALLENGE OF DRAWING ON THE PAST TO BUILD A CUMULATIVE BODY OF KNOWLEDGE

New contributions inevitably face the challenge of balancing what they have to offer with what has come before. Making a novel contribution tends to be reinforced over developing, systematizing, and painstakingly testing existing ideas, at least in the North American scientific community. This can lead to unfortunate outcomes (e.g., recycling of old ideas under new labels, distortions of existing research, overlooking or ignoring relevant literature). As already indicated, there is much to set the taste buds alight in these chapters, and happily they do not suffer from the deficiencies just mentioned. Nonetheless, there are lessons to be culled from past attribution research in considering these chapters.

The Domain of Attributions

Attributions are not attributions are not attributions. I continue to believe that delineation of the domain to which the term *attribution* applies remains the "single most significant barrier to progress" (Fincham, 1985, p. 205). It is quite clear that two distinct (and very familiar) referents, attribution as a cause versus attribution as a property, are considered in these chapters. This is quite understandable when seen in historical perspective. As Kelley openly admits, he stretched the notion of causation in drawing on social comparison ideas to infer entity attributions in his seminal analysis of variance attribution model (Kelley, 1967). Blurring of the boundary between these two foci in the attribution literature is perhaps best illustrated by the other classic attribution statement, Correspondent Inference Theory (Jones & Davis, 1965), in which inferring a trait constitutes causal explanation.

Although understandable, multiple and different referents for the attribution construct have the potential to generate the enemy of progress, namely, confusion. Imputation of meaning is important, in relationships as elsewhere, but not all meaning stems from causal analysis. Using the same term to refer to causal analysis as to other forms of meaning imputation is not inherently problematic, but it surely becomes so when different referents are overlooked or simply treated as equivalent by virtue of sharing a common label. If the potential of the chapters is to be fully realized, greater precision will be needed to ensure that boundary conditions for generalizations about attributions are clear. Delineating and respecting the domain of attributions within and across different analyses remains critical to building a cumulative literature.

Types of Attributions

A closely related challenge concerns clarity about types of attributions. In the relationship domain, distinctions were drawn initially among causal, responsibility, and blame attributions, which is consistent with theoretical and empirical analyses in basic research on attributions. However, empirical analysis showed that spouses did not distinguish responsibility attributions (who is accountable and possibly liable for sanctions for the outcome) from blame attributions, leaving only the distinction between causal attributions (who or what produced an outcome) and responsibility – blame attributions (Fincham & Bradbury, 1992). In my own work, I have emphasized responsibility attributions, as examination of the origins of relationship attribution research in social and clinical psychology shows that the evaluative dimension underlying this type of attribution is essential to understanding attributions in relationships.

This distinction still appears to be problematic. Responsibility attributions have at least three different referents across this set of chapters. One is the usage outlined above. In a second, responsibility is equated with causal locus, and in a third it comprises an attribution dimension equivalent in status to, for example, the stability causal dimension. Although words are merely symbols with admittedly arbitrary referents, usage conventions develop that allow them to be used meaningfully in communication. Linguistic and common sense usage of the term *responsibility* was carefully analyzed by attribution researchers following Fischhoff's (1976) observation that "The incredible confusion in the attribution of responsibility literature ... might serve as an illustrative example of how psychologists' vagueness about their basic concepts can strip their work of its value" (p. 440). These analyses may well be wrong, but it behooves scholars to point out the ways in which they are wrong and to illustrate the advantages of their new (often rarely acknowledged) usage of the concept. Failure to do so raises the real possibility of that field collapsing under the weight of its own confusion.

Levels of Attribution

Continuing the theme of conceptual clarity, it can be noted that attributions exist at different levels, as private and as public events. Further, as private events attributions may occur at the conscious level or they may occur without conscious awareness. Thus far, we have almost exclusively studied private attributions that are consciously available to relationship partners, but even here we have to remember that the manner in which attributions are communicated to the researcher can be influential. As Ned Jones (in Harvey et al., 1978, p. 378) noted, we need "to ask the right kinds of questions, and to be sensitive to the *sequence* of questions," issues that he deemed particularly important in the area of responsibility attribution. This observation reminds us that communication norms (e.g., informativeness, accuracy, politeness) apply to researcher – subject communication and emphasize the need for researchers to provide detailed and precise information concerning how the data were generated. The present chapters do a reasonable job of describing how attributions were obtained, but there is room for greater detail. Indeed, access to verbatim instructions and questions is often necessary to appreciate fully a given attribution data set, yet too often access to such information is not included when the data are reported.

In this context, it is also worth reminding ourselves of the previously drawn distinctions among spontaneous, unsolicited, and solicited attributions. Spontaneous attributions occur without prompts from the researcher and may be found in diaries, essays, conversations, and so on. Unsolicited attributions concern those that occur when the subject is prompted for his or her thoughts, and solicited attributions result from specific requests for them. This should not be confused with the format (e.g., open vs. closed ended format) used to obtain attributions. When open-ended response formats follow a specific request for an explanation, any attributions they contain cannot be considered spontaneous. Thus, whether partners in a relationship spontaneously think about why they experience a certain level of relationship quality remains an open question. If this is not something that happens spontaneously, it may underlie the apparent lack of attributions reported by Berscheid et al.[1]

In drawing attention to levels of attributions and the manner in which attributions are obtained, the present chapters point toward the challenge of specifying the relations among them. Under what conditions do attributions outside of conscious awareness become conscious? And what determines whether a privately held attribution becomes public? In a similar vein, the attention drawn to the manner in which attributions are obtained raises questions about possible systematic influences on our data that might influence the generalizations we make. As these chapters move us forward, it is worth continuing to struggle with rather than to ignore these issues.

CONCLUSION

As a potential dessert to the delectable meal offered by these chapters, I am mindful of becoming the surfeit that upsets digestion. Notwithstanding this risk, I must make one last observation. The satisfaction of a good curry meal rests, in part, on the staple with which it is served, with each component of the meal complementing the other. The rice I have identified may not be the best complement to the curry offered here; that is for the reader to decide. But whatever the outcome, thanks for the curry.

REFERENCES

Berscheid, E. (1983). Emotion. In H. H. Kelley, E. Berscheid, A. Christensen, J. H. Harvey, T. L. Huston, G. Levinger, E. McClintock, L. A. Peplau, & D. Peterson (Eds.), *Close relationships* (pp. 110–168). New York: Freeman.

Berscheid, E., & Reis, H. T. (1998). Attraction and close relationships. In D. T. Gilbert, S. T. Fiske, & G. Lindsey (Eds.), *Handbook of social psychology* (Vol. 2, pp. 193–281). New York: McGraw-Hill.

Bradbury, T. N., & Fincham, F. D. (1988). Assessing spontaneous attributions in marital interaction: Methodological and conceptual considerations. *Journal of Social and Clinical Psychology, 7,* 122–130.

---

[1] However, it needs to be noted that the conclusions of Berscheid et al. regarding attribution frequency rest on a decision to reject described interaction as an explanation for relationship quality. But as Hinde (1997) astutely observes, it is difficult to maintain a clear line between description and explanation in relationships "because some of the characteristics of relationships are to be explained in terms of processes which are themselves characteristics of the relationship" (p. 17).

Fincham, F. D. (1985). Attributions in close relationships. In J. H. Harvey & G. Weary (Eds.), *Attribution: Basic issues and applications* (pp. 203–234). New York: Academic Press.

Fincham, F. D. (in press). Attributions and close relationships: From balkanization to integration. In G. J. Fletcher & M. Clark (Eds.), *Blackwell handbook of social psychology*. Oxford, UK: Blackwell.

Fincham, F. D., & Beach, S. R. (1999). Marital conflict: Implications for working with couples. *Annual Review of Psychology, 50,* 47–77.

Fincham, F. D., & Beach, S. R. (in press). Marriage in the new millenium: Is there a place for social cognition in marital research? *Journal of Social and Personal Relationships.*

Fincham, F. D., & Bradbury, T. N. (1992). Assessing attributions in marriage: The Relationship Attribution Measure. *Journal of Personality and Social Psychology, 62,* 457–468.

Fischoff, B. (1976) Attribution theory and judgment under uncertainty. In J. H. Harvey, W. Ickes, & R. F. Kidd (Eds.), *New directions in attribution research* (Vol. 1, pp. 421–452). Hillsdale, NJ: Erlbaum.

Harvey, J. H., Ickes, W., & Kidd, R. F. (1978). A conversation with Edward E. Jones and Harold H. Kelley. In J. H. Harvey, W. Ickes, & R. F. Kidd (Eds.), *New directions in attribution research* (Vol. 2, pp. 371–388). Hillsdale, NJ: Erlbaum.

Heider, F. (1958). *The psychology of interpersonal relations.* New York: Wiley.

Hinde, R. A. (1997). *Relationships: A dialectical perspective.* Hove, East Sussex, UK: Psychology Press.

Holtzworth-Munroe, A., & Jacobson, N. S. (1988). Toward a methodology for coding spontaneous causal attributions: Preliminary results with married couples. *Journal of Social and Clinical Psychology, 7,* 101–112.

Jones, E. E., & Davis, K. E. (1965). From acts to dispositions: The attribution process in person perception. In L. Berkowitz (Ed.), *Advances in experimental social psychology* (Vol. 2, pp. 219–266). New York: Academic Press.

Kelley, H. H. (1967). Attribution theory in social psychology. In D. Levine (Ed.), *Nebraska symposium on motivation* (pp. 192–238). Lincoln: University of Nebraska Press.

Kelley, H. H., Berscheid, E., Christensen, A., Harvey, J. H., Huston, T. L., Levinger, G., McClintock, E., Peplau, L. A., & Peterson, D. R. (Eds.) (1983). *Close relationships.* New York: W. H. Freeman and Company.

Kelley, H. H., & Michela, J. L. (1980). Attribution theory and research. *Annual Review of Psychology, 31,* 457–501.

Malle, B. F. (1999). How people explain behavior: A new theoretical framework. *Personality and Social Psychology Review, 3,* 23–48.

Miller, S. A. (1995). Parents' attributions for their childrens' behavior. *Child Development, 66,* 1557–1584.

Munton, A. G., Silvester, J., Stratton, P., & Hanks, H. (1999). *Attributions in action: A practical approach to coding qualitative data.* Chichester, UK: Wiley.

Newman, H. (1981). Communication within ongoing intimate relationships: An attributional perspective. *Personality and Social Psychology Bulletin, 7,* 59–70.

Orvis, B. R., Kelley, H. H., & Butler, D. (1976). Attributional conflict in young couples. In J. H. Harvey, W. Ickes, & R. F. Kidd (Eds.), *New directions in attribution research* (Vol. 1, pp. 353–386). Hillsdale, NJ: Erlbaum.

Reis, H. T., & Downey, G. (1999). Social cognition in relationships: Building essential bridges between two literatures. *Social Cognition, 17,* 97–117.

Ross, L. (1977). The intuitive psychologist and his shortcomings: Distortions in the attribution process. In L. Berkowitz (Ed.), *Advances in experimental social psychology* (Vol. 10, pp. 174–221). New York: Academic Press.

PART THREE

NEW DIRECTIONS AND CONTEXTS FOR ATTRIBUTIONS AND COMMUNICATION

Attributions and Regulative Communication by Parents Participating in a Community-Based Child Physical Abuse Prevention Program

Steven R. Wilson and Ellen E. Whipple

Parenting involves frequent attempts to regulate children's behavior. Although setting limits and responding to child misbehavior can be vexing for any parent, the challenges are especially large for parents who live with high levels of stress. Stressors such as young parental age, low education levels, single parenthood, unemployment, and large family size have a significant impact on child rearing practices and are associated with increased incidence of child physical abuse (Kotch, Browne, Dufort, Winsor, & Catellier, 1999; National Research Council, 1993). In response to such stressors, many communities have established parent education and support programs (e.g., Whipple, 1999; Whipple & Wilson, 1996) and home visitation programs (Olds, 1997) designed to prevent child physical abuse.

PARENTAL REGULATIVE COMMUNICATION AND CHILD PHYSICAL ABUSE

Child physical abuse is an interactional event. Parents do not strike their children at random moments but rather at recognizable moments that unfold as part of larger conversations (Reid, 1986). Child physical abuse often escalates from parental attempts to correct perceived child misbehavior and keep the child focused on the parent's agenda. Based on an analysis of protective service agency files, Gil (1970) estimated that 63% of abusive incidents grew out of disciplinary actions taken by parents or other caretakers. In a comprehensive review of the litera-

Note: The authors thank Jennifer Grau for assistance with coding. Please direct correspondence to Steven R. Wilson, Department of Communication, Purdue University, West Lafayette, IN 47907-1366.

ture, Whipple and Richey (1997) argue that physically abusive parents are more likely to "cross the line" in physical discipline episodes with their children than are other parents. A recent nationally representative sample of 1,000 parents found that positive attitudes toward physical discipline, a history of witnessing partner violence, anger mismanagement, and conservative religious ideology placed parents at higher risk for abuse proneness (Jackson et al., 1999).

Most research on regulative communication by physically abusive parents is grounded in Hoffman's (1980) distinction between power-assertive and inductive discipline. *Power assertion* provides the child no rationale for altering his or her behavior other than to avoid punitive consequences (e.g., threats of punishment). *Induction* includes any message that provides explanations or reasons for requiring behavior change. Reasons can appeal to the child's pride, mastery strivings, or concern for others. Especially important for promoting internalization is "other-oriented induction," which highlights implications of the child's behavior for other people.

Physically abusive and nonabusive parents differ in their attempts to regulate perceived child misbehavior (see Wilson, 1999). Physically abusive parents issue more requests and commands than do nonabusive parents during conversations with their children (Oldershaw, Walters, & Hall, 1986, 1989); they also use (1) a larger percentage of requests and commands without any explanation when responding to perceived child misbehavior (Oldershaw et al., 1986); (2) more power-assertive strategies and fewer inductive strategies, both before and after encountering child resistance (Trickett & Susman, 1988); (3) more intense or severe forms of physical discipline, such as slapping or hitting a child (Bousha & Twentyman, 1984; Whipple & Richey, 1997); and (4) primarily power-assertive strategies regardless of how their child has misbehaved, rather than different combinations of power-assertion and induction in response to different types of misbehavior (Trickett & Kuczynski, 1986). Physically abusive parents also display more non-contingent responses than nonabusive parents when attempting to regulate children's behavior (Cerezo, D'Ocon, & Dolz, 1996). Abusive parents are more likely to continue seeking a child's compliance even after the child complies and continue scolding as opposed to praising a child immediately after the child complies (Oldershaw et al., 1986, 1989). Finally, physically abusive parents are less successful than nonabusive parents at gaining their child's compliance (Bousha & Twentyman, 1984).

In light of such findings, most programs designed to prevent or treat child physical abuse include information on parental regulative communication in their curriculum (see Schellenbach, 1998). Altering patterns of regulative communication in physically abusive families is complex, however, because differences between physically abusive and nonabusive parents arise from several sources. In the following section, Milner's (1993, in press) social information-processing model of child physical abuse is used to organize factors that help explain differences in regulative communication by physically abusive and nonabusive parents. Attribution processes are afforded an important role within this model.

MILNER'S SOCIAL INFORMATION-PROCESSING MODEL OF CHILD PHYSICAL ABUSE

Key Concepts and Assumptions

The social information-processing model assumes that all parents possess preexisting schema that shape their perceptions and responses to children's behavior. Abusive parents, however, possess schema that heighten the risk of perceptual bias. Bavelok (1984) proposes that abusive parents are distinguished by four types of dysfunctional beliefs about child rearing: unrealistic developmental expectations (e.g., assuming a 2-year-old will be able to dress herself), lack of empathic awareness of children's emotional needs, strong belief in the necessity of physical punishment, and inappropriate expectations regarding children's abilities to provide social support. Research provides some support for these claims; for example, "high risk" parents possess unrealistic expectations about when children are likely to comply with requests (Chilamkurti & Milner, 1993).

Four stages of information processing are specified within the model. At stage 1 (perception), physically abusive, as compared with nonabusive, parents are believed to be less attentive to and aware of child-related behavior. For example, abusive parents appear less likely than nonabusive parents to distinguish positive and negative child behaviors (Frodi & Lamb, 1980) and are less able to encode their children's emotional states accurately (Kropp & Haynes, 1987). At stage 2 (interpretation and evaluation), physically abusive, relative to nonabusive, parents are assumed to make less charitable judgments about their child's behavior. For example, abusive parents appear more likely than nonabusive parents to make internal, stable, and intentional attributions for their child's negative behavior (Bauer & Twentyman, 1985; Larrance & Twentyman, 1983). Abusive parents also view themselves as less responsible than nonabusive parents for unpleasant interactions with their child and give their child less credit for pleasant interactions (Bugental, Blue, & Cruzcosa, 1989). Parents, in general, report being angrier and more likely to use power-assertive discipline when they perceive that their child's misbehavior is internally caused and intentional and when they believe that the child generally acts this way even though the child is old enough to "know better" (Dix, 1991).

At stage 3 (information integration and response selection), abusive, relative to nonabusive, parents may fail to integrate information adequately and also may possess less complex plans for regulating child misbehavior. For example, parents at high risk for child physical abuse are less likely than low-risk parents to alter their attributions in light of mitigating information even when they are aware of such information (Milner & Foody, 1994). At stage 4 (response implementation and monitoring), abusive parents are thought to be less skilled at implementing, monitoring, and modifying responses. For example, abusive parents are more likely than nonabusive parents to display noncontingent responses (e.g., scolding a compliant child) when regulating child behavior, as previously mentioned.

Application to the Current Study

The study reported here includes data on attributions and regulative communication by parents participating in a community-based child abuse prevention program. Participants described aloud what they would say or do in response to three hypothetical scenarios in which one of their children had misbehaved and later made attributions for each misbehavior. Three classes of variables were assessed: information-processing variables; sociodemographic variables; and indices of parental regulative communication. Milner's (1993, in press) social information processing model was used to organize and justify predictions about relations among these three groups of variables.

Information-processing variables include parents' dysfunctional child rearing beliefs, attributions for child misbehavior, and depression. Each relates to a different component of Milner's model. Dysfunctional child rearing beliefs are one example of preexisting schema. Attributions of *locus* (i.e., whether the child's misbehavior was caused by factors inside versus outside the child), *generality* (i.e., whether the child's misbehavior was caused by factors present only in this situation versus factors present in most situations), *knowledge* (i.e., whether the child was old enough to know how to behave properly), and *blame* fall under Stage 2 of the social information processing model. Finally, chronic depression may result in increased automatic processing during regulative episodes.

Several sociodemographic factors that mark risk status for child physical abuse also were assessed, including parent age and education, family income and structure (e.g., single parent), number of children at home, and level of family growth center involvement. According to Milner (1993, in press), these factors may affect parents' preexisting schema, their attributions for child misbehavior, and/or factors such as depression, which in turn influence mode of information processing (hypothesis 1).

Aside from attributing internality, generality, knowledge, and blame when their child misbehaves, physically abusive parents also appear less sensitive to variation in type of child misbehavior. Parents at high risk for child physical abuse tend to respond in similar fashion regardless of whether their child, for example, is throwing a temper tantrum at a grocery store or refusing to share a new toy with a friend while playing at home (Trickett & Kuczynski, 1986; Wilson, Whipple, & Grau, 1996). Research to date has not explored whether risk status is associated with the degree to which parents vary their attributions in response to different types of child misbehavior. We explore this question here (Research Question 1).

The information processing variables assessed in this study differ in terms of being relatively stable versus episode-specific. Attributions of locus, generality, knowledge, and blame are made during particular regulative episodes. Episode-specific attributions may be driven, in part, by preexisting schema. By increasing automatic processing, chronic depression also may lead to more theory-driven and hence less charitable attributions for child misbehavior in a particular episode (Hypothesis 2). According to Milner's (1993, in press) model, social information processing factors are the immediate antecedents of regulative communication by parents (Hypothesis 3). Finally, we ask the following: Will the degree to which parents vary their attributions across misbehavior situations be associated with their regulative communication? (Research Question 2).

METHOD

Participants and Research Sites

The participants were 30 parents (28 mothers, 2 fathers) who utilized services at one of two family growth centers (FGCs) in a moderate-sized midwestern city. The FGCs offer a range of services at neighborhood sites, including respite day care, social support groups for parents, an early childhood development program preparing 4-year olds for kindergarten, and a structured 15-week parent education program for detailed information regarding FGC services (see Whipple & Wilson, 1996). Participants learned about FGC services primarily through advertising and word-of-mouth contact rather than by referrals from child protective service agencies.

Participants' ages ranged from 23 to 44 years ($M = 34$, SD = 5.6). Of the 30 parents, 25 (83%) were European-American, 3 (10%) were Asian-American, and 2 (7%) were African-American; 17 (57%) were married, 10 (33%) were single mothers, and 3 (10%) lived with an unmarried partner. All but one parent (97%) had completed high school, and 13 (43%) had some college or vocational training. Of the 30 participants, 5 (17%) worked full-time, 9 (30%) worked part-time, and 16 (53%) did not work outside the home; of the 20 partners, 15 (95%) worked full- or part-time, and 5 (25%) were unemployed. Participants on average had 2.27 (range, 1 to 4) children. The majority of households (69%) earned less than $25,000 annually.

Of the 63 parents using FGC services, 30 (48%) volunteered to participate in this study. On average, these parents had attended their FGC just over 2 years ($M = 25.27$, SD = 22.25 months) and had used two or three types of service within the past year ($M = 2.43$, SD = 1.43 services). Participants reported on that one of their children who was most involved in FGC programs. The majority of children were either 4 or 5 years old, although the sample included children aged 1.33 to 8.00 years ($M = 4.50$, SD = 1.30 years). Parents were guaranteed anonymity and received free child care vouchers at the FGCs for participating. Although 30 parents completed the data collection, only 21 to 23 parents generated codable initial or subsequent regulative messages in response to each situation.

Procedures

A second-year graduate student in social work interviewed participants at their FGC after obtaining informed consent and permission to audiotape. Participants then completed a measure of dysfunctional child rearing beliefs and an intake questionnaire. Participants next completed a regulative communication task, responding to three hypothetical regulative scenarios in which their child supposedly (1) threw a temper tantrum during a trip to the grocery store after being told not to touch items on the shelf; (2) refused to share a new toy while playing at home with a friend; and (3) used profanity in response to being teased by a peer. The FGC staff judged that these three regulative situations were realistic and believable for parents with children of varying ages. After parents read each scenario, the interviewer asked them to describe aloud exactly what they would say or do in that situation. If parents provided only an abstract summary, the interviewer prompted them for a word-for-word answer by asking "exactly what would you say to tell (child's name) that?" Following this initial response, the interviewer asked what parents would say or do if they delivered the first message but their child still did not comply (i.e., their response to child resistance).

Parents then completed a depression inventory. Following this, the interviewer presented parents with the same three regulative situations to which they had responded earlier. Parents evaluated the degree to which their child's behavior in each of the three situations was (a) caused by internal versus external factors; (b) caused by specific versus general factors; and (c) inappropriate versus appropriate for a child of that age. Parents also rated the degree to which they blamed their child for misbehaving. They were then thanked for participating and debriefed.

Measures: Social Information-Processing Variables

Dysfunctional Child Rearing Beliefs

Parents' beliefs about child rearing were assessed via Bavelok's (1984) Adult-Adolescent Parenting Inventory (AAPI), a 32-item Likert-type measure, which taps the degree to which parents possess inappropriate developmental expectations for children (e.g., "Children should be able to feed themselves by 12 months"), lack empathetic awareness of their child's needs (e.g., "Children who are given too much love by their parents often grow up to be stubborn and spoiled"), believe physical punishment is vital (e.g., "Children should always be spanked when they misbehave"), and reverse caretaker–dependent roles with their child (e.g., "Young children should be expected to comfort their mother when she is feeling blue"). The mean correlation among these four subscales was quite high ($r = .60$ after r to z transformation); hence, we treated the AAPI as a unidimensional measure. Higher scores reflect inappropriate expectations, limited awareness of children's emotional needs, belief in corporal punishment, and role reversal.

Depression

Parental depression was assessed via the Beck Depression Inventory (BDI), a 21-item instrument designed to assess the severity of depressive symptomatology. Items describe affective, cognitive, motivational, and physiological symptoms of depression. Of our 30 participants, 7 (23%) had a total BDI score of 10 or higher, which indicates at least mild depression (Kendall, Hollon, Beck, Hammen, & Ingram, 1987). Participants' scores on the BDI were positively skewed; hence, we logarithmically transformed total scores to produce a more normal distribution.

Attributions

For each regulative situation, parents completed 3-item, 7-point Likert measures of (1) locus (e.g., "What is the most important reason why your child threw a temper tantrum in this situation? 1 = something outside of your child; 7 = something inside of your child"); (2) generality (e.g., "Is this temper tantrum typical of the way your child normally behaves? 1 = very unusual behavior; 7 = very typical behavior"); (3) knowledge (e.g., "Is your child too young to know how to behave properly in this situation? 1 = definitely too young to know; 7 = definitely old enough to know"); and (4) blame (e.g., "To what degree is your child at fault for throwing a temper tantrum in this situation? 1 = not at all at fault, 7 = totally at fault"). The measures of locus, knowledge, and blame were adapted from Dix, Ruble, and Zambarano (1989). On the basis of item analyses, one question was dropped from the final locus and blame measures. Across the three situations, mean alphas were .86, .78, .85, and .74, respectively, for the locus, generality, knowledge, and blame measures. Total scores on each measure were divided by the number of items to retain the 1 to 7 scale. Higher scores indicate that parents attributed greater internality, generality, knowledge, and blame when their child performed a specific misbehavior.

Measures: Sociodemographic Factors

Parental age, years of education, ethnicity, family structure (two-parent family, single-parent family, or parent and unmarried partner), and number and ages of children living in the household were assessed from the intake questionnaire. Household income was assessed from registration records kept by the FGCs. Degree of FGC involvement was operationalized in four ways. Three indicators of involvement came from parental reports of the number of FGC services they were using currently, FGC services they had used in the past year, and months they had attended the FGC. As a fourth indicator, one of the FGC staff rated all 30 parents for degree of involvement at the centers. Scores on these four measures were standardized and summed into a composite involvement index (alpha = .62).

Coding Procedures: Parental Regulative Communication

Audiotapes of parents' responses to the three hypothetical regulative scenarios were coded by a hierarchical content analysis system developed by Applegate and his colleagues (Applegate, Burke, Burleson, Delia, & Kline, 1985; Applegate, Burleson, & Delia, 1992). Regulative strategies at Level 1, such as commands, threats, and physical punishment, are power-assertive techniques, which offer no reasoning why the child should modify his or her behavior other than to avoid sanctions. Strategies at Level 2 present or demand acceptance of rules that the parent assumes are self-evident. References to rules include any statement about how the child should or should not behave over the long run. At Level 3, parents offer some justification for rules used to change the child's behavior, such as explaining physical consequences or arguing that the rules apply to everyone. Strategies at Level 4 allow the child to deal with parent-controlled options or contingent rewards as a means of modifying child behavior. Regulative strategies reach Level 5 when parents explain psychological causes, consequences, or both of the child's misbehavior to encourage modification. At Level 6, parents use questions to elicit the the child's own account of the psychological causes and consequences of misbehavior. We adapted Applegate's (1985, 1992) coding scheme by including specific regulative technique taught by the FGCs at the relevant hierarchical level. A detailed coding manual is available from the first author.

Categorizing reliability was assessed by having two coders, one of whom was masked to the research hypotheses, independently score 17% ($N = 30$ out of 180) of parents' first and second responses to the three hypothetical scenarios. Coders identified the highest-level strategy used by a parent in each response. Applegate et al. (1985, 1992) argue that this highest-level response reflects a parent's ability to generate inductive strategies under optimal circumstances (i.e., while being interviewed, as opposed to at the moment during a face-to-face regulative episode with her child). Intercoder agreement, as measured by Cohen's kappa, was .75 for first responses and .90 for second responses. Coders resolved disagreements through discussion and then subdivided and coded the remaining responses.

RESULTS

Sociodemographic Factors and Information Processing Variables

Hypothesis 1 predicts that sociodemographic factors associated with child physical abuse risk will be related to social information-processing variables. To assess this prediction, we correlated parental age, education, family structure (coded 1 = single parent status or parent with unmarried partner; 2 = two-parent family), family income, number of children, and level of FGC involvement with dysfunctional childrearing beliefs, parental depression, and parents' attributions of internality, generality, knowledge, and blame. Attributional dimensions were averaged across the three misbehavior scenarios to address the first hypothesis. We also assessed whether age and sex of the child imagined in the scenarios were associated with information-processing variables.

Results of these analyses, which appear in the first six columns of Table 11.1, are consistent with Hypothesis 1. Each sociodemographic factor except sex of the child is associated with one of the social information processing variables. As expected, parents with less education and family income are more likely to possess dysfunctional child rearing beliefs. Parental depression is inversely associated with family income and FGC involvement. Contrary to our prediction, older parents are more likely than younger parents to attribute misbehavior to internal factors within their child. As predicted, parents with a larger

Table 11.1. Correlations Between Sociodemographic Variables and Social Information–Processing Variables

	Sociodemographic Variables		Dysfunctional Parental Variability Across Situations				Information Processing Variables Mean Across Situations			
	Beliefs	Depression	Locus	Gener	Know	Blame	Locus	Gener	Know	Blame
Parent age	-.25	-.23	.35*	-.07	-.25	-.01	-.43*	.22	.07	-.20
Parent education	-.41*	-.07	.24	.08	-.43*	-.13	-.40*	.07	-.07	-.37*
Family structure[a]	.06	-.28	-.08	.12	-.32*	-.05	-.05	.33*	.33*	.10
Family income	-.32*	-.39*	-.02	.05	-.18	-.02	-.09	.25	.48**	.30
Number of children	.05	.21	.03	.45*	.02	.01	-.18	.15	-.15	.05
FGC involvement	-.27	-.33*	-.28	-.11	-.44*	-.24	-.29	-.11	.16	-.05
Child age	-.12	-.06	-.05	-.12	.64**	.34*	-.05	-.01	.05	.34*
Child sex[b]	.15	.05	.12	-.26	.05	-.01	-.11	-.05	-.18	-.49**

N = 27 to 30 parents. * p < .05; ** p < .01 (one-tail).
[a]1 = single parent family or unmarried partner, 2 = two parent family.
[b]1 = boy, 2 = girl. FGC = family growth center; gener = generality; know = knowledge.

number of children at home are more likely to see misbehaviors as reflecting general patterns of behavior for the child in question. Participants are more likely to assume that their child is old enough to know better when they possess less education, are single parents or live with an unmarried partner, or are less involved at their FGC. Parents, in general, attribute more knowledge when the misbehaving child in question is older. Parents also attribute more blame to older children. As is consistent with Milner's (1993, in press) information-processing model, sociodemographic factors that mark risk status for child physical abuse are reflected in parents' cognitions as they imagined regulating their child's behavior.

Research question 1 asks whether sociodemographic factors that mark risk of child physical abuse are associated with the degree to which parents vary their attributions of internality, generality, knowledge, and blame across misbehavior situations. To assess cross-situational variability, we created an absolute-value variability index for each of the four attributional dimensions. Regarding causal locus, for example, each parent's mean level of internality across the three scenarios was calculated. Variability was computed by summing the absolute differences between that parent's attribution of internality within each scenario and overall mean rating of internality. Similar variability indices were created for attributions of generality, knowledge, and blame. Larger scores indicate that parents made different attributions depending on how their child had misbehaved rather than making similar attributions across scenarios. To assess this research question, we correlated parental age, education, family structure, family income, number of children, FGC involvement, and misbehaving child's age and sex with variability in parents' attributions of internality, generality, knowledge, and blame.

Results appear in the final four columns of Table 11.1. Sociodemographic factors that mark risk status for child physical abuse are associated with attributional variability, although the direction of the relationship differs depending on the specific attributional dimension. Parent age and education are associated with less variability in attributions of internality. Participants from two-parent families displayed greater variability in attributions of both generality and knowledge than those who were single parents or lived with an unmarried partner. Household income is positively associated with the degree to which participants vary attributions of knowledge. Parents with more formal education are less likely to vary their attributions of blame across scenarios.

Parents, as a group, also vary attributions of blame more with older children and with boys as opposed to girls. In general, factors that mark reduced risk status for child physical abuse (e.g., more education) are associated with greater variability in attributions of generality and knowledge but less variability in attributions of internality and blame.

Stable and Episode-Specific Information Processing Variables

Hypothesis 2 predicts that stable information-processing factors will be associated with parents' attributions for child misbehavior (i.e., increased attributed internality, generality, knowledge, and blame). To assess this prediction, we correlated dysfunctional child rearing beliefs and parental depression with mean scores for parents' attributions of locus, generality, knowledge, and blame across the three misbehavior scenarios. Dysfunctional child rearing beliefs are positively associated with attribution of greater blame to the misbehaving child, $r = .45$, $p < .05$, but not with the other three attributional dimensions. The finding for blame is consistent with Milner's (1993, in press) contention that preexisting schema (i.e., dysfunctional beliefs) can bias parents' judgments about child behavior during specific regulative episodes.

Level of depression is positively associated with seeing misbehaviors as reflecting the child's general pattern of behavior, $r = .34$, $p < .05$, but not with the other three attributional dimensions. Although no more likely to assume that their child is old enough to "know better," depressed parents also are less likely than nondepressed parents to *vary* attributions of knowledge across different child misbehaviors, $r = -.37$, $p < .05$. This finding is reminiscent of Milner's claim that depression can result in automatic information processing in which parents fail to notice, or integrate, mitigating information.

Information-Processing Variables and Parental Regulative Communication

Hypothesis 3 predicts that information-processing variables associated with risk of child physical abuse (i.e., dysfunctional child rearing beliefs, depression, and attributions of internality, generality, knowledge, and blame) will be inversely associated with the degree to which parents, in general, use inductive rather than only power-assertive regulative strategies and the degree to which they vary their regulative strategies across misbehavior situations. Research question 2 asks whether the degree to which parents' vary their attributions across misbehavior scenarios will be associated with their regulative communication. We created two general indices of parental regulative communication to assess these questions. First, we computed mean scores for each parent's highest-level regulative strategy across the three scenarios. Higher mean scores reflect that parents included inductive strategies from the upper levels of the hierarchical scheme of Applegate et al. (1985, 1992) in their responses rather than including only low-level power-assertive strategies. Mean scores were calculated for each parent both before and after encountering child resistance.

Second, we computed an absolute-value index of variability in parents' highest-level regulative strategy across scenarios. Each parent's mean highest-level regulative strategy across the three scenarios was calculated. Variability was computed by summing the absolute differences between that parent's highest-level strategy within each scenario and his or her overall mean highest-level strategy. Larger variability scores reflect that parents varied their highest-level strategy depending on how their child had misbehaved, rather than generating the same highest-level strategy (usually power-assertive techniques) in all three scenarios. Correlations between social information–processing variables and these indices of parental regulative communication appear in Table 11.2.

Three sets of findings are noteworthy. First, stable information-processing variables are associated with parents' tendency to include inductive rather than only power-assertive strategies in their responses and to vary their highest-level response depending on how their child had misbehaved (see the first two rows in Table 11.2). Depression is inversely associated with these same tendencies both before and after child resistance. Second, mean scores for parents' attributions of knowledge and blame are inversely associated with their highest-level regulative strategies following child resistance. Upon encountering resistance, parents who believe that their child is old enough to know better and who blame the child for misbehaving are more likely than those who attribute less knowledge and blame to include only low-level power-assertive techniques in their responses. Mean scores for locus and generality are not related to parents' highest-level regulative strategies (see rows 3 through 6 in Table 11.2).

Third, variability in parents' attributions across different misbehavior scenarios is related to their regulative communication (see rows 7 through 10 in Table 11.2). After encountering child resistance, parents

Table 11.2.   Correlations Between Information Processing Variables
and Parental Regulative Communication

Information- Processing Variables	Parents' Highest-Level Inductive Strategy			
	Mean Across Situations		Variability Across Situations	
	Before Resistance	After Resistance	Before Resistance	After Resistance
Stable factors				
Dysfunctional beliefs	−.27	−.41*	−.17	−.39*
Parental depression	−.44*	−.56**	−.43*	−.38*
Attributions (mean across situations)				
Locus	.00	.26	−.18	.13
Generality	−.14	−.24	−.28	−.10
Knowledge	−.22	−.42*	−.02	−.31
Blame	−.18	−.37*	−.15	−.30
Attributions (variability across situations)				
Locus	−.12	−.29	−.23	−.11
Generality	.34#	.25	−.21	.35#
Knowledge	.26	.55**	.03	.71**
Blame	−.21	−.21	−.38*	−.06

N = 17 to 21 parents. * p <.05; ** p < .01; # p < .08 (one-tail).

who vary their attributions about whether their child is old enough to know better depending on how the child had misbehaved also are more likely to use inductive rather than only power-assertive regulative strategies. These same parents also vary their highest-level strategy across different scenarios. Parents who vary their attributions of generality display similar trends, although these findings only approached conventional levels of statistical significance. In contrast, parents who vary their attributions of blame depending on how their child has misbehaved are less likely to vary their initial highest-level regulative strategy across scenarios with different child misbehaviors.

DISCUSSION

This chapter reports on attributions and regulative communication by parents participating in community-based FGCs and presents a study couched within a social information–processing model of child physical abuse (Milner, 1993, in press). Parents with less education and from lower-income households were more likely to endorse dysfunctional beliefs such as inappropriate developmental expectations for children and a strong belief in the necessity of physical punishment. Parents who endorsed such beliefs, in turn, blamed the child more for misbehaving. On encountering child resistance, these parents also were less likely to include inductive strategies in their responses to hypothetical scenarios or to vary their regulative strategies depending on how the child had misbehaved.

Depression also affects parents' perceptions of children and was inversely associated with household income and FGC involvement. Parents with higher levels of depression, in turn, were more likely to perceive that specific misbehaviors reflected how their child behaved in general; these parents also were more likely to attribute the same level of knowledge to their child regardless of how the child had misbehaved. As depression increased, parents were less likely to include inductive strategies in their regulative messages or to vary their regulative strategies across different types of child misbehavior, both before and after encountering child resistance.

In addition to these stable information-processing variables, attributions made within specific regulative episodes also affect parents' responses to child misbehavior. Attributions of internality did not relate to sociodemographic factors as expected, and parents' regulative communication did not depend on whether they attributed misbehaviors to internal qualities of their child. In contrast, attributions of generality, knowledge, and blame were affected by factors associated with risk of child physical abuse, such as low education levels, single-parent status, low family income, larger number of children at home, and low FGC involvement, as well as by the age and sex of the misbehaving child (see Table 11.1). Parents altered their regulative communication depending on whether they attributed high levels of generality, knowledge, and blame to their child and on whether they varied these attributions depending on how their child had misbehaved.

Previous research has shown that parents at risk for child physical abuse tend to rely primarily on power-assertive techniques in most situations, whereas lower-risk parents use different combinations of induction and power assertion depending on how their child has misbehaved (Trickett & Kuczynski, 1986; Wilson et al., 1996). Our findings suggest that the relationship between risk status and attributional variability is not so simple. Parents whose sociodemographic profiles suggest higher risk of child physical abuse tended to attribute similar levels of generality and knowledge regardless of how the child had misbehaved, which suggests that these parents were less sensitive to details of how their child actually had misbehaved. Variability in attributions of generality and knowledge also were associated positively with use of inductive as opposed to only power-assertive techniques.

These results for attributions of generality and knowledge are consistent with earlier findings that at-risk parents display little variability in regulative strategies across situations. In contrast, however, parents with less education varied their attributions of blame *more* than did better educated parents, and variability in attributions of blame was *negatively* associated with use of induction. Parents at lower risk for child physical abuse may have tried to avoid blaming regardless of how their child had misbehaved. As is consistent with this speculation, parents who tended not to endorse dysfunctional child rearing beliefs placed less blame on their children across situations. In sum, more *or* less attributional variability may mark risk status for child physical abuse, depending on the dimension of attribution under consideration.

Despite some limitations, our findings raise implications for theories of child physical abuse, as well as for prevention and treatment programs. Our findings suggest that the role of affect within Milner's (1993, in press) model needs further explication. Prior research has shown that physically abusive, relative to nonabusive, parents report higher levels of anger and disgust in response to child misbehavior (Reid, 1986; Trickett & Kuczynski, 1986). Parents in our sample who endorsed dysfunctional child rearing beliefs (i.e., preexisting schema) tended to blame their child for misbehaving; thus, these parents may have felt more anger and disgust. When a child does not comply immediately, however, anger and anxiety may lead physically abusive parents to rely more heavily than nonabusive parents on automatic processing, thereby magnifying attributional differences.

Recent research (Dopke & Milner, in press) shows that parents at high versus low risk for child physical abuse actually make increasingly discrepant attributions after repeated child resistance (i.e., Stage 2 of the model). Once angry, physically abusive parents also may retain their original attributions regardless of how the child or a third party accounts for a misbehavior (i.e., Stage 3). Depressed parents in our sample made similar attributions of knowledge and relied primarily on power-assertive techniques regardless of how the child misbehaved. Depressed parents, in general, appear less attentive than nondepressed parents to their child's behavior (Stage 1) and are less likely to monitor and adjust their own behavior over time (Stage 4) (see Dix, 1991).

Aside from theoretical development, our results also have implications for prevention and intervention programs that target at-risk or abusive families with young children. This study lends a deeper understanding to the findings of our previous program evaluation, where depression and stress were significantly reduced among parents who had a high level of involvement with their FGC, averaging 2 years and completion of three to five programs (Whipple & Wilson, 1996). A second FGC program evaluation with a larger sample ($N = 116$) found that intensity of program involvement was associated with the greatest improvement. Specifically, FGC parents involved in the most intensive program with mandatory parent and child components demonstrated an improved home environment (e.g., fostered their 4-year-old's school readiness), showed clear decreases in parental stress, and learned how to negotiate conflict with their children less violently (Whipple, 1999). Evaluations of child abuse prevention programs with diverse formats increasingly operationalize program involvement in terms similar to those in this study, including a focus on both duration (e.g., number of months involved) and intensity (e.g., frequency of contacts, level of program structure), in order to capture the complexity and flexibility of program structures.

The need to provide at-risk parents with concrete services is clear. Poverty, low education levels, single parenthood, and large family size are especially tenacious risk factors for child abuse and neglect. Parent education and support programs would do well to collaborate closely with high schools and community colleges as well as job training agencies to ensure that young parents have the opportunity to finish their education and find a job within their community. Greater efforts must be made for public and private agencies to work together to provide job training and job opportunities in a flexible framework for families with young children. For example, parent education and support programs could integrate school counselors and employment personnel into the curriculum. Although these suggestions regarding concrete services extend beyond the current study, they make sense in light of our findings that sociodemographic factors such as education and income have an impact on parental attributions and regulative communication in the everyday lives of families at risk for child physical abuse.

REFERENCES

Applegate, J. L., Burke, J. A., Burleson, B. R., Delia, J. G., & Kline, S. L. (1985). Reflection-enhancing parental communication. In I. E. Sigel (Ed.), *Parental belief systems: The psychological consequences for children* (pp. 107–142). Hillsdale, NJ: Erlbaum.

Applegate, J. L., Burleson, B. R., & Delia, J. G. (1992). Reflection-enhancing parenting as an antecedent to children's social-cognitive and communicative development. In I. E. Sigel, A. V. McGillicuddy-DeLisi, & J. J. Goodnow (Eds.) *Parental belief systems: The psychological consequences for children* (Vol. 2, pp. 3–39). Hillsdale, NJ: Erlbaum.

Bauer, W. D., & Twentyman, C. T. (1985). Abusing, neglectful, and comparison mothers' responses to child-related and non-child related stressors. *Journal of Consulting and Clinical Psychology, 53,* 335–343.

Bavelok, S. J. (1984). *Handbook for the Adult-Adolescent Parenting Inventory.* Eau Claire, WI: Family Development Resources.

Bousha, D. M., & Twentyman, C. T. (1984). Mother-child interactional style in abuse, neglect, and control groups: Naturalistic observations in the home. *Journal of Abnormal Psychology, 93,* 106–114.

Bugental, D. B., Blue, J., & Cruzcosa, M. (1989). Perceived control over caregiving outcomes: Implications for child abuse. *Developmental Psychology, 25,* 532–539.

Cerezo, M. A., D'Ocon, A., & Dolz, L. (1996). Mother-child interactive patterns in abusive families: An observational study. *Child Abuse & Neglect, 20,* 573–587.

Chilamkurti, C., & Milner, J. S. (1993). Perceptions and evaluations of child transgressions and disciplinary techniques in high- and low-risk mothers and their children. *Child Development, 64,* 1801–1814.

Dix, T. (1991). The affective organization of parenting: Adaptive and maladaptive processes. *Psychological Bulletin, 110,* 3–25.

Dix, T., Ruble, D. N., & Zambarano, R. J. (1989). Mothers' implicit theories of discipline: Child effects, parent effects, and the attribution process. *Child Development, 60,* 1373–1391.

Dopke, C. A., & Milner, J. S. (in press). Impact of child noncompliance on stress appraisals, attributions, and disciplinary choices in mothers at high and low risk for child physical abuse. *Child Abuse & Neglect.*

Frodi, A. M., & Lamb, M. E. (1980). Child abusers' responses to infant smiles and cries. *Child Development, 51,* 238–241.

Gil, D. G. (1970). *Violence against children: Physical child abuse in the United States.* Cambridge, MA: Harvard University Press.

Goddard, H. W., & Miller, B. C. (1993). Adding attributions to parenting programs. *Families in Society: The Journal of Contemporary Human Services, 74,* 84–92.

Hoffman, M. L. (1980). Moral development in adolescence. In J. Adelson (Ed.), *Handbook of adolescent psychology* (pp. 295–343). New York: Wiley.

Jackson, S., Thompson, R. A., Christiansen, E. H., Colman, R. A., Wyatt, J., Buckendahl, C. W., Wilcox, B. L., & Peterson, R. (1999). Predicting abuse-prone parental attitudes and discipline practices in a nationally representative sample. *Child Abuse & Neglect, 23,* 15–29.

Kendall, P. C., Hollon, S. D., Beck, A. T., Hammen, C. L., & Ingram, R. E. (1987). Issues and recommendations regarding use of the Beck Depression Inventory. *Cognitive Therapy and Research, 11,* 289–299.

Kotch, J. B., Browne, D. C., Dufort, V., Winsor, J., & Catellier, D. (1999) Predicting child maltreatment in the first 4 years of life from characteristics assessed in the neonatal period. *Child Abuse & Neglect, 23,* 305–319.

Kropp, J. P., & Haynes, O. M. (1987). Abusive and nonabusive mothers' ability to identify general and specific emotion signals of infants. *Child Development, 58,* 187–190.

Larrance, D. T., & Twentyman, C. T. (1983). Maternal attributions and child abuse. *Journal of Abnormal Psychology, 92,* 449–457.

Milner, J. S. (1993). Social information processing and physical child abuse. *Clinical Psychology Review, 13,* 275–294.

Milner, J. S. (in press). Social information processing and child physical abuse: Theory and research. In D. J. Hersen (Ed.), *Nebraska symposium on motivation. Vol. 45. Motivation and child maltreatment.* Lincoln, NE: University of Nebraska Press.

Milner, J. S., & Foody, R. (1994). The impact of mitigating information on attributions for positive and negative child behaviors by adults at low-and high-risk for child-abusive behavior. *Journal of Social and Clinical Psychology, 13,* 335–351.

National Research Council. (1993). *Understanding child abuse and neglect.* Washington, DC: National Academy Press.

Oldershaw, L, Walters, G. C., & Hall, D. K. (1986). Control strategies and noncompliance in abusive mother-child dyads. *Developmental Psychology, 57,* 722–732.

Oldershaw, L., Walters, G. C., & Hall, D. K. (1989). A behavioral approach to the classification of different types of physically abusive mothers. *Merrill-Palmer Quarterly, 35,* 255–279.

Olds, D. (1997). The prenatal early infancy project: Preventing child abuse and neglect in the context of promoting maternal and child health. In D. A. Wolfe, R. J. McMahon, & R. DeV. Peters (Eds.), *Child abuse: New directions in prevention and treatment across the lifespan* (pp. 130–156). Thousand Oaks, CA: Sage.

Reid, J. B. (1986). Social interactional patterns in families of abused and nonabused children. In C. Zahn-Waxler, E. M. Cummings, & R. Iannotti (Eds.), *Altruism and aggression: Biological and social origins* (pp. 238–257). Cambridge, UK: Cambridge University Press.

Schellenbach, C. J. (1998). Child maltreatment: A critical review of research on treatment for physically abusive parents. In P. K. Trickett & C. J. Schellenbach (Eds.), *Violence against children in the family and the community* (pp. 419–438). Washington, DC: American Psychological Association.

Trickett, P. K., & Kuczynski, L. (1986). Children's misbehaviors and parental discipline strategies in abusive and nonabusive families. *Developmental Psychology, 22,* 115–123.

Trickett, P. K., & Susman, E. J. (1988). Parental perceptions of child-rearing practices in physically abusive and nonabusive families. *Developmental Psychology, 24,* 270–276.

Whipple, E. E. (1999). Reaching families with preschoolers at risk of physical child abuse: What works? *Families in Society: The Journal of Contemporary Human Services, 80,* 148–160.

Whipple, E. E., & Richey, C. A. (1997). Crossing the line from physical discipline to child abuse: How much is too much? *Child Abuse & Neglect, 12,* 431–444.

Whipple, E. E., & Wilson, S. R. (1996). Evaluation of a parent education and support program for families at risk of physical child abuse. *Families in Society: The Journal of Contemporary Human Services, 77,* 227–239.

Wilson, S. R. (1999). Child physical abuse: The relevance of language and social interaction research. *Research on Language and Social Interaction, 32,* 173–184.

Wilson, S. R., Whipple, E. E., & Grau, J. (1996). Reflection-enhancing regulative communication: How do parents vary across misbehavior situations and child resistance? *Journal of Social and Personal Relationships, 13,* 553–569.

CHAPTER TWELVE

"True Lies"

Children's Abuse History and Power
Attributions as Influences on Deception Detection

*Daphne Blunt Bugental, William Shennum, Mark Frank,
and Paul Ekman*

Skill in detecting deceit has particular value when there is reason to
believe that others cannot be trusted. Concern with such skills has
focused on the lie detection accuracy (i.e., the ability to make accurate
attributions of truth or falsity) of those who are directly or indirectly
involved with law enforcement (Ekman & O'Sullivan, 1991; Ekman,
O'Sullivan, & Frank, 1999). Less empirical attention has been given to
lie detection skills within close relationships, in particular those relationships in which others cannot be trusted. In this paper, we focus on
the attribution skills of children who have experienced unusual levels
of threat in their young lives.

In particular, we are concerned with children who have been physically abused and subsequently removed from their homes. For such children, adults have often been a continuing source of threat, first in the
home environment and then in the disruptions associated with out-of-
home care. As a result, these children have good reason to view adults'
communication patterns as an "early warning system" in detecting possible danger. Subtle features of those adults' facial expressions and voice
quality may serve as signals of the honesty of their words and may provide cues to their future actions. Frequent experience with adults who are
unreliable may lead children to respond with wariness and to be vigilant
for cues indicating that something is not as it seems to be.

The functional adaptiveness of accurate deception detection varies,
not only with the presence of threat: but also with the individual's
unique vulnerability to threat. For example, deception detection varies
with the observer's perceived social power. Children with low perceived

Note: Please send all correspondence to Daphne Blunt Bugental at the Department of
Psychology, University of Santa Barbara, Santa Barbara, CA 93106.

power are more likely than other children to be wary and defensive in their style of interaction with others (Bugental & Martorell, 1998; Cortez & Bugental, 1994). These types of children easily see others as posing a threat and are more emotionally reactive to the possibility of threat than are others. As a result of their vulnerability to potential threat, children with low perceived power may show systematic differences in their response to possible deception.

BACKGROUND

Detecting Lies

Ekman and his colleagues have a long history of research concerned with people's ability to "catch a liar" (Ekman, 1985; Ekman & O'Sullivan, 1991; Frank & Ekman, 1997). Within this literature, there have been differences in findings on the extent to which there indeed are stable differences between individuals in their ability to detect deception. A substantial body of work has shown that observers, even those who are strongly motivated to spot a liar and believe they possess such skills, are very poor lie detectors (e.g., DePaulo, 1994; DePaulo, Stone, & Lassiter, 1985; Kraut & Poe, 1980; Zuckerman, DePaulo, & Rosenthal, 1981). Countering these findings, Ekman and O'Sullivan (1991), as well as Ekman et al. (1999), found that those who have a particularly high-stake investment in catching liars (such as agents within the U.S. Secret Service) are more likely than others to show an ability to detect lies that exceeds chance levels.

As suggested by Frank and Ekman's (1997) research, individual differences in lie detection ability appear to be stable across high-stake situations (i.e., when there are high costs and benefits for both the liar and lie catcher). These findings suggest the importance of focusing on deception detection among those who, within their own lives, have experienced important risks in connection with their responses to deception. In contrast, most of the white lies that constitute a central part of everyday interaction go unnoticed, because failure to read these lies does not pose an important risk to the liar or the lie catcher (e.g., DePaulo, Kashy, Kirkendol, Wyer, & Epstein, 1996).

Research concerned with individual differences in deception detection ability has typically framed the issue as one of accuracy rather than susceptibility to being fooled. In this report we direct attention to individual differences in accurate detection of deception, as well as in the reverse process of susceptibility to misclassifying lies and truths (i.e., the tendency to trust lies more than truth or to see truth as reflecting lies). This second concern redirects the focus of interest to levels of vulnerability to deception.

Abuse and Communication

What do we know about physically abused children that may lead us to predict their ability to detect or misread cues that have relevance for deception? Physically abusive parents have been found to be unreliable communicators (and interpreters) of affective states. For example, Camras and her colleagues (Camras et al., 1988) have observed that abused children and their mothers, when attempting to pose different emotions, produce expressions that are not easily recognized by others. In addition, posed facial expressions are less accurately recognized by abused than by nonabused children (Camras et al., 1990).

Children in abusive homes are exposed to a different communication environment than are those in nonabusive homes (Camras et al., 1990). For example, mothers who are physically abusive or at high risk for physical abuse show (1) a high level of negative responses to their children (DiLalla & Crittenden, 1990; Trickett & Susman, 1989), (2) a low level of positive responses to their children (Bugental, Blue, & Lewis, 1990; Kavanaugh, Youngblade, Reid, & Fagot, 1988), and (3) more inconsistent responses to their children's behaviors (Dolz, Cerezo, & Milner, 1997; Oldershaw, Walters, & Hall, 1986). Message inconsistency has typically been found to serve as a reliable indicator of deception (Burgoon, Buller, & Woodall, 1996). The combined communication pattern (inconsistency plus anger) leads to a situation in which the cues are unreliable but the stakes are high. Abused children may, then, be selectively vigilant to threat cues. As is consistent with this notion, abused children have been found to show selectively greater brain reactions (high amplitude P300 components of event-related potentials) to angry faces than to happy faces (Ekman's Pictures of Facial Affect photo set); no comparable differences have been found for nonabused children (Pollack, Cicchetti, Klorman, & Brumaghim, 1997).

Power Attributions and Communication

Children who have had negative or unreliable life experiences do not necessarily respond in the same way to those experiences. Some will respond with a loss of perceived power, whereas others may respond assertively in an exaggerated effort to maintain control. In addition, those with low perceived power may respond differentially to situations that allow relatively high or low opportunities to regain control. Such opposed response possibilities are consistent with a broad interpretation of the learned helplessness literature (Abramson, Seligman, & Teasdale, 1978). When confronted with lost control, the individual (based on the perceived possibility of regaining control) may respond either with hopelessness and abandonment of effort (Abramson, Metalsky, & Alloy, 1989) or with increased efforts to regain control (Ford & Brehm, 1987).

How, then, will children's differential power attributions influence their deception detection skills? De Paulo's observed findings with respect to sex differences in trust provides one promising lead with respect to the skills of those with low perceived power (DePaulo, 1994; Rosenthal & DePaulo, 1979). That is, girls are more likely than boys to attribute truth to others (even though they do not differ in their actual lie detection ability). In essence, girls follow a polite or accommodating strategy of accepting people's communication at face value. It is possible that the communication acceptance shown by girls reflects a power strategy rather than a specifically gender-based strategy (Henley & LaFrance, 1984).

In the emerging literature on social power, evidence is mixed with respect to the information-processing accuracy of those with high versus low perceived power. Fiske, Morling, and Stevens (1996) have suggested that those in a position of low power are relatively accurate perceivers. In contrast, those in a position of higher power have less reason than those who lack power to be concerned with accurate prediction of others and are, in fact, less accurate. At the same time, however, these findings vary on the basis of opportunities to regain control. In situations that constrain opportunities to regain control, those with low veridical or perceived power are likely to show information-processing deficits (Bugental, Brown, & Reiss, 1996; Bugental, Lin, & Susskind, 1995; Ruscher & Fiske, 1990).

These combined findings suggest the possibility that children with low perceived power are more likely than those with high perceived power to misinterpret deception cues but only in situations in which there is little opportunity to gain control. Children with low perceived power (as measured by the Picture Attribution Test) have been found to be unusually reactive to the possibility of social threat (Bugental,

Cortez, & Blue, 1992). The strategies they use in response to such threat differ, however, according to their opportunity to regain control. For example, they are avoidant with adults who might pose some source of threat; thus, they are more likely than other children to disengage visually from a videotape depicting a child's interaction with a physician during a medical examination (Cortez & Bugental, 1994). As an opposed reaction, they show high engagement and a high level of verbal aggression with potentially competitive friends (Bugental & Martorell, 1999). We suggest that children with low perceived power – in response to unfamiliar or potentially threatening adults – may follow the passive strategy of accepting their messages at face value, with resultant elevations in inaccuracy.

Decoding deficits of children with low perceived power may also be predicted on the basis of their experiences with their parents. Such children are more likely to have parents with low perceived power (Bugental & Martorell, 1999). Thus, children's interpretive style may reflect the deficits and inconsistencies shown in the communication style of parents with low perceived power (e.g., Bugental et al., 1990; Bugental et al., 1996; Bugental & Shennum, 1984).

The parents of children with low perceived power are more likely to show affective inconsistencies. In particular, they are likely to display false positivity or masking, the pattern of interest in the present study (Bugental et al., 1990; Bugental et al., 1996). That is, they are more likely to make use of smiles characteristic of those who are not experiencing enjoyment – smiles that lack the Duchenne marker (Ekman, Davidson, & Friesen, 1990; Ekman, Friesen, & O'Sullivan, 1988). Within O'Hair and Cody's (1994) taxonomy of deceptive acts, such parents can be described as using a concealment strategy in that their expressions act as a facade to disguise their true affect.

Predictions

We predicted that children with low perceived power (across abuse groupings) would be more likely to misread deception cues than would children with high perceived power. This expectation follows either from the avoidance strategies shown by such children in response to adults or from the unreliable communication history that is more common for such children. Children with high perceived power may be more skeptical regarding the truth value of adults' statements, whereas children with low perceived power may passively accept the messages of adults at face value. The skeptical strategy is more adaptive for those who actually have the possibility of gaining control or believe that this possibility exists, and the passive acceptance strategy is more adaptive for those who believe they lack the ability to gain control.

We tested rival hypotheses for the deception detection ability of abused versus nonabused children. Because abused children typically come from family backgrounds that include faulty communication processes, they may show overall deficits in their ability to detect deception. As a rival hypothesis, abused children, because of the high stakes involved in predicting others, may show higher levels of skepticism regarding the truth value of adults' statements. As a third alternative, the deception detection ability of abused children may depend on the interaction of abuse history and perceived power. That is, those with high perceived power may more accurately discriminate between truth and deception cues than do children with low perceived power.

On an exploratory basis, we also compared the effects of institutional history, the reported cues used to detect deception, and the perceived ability to detect deception on children's actual ability to detect deception.

METHOD

Research Participants

The research participants included 22 physically abused and 28 nonabused children from similar demographic backgrounds. The abused children had been removed from their homes and were currently in a residential treatment center for maltreated children. The nonabused children were recruited from a general population within a low income area (by advertisements placed on grocery store bulletin boards). The abused sample included 15 boys and 7 girls; the nonabused sample included 18 boys and 7 girls. Although the relationship between age and abuse has been found to vary, there is some evidence to suggest that boys are overrepresented in abused populations in middle childhood (e.g., Bugental, Blue, & Cruzcose, 1989). The abused sample included 14 white, non-Latino children and 8 Latino children; the nonabused sample included 10 white, non-Latino children and 8 Latino children. The average age in both groups was 9.0 years (range = 7 to 11). The average education of mothers in the abused sample was 11.5 years; the average education of mothers in the nonabused sample was 13.0 years.

Procedure

The Picture Attribution Test

The children were interviewed in a comfortable laboratory setting. They were initially interviewed to assess their attributions for the causes of family outcomes with use of the Picture Attribution Test (PIXAT, Bugental et al., 1992). The interview procedure involves presenting children with pictures that depict a problem in a family followed by pictures that depict a solution. Of the four problems shown, two depict a mother or father who is angry with a child, and two depict a mother or father spanking a child. An array of pictures that could be used in telling a story about events leading up to the problem and the solution were displayed for children's use.

The children were asked to use these pictures in telling a story about the problem and the solution. They were told to use as many or as few pictures as they wished. However, children's picture selections used in coding was limited to their first three choices. Thus, the emphasis was on children's *initial* causal inferences. As our past work has revealed significant effects only for children's attributions for problems (Bugental & Martorell, 1999; Bugental et al., 1992), analyses in the present study were limited to children's attributions for negative events. The sex of the child in the pictures was matched with the sex of the child research participant.

Perceived power was assessed by determining the proportion of pictures selected in which the child (as opposed to other people) was depicted as the primary causal agent in the story. The test–retest reliability of this measure is .71 (Cortez & Bugental, 1994). Past findings for this measure, as well as for the Parent Attribution Test (Bugental et al., 1989) have revealed better predictive power for power categories than for levels of power. Children are categorized as having low perceived power if less than 27% of their causal explanations include the child as agent. Within this sample, 40% of children were categorized as having low perceived power. The frequency of children categorized as having low perceived power did not differ significantly among abused children (45%) and nonabused children (36%).

Deception Detection

After completing the PIXAT, the children were shown a videotape that presented truthful and deceptive messages from 10 adult women (Ekman & Friesen, 1974). Each woman shown lied in one message and told the truth in another message. In contrast, Ekman and O'Sullivan (1991) used a single item rather than a paired item format; that is, separate judgments were made for each item rather than for pairs of items. A lie was shown first in half of the messages, and the truth was shown first in the other half of the messages. The order of presentation of the 10 messages was random.

Children were asked to pick the message in which they believed the woman was lying. Thus, the chance level of performance was .50. Although the judgments made can most accurately be described as reflecting the ability to discriminate between lies and truth, we will use the simpler term *deception detection* in describing the subjects' accuracy of judgment. It is important to recognize, however, that errors may occur because children fail to read either cues to deception or cues to truth accurately.

Of the 10 deceptive messages, 4 included veridical facial cues to deception, 4 included veridical vocal cues to deception, and 2 included both facial and vocal cues to deception. The task of children was to decide which message was a lie in each of the 10 pairs of messages presented to them. The messages were initially drawn from videotaped interviews in which college-aged women either lied or told the truth in response to questions concerning their reactions to a film they were watching. They were shown stimulus tapes that were either pleasant or gory and upsetting. In either case, they were instructed to report positive feelings. Their descriptions of events seen on nature films were truthful, and the descriptions of events seen on upsetting films were lies. The messages were produced by nursing students who had been told that being able to lie about their feelings was important to the success of their nursing careers, and thus they were motivated to lie well.[1]

Before watching the tape, the children were asked to report the clues they used to judge whether someone was lying. The clues reported most commonly included information from smiles, gaze, response latency, and general oddity of response. After seeing the tape, they were again asked what clues they used. Although considerable research attention has been directed to children's increased under-

---

[1] No assumption is made that child judges would equate these young women with their own parents. However, it may be assumed that children's internal working models (of their relationship with parents) influence their expectations of other adults (e.g., George & Main, 1979).

standing of deception and their increasing deception skill across the years of middle childhood (DePaulo, 1992), little is known about changes in the specific cues used to detect deception. Instead, evidence suggests that children are increasingly able to understand integrative rules across these years (e.g., Rosenberg, Simourd, & Moore, 1989).

The children were also asked (before viewing tapes) how good they thought they were at figuring out if someone was lying, and they rated their lie detection ability on a scale from 1 (very good) to 5 (very poor). After watching the tape, they were asked how well they thought they did in telling who was lying; they rated their performance on a scale from 1 (very well) to 5 (very poorly). In order to assess the consistency of children's lie detection skills, we computed the split-half reliability of responses to the 10 items within the test. The analysis yielded an r of .28 (corrected by the Spearman-Brown formula, $r = .44$). Thus, it can be seen that children's responses reflected moderately consistent patterns ($p < .01$).

RESULTS

Deception Detection Skills

Effects of Abuse History and Perceived Power
The deception detection skills of the children were compared in an analysis of variance that included children's abuse history and perceived power as grouping variables. Order of presentation (judgments of paired messages in which a lie was presented first versus paired messages in which the truth was presented first) was included as a repeated measure. Significant main effects were found for abuse, $F (1, 46) = 4.68, p < .04$, and order, $F (1, 46) = 25.03, p < .001$. In addition, a significant interaction was found between abuse and order, $F (1,46) = 7.33, p < .01$. Means (across all variables) are shown in Table 12.1.

Follow-up analyses were conducted separately for those messages in which lies were presented first and those messages in which the truth was presented first. Significant effects for abuse history were only obtained for those message pairs in which lies were presented first, $F (1, 48) = 8.93, p < .01$. Abused children were more accurate ($M = .59$) than were nonabused children ($M = .41$) when the initial message was a lie. However, no significant effects were found for abuse for those message pairs in which the initial message was truthful, $F < 1$.

Table 12.1. Children's Lie Detection Accuracy[a]

	Child Grouping	Messages in Which Lies Presented First		Messages in Which Truth Presented First	
Abuse	Perceived Power	Mean	SD	Mean	SD
Abused	High (n = 12)	.63	.25	.33	.18
	Low (n = 10)	.54	.23	.28	.17
Non abused	High (n = 18)	.44	.18	.38	.18
	Low (n = 10)	.34	.21	.24	.18

[a] Accuracy scores reflect the proportion of correctly selected lies after viewing paired messages in which the speaker tells the truth in one message and lies in the other message. Chance level of accuracy = .50.

In addition, a main effect was found for perceived power, $F (1, 46) = 4.79$, $p < .03$.[2] Children with high perceived power (relative to parents) were more accurate ($M = .45$) than were children with lower levels of perceived power ($M = .37$). A follow-up binomial test was conducted to assess the extent to which children's judgments differed significantly from chance. Children with low perceived power made *inaccurate* judgments (interpreting lies as truth or truth as lies) more frequently than would be expected by chance; that is, the frequency of their *inaccurate* judgments exceeded a chance level of .50 or less ($\chi = 5$, $p < .02$). The judgment accuracy of children with high perceived power did not differ significantly from chance levels.

Effects of Placement History
A follow-up analysis was conducted within the abused group to assess the differential effect of placement history, comparing those children whose prior history, before placement in a residential treatment facility, had included either a home placement with relatives, friends, or foster parents or an institutional placement (group home, detention facility, or psychiatric facility). This distinction between children includes an unavoidable confound between type of placement and

[2] For all comparisons, follow-up analyses were conducted in which mother education was introduced as a covariate. All effects continued to be significant, with the exception that the main effect observed for abuse on lie detection accuracy was reduced to yield an $F (1, 45) = 4.01$, $p = .05$.

possible severity of abuse history. Differences in lie detection skills were compared in an analysis of variance that included two grouping variables, placement history and perceived power.

A significant main effect was found for placement history, F (1, 18) = 6.91, $p < .02$. Children placed in out-of-home care were more accurate ($M = .54$) than were children placed in home care ($M = .41$). A binomial test of the extent to which the higher levels of accuracy shown by children in out-of-home care differed from chance did not reach significance. A binomial test of the extent to which the greater *inaccuracy* shown by children within home placements differed from chance approached significance ($p < .06$). Effects obtained for perceived power and order paralleled those reported above (as a trend). That is, children with higher perceived power were more accurate than children with low perceived power, F (1, 18) = 3.68, $p < .07$; in addition, higher "accuracy" was shown when initial messages were lies than when initial messages were honest, F (1, 18) = 17.01, $p < .001$.

Deception Detection and Demographic Variables

A correlation between age and deception detection accuracy was not significant ($r = .06$). Comparison of the deception detection skills of boys versus girls did not yield significant effects, $t(49) = .05$. In addition, no differences were found between white (Anglo) and Latino children in ability to detect deception, $t(49) = .18$.

Deception Detection Cues and Deception Detection Skills Reported by Children

Additional analyses were conducted to assess children's reported use of cues in detecting deception and their self-perceived skill in ability to detect deception. Chi-square analyses were used to assess the reported frequency of use of different cues (smile type, latency of response, oddness of expression, and gaze behavior) by different child groupings. Significant effects were found only for differences between abused and nonabused groups in their reported reliance on speakers' gaze behavior; chi-square = 10.90, $p < .01$. Of abused children, 46% reported using this cue in making judgments, but only 4% of nonabused children did so.

A test of children's self-reported ability to detect lies was made within a multivariate analysis of variance, which included children's abuse history and perceived power as grouping variables and three types of self-perceived accuracy (perceived ability to lie well in general, expected accuracy before seeing videos, and perceived accuracy after seeing videos). No significant effects or trends were found. An additional analysis was conducted to assess the correlation between children's self-perceived accuracy, the cues in detecting lies, and children's actual accuracy. No significant relationships or trends were found here either.

DISCUSSION

Children were found to differ in their susceptibility to adult deception on the basis of their perceived power, their abuse history, and their placement history. Children with low perceived power showed a generalized pattern of misinterpretation or misattribution of deception (or truth) cues. That is, they typically accepted adult messages at face value. Abused children revealed a pattern suggesting that they expected adult messages to be deceptive. When such children had experienced out-of-home care, however, they also showed a relatively high level of accuracy in their judgments.

Effects of Perceived Power

As predicted, children with low perceived power were found to be particularly susceptible to seeing lies as truth and truth as lies. The paradigm used (choosing between a dishonest and an honest message) does not allow secure inferences regarding their misreading of lies and truth. That is, inaccuracy can follow either from failing to read cues to deception or from failing to read cues to honesty. However, it is reasonable to anticipate that inaccuracies were more likely to reflect the acceptance of false cues to positive affect. That is, it is more likely that they interpreted false positivity as an indication of the speaker's enjoyment than they were to misread honest cues to the speaker's enjoyment. Past research has shown that children more easily understand and make use of false positivity (disguising a negative feeling with a positive display) than false negative messages (disguising a positive feeling with a negative or neutral display) (Shennum & Bugental, 1982). However, it will be important to replicate the findings obtained here with further research that distinguishes between children's use of cues to deception and cues to truth.

So why did powerless children misread cues to deception and honesty? As one possibility, the message style of speakers may have been similar to the message style of their own parents. As noted earlier, powerless children tend to have powerless parents. Parents with low perceived power present a dizzying combination of conflicting affective cues in their communication style. Such children may fail to acquire adequate attribution skills because they are not exposed to sufficient regularities in parents' communication of power and affect.

As a second possibility, the passive acceptance of adults' self-presentations by powerless children may reflect an adaptive coping skill. Just as females were found by DePaulo (1994) to show an accommodating decoding style (by accepting the messages of others at face value), powerless children may accommodate by accepting deceptive displays of positivity as though they were true. Children who believe they lack power vis-à-vis adults have no perceived means of making use of deception information and thus may passively accept lies. In short, if one is helpless in the face of deception, there is no advantage to estimating the truth value of adult messages.

Effects of Abuse History

Differences shown by children from abusive backgrounds reveal a second and very different response to possible deception. Abused children regularly believed that the first message they heard (regardless of its actual truth value) was a lie. Thus, the apparent advantage shown by such children in detecting deception was limited to initial lies; no comparable advantage was found when they were confronted with an initial truth (and a subsequent lie). It appears that abused children make use of a judgment heuristic ("Expect a lie") that yields an accurate judgment only when initial messages are indeed deceptive; or as described in the communication literature, they have a "lie bias" (O'Hair & Cody, 1994). As noted by Burgoon et al. (1996), a suspicious stance may act to overcome the truth bias that is more typically employed.

Even though the apparent advantage of hearing a lie first only reached significance for abused children, all groups showed greater accuracy for initial messages than for second messages. This pattern is exactly opposite to that found for adults (O'Sullivan, Ekman, & Friesen, 1988). Adults were found to be more accurate when the initial message was truthful. This bias was interpreted as reflecting their use of a judgment heuristic to assume honesty. That is, most people are exposed to a higher frequency of honest than dishonest behavior;

thus, thoughts of honesty are more available to them. Further research is needed to determine if indeed there are developmental changes in the judgment heuristics used to interpret the honesty of emotional messages.

Abused children, as a result of their early experiences, may reveal a precocious vigilance for the possibility of deception, a fail-safe strategy that is useful when potential risks are high. This expectation is consistent with the contention that there is a higher level of utility and accuracy in detecting high-stake than low-stake deceptions (Ekman et al., 1988; Ekman & O'Sullivan, 1991; Frank & Ekman, 1997). Supporting this interpretation, abused children were found here to be more likely than nonabused children to show wariness in their response to the messages presented to them. Half of them reported attending to facial features (in particular, gaze) as a way of detecting lies; in contrast, no such facial vigilance was shown by nonabused children. In view of the relatively low utility of visual cues in detecting deception (e.g., Buller & Burgoon, 1994), it does not appear that their response to these cues facilitates accuracy. That is, exaggerated facial monitoring may reflect their skeptical or suspicious view of adult messages rather than a veridical means of detecting deception. In contrast, nonabused children need have little concern about the possibility or consequences of deception. The potential risk and associated costs are very low.

Findings obtained here are not directly comparable with the observations made of abused and nonabused children by Camras and her colleagues (1988, 1990). These investigators found that abused children were less accurate in distinguishing posed emotions and in their ability to detect masked emotions, that is, posed expressions revealing smiles accompanied by facial actions depicting negative affect. No comparable deficits were found in this study.

There are rival explanations for the differences in findings. On the one hand, it may be that the differences reflect the use of posed versus spontaneous emotions. As another possibility, abused children's reduced susceptibility to deception in this study may reflect their history within institutional settings rather than their history of abuse. Abused children who had experienced out-of-home care showed less susceptibility to deception than did abused children in home care. Among those few children who combined an extreme life history (abuse in the home, removal from the home, and placement in an institutional setting) with high perceived power, the levels of accuracy shown approximated those demonstrated by secret service agents in Ekman and O'Sullivan's (1991) research (i.e., their mean accuracy was 63%).

Although the number of such cases was too small to allow any secure statistical inferences to be drawn, this finding suggests the value of exploring the possibility that some children may develop exceptional lie detection skills when there is a profound need to do so. That is, this grouping has both the motivation and the perceived power to challenge the veracity of adult messages. On the other hand, of course, it may be that exceptional lie detection skills are indicative of individual differences that preceded abuse and institutionalization. In future research, it will be important to follow up on the observed findings for children who experienced out-of-home care.

Other Effects

As in previous research on lie detection (DePaulo, Charlton, Cooper, Lindsay, & Muhlenbruck, 1997; DePaulo & Pfeifer, 1986; Ekman & O'Sullivan, 1991; Kohnken, 1987), we found that observers were poor predictors of their own lie detection skills. In addition, children's reported use of specific cues did not serve to predict their actual lie detection accuracy. Thus, the processes of interest do not seem to be known to observers themselves.

No gender or ethnicity (Anglo versus Latino) differences were found in lie detection skills. Absence of gender effects in lie detection accuracy confirms earlier findings (e.g., Ekman & O'Sullivan, 1991; Rosenthal & DePaulo, 1979). The similarity of findings across ethnic groups counters results obtained across cultural groups (Bond, Omar, Mahmoud, & Bonser, 1990). However, these cross-cultural studies did not use high-stake lies and thus may not have elicited emotions on the part of liars, the presence of which can betray deception across cultures (Ekman, 1985; Frank & Ekman, 1997).

CONCLUSION

In conclusion, it appears that vulnerability to deception may reflect different processes. On the one hand, children who lack social power appear to accept messages from adults at face value, whereas children who have higher levels of perceived power are more questioning. As a different process, abused children appear to be on alert for the possibility of deception. On a whole, however, this wariness does not lead to increases in their ability to make accurate attributions for deception. However, there were suggestive indications that children who have been exposed to a series of extreme life circumstances but retain a feeling of social power show higher levels of deception detection accuracy. Most importantly, children have stable differences in their vigilance for deception and the ways in which they respond to potential cues to deception. As a result, it will be useful to give more systematic attention to the bases and the functions of these differences.

REFERENCES

Abramson, L. Y., Metalsky, G. I., & Alloy, L. B. (1989). Hopelessness depression: A theory-based subtype of depression. *Psychological Review, 96,* 358–372.

Abramson, L. Y., Seligman, M. E., & Teasdale, J. D. (1978). Learned helplessness in humans: Critique and reformulation. *Journal of Abnormal Psychology, 87,* 49–74.

Bond, C. F., Jr., Omar, F. A., Mahmoud, A., & Bonser, R. N. (1990). Lie detection across cultures. *Journal of Nonverbal Behavior, 14,* 189–204.

Bugental, D. B., Blue, J., & Cruzcosa, M. (1989). Perceived control over caregiving outcomes: Implications for child abuse. *Developmental Psychology, 25,* 532–539.

Bugental, D. B., Blue, J., & Lewis, J. (1990). Caregiver cognitions as moderators of affective reactions to "difficult" children. *Developmental Psychology, 26,* 631–638.

Bugental, D. B., Brown, M., & Reiss, C. (1996). Cognitive representations of power in caregiving relationships: Biasing effects on interpersonal interaction and information-processing. *Journal of Family Psychology, 10,* 397–407.

Bugental, D. B., Cortez, V., & Blue, J. (1992). Children's affective responses to the expressive cues of others. In N. Eisenberg & R. Fabes (Eds.), *New directions in child development* (pp. 75–90). San Francisco: Josey-Bass.

Bugental, D. B., Lin, E. K., & Susskind, J. E. (1995). Influences of affect on cognitive processes at different ages: Why the change? In N. Eisenberg (Ed.), *Social development review of personality and social psychology* (Vol. 15, pp. 159–184). Thousand Oaks: Sage.

Bugental, D. B., & Martorell, G. (1999). Competition between friends: The joint influence of the perceived power of self, friends, and parents. *Journal of Family Psychology, 13,* 1–14.

Bugental, D. B., & Shennum, W. A. (1984). "Difficult" children as elicitors and targets of adult communication patterns: An attributional-behavioral-transactional analysis. *Monographs of the Society for Research in Child Development, 49* (1, Serial No. 205).

Buller, D. B., & Burgoon, J. K. (1994). Deception: Strategic and non-strategic behavior. In J. Daly & J. Wiemann (Eds.), *Strategic interpersonal communication* (pp. 191–224). Hillsdale, NJ: Erlbaum.

Burgoon, J. K., Buller, D. B., & Woodall, W. G. (1996). *Nonverbal communication: The unspoken dialogue.* New York: McGraw-Hill.

Camras, L. A., Ribordy, S., Hill, J., Martino, S., Sachs, V., Spaccarelli, S., & Stefani, R. (1990). Maternal facial behavior and the recognition and production of emotional expression by maltreated and non-maltreated children. *Developmental Psychology, 26*, 304–312.

Camras, L. A., Ribordy, S., Hill, J., Martino, S., Spaccarelli, S., & Stefani, R. (1988). Recognition and posing of emotional expressions by abused children and their mothers. *Developmental Psychology, 24*, 776–781.

Cortez, V., & Bugental, D. B. (1994). Children's visual avoidance of threat: A strategy associated with low social control, *Merrill-Palmer Quarterly (special issue on Emotion Regulation), 40*, 82–97.

DePaulo, B. M. (1992). Nonverbal behavior and self-presentation. *Psychological Bulletin, 111*, 203–243.

DePaulo, B. M. (1994). Spotting lies: Can humans learn to do better? *Current Directions in Psychological Science, 3*, 83–86.

DePaulo, B. M., Charlton, K., Cooper, H., Lindsay, J. J., & Muhlenbrook, L. (1997). The accuracy-confidence correlation in the detection of deception. *Personality and Social Psychology Review, 1*, 346–357.

DePaulo, B. M., Kashy, D. A., Kirkendol, S. E., Wyer, M. M., & Epstein, J. A. (1996). Lying in everyday life. *Journal of Personality and Social Psychology, 70*, 979–995.

DePaulo, B. M., & Pfeifer, R. L. (1986). Deceiving and detecting deceit. In B. R. Schlenker (Ed.), *The self and social life* (pp. 323–370). New York: McGraw-Hill.

DePaulo, B. M., Stone, J. I., & Lassiter, G. D. (1985). Deceiving and detecting deceit. In B. R. Schlenker (Ed.), *The self and social life* (pp. 323–370). New York: McGraw-Hill.

DiLalla, D. L., & Crittenden, P. M. (1990). Dimensions of maltreated children's home behavior: A factor analytic approach. *Infant Behavior and Development, 13*, 439–460.

Dolz, L., Cerezo, M. A., & Milner, J. S. (1997). Mother-child interactional patterns in high- and low-risk mothers. *Child Abuse and Neglect, 21*, 1149–1158.

Ekman, P. (1985). *Telling lies: Clues to deceit in the marketplace, politics, and marriage.* New York: Norton.

Ekman, P., Davidson, R. J., & Friesen, W. V. (1990). The Duchenne smile: Emotional expression and brain physiology. *Journal of Personality and Social Psychology, 58*, 342–353.

Ekman, P., & Friesen, W. V. (1974). Detecting deception from body or face. *Journal of Personality and Social Psychology, 29*, 288–298.

Ekman, P., Friesen, W. V., & O'Sullivan, M. (1988). Smiles while lying. *Journal of Personality and Social Psychology, 54*, 414–420.

Ekman, P., & O'Sullivan, M. (1991). Who can catch a liar? *American Psychologist, 46*, 913–920.

Ekman, P., O'Sullivan, M., & Frank, M. G. (1999). A few can catch a liar. *Psychological Science, 10*, 263–266.

Fiske, S. T., Morling, B., & Stevens, L. E. (1996). Controlling self and others: A theory of anxiety, mental control, and social control. *Personality and Social Psychology Bulletin, 22*, 115–123.

Ford, C. E., & Brehm, J. W. (1987). Effort expenditure following failure. In C. R. Snyder & C. E. Ford (Eds.), *Coping with negative life events: Clinical and social psychological perspective*. New York: Plenum Press.

Frank, M. G., & Ekman, P. (1997). The ability to detect deceit generalizes across different types of high-stake lies. *Journal of Personality and Social Psychology, 72*, 1429–1439.

George, C., & Main, M. (1979). Social interactions of young abused children: Approach, avoidance, and aggression. *Child Development, 50*, 306–318.

Henley, N. M., & LaFrance, M. (1984). Gender as culture: Difference and dominance in nonverbal behavior. In A. Wolfgang (Ed.), *Nonverbal behavior: Perspectives, applications, intercultural insights* (pp. 351–371). Lewiston, NY: Hogrefe & Huber Publishers.

Kavanaugh, K. A., Youngblade, L., Reid, J. B., & Fagot, B. I. (1988). Interactions between children and abusive versus control parents. *Journal of Clinical Child Psychology, 17*, 137–142.

Kohnken, G. (1987). Training police officers to detect deceptive eyewitness statements: Doe it work? *Social Behavior, 2*, 1–17.

Kraut, R. E., & Poe, D. (1980). Behavioral roots of person perception: The deception judgments of customs inspectors and laymen. *Journal of Personality and Social Psychology, 39*, 181–213.

O'Hair, H. D., & Cody, M. J. (1994). Deception. In W. R. Cupach & B. H. Spitzberg (Eds.), *The dark side of communication* (pp. 181–213). Hillsdale, NJ: Erlbaum.

Oldershaw, L., Walters, G. C., & Hall, D. K. (1986). Control strategies and noncompliance in abusive mother-child dyads: An observational study. *Child Development, 57*, 722–732.

O'Sullivan, M., Ekman, P., & Friesen, W. V. (1988). The effect of comparisons on detecting deceit. *Journal of Nonverbal Behavior, 12*, 203–215.

Pollack, S. F., Cicchetti, D., Klorman, R., & Brumaghim, J. T. (1997). Cognitive brain event-related potentials and emotion processing in maltreated children. *Child Development, 68*, 773–787.

Rosenthal, R., & DePaulo, B. M. (1979). Sex differences in eavesdropping on deceit. *Journal of Personality and Social Psychology, 37*, 273–285.

Rotenberg, K. J., Simourd, L., & Moore, D. (1989). Children's use of a verbal-nonverbal consistency principle to infer truth and lying. *Child Development, 60*, 309–322.

Ruscher, J. B., & Fiske, S. T. (1990). Interpersonal competition can cause individuating processes. *Journal of Personality and Social Psychology, 58*, 832–843.

Shennum, W. A., & Bugental, D. B. (1982). The development of control over affective expression in nonverbal behavior. In R. S. Feldman (Ed.), *The development of nonverbal behavior in children* (pp. 101–118). New York: Springer-Verlag.

Trickett, P. K., & Susman, E. J. (1988). Parental perception of child-rearing practices in physically abusive and nonabusive families. *Developmental Psychology, 24*, 270–276.

Zuckerman, M., DePaulo, B. M., & Rosenthal, R. (1981). Verbal and nonverbal communication of deception. In L. Berkowitz (Ed.), *Advances in experimental social psychology* (Vol. 14, pp. 1–59). New York: Academic Press.

CHAPTER THIRTEEN

HIV-Infected Persons' Attributions for the Disclosure and Nondisclosure of the Seropositive Diagnosis to Significant Others

Valerian J. Derlega and Barbara A. Winstead

The discovery of being infected with the human immunodeficiency virus (HIV) can be a highly stressful and even traumatic experience (Chidwick & Borrill, 1996; Kalichman, 1995; Siegel & Krauss, 1991). Persons who are HIV-infected must cope with a life-threatening disease that has as no known cure. Besides the stress of living with the illness, however, there are social consequences that HIV-infected persons also confront, including changing potentially risky sexual and drug use behaviors, informing previous sexual and drug-using partners about the need for testing, and obtaining emotional and physical support, as well as gauging the reactions of friends and family to news about the diagnosis. How someone deals with the social consequences of HIV depends in part on the decisions that are made about whom to tell about the HIV diagnosis and when and how to tell them.

A review of literature on self-disclosure and coping with HIV (e.g., Derlega & Winstead, 1999; Holt et al., 1998; Wolitski, Rietmeijer, Goldbaum, & Wilson, 1998) indicates considerable variability in who is told about the HIV-positive diagnosis. Men and women who are HIV-positive are likely to disclose their HIV status to sexual partners (Hays

The authors wish to express appreciation to the research participants who provided the material for the interviews and questionnaire research described in this chapter. Thanks are also extended to the HIV–AIDS service organizations and research groups who assisted in the data collection. In particular, we owe a debt of gratitude to the administrative staff and clients at the Tidewater AIDS Crisis Taskforce (TACT) in Norfolk, Virginia, the Peninsula AIDS Foundation (PAF) in Newport News, Virginia, and the Fan Free Clinic in Richmond, Virginia, for their support. We also extend our thanks to Kathryn Greene, William Elwood, and Julianne Serovich for their assistance with the data collection in the questionnaire research. Please address all correspondence to Valerian Derlega, Department of Psychology, Old Dominion University, Norfolk, Virginia, 23529-0267.

et al., 1993; Simoni et al., 1995), but they are more likely to inform a sexual partner with whom they are in a primary or committed relationship than someone to whom they do not feel very close (Norman, Kennedy, & Parish, 1998; Stempel, Moulton, & Moss, 1995). Under certain circumstances, HIV-seropositive persons may fail to disclose the diagnosis to a primary partner (including a spouse or committed partner), particularly if they feel ashamed, embarrassed, or threatened by physical assault (Lie & Biswalo, 1996; Mason, Marks, Simoni, Ruiz, & Richardson, 1995; Rothenberg & Pakey, 1995).

Friends and family members may be selected as disclosure targets by HIV-seropositive persons. However, there is variability in who is told about the diagnosis. For instance, Hays et al. (1993) reported that homosexual HIV-seropositive men were more likely to disclose their seropositivity to a close homosexual than to a close heterosexual friend, and they are more likely to disclose it to a sister or mother than to a father. Research among homosexual and bisexual men also finds that disclosure of HIV infection to parents and close friends is more likely if the mother, father, close male friend, or close female friend knows about their sexual orientation. Also, HIV-seropositive persons are more likely to disclose the diagnosis to family and friends when they have severe physical symptoms associated with HIV and the acquired immunodeficiency syndrome (AIDS) (Hays et al., 1993; Marks et al., 1992; Mason et al., 1995).

In this chapter we present a review of the attributions or reasons why HIV-infected persons disclose or do not disclose their HIV-seropositive status to significant others. Our research is consistent with considerable research and theory in social psychology and communication, confirming that attributions for self-disclosure and communication acts are related to social behavior and perceptions about the quality of one's close relationships (Derlega, Metts, Petronio, & Margulis, 1993; Derlega, Winstead, Wong, & Greenspan, 1987; Harvey & Omarzu, 1997; Taylor, Gould, & Brounstein, 1981).

ATTRIBUTIONS FOR DISCLOSURE OR NONDISCLOSURE OF HIV TEST RESULTS: A CONCEPTUALIZATION AND PERSONAL ACCOUNTS

Our primary goal in this chapter was to discern personal descriptions of attributions for disclosing and for not disclosing. These were derived from two sets of interviews with individuals living with the HIV infection, who were recruited from several HIV–AIDS service organizations in Virginia. A total of 42 men and women participated in the first set of interviews (Derlega & Barbee, 1994; Derlega, Lovejoy, & Winstead, 1998); these first interviews were used for the initial development of our coding scheme of attributions for and against self-disclosure (see Derlega et al., 1998). The participants in the second set of interviews were 25 women (Derlega & Barbee, 1998). The average age of participants in both sets of interviews was in the mid-thirties, and the individuals in both sets of interviews had been living with HIV for various lengths of time. However, in the first interview set, men and women were asked about their attributions or reasons for self-disclosure or nondisclosure about the HIV diagnosis to anyone for the time when they first learned about the diagnosis. In the second interview set, women were asked about their attributions for self-disclosure or nondisclosure about the HIV diagnosis to significant others in their relationships network (e.g., friends, family members, their children, other relatives, intimate partners) for any time after learning about the diagnosis.

A content analysis of the open-ended interviews conducted with men and women living with the HIV infection as well as a review of the HIV self-disclosure literature (Derlega & Winstead, 1999) helped us create a list of attributions for and against disclosing the HIV diagnosis. The attributions emphasize, for the most part, an awareness of the goals, purposes, functions, or possible consequences of disclosure versus nondisclosure for oneself, the other person, or the relationship between the HIV-seropositive person and the other. One attribution, difficulty in communicating as a reason for nondisclosure, on the other hand, is a self-perception of awkwardness or inability to talk with someone about the diagnosis as opposed to a goal or function of nondisclosure.

The attributions for disclosure reflect a self-focus (catharsis, seeking help), an other-focus (duty to inform the other, desire to educate), and an interpersonal focus (testing the other's reactions to the seropositive person, an emotionally close and supportive relationship, similarity with the other person). The attributions for nondisclosure also reflect a self-focus (right to privacy, self-blame or self-concept concerns, fear of rejection or being misunderstood), an other-focus (protect the other person), and an interpersonal focus (superficial relationship). Difficulty in communicating with the other is harder to pin down in terms of the self, other, and interpersonal focus categories. We will present descriptions from our initial interviews with HIV-seropositive persons (Derlega & Barbee, 1994), as well as from more recent interviews (Derlega & Barbee, 1998) to illustrate these attributions for disclosure and nondisclosure.

ATTRIBUTIONS FOR SELF-DISCLOSURE OF HIV TEST RESULTS

Catharsis or Self-Expression

Self-expression or catharsis as an attribution for disclosure emphasizes the opportunity to release or express pent-up feelings. Individuals who experience the trauma of finding out that they have the HIV infection may have strong feelings that they need to share with another. For instance, a male respondent who told his cousin about the diagnosis gave this explanation: "The benefit I would get [from disclosure] would be not having to carry that information around." Another respondent told us that she had not told friends or family about the diagnosis because of a concern about gossip. However, she was nevertheless upset about the diagnosis and decided to tell her supervisor at work: "Well, at first, I was very distraught and I was still in a degree of shock, and it became so overwhelming that I had to share it [the information] with someone."

Seeking Help

Persons who are HIV-seropositive may attribute the decision to disclose to a tangible need for help. For instance, they may have a need for medical advice, transportation, or financial help. This attribution may be mentioned as a reason for disclosing the diagnosis to health workers (Derlega et al., 1998), but seeking help may also be cited as a reason for disclosing it to significant others. For instance, a respondent described informing a friend about the diagnosis "Because she was in the health field and I figured she would be knowledgeable. I thought she could be of help." Another person told his grandmother about the diagnosis, because "I needed a place to stay."

Duty to Inform

Seropositive persons may disclose out of a sense of duty, which may take one of several forms. Individuals may tell someone out of a sense of loyalty, which we found to be cited frequently as an attribution for disclosing to parents and other family members. One person said he disclosed to his parents because "I felt I'm their son, they have the right to know." Another person told his brother because, "He was my only brother. I had to tell him. I felt like I had to at the time." Another facet of the duty to inform as a reason for disclosure derives from a desire to have an honest relationship with another person. For instance, someone mentioned disclosing to his or her lover "to be honest." Another told a girlfriend about the diagnosis "because I thought it was the right thing to do." Some individuals focus on the duty to tell to help prepare another person for what might happen in the future ("I felt he [my father] had to know exactly what my health was in case I got really bad.") or to protect the other from gossip about the disease: "If I didn't tell him [her son] and he found out about it from somebody else, then I was afraid that it might cause some damage in our relationship." Still others may tell family or friends in order to anticipate the needs of their children who might need child care at some point. A woman told her older son, "Because I wanted him to oversee his brother and sister when the time comes [in case the mother became disabled or died from AIDS]."

The duty to inform also appears in the context of health concerns in starting or maintaining a sexual relationship with an intimate partner. Individuals explained disclosure to intimate partners typically in the following terms: "When he wanted to have sex, I had to tell him then," or "I was worried about him catching HIV. It's [for] his safety." Health concerns may also influence disclosure in other social contexts. For instance, some individuals mentioned informing their employers about HIV if they were in a job that required food preparation. Individuals who earned money from babysitting or from taking care of physically disabled persons felt an obligation to tell their employers about being HIV-infected. On the other hand, some individuals believed the right to privacy was greater than the duty to inform (see section on "Privacy") and did not tell their employer.

Desire to Educate

Seropositive persons may disclose to others in order to educate them about who becomes infected and how. The desire to educate others about HIV and AIDS is frequently mentioned as an attribution for disclosure about the diagnosis in relation to talks to community groups. For instance, someone who spoke often to community groups gave this attribution for public disclosure of the HIV diagnosis: "When I am speaking at a seminar, they can hear my experience and what I went through. And, maybe, it will motivate them to go and either have tests or, if they are sexually active with numerous partners, maybe they will realize the danger of what they are doing. Maybe it will stop their high-risk behaviors."

Education may also occur with relatives, friends, or an intimate partner. A person mentioned how she informed her brother's girlfriend about the HIV infection to encourage her to practice safer sex. "I knew she needed some guidance and I wanted to just let her know [about my being HIV positive]. 'I want you to know something. I would not tell you if I didn't feel that I could tell you, and I'm telling you in the hope, not because I want you to feel sorry for me or anything like that, but I want you to see that if it can happen to me, it can happen to you. And I am trusting you to take this information and really listen to what I'm saying and not share it with anybody. This is a really tough thing for me.' So I would tell her and hope that she'd get her life together."

Desire to Test Other's Reactions

Seropositive persons may disclose the diagnosis to test the other's reactions about whether or not to begin or to continue to have a close relationship. The disclosure may serve as a "relationship test" to assess how the other person feels about being in a relationship with someone with HIV. A woman told us of meeting a man to whom she felt attracted. She wasn't sure if he could understand or deal with the fact that she had HIV. She arranged to tell this person by writing him a letter informing him about her HIV diagnosis. She described what she wrote in the letter as follows: "In the letter I told him that if he did not want to call more or talk to me again, I would truly understand. Because some people just cannot deal with it, period. ... Just being positive doesn't mean that you don't have the same desires, the attractions, the needs, whatever. All that's still there, but I felt you have the right to know. You can make a decision, a choice from this." In this case, the man called and thanked her for the letter, expressed his sympathy, and then never called again.

Emotionally Close and Supportive Relationship

This attribution is based on perceptions of trust, love, and affection for the other person, as well as the belief that the other person can provide emotional support. For instance, a male respondent told a friend because, "We were close. We had been close for years. We weren't lovers. We were like brothers, but we lived together. ... He was the very best friend I ever had." One person gave the following attribution for disclosure to relatives based on the importance of a close relationship with them: "I clearly decided that the only time I need to tell someone [about the diagnosis] is when I feel very close to them and I want them to know about all of the important issues in my life. And you have cousins, you have distant cousins, that you only see once a year or whatever. I don't have the desire to tell them. They don't need to know. ... I do have one aunt, she's my uncle's wife. She's so sweet. She's always giving. She just loves to play host. I just feel really good around her. So I told her one day and she was sorry to hear it, but that was that."

Similar Background or Experiences

People who are HIV-seropositive may decide to disclose this fact to someone because they share a common background with that person or they have had similar experiences. For instances, some HIV-infected persons explained that it is easier to talk to someone who has had the same health problems. Illustrations of this attribution for disclosure include "Because he was dying of AIDS, he was in the same boat [as me]"; "We met at the clinic. We were both there and he felt like he could share with me and I could share with him. We discussed our medical problems." Individuals sometimes mentioned that they disclosed to someone who might have a relative with non-HIV health problems that were of a serious nature. A woman noted how she told someone at her church about being HIV-seropositive when the woman said her son had cancer and that he was dying. "I was able to have a one-on-one [talk] with her, to explain to her that there was a lot of suffering going on, that I also had an illness."

ATTRIBUTIONS FOR NONDISCLOSURE OF HIV TEST RESULTS

Individuals make decisions about whom to tell about the diagnosis, but they also make decisions about whom not to tell. These attributions for nondisclosure of the HIV diagnosis include privacy, self-blame or self-concept concerns, fear of rejection or being misunderstood, protecting others, superficial relationship, and communication difficulties.

Privacy

Individuals who decide not to tell someone about the diagnosis may attribute their decision to a personal right to privacy. For instance, HIV-infected, as compared with HIV-noninfected, persons express a greater desire to restrict access to HIV test results from immediate family (e.g., spouse, lover, parent, or child) or nonfamily (e.g., a coworker) (Greene & Serovich, 1996). The assertion of a right to privacy may derive from a claim to ownership over the information about the self. For instance, a woman explained that she did not tell anyone at her church about being HIV-seropositive "because I didn't want anybody to know my business." Another aspect of the right to privacy derives from concern about the spread of the information about being HIV positive to "unwanted" other persons. Some individuals may not tell particular family members or even friends about the diagnosis because of a concern that "this person" might leak the information or gossip to others. For instance, someone didn't tell a friend because "[I] worried that she would tell other people." Another person didn't tell siblings "because once they find out, they will call all over and tell all my family."

Self-Blame or Self-Concept Difficulties

Some HIV-seropositive persons may feel morally tainted or personally stigmatized by the diagnosis. They may conceal the information, because they feel ashamed or personally at fault for having contracted HIV. A woman we interviewed had delayed telling her son's father about being HIV-positive. She said, "As far as the chain of people who I told, he was the last person I told. It was a little bit to do with guilt, feeling like a failure."

Communication Difficulties

One aspect of difficulty in communicating reflects a lack of confidence or low self-efficacy about talking with a particular person about the HIV-positive diagnosis. Typical explanations included, "I just didn't know how to tell him, so I just hid from him most of the time and avoided him." "I just can't [tell him – a son referring to his father]. Every time I want to tell him I just can't."

A second aspect of difficulty in communicating may reflect denial or an inability to face the future after learning about the HIV infection. Finding out about the diagnosis may be so traumatic that the HIV-infected person is not ready to talk about the diagnosis with anyone. For instance, a woman with HIV who didn't tell anyone initially about the diagnosis explained her decision in the following way: "I think first I had to deal with it myself so I went through a time period of fear of telling anyone." Another woman we interviewed said, "It took [me] two years to tell anybody. I didn't even go to the doctor. I was in denial. I was using drugs and my use had progressed a lot. A couple of years later it finally hit me that it was true that I had it, so I admitted myself into a drug treatment program. When I was there I told my mother. That was the first person I told."

Fear of Rejection or Being Misunderstood

Concerns about being misunderstood, discriminated against, ridiculed, or rejected are frequently cited as an attribution for not disclosing the HIV diagnosis (Derlega et al., 1998). Illustrative statements of this reason for nondisclosure include "They [uncles and aunts] are an old-fashioned country family who are set in their ways. It is better that they don't know because they are the type that I know would turn their back on me instead of be there for me"; "Because they [family] would reject me"; "For the fear of repercussions [from sexual partners] of being hurt, killed, or friendless"; and "She [a sister] would treat me like a plague. She would not understand."

Persons who are HIV-infected may be concerned not only about being misunderstood or rejected because of their HIV status – the fear of rejection may be associated with concerns that people would reject them for practicing a socially unacceptable life style by being homosexual or using illegal drugs. For instance, a homosexual man did not disclose his HIV-seropositive status to his aunt and her family because "They don't believe that people should be gay. I felt that they would be very judgmental and not understand." Some people are also afraid of being physically abused and harmed (Rothenberg & Pakey, 1995). A woman mentioned her "fear of getting physically hurt. I mean physically. I know some people that if they tell a guy, the guy might beat them up. I know a girl that told a guy and he beat her up badly. That [is] what happens when you get in a relationship and don't tell them first."

Protect the Other Person

The need to protect someone is often given as an attribution for a possible, new intimate partner because "It is not right to jump right in and scare them to death." Another person didn't tell an aunt "to keep her from being more hurt." A parent didn't tell her son so he wouldn't worry about her: "I didn't want him to give up things he had going on in his life." Another person didn't tell family members because "I did not want them to worry about me." The desire to protect others as an attribution for nondisclosure may originate with the HIV-infected person, but it may also originate from others in one's social network. Several individuals whom we interviewed explained that the wish to protect someone, as a reason for not disclosing, began with the request of a relative or friend. For instance, a mother was asked by the father of her adolescent son to keep the diagnosis from their son. She said, "His daddy didn't want me to tell him that I was positive. He felt like he [the son] couldn't handle it. So I gave his father one year. If he doesn't tell him, then I'm going to tell him."

Superficial Relationship

Some individuals attribute the decision not to disclose their HIV-positive status to the fact that they don't feel close to a particular person or that there is a superficial relationship. For instance, a person told no one at work about the HIV diagnosis because he didn't feel close to anyone: "If it's just people you work with and you don't see them after you leave and you don't see them before you get there, then maybe they don't need to know your personal business, no matter what it is." Another person didn't tell his father "Because we have never had a relationship, so I didn't see any reason to tell him."

Section Summary

In this first section we have reviewed the types of attributions that are given for the decision to disclose or not disclose to other persons about the HIV-seropositive diagnosis. This information helps to understand individuals' motivations for why they did or did not tell someone. But, as many of the anecdotes illustrated, the endorsement of various attributions may be affected by the nature of the relationship with significant others. We examine this issue in the following section.

ENDORSEMENT OF ATTRIBUTIONS FOR DISCLOSURE AND NONDISCLOSURE ABOUT HIV TO SPECIFIC PERSONS

Along with identifying, on the basis of interviews, categories of attributions for disclosing and not disclosing the HIV-positive diagnosis, we examined more recently, via paper-and-pencil questionnaire research, the degree to which individuals endorse various attributional categories in deciding whether or not to inform significant others about the diagnosis. Scales were constructed to measure the influence of several factors on the decision to disclose or not disclose HIV seropositivity to particular persons. These scales (available from Valerian J. Derlega) were used to examine what attributions may have motivated disclosure or nondisclosure to a parent, friend, and an intimate partner among HIV-infected persons. (An earlier, longer version of these scales, constructed to examine attributions for self-disclosure or nondisclosure about the HIV-positive diagnosis to an intimate partner, appears in Derlega, Winstead, & Folk-Barron, in press.) We expected differences in reasons given for informing or not informing particular persons about the HIV diagnosis to be based on the nature of the relationship.

The research participants for the data analyses to be reported from this study consisted of 80 men and 26 women with the HIV infection who were recruited from several HIV–AIDS service organizations and from two sites with ongoing research on psychosocial issues in coping with HIV. The men and women who participated were, on average, in their mid-thirties. The men in this data set identified themselves as either homosexual or bisexual. The women identified themselves as heterosexual. The data analyses to be reported are presented separately for the two samples. (In the data collection for the questionnaire study, there were some men who identified themselves as heterosexual and some women who identified themselves as lesbian or bisexual. Some other men and women did not identify themselves according to sexual orientation. The numbers of these groups were too small to permit analysis, however.)

In presenting the questionnaire, we asked the participants to think about the time when they learned about the HIV diagnosis and about their decision making about informing or not informing a parent, close friend, and an intimate partner about the diagnosis. They were asked to indicate on 5-point scales how much the various reasons influenced their decision to tell or not to tell this particular person about the diagnosis.

A preliminary analysis of the participants' responses for the endorsement of reasons for disclosure or nondisclosure indicated a high correlation between the "closeness and emotional support" and "help" scales, as well as between the "duty to inform" and the "desire to educate" categories, regardless of friend, intimate partner, or parent as the target person. There was also a high correlation among the specific items that composed the "closeness and emotional support" scale and the "help" scale, as well as among the specific items that composed the "duty to inform" and the "desire to educate" scales. It was decided, for this data set, to combine the items from the "closeness and emotional support" and the "help" scales into a single scale, the "close–supportive" attributional category. We also combined the items from the "duty to inform" and "educate" scales into a single scale, the "duty to inform–educate" category. The duty–educate attribution still reflects another focus as a reason for disclosure. However, the close–supportive attribution somewhat blurs the distinction between a relationship focus (being in a close relationship with someone) and a self-focus (needing help). It may be that the specific items for the help category ("My ___ could be of help"; "My ___ would be able to provide support"; and ""My ___ would provide me with assistance") reflect less a perception of one's need for help than a perception about how helpful the target person might be when help is needed.

Endorsement of Attributions for Disclosure

For the male participants, we found that the endorsement of specific attributions for disclosure was moderated by the relationship with the target person. The men endorsed duty to inform or educate as a reason for disclosure to an intimate partner and a parent more than to a friend. The desire to test the other person's reactions about the HIV test, although not rated as very influential in their decision making, was also endorsed more for an intimate partner than for either a friend or parent. Similarity with the other person was endorsed more as an explanation for disclosure to a friend or an intimate partner than to a parent.

For the men, we also examined separately the endorsement of types of attributions for disclosure to a friend, intimate partner, and parent. For the intimate partner, duty to inform or educate was rated higher as an attribution for disclosure than was catharsis. For the friend, a close or supportive relationship was rated highest as an attribution for disclosure, whereas the desire to test the other's reaction was rated lowest. For the parent, duty to inform or educate was endorsed more as an attribution for disclosure than was either testing the other's reactions or similarity.

For the women, there was no interaction of type of reason with relationship on endorsement of the attributions for disclosure. Only the type of attributions themselves influenced endorsement. Catharsis, duty to inform or educate, and close or supportive relationship were more highly endorsed as attributions for disclosure than was similarity. Testing the other's reactions as a reason for disclosure was endorsed midway between the highest and least endorsed attributions (see Table 13.1).

Endorsement of Attributions for Nondisclosure

For the men, the endorsement of types of attributions for nondisclosure was moderated by the relationship with the other person. Privacy as an attribution for not disclosing was endorsed more for a friend than for an intimate partner or a parent. There was also a greater endorsement of protecting the other as an attribution for not disclosing

Table 13.1. The Most and Least Endorsed Attributions for Disclosure by the Men and Women in Different Relationships

	Most Important Attribution(s) for Disclosure	Least Important Attribution(s) for Disclosure
For men		
Friend as target	Close–supportive relationship	Test other's reactions
Intimate partner as target	Duty to inform–educate	Catharsis
Parent as target	Duty to inform–educate	Similarity; test other's reactions
For women		
Same impact of type of reasons regardless of friend, intimate partner, or parent as target	Catharsis; duty to inform–educate; close–supportive relationship	Similarity

Note: These findings are based on type of attributions for disclosure simple effects within relationships. They do not represent significant differences between relationships.

to a parent than for not disclosing to a friend. Concern for protecting an intimate partner as an attribution for nondisclosure was endorsed midway between the ratings for a parent and for a friend.

Among the men, we examined separately the endorsement of types of attributions for nondisclosure to a friend, intimate partner, or a parent. For the friend as target person, privacy was endorsed most strongly as an attribution for not disclosing, whereas communication difficulties were endorsed least. Superficial relationship, concern for others, self-blame, and fear of rejection were endorsed midway between privacy and communication difficulties as attributions for not disclosing to a friend. For an intimate partner, self-blame, protecting the other, and fear of rejection were endorsed more as attributions for not disclosing, whereas communication difficulties was endorsed the least. For a parent, protecting the other was endorsed the most as an attribution for not disclosing, whereas communication difficulties and having a superficial relationship were endorsed the least (see Table 13.2).

Table 13.2. The Most and Least Endorsed Attributions for Nondisclosure by the Men and Women in Different Relationships

	Most Important Attribution(s) for Nondisclosure	Least Important Attribution(s) for Nondisclosure
For men		
Friend as target	Privacy	Communication difficulties
Intimate partner as target	Self-blame; protect the other; fear of rejection	Communication difficulties
Parent as target	Protect the other	Communication difficulties; Superficial relationship; fear of rejection
For women		
Friend as target	Protect the other; privacy; fear of rejection	Superficial relationship
Intimate partner as target	No effect	No effect
Parent as target	Protect the other	Superficial relationship

Note: These findings are based on type of attributions for nondisclosure simple effects within relationships. They do not represent significant differences between relationships.

For the women, there was also an interaction of type of attribution by nature of relationship on endorsement of attributions for nondisclosure. Comparing the endorsement of each attribution for nondisclosure across relationship types, there was only one effect, namely superficial relationship was endorsed more as an attribution for not disclosing to an intimate partner than to a parent.

Separate examination of the effects of type of attributions for nondisclosure to friends, intimate partners, and parents revealed the following patterns. For a friend, protecting the other, privacy, and fear of rejection were endorsed the most, and superficial relationship was endorsed the least as attributions for not disclosing. For an intimate partner, there was no difference in endorsement of attributions as a function of type of attribution. For a parent, protecting the other was endorsed the most as an attribution for not disclosing, and superficial relationship was endorsed the least.

DISCUSSION

The results of the questionnaire research tell us something about why people choose to tell, or not to tell, about how the nature of relationships influences attributions, and possibly about how attributions can affect relationships. Both men and women cited the importance of a close–supportive relationship and the duty to inform or educate as reasons for disclosure, reflecting the importance across the sexes of affectional and trustworthy ties as well as a sense of obligation to significant others as reasons for disclosure. However, women, as compared with men, strongly endorsed catharsis as a reason for disclosure.

It is most likely that this difference between the men and women in this sample on endorsement of the catharsis category reflects not a gender difference but a difference in circumstances. The men were homosexual or bisexual, and they generally acquired HIV through sexual contact with other men. They would be aware that they were at some risk for acquiring HIV. The women in the sample were heterosexual, and most acquired HIV from their male partner. They often were surprised by the discovery of their HIV status, having assumed that they were not at risk. This unexpected, and perhaps at first inexplicable, negative information may lead to a feeling of needing to share and unburden. The women, as compared with the men, might feel a greater need to talk about this event in order to understand it as much as to seek solace. Of course, the women were not unaffected by their perceptions of trust for a prospective disclosure target. The women, like the men, endorsed having a close and supportive relationship as an important reason for disclosure.

Attributions for not disclosing in the questionnaire research were similar for women and men. Both endorsed privacy, fear of rejection, and protecting the other as important attributions for not disclosing. Privacy, or concerns about keeping personal information contained within a specified social network or to one's self, is an issue for any self-disclosure. Releasing information to others means that they can, even if asked not to, pass that information on to people whom the discloser does not want to know. Fear of rejection reflects the continuing social stigmatization of HIV-positive persons and their awareness of this. Like privacy, it is a self-focused attribution for not disclosing. Concern about protecting others, on the other hand, is a prosocial attribution for not disclosing. Individuals may decide that information would lead to distress for another.

Our findings also reveal something about how relationships influence the attributions people give for disclosure and nondisclosure. Men were more likely to endorse duty to educate for disclosure to their intimate partners or parents than to friends. They also endorsed testing the other's reactions as a reason for disclosure more for an intimate partner than for a friend or parent. These attributions suggest a sense of obligation but also a wariness or uncertainty in their intimate relationships. Men give similarity as an attribution for intimate partner and friend more than for parent. This may reflect their feeling of belonging to a social group (homosexuals or bisexuals) that is distinct from that of their parents. It may also be that they know others who are HIV-seropositive and that these others become confidants because of their similarity. Women do not make these distinctions among relationships in their attributions for disclosure. Women may have less informal or hearsay knowledge about how others will react to the disclosure and thus have no reason to differentiate between intimate partner, friend, or parent in terms of attributions for disclosure.

For not disclosing, the men endorsed protecting the other more for parents than for friends. This same trend, albeit nonsignificant, occurred for the women. One might regard this as a rationalization, that is, the men may transform a concern for how they would feel disclosing this information to their parents into a concern for their parents' well-being. However, our interviews suggest that many individuals do recognize that parental concern for children is a genuine source of stress, and they want to spare their parents the worry that comes with know-ing their child is ill. We found, for the women but not for the men, that superficial relationship was endorsed more as a reason for not disclos-ing to an intimate partner than to a parent. The women, in weighing decisions not to disclose, may see intimate partners as less emotionally connected to them or less committed to them than their parents, at least when thinking about whom not to tell about the HIV diagnosis.

While the type of relationship will influence how disclosing or not disclosing information is explained, the attribution itself could also influence the relationship. To some extent, not disclosing leads to a self-fulfilling prophecy. A superficial relationship remains superficial, because the other does not know something very important about the would-be discloser. Not telling out of fear of rejection can leave per-sons feeling unwanted or disliked without ever having given the other person a chance to respond (positively or negatively). Not disclosing out of concern for someone also means not finding out how well (or poorly) the target person will handle the information. However, whereas other attributions tend to portray the relationship as negative in some way (e.g., superficial, rejecting, not trustworthy), protecting someone suggests positive feelings for the person.

Attributions for disclosing the information can also influence a rela-tionship. Having disclosed because one feels close to someone else establishes an expectation that the other will live up to one's standards for closeness. Thinking of testing the reaction of the other as an attribu-tion for telling may reinforce the feeling that this is a person whom one could not implicitly trust (even if they pass your "test"). A disclosure made to seek help defines the relationship in terms of the discloser's needs; a disclosure made to educate suggests that the discloser has something to offer the other. In each case, the explanation for the dis-closure helps to define the self in relation to the other.

CONCLUSIONS

Overall, this chapter indicates that HIV-infected individuals generate and differentially endorse attributions for and against self-disclosure of their diagnosis to others. These attributions reflect, in part, the tensions and conflicts people experience over whom to tell about the diagnosis. Examining these reasons helps us to understand the thinking of HIV-infected persons during a critical time of life, as well as the importance of the nature of the relationship in making these decisions. The attributional processes of HIV-positive persons regarding disclosure or nondisclosure may also reflect the psychological reasoning in other populations (e.g., cancer patients, victims of abusive relationships) regarding disclosure of highly personal and potentially stigmatizing information.

REFERENCES

Chidwick, A., & Borrill, J. (1996). Dealing with a life-threatening diagnosis: The experience of people with the human immunodeficiency virus. *AIDS Care, 8,* 271–284.

Derlega, V. J., & Barbee, A. P. (1994). *Unpublished transcripts of interviews with HIV-infected persons in southeastern Virginia about self-disclosure and social support issues.* Old Dominion University, Norfolk, VA.

Derlega, V. J., & Barbee, A. P. (1998). *Unpublished transcripts of HIV-infected mothers about HIV and personal relationships.* Old Dominion University, Norfolk, VA.

Derlega, V. J., Lovejoy, D., & Winstead, B. A. (1998). Personal accounts of disclosing and concealing HIV-positive test results: Weighing the benefits and risks. In V. J. Derlega & A. P. Barbee (Eds.), *HIV and social interaction* (pp. 147–164). Thousand Oaks, CA: Sage Publications.

Derlega, V. J., Metts, S., Petronio, S., & Margulis, S. T. (1993). *Self-disclosure.* Newbury Park, CA: Sage Publications.

Derlega, V. J., & Winstead, B. A. (1999). *Self-disclosure of HIV infection: A functional analysis of the reasons for and against disclosure from the perspective of the HIV-infected person.* Manuscript submitted for publication.

Derlega, V. J., Winstead, B. A., & Folk-Barron, L. (2000). Reasons for and against disclosing HIV-seropositive test results to an intimate partner: A functional perspective. In S. Petronio (Ed.), *Balancing secrecy, self-disclosure, and privacy.* Mahwah, NJ: Erlbaum.

Derlega, V. J., Winstead, B. A., Wong, P. T. P., & Greenspan, M. (1987). Self-disclosure and relationship development: An attributional analysis. In M. E. Roloff & G. R. Miller (Eds.), *Interpersonal processes: New directions in communication research* (pp. 172–187). Newbury Park, CA: Sage Publications.

Greene, K., & Serovich, J. M. (1996). Appropriateness of disclosure of HIV testing information: The perspective of PLWAs. *Journal of Applied Communication Research, 24,* 50–65.

Harvey, J. J., & Omarzu, J. (1997). Minding the close relationship. *Personality and Social Psychology Review, 1,* 224–240.

Hays, R. B., McKusick, L., Pollack, L., Hilliard, R., Hoff, C., & Coates, T. J. (1993). Disclosing HIV seropositivity to significant others. *AIDS, 7,* 1–7.

Holt, R., Court, P., Vedhara, K., Nott, K. H., Holmes, J., & Snow, M. H. (1998). The role of disclosure in coping with HIV infection. *AIDS Care, 10,* 49–60.

Kalichman, S. C. (1995). *Understanding AIDS: A guide for mental health professionals.* Washington, DC: American Psychological Association.

Lie, G. T., & Biswalo, P. M. (1996). HIV-positive patients' choice of a significant other to be informed about the HIV-test result: Findings from an HIV/AIDS counselling programme in the regional hospitals of Arush and Kilimanjaro, Tanzania. *AIDS Care, 8,* 285–296.

Marks, G., Bundek, N. I., Richardson, J. L., Ruiz, M. S., Maldonado, N., & Mason, R. C. (1992). Self-disclosure of HIV infection: Preliminary results from a sample of Hispanic men. *Health Psychology, 11,* 300–306.

Mason, H. R. C., Marks, G., Simoni, J. M., Ruiz, M. S., & Richardson, J. L. (1995). Culturally sanctioned secrets? Latino men's nondisclosure of HIV infection to family, friends, and lovers. *Health Psychology, 14,* 6–12.

Norman, L. R., Kennedy, M., & Parish, D. (1998). Close relationships and safer sex among HIV-infected men with haemophilia. *AIDS Care, 10,* 339–354.

Rothenberg, K. H., & Pakey, S. J. (1995). The risk of domestic violence and women with HIV infection: Implications for partner notification, public policy, and the law. *American Journal of Public Health, 11,* 1569–1576.

Siegel, K., & Krauss, B. (1991). Living with HIV infection: Adaptive tasks of seropositive gay men. *Journal of Health and Social Behavior, 32,* 17–32.

Simoni, J. M., Mason, H. R. C., Marks, G., Ruiz, M. S., Reed, D., & Richardson, J. R. (1995). Women's self-disclosure of HIV infection: Rates, reasons, and reactions. *Journal of Consulting and Clinical Psychology, 63,* 474–478.

Stempel, R. R., Moulton, J. M., & Moss, A. R. (1995). Self-disclosure of HIV-1 antibody test results: The San Francisco General Hospital cohort. *AIDS Education and Prevention, 7,* 116–123.

Taylor, D. A., Gould, R. J., & Brounstein, P. J. (1981). Effects of personalistic self-disclosure. *Personality and Social Psychology Bulletin, 7,* 487–492.

Wolitski, R. J., Rietmeijer, C. A. M., Goldbaum, G. M., & Wilson, R. M. (1998). HIV serostatus disclosure among gay and bisexual men in four American cities: General patterns and relation to sexual practices. *AIDS Care, 10,* 599–610.

CHAPTER FOURTEEN

Attributions About Communication Styles and Strategies

Predicting Dating Couples' Safe-Sex Discussions and Relationship Satisfaction

Candida C. Peterson, Ashlea Troth, Cynthia Gallois, and Judith Feeney

Most adults are skilled conversationalists who are not only adept at speaking and listening but also at monitoring the nature and success of the communicative exchange itself. In doing this monitoring, adults are likely to engage in processes of causal attribution (Weiner, 1985; Wong & Weiner, 1981). Attributions can be viewed as the meanings people impose on their own and others' overtly observable actions (Manusov, Floyd, & Kerssen-Griep, 1997). An attributional approach to conversation posits this search for meaning, intent, and underlying causality in discourse as just one element in a broader human tendency to seek meaning for all instances, forms, and variations in human social exchange (Heider, 1958). The discovery of reliable patterns of association and causal connection between cognitions and communicative acts facilitates the accurate understanding of self and others, as well as assisting the progress of a close relationship toward increasing levels of intimacy, mutuality, and the skilled exchange of views. Given the vast range of possible personal or situational influences on any speech act, the possibilities for causal thinking about conversation and communication are almost limitless.

COUPLES' ATTRIBUTIONS FOR COMMUNICATION DIFFICULTIES

Applied to couple communication, the suggestion that cognitive attributional activity is triggered by difficulties or disconfirmations of

Note: Address all correspondence about this manuscript to Professor C.C. Peterson, School of Psychology, The University of Queensland, Brisbane, Australia, 4072, Fax: 617-3365-4466, E-mail: candi@psy.uq.edu.au.

interlocutors' expectations (Wong & Weiner, 1981) implies that these difficulties will inspire deeper and more frequent attributional thoughts than will harmonious discussions that provide no challenges or unpleasant surprises. The motivation to seek causal explanations may likewise be heightened by the negativity and personal importance of social events (Weiner, 1985). Consequently, in couples' everyday interactions with one another, communication difficulties may be bound up with tasks of central importance to relationship quality. These include the expression of negative emotions (anger, fear, sadness); the resolution of conflict; the disclosure of highly personal information; the discussion of topics that are socially, culturally, or personally taboo; and the need to probe for information that the partner is unwilling to reveal. In addition, difficulties in spontaneous couple communication are likely to arise when partners either accidentally misunderstand or strive to deliberately deceive one another or when the information they transmit through verbal and nonverbal channels is discordant (Noller, 1984).

From a methodological standpoint, the negativity–expectancy violation hypothesis of attribution arousal (Weiner, 1985; see also Burgoon, Stern, & Dillman, 1995) highlights the usefulness of observing romantic partners' spontaneous cognitive attributional activity while they are engaged in inherently difficult communication tasks (e.g., discussing condoms or a past sexual experience). Several separate lines of evidence from a range of distinct research traditions converge in support of the proposition that couples engage spontaneously in cognitive attribution when their relationships are faced with challenging conversational hurdles such as these. Consequently, these situations present an ideal empirical setting in which to test hypotheses about the nature and consequences of couples' attributional thought processes.

With no attempt to provide an exhaustive listing, a number of examples can be provided to support this proposition. These examples illustrate the wide range and rich diversity of the cognitive attributions that couples engage in before, during, or after a communication problem has disrupted the normal flow of intimate conversation. Manusov (1995), for instance, investigated how romantic partners reacted to the intrusion of unexpected nonverbal emotional expressions into their discussions. She discovered that negative nonverbal behaviors were noticed more often than positive ones, even though the experimental manipulation ensured that both types were actually equally frequent. When the partner's nonverbal expression of negative affect was noticed, attributional activity commonly followed, suggesting that "people do ascribe interpretations to their partners' [nonverbal] behavior" (Manusov, 1995, p. 473). The attributions couples initially made for negative nonverbal affect were often relationship-enhancing in that they ascribed the unpleasantness to temporary personal characteristics or situational factors, rather than to enduring difficulties that would be likely to generalize outside this individual instance of problematic communication.

Extending this procedure to include the assessment of couples' attributions for nonverbal communicative acts, Manusov et al. (1997) designed a study in which video recordings of their naturalistically engineered positive and negative nonverbal communication were played back to a sample of romantically involved participants. The couples gave judgments about what the nonverbal behaviors meant and what was being communicated. A comparison of their own with their partners' ratings of the same instances of negative nonverbal behavior gave evidence of self-serving attributional biases, which were particularly pronounced in unhappy couples. In other words, when viewing the videotapes, individuals ascribed less deliberate intent, less control, and less internality to their own negative communicative acts than their partners did when rating the same nonverbal acts from the perspective of receiver. Furthermore, the partners who reported the highest levels of relationship distress were the ones most likely to attribute responsibility for nonverbal negativity in this self-serving manner. This result suggests that attributional thinking about the important relationship dimension of nonverbal communication is likely to shape not only the couple's momentary feelings about the success of a conversation but also, more broadly, their relationship satisfaction as a whole.

The effects of cognitive attributions about conversations on communication outcomes may be specific to close relationships in which the attributors know each other well enough to make reasonable inferences. In a study that was designed to compare strangers with friends and to investigate the associations between the attribution process and the depth of adults' disclosure of personal information to conversational partners of the opposite sex, Derlega, Winstead, Wong, and Greenspan (1993) compared strangers with friends in terms of three types of attributions, namely self-based, partner-based, and relationship-based. Instances of these three types of causal attribution were further differentiated according to their affective valence (positive or negative).

The results indicated that there was little or no association between attributions and the self-disclosure process in conversations between strangers. However, when the male and female conversational partners were close friends, clear patterns of association between cognitive attributions and intimate disclosure emerged. Positively valenced attributions to self, to partner, and to the relationship were all linked with greater intimacy of self-disclosure about personal feelings and problems. This result suggests that friends who liked and trusted one another and their relationship well enough to confide were inclined to attribute to positive friendship qualities the responsibility for the somewhat unexpected communication event of a highly intimate disclosure of confidential information. To the extent that disclosure itself is a rewarding relationship input (Altman & Taylor, 1973), a cycle of favorable attributions along with increasingly intimate communication may become self-perpetuating in close friendships and other intimate relationships. The lack of a knowledge base from which to frame attributions, however, means that disclosure may have little bearing on conversations among people who are not well acquainted.

The problematic communication that arises when intimate partners deceive one another or suspect one another of practicing deceit is a highly negative input that is especially likely to trigger cognitive attributional activity, according to Wong and Weiner's (1981) expectancy violation hypothesis. In a study of 40 heterosexual Australian couples, Peterson (1996) examined attributions of responsibility for deceptive communications, including white lies (e.g., an insincere compliment), omissions and half truths (e.g., failing to mention something the partner will find upsetting), and blatantly self-serving lies. Adults' attributions of blame to the speaker (self or partner) were found to vary with the degrees of self-interest, deliberation, and departure from truth that each deceptive communication entailed. White lies attracted little blame and were perceived, on average, as neither particularly constructive nor particularly destructive for the communication process. However, each of the other forms of intimate deception attracted attributions of partner blame and personal guilt, and the partners who exchanged these forms of deceit most frequently were the ones who reported the lowest levels of satisfaction with their couple relationship. Frequent deception was also associated with the defensive avoidance of conflict and with romantic partners' preferences to deceive one another rather than to argue about a troubling issue. When attributing guilt or blame for identical acts of deception, evidence of a self-serving bias (Zuckerman, 1979) was observed, in line with the findings of Manusov et al. (1997).

Bradbury and Fincham (1992) also studied causal and responsibility attributions for marital problems (e.g., difficulties with in-laws, finances, and mutual trust) in relation to the actual communication strategies they used during a videotaped problem-solving discussion. The communication task was rendered more difficult by the fact that its topic was also a marital problem. Individual attribution ratings were summed to create two indices of maladaptive thinking, causality and responsibility. Higher levels of marital distress were linked with higher causal and responsibility attribution index scores, reflecting a stronger tendency in unhappy marriages to blame the spouse for difficulties in marriage and to view the spouse as their cause. Avoidance of communication during the interaction task was also a predictor of marital distress.

The link between the marital communication problem of conflict avoidance and spouses' irrationally self-serving biases in their attributions for marital problems that are not directly communication-related is a provocative and important one, warranting further investigation. As will be explained in more detail subsequently, we examined romantic couples' attributions about conflict-avoidance in the present study, exploring the possibility that partners who attribute avoidance to self and partner will (a) follow this through in their actual conversational behavior and (b) be less satisfied with their relationship than other couples.

THE DIFFICULTY OF COMMUNICATING ABOUT SAFE SEX

The task of communicating with a dating partner about safe-sex precautions for protection against sexually transmitted diseases (STDs), including human immunodeficiency virus (HIV), is exceptionally difficult for adolescents and young adults. Young people in the early stages of mutual acquaintance may feel threatened by any topics connected with sex or may perceive that frank discussions of condoms or past sexual partners represent too high a level of self-disclosure to enable their intimacy to grow naturally. Indeed, a number of recent studies suggest that young people find the challenge of communicating about condoms and other safe-sex strategies an almost impossibly difficult one (Cline, Freeman, & Johnson, 1990; Crawford, Turtle, & Kippax, 1990; Pittam & Gallois, 1997; Rosenthal & Peart, 1996).

Young people in the early stages of a relationship may also lack the conversational skill to persuade and negotiate with one another over issues about which they initially disagree. Conflict resolution skills acquired in arguments with their parents and siblings while growing up are carried forward into young peoples' first sexual relationships (Peterson, 1990; Troth & Peterson, 2000). These skills vary widely in their breadth and effectiveness. In some families, open discussion, relaxed exchanges of intimate disclosures, and a thoughtfully involved approach to the resolution of parent–adolescent conflicts are all routinely practiced (Peterson, 1990). This is likely to lead to the acquisition of effective communication strategies that can readily be applied to such tasks as persuading a sexual partner to use a condom.

On the other hand, young people who grew up in families in which disagreements and conflicts were routinely avoided and in which sensitive topics such as drugs, alcohol, or sexual intimacy were rarely broached may embark on dating relationships with no such skills at their disposal. Troth and Peterson (2000) discovered a link between young adults' inability to discuss condom use with their dating partners and their parents' earlier use of avoidant or hostile conflict resolution strategies when arguing with them as they grew up. Anxious conflict avoidance, in particular, was a predictor of subsequent difficulties with safe-sex communication as a couple. Young daters who reported that their mothers or fathers had generally avoided discussing issues of disagreement with them during earlier adolescence were subsequently very reluctant to discuss safe sex with their partners and often failed to use condoms when they wanted to, simply out of conversational anxiety. Offspring from avoidant families of origin often reported beliefs that simply talking about condoms, HIV, or STDs with a dating partner would damage their relationship and promote suspicion about past sexual practices or sexual orientation. Independently of destructive parent–adolescent conflict avoidance, two positive predictors of young people's motivation and skill in discussing condoms and safe sex were frequent discussions with their mothers about sexual health and communicative assertiveness skills outside of the sexual context (e.g., ease of asking a stranger for help).

Effective communication about safe sex is often a necessary but missing ingredient in safe sexual practice. Furthermore, the inability to communicate effectively about condoms and other health precautions significantly predicts couples' actual unsafe sexual behavior (Boldero, Moore, & Rosenthal, 1992). Many recent studies likewise show that young adults continue to behave in ways that place themselves and their sexual partners at risk for the spread of HIV and other STDs in spite of high levels of knowledge about these diseases and their modes of transmission (Desiderato & Crawford, 1995; Gallois, Terry, Timmins, McCamish, & Kashima, 1994; Kelly, St. Lawrence, Hood, & Brasfield, 1989; Reitman, St. Lawrence, Jefferson, & Allyne, 1996).

Effective communication about safe sex is a necessary precursor of consistent condom use (Fisher & Fisher, 1992). Therefore, the facilitation of couples' discussions about their sexual and health needs, their preferences for condoms or other safe-sex strategies, their anxieties and uncertainties, and their past sexual histories may all contribute productively to curbing the risk of HIV and other STDs. In the study mentioned earlier, Troth and Peterson (2000) discovered that condoms were rarely or never used by those sexually active young adults whose attitudes to discussing safe sex were fearful or antagonistic. Using a similar population of heterosexual Australian university students as subjects, Troth and Peterson found that adults' frequency of condom use for intercourse with casual sex partners was positively correlated with favorable attitudes to discussing safe sex with romantic partners generally. In support of the suggestion that the acquisition of constructive conflict resolution strategies in the family of origin may also facilitate the adoption of safe sex practices, the results showed that failure to use a condom for casual sex was predicted by the mother's frequent use of conflict avoidance in disputes with the respondent at home. In addition, this maladaptive conflict resolution style exerted an independent influence on unsafe sex, over and above its joint association with attitudes unfavorable to discussion.

Although these findings are provocative, further research is clearly warranted in order to discover the proximate factors that create a bridge between a young person's modes of sexual conversation and behavior. Young adults' attributional cognitions about their own communication styles and patterns and those of their romantic partners may serve as one point of interconnection between developmental origins and mature conversational outcomes.

THE PRESENT STUDY

During their early opportunities to converse, dating partners are likely to gain increasingly sophisticated insights into the skills and strategies they each bring to bear on such difficult communication challenges as the need to disclose intimately confidential information (e.g., about sex), the need to persuade a partner to do something he or she will not like (e.g., use condoms), the resolution of disagreements, and the revelation of personal problems, anxieties, or transgressions. These insights are likely to contribute to future conversational encounters and may ultimately promote satisfaction with the communication process and the relationship itself. To the extent that partners perceive their own and the other person's communication goals and strategies accurately, these conversational experiences may selectively modify communication patterns in favorable directions. Appreciation of the benefits deriving from constructive approaches may enhance their frequency at the same time that partners learn to curb or modify such destructive communication patterns as deception, anxious avoidance of discussion, or angry escalation.

As Bradbury and Fincham (1992) have pointed out, spouses' maladaptive attributions of causality for problems in their relationships are a frequent occurrence. Vangelisti, Corbin, Lucchetti, and Sprague (1999) recently reported a similar association between relationship quality and pattern of attributions. Romantic partners may be more inclined to attribute destructive communicative goals to one another than would an outsider judging their conversation. In line with these earlier findings regarding maladaptive attributions of blame, a lover's misperception of the partner's communicative intentions and tactics during communication about safe sex and STDs may undermine relationship satisfaction while at the same time interfering with the communication process itself.

The present study was designed to test these possibilities. We looked for correlations between attributions and satisfaction with the process and outcome of the communication episode and how difficult versus enjoyable this task was for couples to perform. Finally, attributions about one's own and partner's communication were examined, along with the speaker's gender and attitudes to discussing safe sex and the actual outcomes of the discussion, for their role in predicting young people's overall levels of satisfaction with their couple relationship.

Method

Participants
A total of 96 Australian young adults comprising 48 heterosexual dating couples took part. Their ages ranged from 17 to 28 years ($M = 19.41$). The participants were recruited from introductory psychology classes on condition that at least one partner was no older than 23 and

that they had been dating each other for a minimum of 2 months. Actual relationship durations ranged from 3 months to 4 years ($M = 14$ months). Of the 96 respondents, 86 (90%) were not virgins. Of the 10 virgins, 7 were female. Of the sexually experienced respondents, 79 (92%; 82% of sample) reported having had sexual intercourse with their current partner; 51 (59%) of nonvirgins reported that they had engaged in at least one previous committed relationship that had included sexual intimacy; and 40 (46%) had also experienced casual sex. Of the total sample, 67 (70%) currently lived with a member of their family of origin; the remainder lived with friends, roommates, or extended kin or in university halls of residence. Twenty-four respondents (25%) reported some form of religious affiliation.

Interaction Task

The couples were escorted to the laboratory and given a written scenario about a hypothetical unmarried couple who had been dating for several months and were contemplating their first sexual encounter. One partner (Ann) wished to use a condom for sexual intercourse, but her partner (Rick) did not. After the couples read the scenarios, the video was turned on, and they were asked to discuss Ann's and Rick's options, how these individuals might persuade each other and, in terms of their own relationship, their beliefs about condom use and safe-sex precautions, along with factors that would contribute to their own decision and any additional relevant issues. Under instruction to try to reach consensus, most spoke for about 11 minutes (range, 4 to 28 minutes). The 48 conversations were transcribed and broken down into conversational units, with simple sentences chosen as the coding unit (Kane, 1983).

Observers' ratings were developed on the basis of Bales's (1950, 1970) Interaction Process Analysis (IPA) system. Each unit was coded during the final 5 minutes of the interaction, the point at which couples were most relaxed and most likely to be discussing safe-sex issues in the context of their own relationship. A researcher trained in the use of IPA coded the written transcripts while watching the videotape. When more than one category was used in a conversational unit, all categories were listed, but the primary code was specified. A second trained coder categorized a randomly chosen 20% of the transcripts independently. Cohen's (1960) kappa coefficient was used to compute their agreement. The resulting coefficient, .91, indicated adequate reliability. Discrepancies in IPA coding between the two coders were resolved by discussion. The percentage of conversational units assigned to each category was calculated for each partner, only the primary category being used for each unit. These percentage scores were then used in all subsequent statistical analyses. Table 14.1 shows the IPA coding categories used, along with examples taken from the transcripts.

Questionnaire Measures

Satisfaction. Respondents' overall level of satisfaction with their relationship was measured by a modified version of the Quality Marriage Index (Norton, 1983). Cronbach's alpha coefficient for the totals was .83, indicating adequate internal consistency for this measure. An additional satisfaction scale was administered immediately after the videotape task to assess the following dimensions on 5-point scales: (1) satisfaction with the interaction process, (2) satisfaction with the interaction outcome, (3) level of comfort felt during the conversation, and (4) degree of upset felt during the conversation.

Attributions. Respondents made attributional judgments about their own and their partner's motivations and conversational strategies during the interaction task, using the dimensions friendly versus hostile intent, open versus closed communication, topic avoidance versus involvement, competitive versus cooperative orientation, and calm versus emotional mood. Each person rated self and partner on each of the five 6-point scales, with higher scores reflecting more positive attributions. As a way of assessing self-serving biases in couples' attributions, we compared self and partner ratings on each of the five attributional dimensions, using one of three categories for each dimension. These categories were (1) a higher rating given to self than partner on that dimension, (2) identical rating given to both partners, and (3) a higher rating given to partner than self. For the positive attributions, type (1) categorizations were labeled *self-serving,* and type (3) categorizations were labeled *partner-enhancing.* The reverse was done for the negative attributions. Identical ratings for self and partner were called an *equality* pattern. In order to compare outside observers' IPA ratings with respondents' attributions, we matched by common dimensions of communication (e.g., friendly overture equals friendly intent) and then correlated the two sets of ratings.

Results and Discussion

The hypothesis that romantically involved partners might show self-serving biases in their attributions of communicative intentions and

Table 14.1. Interaction Process Analysis (IPA) Categories Used in the Data Analyses

IPA Code No.	Category Label	Definition	Example
1	Friendly overture	Gives help, gives reward, or other's status	"You were great when we first started going out"
3	Cooperates	Shows passive acceptance, concurs, complies, agree	"Absolutely"
5	Gives opinion	Expresses own viewpoint, wish or feeling; evaluates or analyzes topic or partner's statement	"Condoms feel awful"
6	Directs conversation by giving information or orientation	Leads or guides discussion or conclusion	"Okay, is there anything you want to add?"
7	Seeks information or orientation	Asks partner to supply informational content or direction	"How do you get herpes?"
8	Seeks opinion	Asks partner to judge, evaluate, validate or confirm	"Do you think we've made up our mind?"
10	Uncooperative move	Shows passive rejection, formality, withholds, help, expresses disagreement	"No, that's not true"
11	Avoidant move via tension or withdrawal	Withdraws, shows nervous tension or distress, escapes from argument, clams up	Nervous laughter (not part of a joke) Silence (in response to direct query)
12	Hostile overture	Attacks, criticizes, deflates other's status	"Well, I don't trust you."

tactics was tested by comparing the frequencies of partner-enhancing, self-serving, and equality categorizations for and male and female respondents separately, as shown in Table 14.2. For each of the dimensions of attribution that we looked at, the equality pattern was predominant. Most participants believed that they displayed the same amounts of friendly intent, open communication, avoidance, cooperation, and emotionality as their partner. Though reflecting cognitions rather than the actual behaviors studied by Bradbury and Fincham (1992), our findings are in line with their observations of reciprocity. These authors found that partners tended to reciprocate one another's friendly, hostile, and avoidant communication behaviors, although their extent of doing so was moderated by their causal attributions for marital problems.

There were no statistically significant sex differences in frequencies of self-enhancing, partner-enhancing, or equality attributions of friendly intent, avoidance, competitiveness, or openness of communication $\chi^2(2) = 3.89, .57, 1.62$ and 1.42, respectively, all nonsignificant. There was, however, a statistically significant difference for attributions of emotionality, $\chi^2(2) = 12.75, N = 96, p < .01$. Assuming that calmness is deemed to be the positive pole of this attributional continuum, female subjects were significantly more likely than males to make self-serving attributions, judging their own communication to be calmer than their partners' during the safe-sex discussion task. In general, however, these results give very little evidence either of sex differences or of self-serving biases, suggesting that most communication characteristics were attributed similarly by these romantically involved partners during discussion of a difficult topic.

The possibility that couples in unsatisfactory relationships may make negative attributions about their interactions more frequently than satisfied couples (Bradbury & Fincham, 1992) was examined for the present sample by comparing the relationship distress scores derived from our modified Quality Marriage Index (Norton, 1983) satisfaction index with attribution patterns. The hypothesis predicted more frequent self-serving attributions by participants whose overall relationship satisfaction was low. For each dimension of communicative attributional judgment, a separate 2 (sex) × 3 (attribution pattern) analysis of variance on relationship satisfaction scores was performed. Two of these yielded statistically significant results. For attributions of friendly communicative intent, there was a statistically significant main effect of attribution pattern, $F (2, 90) = 3.58, p < .05$. Participants

Table 14.2. Frequency of Biased Patterns of Communication Attributions for 48 Couples

Attributional Dimension	Male			Female		
	Self-Serving Pattern	Equality Pattern	Partner-Enhancing Pattern	Self-Serving Pattern	Equality Pattern	Partner-Enhancing Pattern
Friendly	6% (3)	71% (34)	23% (11)	2% (1)	87% (42)	11% (5)
Open	23% (11)	56% (27)	21% (10)	17% (8)	68% (33)	15% (7)
Avoidant*	27% (13)	54% (26)	19% (9)	28% (13)	59% (28)	13% (6)
Competitive*	13% (6)	67% (32)	21% (10)	19% (9)	67% (32)	13% (6)
Emotional*	8% (4)	56% (27)	35% (17)	19% (9)	75% (36)	6% (3)

Note: Numbers (out of 48 for each sex) are in parentheses, reflecting a missing value on a few items; an asterisk denotes negative attributional dimensions that were scored so that a lower-self-than-partner-rating was self-serving.

who made self-serving attributions were significantly less satisfied with their couple relationship ($M = 26.1$), than those who used an equality pattern ($M = 36.1$) or a partner-enhancing pattern ($M = 37.4$), which supports the hypothesis. There was also a statistically significant interaction between sex and attribution pattern, $F (2, 90) = 5.14$, $p < .05$, owing to the fact that low levels of satisfaction were more pronounced for females than males who used the self-serving pattern for friendly intent. For attributions of open communication, only the main effect of attributional pattern reached significance, $F (2, 90) = 3.52$, $p < .05$. Respondents who attributed openness equally to self and partner scored significantly higher in relationship satisfaction ($M = 37.5$) than those who attributed self-servingly ($M = 32.5$) or in a partner-enhancing manner ($M = 33.5$).

Partners' own attributions about the communication intentions and characteristics to self and partner were also compared with the ratings the trained observers had assigned using IPA. Table 14.3 shows how we matched the categories derived from the IPA coding with corresponding dimensions of attribution about communication. Predicted interconnections appear as the intersections of the rows and columns, and observed correlation coefficients appear beneath the verbal

Table 14.3. Correlations Between Outsiders' IPA Ratings Units and Respondents' Attributions

Observers Ratings of Communications Units	Respondents' Attributions of Communication Tactics	
	Self-Attribution	Partner Attribution
Friendly overture (1)	Friendly .01	Friendly .06
Hostile overture (12)	Unfriendly .28**	Unfriendly .23*
Cooperates (3)	Cooperative .00	Cooperative −.04
Uncooperative move (10)	Competitive .21*	Competitive .17
Avoidant move (11)	Avoidant .10	Avoidant .20*
Directs conversation (6)/ Gives opinion (5)	Actively involved −.14/.07	Actively involved −.22*/.01
Seeks information (7)/ Seeks opinion (8)	Open .01/−.08	Open .10/.03

Note: Numbers in parentheses refer to IPA code numerals as also shown in Table 14.1; * denotes significance at $p < .05$ and ** at $p < .01$.

description of each attribution dimension. Apart from a clear correspondence between attributions of hostility to self and partner and the observers' coding of hostile conversational turns, very few significant associations emerged in these data. It appears that partners' attributions of communication characteristics to one another reflect interpretations that either go beyond the evidence available to trained observers who code only individual units of dyadic conversation or else are based on cognitions that are relatively independent of overt conversational behavior.

Even if a partner's attributions of communication characteristics are not objectively accurate, they may nevertheless be associated with feelings of satisfaction both with their conversations and with their relationship more generally. To test this possibility, we computed correlations between self and partner attributions and the four dimensions of satisfaction that we measured. The results of these analyses appear in Table 14.4. Levels of satisfaction both with the communication process and with the couple relationship in general were significantly correlated with respondents' attributions of communication qualities to self and partner, as shown in Table 14.4. In particular, open communication and friendly communicative intent were positive correlates of satisfaction with the communication process, with the communication outcome, and with the relationship as a whole. In line with Bradbury and Fincham's (1992) finding of lower marital satisfaction in couples practicing avoidant modes of communication, participants who attributed avoidant communication strategies either to themselves or their partners were less satisfied with the overall relationship, as well as with this particular safe-sex discussion. This latter result is also keeping with Troth and Peterson's (2000) finding that young people who had practiced conflict avoidance in the family of origin reported greater discomfort with safe-sex discussions.

Participants' attributions of hostile versus friendly intent to their partners were strong predictors of levels of satisfaction with the conversation and the entire relationship (see Vangelisti, this volume). Interestingly, however, self-attributions of friendliness influenced only the former. The attribution of a competitive versus cooperative approach to the conversation similarly influenced couples' feelings mainly during the conversation itself, with little overall effect on their satisfaction either with their relationship or with the final outcome of this conversation.

Table 14.4. Correlations Between Respondents' Attributions to Self and Partner and Satisfaction with Conversation and Relationship.

Outcomes	Self-Attributions					Partner Attributions				
	Friendly	Open	Avoidant	Competitive	Emotional	Friendly	Open	Avoidant	Competitive	Emotional
Satisfaction with conversation process	.32**	.32**	-.24*	-.05	-.10	.31**	.32**	-.30**	-.12	-.06
Comfort during conversation	.43**	.34**	-.11	-.14	-.10	.39**	.32**	-.21*	-.25*	-.23*
Upset during conversation	-.22*	.03	.03	.22*	-.00	-.25*	.04	.10	.30**	.01
Satisfaction with conversation outcome	.32**	.36**	-.11	-.15	-.09	.24*	.28*	-.21*	-.17	-.08
Relationship satisfaction	.12	.32**	-.36**	-.17	-.06	.23*	.31**	-.21*	.12	.13

* $p < .05$; ** $p < .01$.

Finally, to examine the independent contribution that attributions made to respondents' overall feelings of satisfaction or distress with their couple relationships, two separate hierarchical multiple regressions were performed. The first examined the influence of self-attributions on Quality Marriage Index satisfaction scores. Participant sex was entered at step 1 as a control variable. The resulting equation was not significant, $R^2 = .00$, adj. $R^2 = -.01$, $F < 1$, indicating that men and women reported comparable levels of overall contentment with their couple relationship. After step 2, with all of the self attributions entered, the equation differed significantly from zero, $R^2 = 19$, adj. $R^2 = .12$, $F(6, 86) = 3.79$, $p < .01$, F (change) $= 4.46$, $p < .01$. Only two of the six attribution dimensions varied significantly to this effect, namely avoidance, with a beta weight of .26, $p < .05$, and openness, with a beta weight of .28, $p < .05$. Respondents' self-attributions of topic avoidance and of failure to communicate openly were significant independent predictors of overall dissatisfaction with their couple relationship.

Self-attributions of avoidance of difficult communication tasks emerged as a significant predictor of discontent with the relationship. This result is also in line with earlier research by Bradbury and Fincham (1992) showing that avoidant behavior is a negative predictor of satisfaction. It is also consistent with these authors' suggestion that avoidant communication strategies may not only limit couples' opportunities to discuss difficult issues in enough depth to achieve a solution but may also exacerbate a tendency for partners to attribute their marital or communication problems in maladaptive ways. To the extent that self-defeating attributions of relationship difficulties to communication style rather than to immediate situational factors is irrational yet distressing, open communication between partners about their attributions could help to improve relationship satisfaction.

In order to examine the influence of the communication characteristics attributed to partners on relationship satisfaction, a second hierarchical multiple regression analysis was performed. With the inclusion of the control variable sex at step 1, the equation was again not significant, $F < 1$. At step 2, with all of the partner communication attributions entered, a marginally significant increment in explained variance emerged, F (change) $= 2.20$, $p < .06$, but the overall regression equation failed to reach significance, $F (6, 88) = 1.90$, $p = .09$.

CONCLUSIONS

Our results suggest that self-attributions of communication may be more potent overall than partner attributions as predictors of relationship quality, even though both types of attribution showed significant correlations with satisfaction scores. In line with the relatively weak evidence for self-serving patterns of attribution cited earlier and with the strong suggestion of reciprocity in partners' attributions of communication strategies such as openness, avoidance, and hostility, it is conceivable that young couples' relationship satisfaction is mediated by reasonably accurate perceptions of their own and partners' communicative goals, intentions, and abilities. Nevertheless, as previous researchers have found, young adults in the early stages of a couple relationship vary widely in their communication abilities, and such variations are likely to have a profound impact on the quality both of safe-sex discussions in particular and relationship quality in general. Avoidant communication strategies have emerged as negative predictors of satisfaction in previous research, reinforcing the finding of the present study that young adults who attributed avoidant communication intentions to themselves scored low in satisfaction both with their couple relationship and with their videotaped safe-sex discussion.

Of course, suggestions such as these remain tentative until confirmed in future research by using a wider and more diverse sample of couples and a broader sample of communication behaviors and attribution dimensions. Researchers might also explore a varied set of alternative windows into lovers' attributions of causality to the communication process and the attributional outcomes of such challenging tasks as revealing their sexual histories, their anxieties about safe sex and STDs, and their desires to use (or not to use) condoms in their relationship. The importance of these issues, both for intimate relationships and for public health, cannot be overestimated.

REFERENCES

Altman, I., & Taylor, D. A. (1973). *Social penetration: The development of interpersonal relationships.* New York: Holt, Rinehart & Winston.

Bales, R. F. (1950). A set of categories for the analysis of small group interaction. *American Sociology Review, 15,* 257–263.

Bales, R. F. (1970). *Personality and interpersonal behavior.* New York: Holt, Rinehart, & Winston.

Boldero, J., Moore, S., & Rosenthal, D. (1992). Intention, context, and safe sex: Australian adolescents' responses to AIDS. *Journal of Applied Social Psychology, 22*, 1374–1396.

Bradbury, T. N., & Fincham, F. D. (1992). Attributions and behavior in marital interaction. *Journal of Personality and Social Psychology, 63*, 613–628.

Burgoon, J. K., Stern, L. A., & Dillman, L. (1995). *Interpersonal adaptation: Dyadic interaction patterns.* Cambridge, UK: Cambridge University Press.

Cline, R. J., Freeman, K., & Johnson, S. J. (1990). Talk among sexual partners about AIDS: Factors differentiating those who talk from those who do not. *Communication Research, 17*, 792–808.

Cohen, J. (1960). A coefficient of agreement for nominal scales. *Educational and Psychological Measurement, 20*, 37–46.

Crawford, J., Turtle, A., & Kippax, S. (1990). Student favored strategies for AIDS avoidance. *Australian Journal of Psychology, 42*, 123–137.

Derlega, V. J., Winstead, B. A., Wong, P. T. P., & Greenspan, M. (1993). Self-disclosure and relationship development: An attributional analysis. In V. J. Derlega, S. Metts, S. Petronio, & S. T. Margulis (Eds.), *Self-disclosure* (pp. 172–187). Newbury Park, CA: Sage.

Desiderato, L. L., & Crawford, H. J. (1995). Risky sexual behavior in college students: Relationships between number of sexual partners, disclosure of previous risky behavior, and alcohol use. *Journal of Youth and Adolescence, 24*, 55–68.

Fisher, J. D., & Fisher, W. A. (1992). Changing AIDS-risk behavior. *Psychological Bulletin, 111*, 455–474.

Gallois, C., Terry, D., Timmins, P., Kashima, Y., & McCamish, M. (1994). Safe sexual intentions and behavior among heterosexuals and homosexual men: Testing the theory of reasoned action. *Psychology and Health, 10*, 1–16.

Heider, F. (1958). *The psychology of interpersonal relations.* New York: Wiley.

Kane, T. S. (1983). *Oxford guide to writing: A rhetoric handbook for college students.* Oxford: Oxford University Press.

Kelly, J. A., St. Lawrence, J. S., Hood, H. V., & Brasfield, T. J. (1989). Behavioral intervention to reduce AIDS risk activities. *Journal of Consulting and Clinical Psychology, 57*, 60–67.

Manusov, V. (1995). Reacting to changes in nonverbal behaviors: Relational satisfaction and adaptation patterns in romantic dyads. *Human Communication Research, 21*, 456–477.

Manusov, V., Floyd, K., & Kerssen-Griep, J. (1997). Yours, mine, and ours: Mutual attributions for nonverbal behaviors in couples' interactions. *Communication Research, 24*, 234–260.

Noller, P. (1984). *Nonverbal behavior in marital interaction.* Oxford, UK: Pergamon.

Norton, R. (1983). Measuring marital quality: A critical look at the dependent variable. *Journal of Marriage and the Family, 45*, 141–152.

Peterson, C. C. (1990). Disagreement, negotiation and conflict resolution in families with adolescents. In P. Heaven & V. Callan (Eds.) *Adolescence: An Australian perspective* (pp. 66–82). Sydney: Harcourt/Brace, Jovanovich.

Peterson, C. C. (1996). Deception in intimate relationships. *International Journal of Psychology, 31*, 279–288.

Pittam, J., & Gallois, C. (1997). Attribution of blame in conversations about HIV and AIDS. *Communication Monographs, 64,* 201–218.

Reitman, D., St. Lawrence J. S., Jefferson, K. W., & Allyne, E. (1996) Predictors of African American adolescents' condom use and HIV risk behavior. *AIDS Education & Prevention, 8,* 499–515.

Rosenthal, D., & Peart, R. (1996). The rules of the game: Teenagers communicating about sex. *Journal of Adolescence, 19,* 321–332.

Troth, A., & Peterson, C. (2000). Factors prediciting safe-sex talk and condom use in early sexual relationships. *Health Communication, 12,* 195–218.

Vangelisti, A. L., Corbin, S. D., Lucchetti, A. E., & Sprague, R. J. (1999). Couples' concurrent cognitions: The influence of relational satisfaction on the thoughts couples have as they converse. *Human Communication Research, 25,* 370–398.

Weiner, B. (1985). "Spontaneous" causal thinking. *Psychological Bulletin, 97,* 74–84.

Wong, P. T. P., & Weiner, B. (1981). When people ask "why" questions, and the heuristics of attributional search. *Journal of Personality and Social Psychology, 40,* 650–663.

Zuckerman, M. (1979). Attribution of success and failure revisited: The motivational bias is alive and well in attribution theory. *Journal of Personality, 47,* 245–287.

CHAPTER FIFTEEN

Why Do People Have Affairs?

Recent Research and Future Directions About Attributions for Extramarital Involvement

David C. Atkins, Sona Dimidjian, and Neil S. Jacobson

Recent representative national surveys estimate that 20 to 25% of contemporary married persons will have an affair at some point in their lives (Greeley, 1994; Laumann, Gagnon, Michael, & Michaels, 1994; Wiederman, 1997). Yet, despite the long history and wide prevalence of extramarital involvement (EMI), social scientists have only begun to study the phenomenon in earnest over the last 25 years. This work comes from a number of disciplines representing a number of research perspectives, leading Parker (1997) to comment that the study of non-monogamy "has been unsystematic and does not lend coherence to a theoretical understanding of [nonmonogamy]; rather, it may more closely approximate unfocused empiricism" (p. 2).

One route to synthesizing the literature is through examining the central and organizing questions in the field. A central question in the study of EMI is, why do people have affairs? The question of why is often foremost on the minds of individuals whose lives are affected by EMI, and lay theories of why people have affairs abound in the culture at large. To date, empirical investigations of why have been approached in two primary ways: through studies examining popular theories about reasons for EMI and through research that focuses explicitly on reason giving or causal attributions for EMI.

Popular theories regarding reasons for EMI often reference two factors, gender and marital satisfaction. For instance, men and women are frequently assumed to have affairs for different reasons. Sexual motivations are more commonly ascribed to men, while women are assumed to be motivated primarily by forces of love and emotional

Correspondence should be addressed to David Atkins, Center for Clinical Research, University of Washington, Seattle, WA 98195.

attachment. In the area of marital satisfaction, individuals are thought to have affairs because their primary relationships are discordant or dissatisfying. Much of the research on EMI has focused on investigating whether these commonly held beliefs can be supported by empirical data.

An explicit focus on causal attribution in the area of EMI has also provided important contributions to our understanding of why people have affairs. In fact, since the "cognitive revolution" in psychology in the 1970s, attributions—or how people account for and explain the events in their own and others' lives—have attracted great research interest. It is, however, only in the last decade that researchers have addressed the issue of attribution in nonmonogamy specifically. These studies investigate directly how people might explain their own (usually hypothetical) nonmonogamy or the attributions one makes about the hypothetical nonmonogamy of an intimate partner.

In general, this chapter reviews the literature on gender and marital satisfaction in relation to EMI. We focus on the contributions and shortcomings of these areas of research, highlighting how the research to date has influenced our understanding of why people engage in nonmonogamy. Finally, we also examine some of the methodological difficulties that arise in studying nonmonogamy and suggest directions for future research.

THE ROLE OF GENDER

Numerous research studies have identified gender as a critical variable in extramarital behavior, which is consistent with popular assumptions about EMI. For instance, such assumptions often suggest that affairs are most frequently a male phenomenon, and that as previously mentioned, when women do engage in EMI, their reasons for so doing differ significantly from men's reasons. Some data suggest that more men than women *have* engaged in extramarital involvement (Wiederman, 1997). Moreover, of those men and women who do engage in nonmonogamy, it is reported that men are likely to have a greater number of liaisons (Lawson, 1988; Spanier & Margolis, 1983) and to express greater interest in affairs (Buunk & Bakker, 1995; Seal, Agostinelli, & Hannett, 1994; Thompson, 1984) than do women. Additionally, some studies report that men express more liberal attitudes toward EMI than do women (Christensen, 1973, cited in Thompson, 1984; Reiss, Anderson, & Sponaugle, 1980; Sheppard, Nelson, & Andreoli-Mathie,

1995). In their meta-analysis of gender differences in sexuality, Oliver and Hyde (1993) reported that men held more permissive attitudes toward extramarital sex than women did, although the effect size was small ($d = .29$).

Some recent research suggests, however, that the gender gap in EMI may be decreasing (Greeley, 1994; Laumann et al., 1994; Thompson, 1983; Wiederman, 1997; also see Parker, 1997, for a recent study that failed to find gender differences). Oliver and Hyde's (1993) meta-analysis examined gender differences by the year of data collection, and their results suggested that rates of affairs are becoming more similar among younger cohorts. Recent findings also indicated that gender differences in attitudes toward extramarital sex have an inverse relationship with age, with younger cohorts expressing more similar attitudes (Oliver & Hyde, 1993). This finding is similar to other research that has found no gender differences for individuals under the age of 40 (Wiederman, 1997).

Lawson (1988) provides further evidence that, as with behavior, the gender gap in attitudes towards EMI is diminishing. In her study, participants were asked to comment retrospectively on their attitudes towards fidelity at the time of their first marriage, at the time of their most recent marriage, and at the time the survey was conducted. Results demonstrated that at the time of their first marriage, participants overwhelmingly believed that they should be sexually faithful (90%), and women were more likely to support sexual fidelity (94%) than were men (84%). However, results for current attitudes suggest that there was a large increase in permissiveness over time; only 63% of men and women believed in sexual exclusivity at the time of the interview (Lawson, 1988). Moreover, differences between men and women with regard to present attitudes were not significantly different.

Multiple studies have also addressed the relevance of gender to the causal attributions individuals make about EMI. Overall, these studies provide some evidence supporting the conclusion that women and men seek different "types" of extramarital involvement and engage in extramarital relationships for different reasons (Glass & Wright, 1977, 1992; Spanier & Margolis, 1983; Thompson, 1984). Results from a questionnaire-based study (Glass & Wright, 1985) suggest that men describe their affairs as more sexual than emotional, whereas women describe their affairs as more emotional than sexual. In addition, the actual degree of sexual involvement is greater among men, and more men report engaging in extramarital sexual intercourse.

Although no sex differences exist in the *incidence* of emotional involvement, the *degree* of emotional involvement is greater among women. Among those participants who had engaged in extramarital intercourse, men were more likely than women to have slight or no emotional involvement: 44% versus 11%, respectively (Glass & Wright, 1985). These findings are similar to those of Spanier and Margolis (1983), who found that women who had been involved in an affair tended to be more emotionally involved with their affair partners than had men; 40.5% of women versus 11.5% of men described their last extramarital relationship as a more long-term love relationship. The involved women also reported greater feelings of guilt.

Glass and Wright (1992) addressed the issue of causal attributions directly by exploring men's and women's justifications for EMI. Participants completed a self-report questionnaire asking them to rate the extent to which they would feel justified engaging in EMI based on 17 possible reasons, and the authors used factor analysis to analyze responses. Four factors summarizing participants' justifications for affairs emerged, accounting for 74% of the total variance. The authors named these factors *sexual* (sexual enjoyment, curiosity, excitement, and novelty); *emotional intimacy* (intellectual sharing, companionship, ego-bolstering aspects of enhancing self-esteem, and respect); *extrinsic motivation* (getting even with spouse and career advancement); and *love* (receiving love and affection and falling in love).

Both men's and women's responses clustered into these four factors; however, the sexual dimension was the first factor to emerge for men and the second to emerge for women, whereas the emotional intimacy factor was the first to emerge for women and the second to emerge for men (Glass & Wright, 1992). Results also suggest that men were more approving of sexual justifications than were women. Involved women approved of love justifications more than did involved men, although no gender differences existed for noninvolved participants. This may suggest that justifications change as a result of one's EMI or that individuals with different attitudes engage in nonmonogamy. Moreover, no gender differences were found with regard to approval of emotional intimacy justifications (Glass & Wright, 1992).

Related studies also demonstrate that others perceive men's and women's extramarital behavior to be differently motivated. Results from a person perception experiment with undergraduates indicated that participants' perceptions of the likely outcome of the extramarital relationship were influenced by the sex of the involved spouse

(Sprecher, Regan, & McKinney, 1998). In particular, married women engaging in extramarital relations were perceived as experiencing more love and commitment for their affair partners and were perceived as more likely to marry the affair partner. "These results are consistent with other research indicating that people believe that the love-sex association is stronger for women than for men" (Sprecher et al., 1998, p. 308).

Kitzinger and Powell (1995) examined possible sex differences in motivations to engage in nonmonogamy. They administered a story completion task to undergraduate students in which a narrative describes an affair by either a male or female partner. Content analysis of the students' stories suggested that men more frequently perceived the affair relationship in primarily sexual terms. Male participants saw the female perpetrator as motivated by sexual dissatisfaction with their partner, and men did not perceive the perpetrator of either sex as motivated by emotional factors. Male participants also tended to minimize the emotional impact of EMI on men in the stories and included male physical violence in their written reactions to the stories (36% of male responses). Female participants, on the other hand, more frequently relied on emotional factors to explain motivation for men and women to engage in EMI and tended to emphasize the negative emotional impact of EMI on men and women (Kitzinger & Powell, 1995).

Mongeau, Hale, and Alles (1994) used a person perception experiment to investigate participants' responses to an extramarital sexual involvement. In their study, the researchers controlled whether the sexual involvement was revenge-motivated (i.e., based on discovering that the partner was having an affair) and whether the affair was intentional or accidental. They also considered the sex of the participant and that of the character in the vignette. After reading the scenario, participants were asked about the intent, responsibility, blame, and guilt of the perpetrator in the story. Participants also gave accounts of why they may have had the affair: "What would you say to [partner's name] in an attempt to explain your behavior?" (p. 333).

As is consistent with past research, the sex of the character in the story influenced participants' attributions of the nonmonogamy. Participants evaluated female perpetrators as being more responsible and as experiencing more guilt for the affair than male perpetrators. Furthermore, participants perceived perpetrators of the opposite sex as acting more intentionally than perpetrators of their own sex. Several writers have noted that there is a sexual double standard in our society such that men and women are evaluated differently in terms of their sexuality (Schwartz & Rutter, 1998; Sprecher & McKinney, 1993). This study supports such a contention. Finally, regardless of the perpetrator's sex, if the affair in the vignette was seen as retaliatory for a partner's affair, participants rated the perpetrator lower in blame, responsibility, and guilt (Mongeau et al., 1994).

Although gender differences such as the ones reported above are highlighted consistently in the literature, much of the research on EMI has failed to provide a comprehensive or convincing explanatory model that accounts for the role of gender in EMI. Attempts to explain why gender influences who has affairs and how people perceive extramarital involvement have typically relied on sociobiological or sex-role–socialization theory.

Sociobiologists (e.g., Buss & Schmitt, 1993; Shackelford & Buss, 1997) suggest that gender differences in EMI are a natural by-product of human evolution. They theorize that the human species, through the process of natural selection, is motivated primarily by the drive to reproduce and thus ensure continuation of the species. Based on this premise, most sociobiologists argue that men are by nature less monogamous, because it is evolutionarily advantageous. A non-monogamous mating strategy allows men to pass on as much of their genetic material as possible to succeeding generations. Women, however, are assumed to be by nature monogamous given a presumed motivation to find a stable mate who will provide the resources necessary to support gestation and child rearing. However, Fisher (1993) uses evolutionary arguments to present a view of how women might be influenced to engage in EMI. She contends that women may search for new partners (roughly every 4 years) – often engaging in a process of serial monogamy – in order to secure more resources for themselves through a more powerful mate.

In contrast to the evolutionary perspective, other researchers have explained gender differences in nonmonogamy by relying on sex-role–socialization theories. For example, in an effort to explain their assertion that men and women participate in different types of affairs, Glass and Wright (1992) point to socialization theories, such as that of Gilligan (1982), who argues that men and women possess fundamentally different moral and psychological perspectives. Women are posited to be more "relational" and contextually oriented, whereas men are more oriented toward individual rights and abstract conceptions of right and wrong. Glass and Wright (1992) state, "One could infer that the attitudinal differences between men and women regarding sexual justifications for EMI represent an individualistic motivation by men and a relational motivation by women that parallels Gilligan's (1982) differentiation of male–female ethics" (p. 379). Fundamental psychological differences between men and women are assumed to shape the gender-determined experience of non-monogamy.

A common theme in both sociobiology and sex-role–socialization theories is that gender differences in EMI result from stable, internal, and enduring characteristics of men and women. The narrow focus on stable individual characteristics (i.e., biology and psychology), however, may risk underestimating the influence of potentially critical environmental and structural variables. Yet, multiple environmental or sociocultural variables may be relevant to a discussion of the role of gender in EMI. For instance, economic disparities and other social structural differences between men and women are likely to shape men and women's experiences of, and reasons for, nonmonogamy. Women may risk more than men do by participating in EMI. Women are more likely to be economically vulnerable following divorce, given that they tend to earn less than men do and to retain primary child rearing responsibilities. These factors may make women less likely to pursue or participate in EMI or to hold positive attitudes toward EMI. Women's vulnerability to pregnancy and sexually transmitted diseases may also make participation in EMI a more risky proposition for women than for men. Furthermore, society has traditionally censured women far more harshly for EMI than men. For instance, Schwartz and Rutter (1998) note that until 1960, a wife's affair was cause for justifiable homicide in the state of Texas.

Finally, a range of factors also limits women's opportunity to engage in nonmonogamy. The fact that women are traditionally more likely to be primarily responsible for child care and housework means that women will have less opportunity (and perhaps less energy) to participate in EMI. Social forces that tend to constrain women's level of comfort with active expression of sexual desire also are likely to influence their degree of opportunity. For instance, Schwartz and Rutter (1998) describe a study by Heiman (1977) in which the researcher measured both men's and women's physiological responses to erotic material and collected self-report data on their level of arousal. Results suggested that women underreported their level of arousal in the self-report data, whereas men provided more accurate measures. Moreover, researchers have found differences in sexual initiation, suggesting that women are likely to receive negative responses from their partners if they initiate sexual activity more than do their male partners (Blumstein & Schwartz, 1983). These data imply that social forces may place women in a more passive position regarding the initiation of EMI, thus creating less opportunity for women than for men.

In summary, gender appears to be a powerful factor influencing EMI. Gender has been associated with the prevalence of affairs, types of affairs, as well as attitudes toward and justifications or attributions for affairs. Yet there are still aspects of the relationship between gender and EMI that remain unclear. Those studies that have taken the age of their participants into account have generally found differences in both attitudes and behaviors among separate cohorts, possibly indicating that the impact of gender is changing over time.

THE ROLE OF MARITAL SATISFACTION

Oscar Wilde wrote, "The one charm of marriage is that it makes a life of deception absolutely necessary for both parties." One of the most popular causal attributions regarding EMI is that unhappiness or conflict in the primary relationship leads to the affair. The association between relationship satisfaction and affairs has frequently been studied in the non-monogamy literature; however, the research findings to date have not clearly supported or disproved the influence of marital dissatisfaction on affairs. Thompson (1984) refers to a "deficit model" of extramarital involvement, in which deficiencies of the primary relationship are perceived to have a role in precipitating and sustaining EMI. He reviewed 10 studies that examined the association between marital variables and nonmonogamy and found only one study (Neubeck & Schletzer, 1969) that failed to find a significant relationship between marital satisfaction and EMI. However, other researchers have commented that this study used a small sample with a low incidence of nonmonogamy (Glass & Wright, 1988). Based on his review, Thompson estimated that characteristics of the marriage (low marital satisfaction and low sexual frequency) reliably account for 25% of the variance in EMI. Other, more recent studies have found that marital conflict may make a couple more susceptible to an extramarital affair (Buss & Shackelford, 1997) and that relational dissatisfaction may increase the desire to become involved in an affair (Prins, Buunk, & Van Yperen, 1993).

On the other hand, some studies have failed to find a relationship between affairs and marital satisfaction (Cuber, 1969). Blumstein and Schwartz (1983), in their large sample survey of American couples, did not find an association between either marital satisfaction or sexual frequency and nonmonogamy. Spanier and Margolis (1983), in their study of divorced individuals, reported that quality of marital sex was unrelated to occurrence of extramarital sex among a sample of recently separated and divorced respondents. In addition, several therapists support the idea that affairs do not automatically imply the presence of a bad marriage (Elbaum, 1981; Finzi, 1989).

Despite these latter findings, people believe that there is a link between dissatisfaction and EMI. In a study focusing specifically on attributions, for example, Wiederman and Allgeier (1996) conducted interviews with young married couples, inquiring about the couples' expectations regarding monogamy and attributions for a hypothetical affair. The overwhelming majority of their sample expected that their partner would remain sexually monogamous, and the most likely reason given for a potential affair was that the spouse was dissatisfied and unfulfilled with the marriage.

These findings, however, conflict with those reported by Buunk (1984). He studied 218 men and women from the Netherlands whose partner had had an affair within the last 2 years, and the majority of participants (85%) had been involved in an affair themselves. Participants in this study reported attraction to the affair partner, the circumstances, and the need for variety as the most common reasons for their partners' affairs. Fewer of the study participants mentioned problems in their relationship as a reason for their partners' affairs. When study participants did report relationship problems as a cause for their partners' affairs, this attribution was highly related to their own, self-reported jealousy. Thus, Buunk found that other reasons besides relationship dissatisfaction were more commonly reported as the cause of an affair. However, problems in the relationship may be a more distressing reason for the noninvolved partner.

Interestingly, Buunk's (1984) findings suggest that studies with people who have experienced an affair may yield quite different results from those of studies with participants who simply imagine their reaction to, or reasons for, a hypothetical affair. Moreover, as we discuss in the following section below, interpretation of many of the studies on EMI and relationship satisfaction are hindered by the fact that satisfaction is often studied retrospectively, which makes it difficult to determine whether relationship dissatisfaction preceded or followed the affair. In addition, a self-report bias may be evident in such studies. One study with recently separated and divorced individuals found that 52% of men and 46% of women thought that their partners' affair caused their marital problems. In contrast, only 6% of respondents thought their own affair caused marital problems. The majority (70% of respondents) thought that their own EMI was a result of preexisting marital dissatisfaction (Spanier & Margolis, 1983).

Finally, there is some evidence that other variables may moderate the association of relationship dissatisfaction with nonmonogamy. Glass and Wright (1985) have suggested that the type of affair may interact with marital satisfaction. In particular, they found that "sexual only" affairs are less likely to be related to marital dissatisfaction than "combined-type" affairs that include both sexual and emotional components. They note that "since women are more likely than men to participate in a combined-type involvement, there is often a greater association between the state of the marriage and EMI for women than for men" (Glass & Wright, 1988, p. 308). In their sample, they reported that approximately half of men and one-third of women with EMI report happy marriages, which is very similar to earlier data from Hunt (1974).

Another potential mediator of marital satisfaction may be religiosity. A survey study using a nationally representative sample found a significant interaction between religiosity and marital satisfaction. Respondents who reported high marital satisfaction and did not attend religious services were more likely to have had an affair than those who reported high marital satisfaction but frequently attended religious services. Couples with moderate or low marital satisfaction reported higher rates of affairs than highly satisfied couples, but their religiosity did not influence their likelihood of an affair (Atkins & Jacobson, 1999).

In summary, the literature provides mixed support for the influence of relationship satisfaction on nonmonogamy. Unfortunately, numerous methodological problems, which we detail in the following section, limit our ability to understand definitively whether relationship satisfaction does have an impact on affairs and the nature of its influence.

CRITIQUE AND FUTURE DIRECTIONS

Many research studies have explored the area of EMI and associated attributions, and their findings point to some reasons why people have affairs. However, extramarital involvement is inherently difficult to study. Researchers have used various methodologies to address and study affairs, and unfortunately, many of these studies are hampered by methodological problems. In this section we examine some of the methodological issues that are endemic to the field of non-monogamy research.

As already noted, one issue that has been a significant problem in much of the existing research on EMI is sample selection. Spouses are often unaware of their partners' affairs, and it is reasonable to assume that someone involved in an affair might be reticent to participate in a research study. Most researchers find that it is especially challenging to recruit participants who are involved in an affair, and likely as a result, many studies have opted for samples of convenience. Depending on the specific focus of the research, this can drastically affect the findings of the study as well as limit its generalizability.

One popular method of dealing with this participant problem is using person perception studies, in which participants are presented with a scenario portraying the discovery of an affair, and they are then asked for their attributions as to why this may have occurred. This methodology is very flexible, as the researcher may vary certain elements of the scenario and see how the participants (or different types of participants) respond to the varying vignettes. However, many of the studies using this methodology employ college undergraduates. While such samples provide one window into society's response to, or attributions about, EMI, 19 to 20-year-old students, who may have never had a serious or committed intimate relationship, are not representative of society at large. Moreover, such samples tell us little about the actual experiences of individuals who have engaged in EMI.

Another common strategy for those interested in variables that may influence EMI is to have one or both spouses rate the likelihood that they will have an affair or engage in a certain number of extramarital behaviors (Shackelford & Buss, 1997). This practice itself is not problematic if the aim is to study people's hypothetical propensity to engage in nonmonogamy; however, often there is a tendency for researchers to discuss their findings as if they were studying couples in which an affair had occurred. The few studies that have used split samples, in which some individuals have had affairs and others have not, have generally found significant differences between these two classes of participants (Buunk & Bakker, 1995; Glass & Wright, 1992; Roscoe, Cavanaugh, & Kennedy, 1988). To study many of the issues related to EMI, samples of individuals who have engaged in EMI will be required. At the very least, there is a need for studies using participants who have had affairs to replicate the findings of studies that have used a "likelihood" measure or person perception methodology.

The study of nonmonogamy would also benefit from a greater attention to longitudinal design. Despite a thorough review of the literature in this area, we are familiar with no longitudinal studies of extramarital behavior. Prospective longitudinal designs are required for the investigation of "causes" of EMI. For example, as we noted earlier, one of the most frequently cited findings is that deficits in the primary relationship lead to affairs via marital dissatisfaction. At present, however, the field lacks data on the temporal order of EMI and marital dissatisfaction. Does marital dissatisfaction precede an affair, or do affairs typically precede marital satisfaction? The absence of longitudinal data prohibit us from drawing any definitive conclusions about causal associations between dissatisfaction in the primary relationship and EMI. Spanier and Margolis (1983) have demonstrated that affairs can be significantly disruptive events for the primary relationship and can distort retrospective causal attributions.

Another area where nonmonogamy research can move forward is in understanding the influences of gender on extramarital involvement. Numerous studies have shown that gender can have an important influence on affairs, but researchers need to be more precise about how this influence is exerted. Consider, for example, Glass and Wright's (1985) conclusions about how men and women characterized their affairs along sexual and emotional dimensions. They conclude, "Men and women differ in type of extramarital involvement in ways that reflect traditional sex roles: Men are more sexual and women are more emotional" (Glass & Wright, 1985, p. 1113). In fact, it seems highly possible that men and women are more similar than different, particularly if potential reporting biases are considered.

Most studies of EMI utilize self-report data, and men's and women's actual attitudes and behaviors may not be the same as their reported attitudes and behaviors. In their meta-analysis of gender differences in sexuality, Oliver and Hyde (1993) conclude, "Males may have a tendency to exaggerate their sexual experiences (at least the socially approved ones). Females may underreport their sexual experiences. Either or both trends could create gender differences in self-reports where no actual differences in behaviors or attitudes exist or could magnify a small gender difference" (p. 45). The adoption of dichotomous terms such as *emotional* and *sexual* obscures the importance of sex in women's experiences of EMI and likely obscures the presence of emotion in men's experiences as well.

When an area of research is new, methodological concerns often are not the foremost focus. Reliance on samples of convenience, quasi-experimental designs, or unvalidated measures can be common in the exploratory phases of research. Nonmonogamy research, however, is no longer in its nascent phase, and there is a need to address and improve on the methodological problems that come with research in this area. As our review of the EMI literature suggests, research to date has provided important information about why people have affairs, yet many questions remain.

The investigation of gender and relationship satisfaction, in particular, has yielded insights into why people have affairs. But even these well researched topics still pose questions. Are men's and women's behavior and attitudes changing with regard to affairs? What is the interaction of opportunity to engage in EMI, gender, and causal attribution for EMI? Does relationship distress precede or follow EMI? Moreover, there is clearly much to explore and study beyond these areas. For instance, we have little data about factors specific to the affair relationship and how these factors influence one's propensity to engage in EMI. Future research likely will benefit from a focus on these questions and areas as well as attention to the methodological critiques presented in this chapter. The study of EMI is often complicated and controversial; however, further research in this area holds great importance both for basic research on close and intimate relationships and for clinical intervention.

REFERENCES

Amato, P. R., & Rogers, S. J. (1997). A longitudinal study of marital problems and subsequent divorce. *Journal of Marriage and the Family, 59,* 612–624.

Atkins, D. C., & Jacobson, N. S. (2000). *Why do people have affairs? Modeling the influences of infidelity*. Manuscript submitted for publication.

Blumstein, P., & Schwartz, P. (1983). *American couples: Money, work, and sex.* New York: William Morrow.

Buss, D. M., & Shackelford, T. K. (1997). Susceptibility to infidelity in the first year of marriage. *Journal of Research in Personality, 31,* 193–221.

Buss, D. M., & Schmitt, D. P. (1993). Sexual strategies theory: An evolutionary perspective on human mating. *Psychological Review, 100,* 204–232.

Buunk, B. P. (1984). Jealousy as related to attributions for the partner's behavior. *Social Psychology Quarterly, 47,* 107–112.

Buunk, B. P., & Bakker, A. B. (1995). Extradyadic sex: The role of descriptive and injunctive norms. *The Journal of Sex Research, 32,* 313–318.

Cuber, J. F. (1969). Adultery: Reality versus stereotype. In G. Neubeck (Ed.), *Extramarital Relations* (pp. 190–196). Englewood Cliffs, NJ: Prentice-Hall.

Elbaum, P. L. (1981). The dynamics, implications and treatment of extramarital sexual relationships for the family therapist. *Journal of Marital and Family Therapy, 7,* 489–495.

Finzi, S. C. (1989). Cosi fan tutte: So does everyone. *The Family Therapy Networker 13,* 31–33.

Fisher, H. E. (1993, March 1). After all, maybe it's biology. *Psychology Today.*

Gilligan, C. (1982). *In a different voice.* Cambridge, MA: Harvard University Press.

Glass, S. P., & Wright, T. L. (1977). The relationship of extramarital sex, length of marriage, and sex differences on marital satisfaction and romanticism: Athanasiou's data reanalyzed. *Journal of Marriage and the Family, 39,* 691–703.

Glass, S. P., & Wright, T. L. (1985). Sex differences in types of extramarital involvement and marital dissatisfaction. *Sex Roles, 12,* 1101–1119.

Glass, S. P., & Wright, T. L. (1988). Clinical implications of research on extramarital involvement. In R. Brown & J. Field (Eds.), *Treatment of sexual problems in individual and couple's therapy.* New York: PMA Publishing Corp.

Glass, S. P., & Wright, T. L. (1992). Justifications for extramarital involvement: The association between attitudes, behavior, and gender. *Journal of Sex Research, 29,* 361–387.

Greeley, A. (1994). Marital infidelity. *Society, 31*(4), 9–13.

Heiman, J. R. (1977). A psychophysiological exploration of sexual arousal patterns in females and males. *Psychophysiology, 14,* 266–274.

Hunt, M. (1974). *Sexual behavior in the 1970's.* New York: Playboy Press.

Kitzinger, C., & Powell, D. (1995). Engendering infidelity: Essentialist and social constructionist readings of a story completion task. *Feminism & Psychology, 5,* 345–372.

Laumann, E. O., Gagnon, J. H., Michael, R. T., & Michaels, S. (1994). *The social organization of sexuality: Sexual practices in the United States.* Chicago: University of Chicago Press.

Lawson, A. (1988). *Adultery: An analysis of love and betrayal.* New York: Basic Books.

Mongeau, P. A., Hale, J. L., & Alles, M. (1994). An experimental investigation of accounts and attributions following sexual infidelity. *Communication Monographs, 61,* 326–344.

Neubeck, G., & Schletzer, V. M. (1969). A study of extramarital relationships. In G. Neubeck (Ed.), *Extramarital relations* (pp. 146–152). Englewood Cliffs, NJ: Prentice-Hall.

Parker, R. G. (1997). The influence of sexual infidelity, verbal intimacy, and gender upon primary appraisal processes in romantic jealousy. *Women's Studies in Communication, 20,* 1–24.

Prins, K. S., Buunk, B. P., & VanYperen, N. W. (1993). Equity, normative disapproval and extramarital relationships. *Journal of Social and Personal Relationships, 10,* 39–53.

Reiss, I. L., Anderson, R. E., & Sponaugle, G. C. (1980). A multivariate model of the determinates of extramarital sexual permissiveness. *Journal of Marriage and the Family, 42,* 395–411.

Roscoe, B, Cavanaugh, L. E., & Kennedy, D. R. (1988). Dating infidelity: Behaviors, reasons and consequences. *Adolescence, 23,* 35–43.

Schwartz, P., & Rutter, V. (1998). *The gender of sexuality.* Thousand Oaks, CA: Pine Forge Press.

Seal, D. W., Agostinelli, G., & Hannett, C. (1994). Extradyadic romantic involvement: Moderating effects of sociosexuality and gender. *Sex Roles, 31,* 1–22.

Shackelford, T. K., & Buss, D. M. (1997). Cues to infidelity. *Personality and Social Psychology Bulletin, 23,* 1034–1045.

Sheppard, V. J., Nelson, E. S., & Andreoli-Mathie, V. (1995). Dating relationships and infidelity: Attitudes and behaviors. *Journal of Sex & Marital Therapy, 21,* 202–212.

Spanier, G. B., & Margolis, R. L. (1983). Marital separation and extramarital sexual behavior. *The Journal of Sex Research, 19,* 23–48.

Sprecher, S., & McKinney, K. (1993). *Sexuality.* Newbury Park, CA: Sage Publications.

Sprecher, S., Regan, P. C., & McKinney, K. (1998). Beliefs about the outcomes of extramarital sexual relationships as a function of the gender of the "cheating spouse." *Sex Roles, 38,* 301–311.

Thompson, A. P. (1983). Extramarital sex: A review of the research literature. *The Journal of Sex Research, 19,* 1–22.

Thompson, A. P. (1984). Extramarital sexual crisis: Common themes and therapy implications. *Journal of Sex & Marital Therapy, 10,* 239–254.

Wiederman, M. W. (1997). Extramarital sex: Prevalence and correlates in a national survey. *The Journal of Sex Research, 34,* 167–174.

Wiederman, M. W., & Allgeier, E. R. (1996). Expectations and attributions regarding extramarital sex among young married individuals. *Journal of Psychology and Human Sexuality, 8,* 21–35.

CHAPTER SIXTEEN

Attribution in Social and Parasocial Relationships

Rebecca B. Rubin and Alan M. Rubin

People use basic attribution processes in forming impressions during initial interactions and when developing social relationships with others. As relationships grow, people develop explanations that take into account both situational influences and personality or dispositional influences for others' behavior. Attribution processes also apply to parasocial relationships that people develop with media personalities. Media consumers such as television viewers often form pseudofriendships with television characters or personalities and make attributions about the actions of these characters.

In this chapter we review basic principles of attribution and how they influence social relationships. We also discuss how these principles affect uncertainty reduction, which is a foundation of both social and parasocial relationships, and note its connection to attribution processes. We then discuss the concept of parasocial interaction and conclude by proposing research directions that apply principles of attribution theory to parasocial relationships.

ATTRIBUTION THEORY

Seibold and Spitzberg (1982) provided a coherent summary of attribution theory etymology, research, and application to the communication discipline. As they explained, current interest in attribution stemmed from person perception research prominent in social psychology in the 1940s and 1950s. Initial impressions that people form of others are based on perceptual data organized into consistent meaningful units.

For correspondence about this chapter, please contact Rebecca B. Rubin, School of Communication Studies, Kent State University, P. O. Box 5190, Kent, OH 44242-0001.

Cognitive psychologists and communication researchers alike are concerned with how people glean information from the situation during interaction, how attributions shape relationships, and how attributions influence future communication.

Attribution theory operates from a perspective of information needs. People try to understand why actions occur by attributing the actions either to the circumstances surrounding an event or to personality or dispositional elements (Heider, 1958). Heider argued that observers first consider if the other's actions could be unintentional or caused by the situation and later consider actions a result of the actor's disposition. Ross (1977) called the tendency to emphasize traits and to disregard situational influences a fundamental attribution error.

A key feature in attribution theory is who is making the attribution, the actor or the observer (Jones & Nisbett, 1972). *Actors,* who are dynamically involved with the environment, perceive situational or environmental factors as the cause of their own behaviors. *Passive observers,* on the other hand, see dispositional or personality factors as the cause of an actor's behaviors. For example, an actor will interpret a social blunder, such as not shaking another's outstretched hand, to be the result of not seeing the hand. An observer, though, might see the action as social incompetence or intentionally rude behavior. Actors have more knowledge of the circumstances, motives, and history of the situation, and therefore they are more likely to make situational attributions about themselves. In close relationships, attributions to the other's disposition decrease over time; longer-term relationships are marked by language requiring interpretation from prior experiences and interactions (Fiedler, Semin, Finkenauer, & Berkel, 1995).

Herzog (1994) extended attribution theory by considering both active and passive observers, noting that active observers are much like actors in that they interact and observe at the same time. Passive observers, however, have less information about the context to consider, so they rely on perceived dispositional qualities. In general, however, when actors judge their own behavior, they attribute causes to external factors. Like observers, though, when judging others, actors are more likely to attribute causes to internal factors.

UNCERTAINTY REDUCTION THEORY

Charles Berger brought attribution to the forefront of interpersonal communication in his uncertainty reduction theory. Berger (1979) described passive, active, and interactive strategies for gaining information about others during initial interactions.

Passive strategies include unobtrusive observation in reactive situations (Berger, 1979). Reactivity can range from a being alone in a context to interacting (reacting) with several others. Being alone in a context provides less information than does interacting with others because the latter allows for greater prediction. Social comparison is another passive strategy. People look for validation of their own actions or attitudes from similar others. Increased confidence or certainty occurs when the observed interacts with known others, especially if these others are similar to the observer. Disinhibition search is a third passive strategy. Observers prefer to observe strangers in social situations that are less constrained by rules or norms. Contexts that allow a greater range of behavior permit actors to behave in uninhibited ways; this provides additional information about the observed.

Active strategies require actions and energy on the part of the observer (Berger, 1979). Observers can ask others to report about the target or to structure the environment in such a way as to glean more information about the other. By asking those who know the other, observers gain additional knowledge, which may be distorted. Reporters may distort the information intentionally, may do so unintentionally, or may report to the target that another is asking for information, resulting in changes in the target's behavior. Environmental structuring occurs when the observer alters aspects of the situation and observes the target's behavior. Seating the target next to a good friend at a dinner party, for example, might combine both of these active strategies.

Interactive strategies require actual interaction with the target. Verbal interrogation, self-disclosure, and deception detection are three types of interactive strategies (Berger, 1979). When people meet for the first time, they ask questions, either directly or indirectly. There are social rules about how many questions people can ask without drawing suspicion and social norms about which questions are asked before others. There is a reciprocity norm that the questioner must also be willing to answer the questions asked (Berger, 1979). This norm also applies to self-disclosure. As one person discloses more intimate information, he or she expects the other to disclose more intimate information as well. Instead of asking, disclosing one's own views might lead to the same result, more information. Finally, people often withhold or distort information when they interact. Several strategies can be used to distort or deceive. Likewise, strategies exist to detect deception and present further false information. Many of these detection and deception strategies are similar to the information strategies described above.

Attribution in Social Relationships

Berger and Calabrese (1975) proposed that strangers need to reduce uncertainty when they meet. Strangers seek information about the other and the situation so they can act in socially appropriate ways. They use proactive and retroactive attributions to explain and predict others' behavior (Berger, 1975). Proactive attribution occurs when people use past behavior to predict future behavior. In retroactive attribution, people use past actions to explain present actions. Uncertainty depends on how many plausible explanations one has for another's behavior. Berger, Gardner, Parks, Schulman, and Miller (1978) proposed that higher levels of uncertainty reduction require more cognitive effort, and more advanced relationships allow for higher levels of attribution.

Berger's (1979) uncertainty reduction theory attempts to explain how understanding actions and predicting future actions decrease uncertainty. "When cognitive uncertainty is decreased, persons are more likely to assert that they know and understand each other. The extent of their knowledge and understanding is determined by the level of knowledge reached and the opportunities available for verifying that knowledge" (Berger, 1979, p. 126). The formal roles in which the actors are situated sometimes reduce this cognitive state of uncertainty. As Jones and Davis (1965) argued in their correspondent inference theory, these formal roles provide information that encourages people to make attributions that the actors are not unique. When actors do not conform to the demands of the roles, however, observers make attributions about the actors' personalities and try to understand them as individuals. Observers form impressions about the mental health and attractiveness of the actor.

Clatterbuck (1979) developed measures of attributional certainty. In various studies researchers have sought to explain how certainty increases as a function of the amount of self-disclosure, nonverbal affiliative expressiveness, amount of verbal communication, information-seeking behavior, intimacy level, reciprocity rate, and similarity (Berger & Calabrese, 1975). Research in this tradition has shown that certainty increases when self-disclosure, information seeking, and verbal communication increase.

Antecedents of Uncertainty Reduction

Berger (1979) also speculated that several antecedents affect interpersonal knowledge generation. Awareness of one's own and another's behavior is most essential. Paying close attention to what the other says and does allows for greater knowledge over time. The incentive, or belief that the other can increase rewards through need satisfaction, is also influential. Friendships, in particular, can function as mechanisms for alleviating loneliness, satisfying needs for inclusion, and providing support. Deviation from expectations or norms is another antecedent. If behavior deviates from the expected, it will be monitored more closely, and finer perceptual units will be needed to increase predictability. Negative feelings often result with unexpected norm violation, whereas positive affect occurs with conformity to norms, especially during initial interactions. However, relationships will not grow if people treat all others in the same way. Individuation is needed to move toward personal relationships that emphasize the uniqueness of the individual, so some deviation also helps to move relationships forward.

Anticipated future interaction also affects relationship development. Monitoring and awareness of the other increase when people believe interaction will occur again in the future. People exchange more biographic or demographic information about themselves when they believe they will interact with one another in the future (Berger & Calabrese, 1975).

Attraction

Berger (1973b) linked Heider's (1958) attribution theory to communication transactions by identifying several questions interactants ask about others. He investigated the last of these questions (Is someone who has similar attributions more attractive?) by having "partners" give feedback to test-taking subjects who either did or did not perform well on the test. The feedback provided either a personal or environmental attribution for success or failure. People attributed failure to factors in the environment and success to their own abilities. They were more attracted to those who agreed with these attributions. In a second study, students' professors provided the feedback, and attraction to the professor was measured (Berger, 1973a). Self-esteem seemed to be a moderating variable. Those with moderate levels of self-esteem were less attracted to the professor than those with very low self-esteem when their failure was attributed to excessive task difficulty, but more attracted to those who attributed success to task easiness.

These attributions are mainly retroactive in nature. They are made after the action to explain why the behavior occurred. Manusov, Floyd, and Kerssen-Griep (1997) examined attributions that couples make for nonverbal and verbal behaviors. Although nonverbal behaviors were interpreted like other behaviors, positive behaviors were not noticed as much as negative nonverbal cues. Relational satisfaction seemed to enhance differences in self and other attributions. As Clatterbuck (1979) suggested, confidence in one's attributions increases one's certainty about the other's personality and future interactions.

Other researchers have examined attributions of credibility and related impressions (McKillip, 1975). Hosman and Tardy (1980) found that the perceptions of another's competence diminished when the other person violated expectations for high disclosure reciprocity in initial situations that contained high disclosure. The focus on competence came from credibility research that had identified up to five dimensions of credibility: sociability, extroversion, competence, composure, and character (McCroskey, Jenson, & Valencia, 1973). Credibility and competence are impressions that observers make about targets on the basis of mostly dispositional attributions. It is not the situation that makes someone credible but, typically, an attribute of the person.

Interpersonal attraction, then, results in large part from interpersonal attribution. People use verbal and nonverbal information to form impressions of others and often compare the resultant image to their self-views. Many interpersonal communication theories suggest that homophily (similarity in attitudes, behavior, and personality) increases attraction (Berger & Calabrese, 1975; cf. Sunnafrank, 1991). Homophily, in turn, motivates future interaction. Both social and parasocial relationships may develop in this way.

PARASOCIAL RELATIONSHIPS

The media provide an illusion of a face-to-face relationship, that is, a parasocial relationship, with media personalities (Horton & Wohl, 1956). Some media have greater social presence and are able to involve us in their presentations to a greater extent than others. Media and their content, then, vary as to their parasocial potential (Nordlund, 1978).

Media such as television use various techniques to foster parasocial relationships. Television characters use techniques similar to those used in interpersonal relationships to help decrease uncertainty and foster the feeling that people know and understand each other. These characters use gestures, gaze, conversational style, small talk to other cast members or to the viewer (acknowledging a viewer's perspective), and informality to encourage feelings of relationship and intimacy. Television producers use spatial arrangements and visual composition such as close-up camera shots (displaying reactions and emotions) to provide a sense that viewers are part of an interpersonal conversation or friendship (e.g., Cathcart & Gumpert, 1986; Rubin, Perse, & Powell, 1985). Meyrowitz (1986) suggested that camera shot composition and distances affect parasocial interaction as viewers interpret and react to paraproxemic relationships.

Characteristics of Parasocial Relationships

Parasocial interaction is a relationship of friendship or intimacy with a media personality based on a person's felt affective ties with that personality (Horton & Wohl, 1956). It may be experienced as "seeking guidance from a media persona, seeing media personalities as friends, imagining being part of a favorite program's social world, and desiring to meet media performers" (Rubin et al., 1985, pp. 156–157). Viewers participate mentally in the lives of these characters and personalities and may even feel that they know these celebrities as they do their own friends. In so doing, they use the three levels of knowledge by which people come to know others, that is, description, prediction, and explanation (Berger et al., 1978). Not only do they make baseline observations but they also form inferences about the attitudes and behaviors of media personalities and develop attributions or explanations for their behavior.

Parasocial interaction is grounded in interpersonal notions of attraction, perceived similarity or homophily, and empathy. Horton and Wohl (1956) suggested that such elements should remind us of face-to-face interaction. As the relationship evolves, we feel that we know the celebrities better and have a personal bond with them. Although such a relationship is actually one-sided, media personae often anticipate audience responses and use informal gestures and a conversational style that mirror interpersonal communication and invite audience interaction (Rubin et al., 1985). Parasocial interaction appears to parallel "interpersonal interaction so that a sense of intimacy and self-disclosure should follow from increased and regular interaction"

(Rubin, 1994, p. 273). We attribute motives to and develop expectations about the behavior of parasocial partners.

Some researchers have suggested that parasocial relationships evolve over time, with a history of shared experiences and regular, dependable visits (e.g., Horton & Wohl, 1956; Levy, 1979). There has been some support for the length of a parasocial relationship leading to greater attributional confidence and in turn to greater parasocial interaction (Perse & Rubin, 1989). However, the quality of the relationship rather than the quantity of interaction seems to matter most. Researchers have typically been unable to find that the amount or duration of exposure to the parasocial partner leads to stronger parasocial relationships directly (e.g., A. M. Rubin et al., 1985; R. B. Rubin & McHugh, 1987). Perhaps the length of interaction plays a different role in parasocial relationships than it does in interpersonal relationships. If so, this might speak against developing socially learned expectations, achieving deeper states of intimacy, and increasing the amount of self-disclosure in parasocial relationships as compared with interpersonal relationships (see Altman & Taylor, 1973). It also might suggest that the opportunities for or strength of proactive and retroactive attributions are limited in parasocial relationships (see Berger & Calabrese, 1975).

Functional Alternatives

According to theoretical orientations such as uses and gratifications, people will seek alternative means of fulfilling their needs if their primary needs are not met (e.g., Nordlund, 1978; Rubin & Rubin, 1985). They might, for example, turn to the media to fill needs for social interaction if face-to-face interaction does not meet these needs. Findings from several studies suggest that various media serve as functional alternatives to face-to-face interaction. For example, Armstrong and Rubin (1989) observed that telephoning a talk-radio host was an accessible and nonthreatening alternative to interpersonal communication for those who were apprehensive or anxious about face-to-face communication. Similarly, Papacharissi and Rubin (1998) found that the Internet may serve as a functional alternative to face-to-face communication for those who do not find face-to-face interaction to be rewarding. Earlier, Rubin and Perse (1987) noted that parasocial interaction with favorite soap opera characters linked negatively to social utility reasons for watching televised soap operas. Perhaps those lacking an interpersonal context for face-to-face interaction sought parasocial involvement with media characters.

Other studies also support the interpersonal nature of parasocial interaction by depicting a process similar to the one by which we come to know other people. In separate studies, R. B. Rubin and her colleagues found that parasocial interaction related positively to (1) perceiving the relationship to be important; (2) being socially and task-attracted to a favorite personality (Rubin & McHugh, 1987); (3) reducing uncertainty; and (4) predicting the attitudes and feelings of the persona accurately (Perse & Rubin, 1989). Perse and Rubin used uncertainty reduction and personal construct theories in developing their conclusions about the need to base parasocial interaction on attributional confidence and on predicting others' attitudes or feeling. Reducing uncertainty about characters, then, can help explain the development of parasocial relationships. The relationship may give meaning to the media experience for the viewer (Alperstein, 1991). In addition, Turner (1993) found that attitude homophily was a sizable predictor of parasocial interaction with television news and entertainment personalities.

Horton and Wohl (1956) argued that parasocial interaction might connote "the formation of compensatory attachments by the socially isolated, the inept, the aged and the invalid, the timid and the rejected" (p. 223). Although parasocial interaction might provide "a functional alternative for inadequate interaction opportunities" (Levy, 1979, p. 70), a compensation model has failed to provide an adequate depiction of developing parasocial relationships. Being lonely, for example, has not predicted greater parasocial interaction (Rubin et al., 1985). Media personalities do not seem to substitute for personal interaction lacking in the lives of the lonely.

Antecedent or Consequent

An additional issue is whether parasocial interaction is an antecedent of or is consequent to communication behavior or media use. Researchers have often treated parasocial interaction as an outcome of behavior (e.g., Rosengren & Windahl, 1972). Levy (1979) argued that the causal direction is from media exposure to parasocial interaction. In addition, parasocial interaction seems to follow from instrumental media use. Involved viewers, but not necessarily heavy viewers, appear likely to form parasocial relationships. For example, a greater sense of parasocial interaction with news personalities and soap opera characters follows from instrumental motivation (i.e., information, exciting entertainment, and social utility) to use media. Active media orientations have implications for active versus passive strategies for gaining information and for how much accurate information may be acquired about the actor (Berger, 1979).

Scholars have also identified gender relationships in the degree of parasocial interaction. Hoffner (1996) found that perceived character traits differentially predicted parasocial interaction with a favorite male or female television character for boys and girls. For both girls and boys, attractiveness and intelligence significantly predicted parasocially interacting with favorite male characters. However, for girls, attractiveness was the only significant predictor of parasocial interaction with favorite female characters. Cohen (1997) also found that males and females differed when focusing on dating relationships. Males who felt more attachment anxiety about their dating relationships had stronger parasocial relationships, whereas women who were more secure about their dating relationships exhibited stronger parasocial relationships with favorite television characters. Cohen explained the differences on the basis of diversity in media audience reactions, whereby people experience attachment needs and parasocial relationships differently in various situations. In this case, reactions are based on gender differences in romantic relationships.

Parasocial interaction may also be more important than a program's content for determining viewing intent, selection, and expectations (Conway & Rubin, 1991). Grant, Guthrie, and Ball-Rokeach (1991) suggested that those who "already have a strong dependency relationship with a new media genre, such as television shopping, in turn develop parasocial relationships with television shopping personalities" (p. 793). These parasocial relationships lead to television exposure and to purchase behavior.

Parasocial interaction, then, can influence media uses and outcomes. It affects content or message selection and attention, having implications for "the different functions TV persons can have for the viewer" (Gleich, 1997, p. 50). Because parasocial interaction reflects involved media use, it should accentuate potential effects. This is supported by several studies in which parasocial interaction had positive links to (1) instrumental news viewing motivation, (2) perceived news realism and affinity (Rubin et al., 1985), and (3) cognitive and emotional involvement with television news (Perse, 1990) and soap operas (Rubin & Perse, 1987).

As affective emotional involvement, parasocial relationships affect attitudes and behavior. Brown and Basil (1995) found that emotional involvement with a celebrity (Magic Johnson) mediates persuasive communication and can increase personal concern about health messages (about AIDS and high-risk sexual behaviors). For example, attributions about Johnson's personality or what elements in the situation might have caused his HIV-positive state could influence how receivers treat his messages encouraging safe-sex practices.

In a study of television home shopping, Stephens, Hill, and Bergman (1996) found that Quality Value Convenience Network (QVC) hosts seek to establish parasocial relationships with their audiences and to use these relationships to encourage viewers to purchase products. In another recent study of public affairs talk radio, parasocial interaction with a talk radio host predicted (1) planned and frequent listening to that host, (2) treating the host as an important source of societal information, and (3) feeling that the host influenced how listeners felt about and acted on societal issues (Rubin, Step, & Hofer, 1996). In contrast, however, Hofstetter and Gianos (1997) suggested that listening to political talk radio serves companionship needs through parasocial interaction, along with needs to seek political information and to interpret reality. They argued that these more active listeners would be less susceptible to propaganda appeals because they were less dependent on the medium for information.

FUTURE DIRECTIONS

Considering the interface between personal and mediated contexts is important for understanding communication processes and behavior (Rubin & Rubin, 1985). As Bente and Vorderer (1997) and others have argued, parasocial interaction is a key concept for future research on the emotional component of communication and media use. Principles of attribution theory suggest several research directions.

First, we need to understand the functions served by parasocial interaction (e.g., social utility, companionship, information acquisition) and the links between media–person interaction and face-to-face interaction (e.g., functional alternatives). Basic interpersonal and media needs might help explain why these relationships develop as they do. Some of these needs might be primary in nature, and others might be situation-specific or secondary (Rubin & Martin, 1998). For example, people may feel they lack interpersonal control when they sense that others do not value what they have to contribute to a face-to-face encounter. Using talk radio and the Internet seems to provide alternative vehicles for those lacking interpersonal reward and sensing face-to-face anxiety (Armstrong & Rubin, 1989; Papacharissi & Rubin, 1998). Consequently, those who believe that they lack interpersonal control might seek to gratify their need for control by interacting with others via calling a talk radio show or by using the Internet.

Second, we should explain the similarities and differences between interpersonal and parasocial relationships (e.g., notions of intimacy, self-disclosure, uncertainty reduction, impression formation). Interpersonal relationships develop as a result of increased knowledge. As knowledge of the other increases, descriptive and predictive levels of knowledge give way to explanatory levels. Are those who form parasocial relationships engaging in active or interactive observation and those who do not form parasocial relationships more like passive observers (Herzog, 1994)? People who are active might buy fan magazines, visit a personality's website, or find other ways of seeking information (e.g., watching *Entertainment Tonight*). Or they may become interactive and telephone a call-in talk radio host, go to a shopping mall to see their favorite soap opera character, become a member of a studio audience, or e-mail the personality with a question or a request for a photo. The information gleaned about the target, as with social attribution, might depend on whether the personality is viewed in a context or alone and whether the situation allows for uninhibited, unscripted action or is constrained by rules and norms (Berger, 1979).

Third, we should address questions of development of such mediated relationships over time, including the idea of whether we are addressing notions of parasocial interaction or parasocial relationships. As social relationships develop, observers come to know their targets as individuals. We would expect parasocial relationships to differ accordingly, with some being more individualized and personal than others. Although some have suggested that time, history, and evolution are important to the development of parasocial relationships, just as they are to interpersonal relationships, research has yet to provide much support for this premise.

Fourth, we should examine the effects of parasocial interaction on individuals' attitudes and behavior. Does being in a parasocial relationship mean being influenced by or complying with the attitudinal expressions or behavioral suggestions of the media partner? Ellis, Streeter, and Engelbrecht (1983) suggested that television images influence viewers' behaviors because viewers "take the roles of television personalities or characters that they perceive as significant" and "through vicarious television role taking" acquire social skills that can "indirectly enhance their social relationships" (p. 381). Parasocial relationships would seem to be asymmetrical in that the media personality maintains a one-up position.

Fifth, by investigating parasocial interaction with those who may not be well liked or those not felt to be particularly attractive, the nature of parasocial relationships might be altered (from how it has been depicted in the literature). We also might locate additional dimensions of parasocial interaction. This suggests that, like interpersonal friendships, parasocial relationships are multidimensional rather than unidimensional. Rubin et al. (1985) noted that parasocial interaction contains elements of similarity, attraction, and empathy. Gleich (1997) thought that parasocial interaction could have three dimensions, namely, companionship, person–program interaction, and empathic interaction. Bente and Vorderer (1997) described three different dimensions of the concept: personal (i.e., "virtual interaction with a person on the screen"), mood machine (i.e., "interacting with the screen as a virtual person"), and virtual reality (i.e., "interacting with a virtual person on the screen") (p. 134).

Sixth, we should compare the role of parasocial interaction or relationships in different cultures. From a small pilot test of 24 Finnish speech communication students, for example, Isotalus (1995) suggested that the empirical indicators of parasocial interaction might be culture-bound – that is, the levels of parasocial interaction might vary for different cultures. Social relationships in other cultures likewise might differ based on amount and type of information and amount of uncertainty communicators are willing to tolerate (Gudykunst & Nishida, 1986).

Seventh, we should more closely examine the differences among parasocial and other types of relationships. For example, Horton and Strauss (1957) identified three types of interaction: (a) personal interaction, in which each participant fully takes other participants into account and adjusts his or her behavior on the basis the other persons; (b) vicarious interaction, in which people are spectators, following the interaction of others without taking part in the interaction; and (c) parasocial interaction, which resembles personal interaction as one party "appears to address the other(s) directly, adjusting his course of action to the latter's response" (p. 580), but the qualities of the encounter–immediate, personal, and reciprocal–"are illusory and presumably not shared by the speaker" (p. 580).

Eighth, we should further examine antecedent personality factors and individual differences. Research showing that men and women differ in their attributions of success and failure (Andrews, 1987) and in their feelings in social relationships (Johnson & Shulman, 1988) suggests that such differences might exist for men and women as observers and targets. Other individual differences might also exist (Herzberger & Clore, 1979). For instance, Fletcher, Danilovics, Fernandez, Peterson, and Reeder (1986) thought that people with more complex causal schema can consider multiple causes for behavior, whereas those with less attributional complexity are limited to single causes. Murphy (1994) found that less complex people attributed causation to the situation. Cognitive complexity, then, might differ among audience members, as it does with social interactants (Perse & Rubin, 1987). In addition, Berger (1973a) found that self-esteem mediates reactions to ego-threatening communication. People with high or low self-esteem were more defensive when receiving such messages. Those with moderate self-esteem were not attracted to those who attributed their failure to situational factors. Following from uncertainty reduction theory, anticipated future interaction with media personae might enhance parasocial interaction development. These individual personality differences and expectations, then, may influence parasocial relationship development.

Ninth and finally, we should consider the effects of assumed similarity and homophily (real similarity) on parasocial relationship development. Given the research in social relationships, we might expect higher levels of parasocial interaction with similar others. In fact, people assume they are more similar to friends on personality characteristics (Furnham & Henderson, 1983) and that friends are more consistent in their traits (Kammer, 1982) than are strangers. Turner (1993) did find that attitude homophily predicted parasocial interaction with television personalities. We do not know, though, whether observers of parasocial relationships are forming friendships or acquaintanceships based on amount of knowledge and assumed similarity (Johnson, Struthers, & Bradlee, 1988).

People use attribution processes when forming initial impressions of and when developing interpersonal and parasocial relationships with others. They use active and passive strategies seeking to gain information in order to reduce uncertainty, understand others, and develop explanations for others' present and future actions. The principles of attribution theory can help us understand the similarities and differences in the formation and development of interpersonal and parasocial relationships. We know that a sense of relationship follows from exposure to the personality and that, as in interpersonal communication, this sense of relationship or friendship influences how and why people subsequently interact. The real questions are (1) In what ways do parasocial relationships affect media use? and (2) What impact, if any, do such relationships have on the cognitions, attitudes, and behavior of interactants? We expect that the principles of attribution and uncertainty reduction can inform our understanding of these processes.

REFERENCES

Alperstein, N. M. (1991). Imaginary social relationships with celebrities appearing in television commercials. *Journal of Broadcasting & Electronic Media, 35,* 43–58.

Altman, I., & Taylor, D. A. (1973). *Social penetration: The development of interpersonal relationships.* New York: Holt, Rinehart & Winston.

Andrews, P. H. (1987). Gender differences in persuasive communication and attribution of success and failure. *Human Communication Research, 13,* 372–385.

Armstrong, C. B., & Rubin, A. M. (1989). Talk radio as interpersonal communication. *Journal of Communication, 39,* 84–94.

Bente, G., & Vorderer, P. (1997). The socio-emotional dimension of using screen media: Current perspectives in German media psychology. In P. Winterhoff-Spurk & T. H. A. van der Voort (Eds.), *New horizons in media psychology: Research cooperation and projects in Europe* (pp. 125–144). Wiesbaden, Germany: Westdeutscher Verlag.

Berger, C. R. (1973a). Attributional communication, situational involvement, self-esteem and interpersonal attraction. *Journal of Communication, 23,* 284–305.

Berger, C. R. (1973b). Task performance and attributional communication as determinants of interpersonal attraction. *Speech Monographs, 40,* 280–286.

Berger, C. R. (1975). Proactive and retroactive attribution processes in interpersonal communications. *Human Communication Research, 2,* 33–50.

Berger, C. R. (1979). Beyond initial interaction: Uncertainty, understanding, and the development of interpersonal relationships. In H. Giles & R. St. Clair (Eds.), *Language and social psychology* (pp. 122–144). Oxford, UK: Blackwell.

Berger, C. R., & Calabrese, R. J. (1975). Some explorations in initial interaction and beyond: Toward a developmental theory of interpersonal communication. *Human Communication Research, 1,* 99–112.

Berger, C. R., Gardner, R. R., Parks, M. R., Schulman, L., & Miller, G. R. (1978). Interpersonal epistemology and interpersonal communication. In G. R. Miller (Ed.), *Explorations in interpersonal communication* (pp. 149–172). Beverly Hills, CA: Sage.

Brown, W. J., & Basil, M. D. (1995). Media celebrities and public health: Responses to "Magic" Johnson's HIV disclosure and its impact on AIDS risk and high-risk behaviors. *Health Communication, 7,* 345–370.

Cathcart, R., & Gumpert, G. (1986). Mediated interpersonal communication: Toward a new typology. In G. Gumpert & R. Cathcart (Eds.), *Inter/media: Interpersonal communication in a media world* (3rd ed., pp. 26–40). New York: Oxford University Press.

Clatterbuck, G. W. (1979). Attributional confidence and uncertainty in initial interaction. *Human Communication Research, 5,* 147–157.

Cohen, J. (1997). Parasocial relationships and romantic attraction: Gender and dating status differences. *Journal of Broadcasting & Electronic Media, 41,* 516–529.

Conway, J. C., & Rubin, A. M. (1991). Psychological predictors of television viewing motivation. *Communication Research, 18,* 443–464.

Ellis, G. J., Streeter, S. K., & Engelbrecht, J. D. (1983). Television characters as significant others and the process of vicarious role taking. *Journal of Family Issues, 4,* 367–384.

Fiedler, K., Semin, G. R., Finkenauer, C., & Berkel, I. (1995). Actor-observer bias in close relationships: The role of self-knowledge and self-related language. *Personality and Social Psychology Bulletin, 21,* 525–538.

Fletcher, G. J. O., Danilovics, P., Fernandez, G., Peterson, D., & Reeder, G. D. (1986). Attribution complexity: An individual difference measure. *Journal of Personality and Social Psychology, 51,* 875–884.

Furnham, A., & Henderson, M. (1983). The mote in thy brother's eye, and the beam in thine own: Predicting one's own and others' personality test scores. *British Journal of Psychology, 74,* 381–389.

Gleich, U. (1997). Parasocial interaction with people on the screen. In P. Winterhoff-Spurk & T. H. A. van der Voort (Eds.), *New horizons in media psychology: Research cooperation and projects in Europe* (pp. 35–55). Wiesbaden, Germany: Westdeutscher Verlag.

Grant, A. E., Guthrie, K. K., & Ball-Rokeach, S. J. (1991). Television shopping: A media system dependency perspective. *Communication Research, 18,* 773–798.

Gudykunst, W. B., & Nishida, T. (1986). Attributional confidence in low- and high-context cultures. *Human Communication Research, 12,* 525–549.

Heider, F. (1958). *The psychology of interpersonal relations.* New York: Wiley.

Herzberger, S. D., & Clore, G. L. (1979). Actor and observer attributions in a multitrait-multimethod matrix. *Journal of Research in Personality, 13,* 1–15.

Herzog, T. A. (1994). Automobile driving as seen by the actor, the active observer, and the passive observer. *Journal of Applied Social Psychology, 24,* 2057–2074.

Hoffner, C. (1996). Children's wishful identification and parasocial interaction with favorite television characters. *Journal of Broadcasting & Electronic Media, 40,* 389–402.

Hofstetter, C. R., & Gianos, C. L. (1997). Political talk radio: Actions speak louder than words. *Journal of Broadcasting & Electronic Media, 41*, 501–515.

Horton, D., & Strauss, A. (1957). Interaction in audience participation shows. *American Journal of Sociology, 62*, 579–587.

Horton, D., & Wohl, R. R. (1956). Mass communication and para-social interaction: Observations on intimacy at a distance. *Psychiatry, 19*, 215–229.

Hosman, L. A., & Tardy, C. H. (1980). Self-disclosure and reciprocity in short- and long-term relationships: An experimental study of evaluational and attributional consequences. *Communication Quarterly, 28*, 20–30.

Isotalus, P. (1995). Friendship through the screen: Review of parasocial relationship. *Nordicom Review, 1*, 59–64.

Johnson, J. T., & Shulman, G. A. (1988). More alike than meets the eye: Perceived gender differences in subjective experience and its display. *Sex Roles, 19*, 67–79.

Johnson, J. T., Struthers, N. J., & Bradlee, P. (1988). Social knowledge and the "secret self": The mediating effect of data base size on judgments of emotionality in the self and others. *Social Cognition, 6*, 319–344.

Jones, E. E., & Davis, K. (1965). From acts to dispositions: The attribution process in person perception. *Advances in Experimental Social Psychology, 2*, 219–266.

Jones, E. E., & Nisbett, R. E. (1972). The actor and the observer: Divergent perceptions of the causes of behavior. In E. E. Jones, D. E. Kanouse, H. H. Kelley, R. E. Nisbett, S. Valins, & B. Weiner (Eds.), *Attribution: Perceiving the causes of behavior* (pp. 79–94). Morristown, NJ: General Learning Press.

Kammer, D. (1982). Differences in trait ascriptions to self and friend: Unconfounding intensity from variability. *Psychological Reports, 51*, 99–102.

Levy, M. R. (1979). Watching TV news as para-social interaction. *Journal of Broadcasting, 23*, 69–80.

Manusov, V., Floyd, K., & Kerssen-Griep, J. (1997). Yours, mine, and ours: Mutual attributions for nonverbal behaviors in couples' interactions. *Communication Research, 24*, 234–260.

McCroskey, J. C., Jenson, T., & Valencia, C. (1973, April). *Measurement of the credibility of peers and spouses.* Paper presented at the meeting of the International Communication Association, Montreal.

McKillip, J. (1975). Credibility and impression formation. *Personality and Social Psychology Bulletin, 1*, 521–524.

Meyrowitz, J. (1986). Television and interpersonal behavior: Codes of perception and response. In G. Gumpert & R. Cathcart (Eds.), *Inter/media: Interpersonal communication in a media world* (3rd ed., pp. 253–272). New York: Oxford University Press.

Murphy, R. (1994). Attributional complexity: Information search and integration during causal reasoning. *Journal of Research in Personality, 28*, 382–394.

Nordlund, J. (1978). Media interaction. *Communication Research, 5*, 150–175.

Papacharissi, Z., & Rubin, A. M. (1998, November). *Uses of the Internet.* Paper presented at the annual meeting of the National Communication Association, New York.

Perse, E. M. (1990). Media involvement and local news effects. *Journal of Broadcasting and Electronic Media, 34*, 17–36.

Perse, E. M., & Rubin, R. B. (1989). Attribution in social and parasocial relationships. *Communication Research, 16,* 59–77.

Rosengren, K. E., & Windahl, S. (1972). Mass media consumption as a functional alternative. In D. McQuail (Ed.), *Sociology of mass communications* (pp. 166–194). Harmondsworth, England: Penguin.

Ross, L. (1977). The intuitive psychologist and his shortcomings: Distortions in the attribution process. *Advances in Experimental Social Psychology, 21,* 57–96.

Rubin, A. M. (1994). Parasocial interaction scale. In R. B. Rubin, P. Palmgreen, & H. E. Sypher (Eds.), *Communication research measures: A sourcebook* (pp. 273–277). New York: Guilford Press.

Rubin, A. M., & Perse, E. M. (1987). Audience activity and soap opera involvement: A uses and effects investigation. *Human Communication Research, 14,* 246–268.

Rubin, A. M., Perse, E. M., & Powell, R. A. (1985). Loneliness, parasocial interaction, and local television news viewing. *Human Communication Research, 12,* 155–180.

Rubin, A. M., & Rubin, R. B. (1985). Interface of personal and mediated communication: A research agenda. *Critical Studies in Mass Communication, 2,* 36–53.

Rubin, A. M., Step, M. M., & Hofer, C. (1996, November). *Impact of motivation, attraction, and parasocial interaction on talk-radio listening effects.* Paper presented at the annual meeting of the Speech Communication Association, San Diego.

Rubin, R. B., & Martin, M. M. (1998). Interpersonal communication motives. In J. C. McCroskey, J. A. Daly, M. M. Martin, & M. J. Beatty (Eds.), *Communication and personality: Trait perspectives* (pp. 287–307). Cresskill, NJ: Hampton Press.

Rubin, R. B., & McHugh, M. P. (1987). Development of parasocial interaction relationships. *Journal of Broadcasting & Electronic Media, 31,* 279–292.

Seibold, D. R., & Spitzberg, B. H. (1982). Attribution theory and research: Review and implications for communication. In B. Dervin & M. J. Voight (Eds.), *Progress in communication research* (Vol. 3, pp. 85–125). Norwood, NJ: Ablex.

Stephens, D. L., Hill, R. P., & Bergman, K. (1996). Enhancing the consumer-product relationship: Lessons from the QVC home shopping channel. *Journal of Business Research, 37,* 193–200.

Sunnafrank, M. (1991). Interpersonal attraction and attitude similarity: A communication-based assessment. In *Communication yearbook* (Vol. 14, pp. 451–483). Newbury Park, CA: Sage.

Turner, J. R. (1993). Interpersonal and psychological predictors of parasocial interaction with different television performers. *Communication Quarterly, 41,* 443–453.

Extending Attribution Theory

Contributions and Cautions

Sandra Metts

The six chapters in this section invite readers to enter very different domains of application for attribution theory and principles. Each is informative in its own right, and together they offer a vision of where attribution research might move in the coming years. In this commentary, I review each chapter briefly and offer comments relevant to its conceptual and methodological approach to attribution theory, principles, or processes. I then propose several insights about attributions that were prompted by the research reported in these chapters. Finally, I close with a note of caution concerning the extent to which we can usefully extend attribution theory and research independently of its original formulation and from the related constructs that are evident in the literature.

CHAPTER REVIEWS

The Wilson and Whipple study of parental regulative communication is a fitting piece to initiate this section. It is the most explicitly indebted to the traditional notion of attributional principles. Parents were asked to imagine their child in two situations (temper tantrum at a grocery story or refusing to share a new toy with a friend at home) and to make judgments along several dimensions that reflect features common to traditional attributional research. In addition, however, Wilson and Whipple embed these attributions in a larger model of information processing stages, illustrating how patterns of attributions about a child's behavior can be influenced by demographic risk factors, dysfunctional child rearing beliefs, and depression and, in turn, how attribution patterns may influence the enactment of regulative behavior.

This research not only extends the previous work done by the authors in parental regulative communication but also begins to explore the systematic nature of the cognitive processes that lead to abusive forms of discipline. Wilson and Whipple, drawing on the earlier work by Milner, suggest that at any of the four stages of information processing – perception, interpretation and evaluation (where attributions are most salient), information integration and response selection, and response implementation and monitoring – certain variables may shift parents toward automatic processing at the expense of data-driven judgments about a child's behavior. Indeed, particular factors in specific combinations may even lead to parents skipping stages.

Wilson and Whipple's findings are, however, a conservative estimate of how various factors infringe upon or short-circuit the information processing stages. In the chaos and pressure of actual family life, – for example, where a single parent is trying to get dinner ready or trying to quiet a crying toddler while putting the baby to bed, or where two parents are trying to work through a stressful conversation while a child is taunting his or her sibling – automatic processing is even more likely to engage and violent discipline more likely to result.

In addition, Wilson and Whipple's delineation and application of Milner's information processing model illustrates clearly the interdependence of cognition and behavior. Scholars working in the area of intimate relationships have begun to articulate similar processes in dating and married couples, which seem to be the positive side of Milner's coin. For example, Rusbult, Yovetich, and Verette (1996) proposed that an accommodation bias operates in satisfying relationships such that constructive responses and charitable attributions are more likely to follow partner's untoward behavior than are self-interested or self-protective responses. Similarly, Murray and Holmes (1997) propose the notion of "positive illusions," which function as a positive self-fulfilling prophecy: Partners expect a satisfying relationship, interpret events in that light, enact behaviors that manifest that assumption, and find their relationship to be satisfying. These and other authors linking cognitions and behavior will find Wilson and Whipple's piece of interest.

Bugental, Shennum, Frank, and Ekman's chapter is a perfect sequel to Wilson and Whipple's; these authors might well be studying the children of Wilson and Whipple's parental sample. The proximity of these chapters makes painfully clear how family systems perpetuate dysfunctional information processing practices. Noting that children of abusive parents may adopt deception detection schema that make them more (or less) perceptive to deception clues than other children, Bugental et al. examine patterns of truth versus deception attributions made by children to videotaped displays of adults telling the truth and telling lies. The authors' concern is not simply with children's ability to detect deception but also with their ability to detect truthful messages and their tendency to misclassify lies as truth or truth as lies. The results indicate that abused children tend to misclassify initial truthful messages as lies; in essence, they forego the fundamental Grician principle of assuming the truth in favor of assuming the lie. Abused children also acquire the practice of monitoring facial cues, particularly eye gaze, in their (often unsuccessful) attempts to discern truthful and deceptive messages.

Although the attributional patterns of children viewing the videotapes is the most obvious application of attributional principles in this study, Bugental et al. make use of attribution principles in a second way. They use attributions to assess the child's perceived level of power. On the basis of the first three pictures chosen by a child to describe the events leading up to the scene depicted (a parent angry or a parent spanking a child), the authors assess power as the proportion of pictures selected in which the child (rather than someone else) is portrayed as the primary causal agent. Although this procedure serves the authors as a useful empirical analogue for power, the conceptual link to power is less apparent. This procedure seems to tap into a child's sense of responsibility for, rather than control over, a parent's displeasure. These are different constructs; the former implies blame, and the latter implies efficacy or potency. In fact, high power would seem more logically reflected in the data that were not used here, namely, the pictures chosen to provide a solution for the problem depicted. That is, if a child selected pictures in which he or she were the primary causal agent in abating a parent's anger or in convincing a parent to select a punishment other than spanking, the connection to efficacy would seem stronger.

A reader might wonder whether the children categorized as having low perceived power may be children who have not developed a carefully differentiated understanding of the link between their behavior and parental responses. Indeed, efforts of abused children to establish an information-processing heuristic that reliably differentiates among those behaviors that "definitely make Mom angry," or "probably make Mom angry," or "make Mom hit me," or "make Mom stop hitting me" may eventually yield to a simple random model: "Mom (or Dad) gets angry or spanks me regardless of what I do or don't do, and regardless of what others do and don't do." This is consistent with Wilson and Whipple's observation that abusive parents sometimes fail to process and respond appropriately to a child's exhibited behavior, for example, displays of positive interactional behavior or compliant behavior following an initial regulative message.

The Derlega and Winstead study moves attribution theory out of the laboratory, figuratively speaking, and into the field. The focus remains, however, on attributional processes in the domain of significant social and relational problems. Reasons for disclosing or not disclosing one's HIV diagnosis were obtained from interviews and then rated on importance in questionnaires given to the same population. The general categories into which these reasons fall – self-focus, other focus, interpersonal–relationship focus, and message focus – indicate the multiple and sometimes conflicting impulses that both motivate and prohibit disclosure of important information. Although Derlega and Winstead are not concerned with dimensions that might underlie categorical distinctions, the numerous examples of respondents' own accounts provide compelling evidence that persons make fine-grained distinctions when deciding to reveal or conceal information. For example, respondents' reasons implied such dimensions as opportunity, conversational reciprocity norms, comforting rules, relationship rules, and so forth.

Of interest in this study is not only the careful description of post hoc explanations provided by the respondents but also the implicit indication that these respondents used projected and emergent attributions. For example, choosing to disclose one's HIV diagnosis to a particular person in order to receive support and comfort presumes that the recipient of this disturbing news is capable of and willing to give the desired comfort. Likewise, not disclosing to someone who might gossip presumes a certain dispositional quality of the other. In those circumstances where the revelation was used as a litmus test for the resilience of the relationship, attributional projections may have produced ambiguous conclusions or low attributional confidence. Although it is not often mentioned in traditional attribution research, the evidence presented here that people "explain" their own and others' envisioned or anticipated behavior is an important element in the sense-making process.

Given the obviously rich source of information provided by the interviews, two questions seem relevant. First, it appears that separate reasons were bracketed in the transcripts and then treated as the unit of analysis for coding into categories and creating items for the questionnaire study. Given the intricate formation of personal accounts for relationally embedded behavior (e.g., Burnett, McGhee, & Clarke, 1987) and behavior that involves disclosing or not disclosing information to the social network (Baxter & Widenmann, 1993), a reader might wonder whether these respondents were asked if multiple reasons existed for telling or not telling the same person.

A second observation is that no respondents attributed their decision to disclose their HIV status to the effects of the disease (e.g., the need to account to others for missing work for medical appointments, visible weight loss, or the appearance of skin lesions). Although the instructions to respondents during the first interview (42 men and women) directed them to recall the reasons that were salient during the time they first received their diagnosis, it is still reasonable to expect that some symptoms were present and perhaps motivated the initial doctor visit. Moreover, the second interview (25 women) asked respondents to consider the entire span of time after receiving their diagnosis to the present. Although no data are provided to indicate the range or mean of time since diagnosis, it is reasonable to expect that in some cases, considerable time may have passed since the diagnosis. It is therefore somewhat surprising that no reference was made to the appearance of physical symptoms as a reason to reveal one's HIV status.

In a study of social support and depression in a sample of seropositive individuals (Metts, Manns, & Kruzic, 1996), disclosure targets varied significantly according to progressive symptomology. Nonsymptomatic seropositive individuals reported that family members were much less likely to be used for support than were members of the individuals' intimate network (e.g., partners, friends, lovers) and even less likely to be used than persons with weak ties (e.g., support groups and ministers). However, for those respondents who indicated that they had visible symptoms of the disease (e.g., facial lesions or weight loss), family members were as likely to be used as sources of support as were intimate network members. Certainly the questions that concern Derlega and Winstead (why or why not disclose) are different from questions about patterns of social support, but it is surprising that no respondent mentioned visible physical changes as an external factor that motivated disclosure even when privacy would have been preferred.

Peterson, Troth, Gallois, and Feeney are, like Derlega and Winstead, interested in the influence of relationship features on the sharing of problematic information. Their focus is more explicitly on the attributions made during the problematic episode, in this case, a discussion of condom use with a romantic partner. Couples are asked to engage in a conversation stimulated by a hypothetical situation in which a couple is contemplating their first sexual encounter and "Ann" wishes to use a condom, but "Rick" does not. This procedure offers an interesting vehicle for examining attributional processes during a very private moment, one that is more typically studied with retrospective self-report data. In addition, this procedure allows the researchers to assess both relatively stable affect, in this case relationship satisfaction, and situationally contingent affect, in this case, satisfaction with the conversation. Attributions are operationalized as ratings for self and partner on five dimensions of conversational involvement: friendly versus hostile interest, open versus closed communication, topic avoidance versus involvement, competitive versus cooperative orientation, and calm versus emotional mood. Attributional biases are then derived from a respondent's self-assessment relative to assessment of the partner: Relatively more favorable ratings for self are considered self-serving biases, and relatively more favorable ratings for partner are considered partner-enhancing biases. Identical ratings are considered equality attributions.

The findings indicate that, in general, attribution patterns among these college-aged couples reflected an equality pattern rather than a self-serving bias or a partner-enhancing bias. However, partners who did exhibit a self-serving bias in friendly intent were less satisfied than those exhibiting an equality or partner-enhancing pattern (although according to Table 14.2, this included only three men and one woman). A more robust, and certainly intuitive, finding is that partners who are satisfied are more likely to make equitable attributions of openness than to make self-serving or partner-enhancing attributions.

Correlation analyses using the attributional scales as continuous variables indicate that overall higher scores on perceptions of openness and friendly intent are associated with both relationship and conversational satisfaction. More specifically, ratings of partner's friendly intent were associated with both conversational and relational satisfaction, but ratings of one's own friendly intent were associated only with conversational satisfaction. Higher ratings on the avoidant scale for either self or partner correlated with lower ratings on satisfaction. The regression analyses revealed that ratings of one's own conversational attributes on avoidance–lack of involvement and closedness–lack of openness contributed to dissatisfaction, whereas ratings of partner were not significant predictors.

The regression finding is especially interesting because it points to one of the problems in extending attribution concepts to new contexts. Of all possible predictors for both self- and partner ratings, the only two that emerged were self-ratings on the avoidance and closedness attribution scales for self's satisfaction. Given that behaviors *not* displayed are difficult to detect, it is logical that only one's self would be aware of moderating one's talk to avoid making certain comments. Hence, the close connection between one's own dissatisfaction and one's own on-line editing makes sense, as does the absence of such a connection in assessing partner's avoidant behavior.

Peterson et al.'s chapter is a noble effort to uncover dynamics of attributional processes exploring associations among preexisting relational satisfaction, emergent conversational satisfaction, attributions about conversational qualities, and even observer ratings of conversational qualities. Scholars have long recognized that the impact of conversations between relational partners is inevitably as much about the relationship as about a given area of content (Watzlawick, Beavin, & Jackson, 1967). Indeed, Duck (1990) argues that relationships are "talked into being" during the mundane moments of daily conversation. Peterson et al.'s study of attributions made during a conversation about a relationally charged issue such as condom use contributes to our understanding of these dynamics.

The final two chapters in this section are summaries of existing research and push the reader to think even more broadly about attribution principles in practice. Atkins, Dimidjian, and Jacobson explore attributions at two levels. The first is what might be called the cultural-level script for affairs – who is expected to do what with whom and with what consequences. Embedded within this schema are also classes or types of attributions that would be considered normative and "legitimate" reasons for engaging in extramarital affairs. These cultural norms are inferred from studies of respondents' attributions to explain why people in general might have affairs, why they might themselves hypothetically engage in an extramarital affair, or both. The second level of attributions resides in individual motivations offered by persons who have had affairs to explain their actions or decisions. These are usually gathered from self-report data. These data illustrate the classical attribution causal link: Partners' affairs are seen as the cause of problems in the marriage, whereas respondents' affairs are seen as the response to preexisting problems in the marriage.

Together, these two levels of analysis suggest four motivations that most members of this society recognize or report to be reasons to engage in extramarital affairs: sexual excitement, emotional intimacy, extrinsic motivation, and love. These justifications reflect patterns consistent with traditional sex role expectations. In general, sexual motivations are assumed and often reported to be more prominent in the motivational profiles of men, and emotional intimacy is assumed and often reported to be more prominent in the motivational profiles of women. Further, men report more approval of sexual justifications than do women. Women who have been involved in an extramarital affair report greater approval of love justifications than do men who have also been involved in an extramarital affair.

It is not surprising that the attributional profiles gathered from men and women who have had affairs closely resemble those gathered from persons who are asked to report about hypothetical situations. After all, attributions for relational conduct need to "make sense" to others who share the same social world. Indeed, one of the challenges in studying attributions for extramarital affairs and similar relationship misconduct is that we organize attributional structures as we organize all information, according to the linguistic conventions available for talking about them.

As Antaki (1987) observes, most accounts are performable, that is, they can be rendered in common language for access by other members of the social network; however, some accounts are unperformable, below the level at which they can be transformed into common language. This suggests that self-reports of attributions for affairs may be closer to normative scripts, particularly sex role expectations, than to the truth of the event. The situation is complicated further by the fact that cultural level expectations shape individual information processing. If Milner's model is imported here from Wilson and Whipple's chapter, we could argue that sex role expectations influence perception and interpretation in such a way that men misclassify emotional markers as sexual, and women misclassify sexual markers as emotional; in other words, is it possible that affairs are understood by men as sexual because those attributions are indigenous to the male sex role and understood by women as emotional because those attributions are indigenous to the female sex role? Although the data would be difficult to obtain, asking couples who are partners in the same extramarital relationship to reflect on the same behavior or event and provide explanatory attributions would be a possible way to identify the influences of cultural level sex role expectations on individual level and couple level attributions.

The final paper by Rubin and Rubin is a review of the research that has been conducted on the interesting phenomena known as parasocial interaction and parasocial relationships. Contrary to what might be expected, at least by readers previously unfamiliar with this line of research, the compensation model does not adequately account for the emergence of parasocial relationships; being lonely does not necessarily predict greater parasocial interaction. In fact, a better explanation for the emergence and maintenance of a parasocial relationship consists of those very factors that explain the development of face-to-face relationships: perceiving the relationship as important, being socially attracted and task-attracted to a media personality, and believing that one can predict the attitudes and feelings of the media person accurately.

This latter notion, the belief by a viewer that he or she is able to predict the attitudes and feelings of the media person, seems to be central to the parasocial relationship and the basis of the link between attribution theory and uncertainty reduction theory as articulated by Rubin and Rubin. It is a source of comfort and relational identification for some viewers when they believe they have reduced their uncertainty about and come to know a media personality. It is not surprising that the literature reviewed by Rubin and Rubin indicates that parasocial relationships, whether as cause or effect, tend to be associated with instrumental media use, an active orientation to viewing, and electronic correspondence when possible. We see the same use of information-seeking strategies in developing face-to-face relationships.

The particularly interesting contribution of this chapter is that it reveals the intersection between, or perhaps the fuzzy boundaries separating, mass communication theory and interpersonal communication theory. Rubin and Rubin describe the ways in which media personalities and their producers use camera angles, close-up shots, and other technical devices to capitalize on the same aspects of interaction that are associated with attractiveness in face-to-face encounters – nonverbal immediacy, directed eye gaze, smiling, relaxation, expressed interest in other's views, and so forth. Because repeated exposure tends to confirm rather than disconfirm initial positive attributions to stable personality traits, parasocial interactions lead as logically to parasocial relationships as do positively attributed (and subsequently confirmed) face-to-face interactions. The ten directions for future research proposed by these authors indicate the challenges and potential this area offers as contributions to our understanding of face-to-face relationships by studying the intersection of reality and media in the parasocial relationship.

CONTRIBUTIONS

At first read, the wide range of interests and varied domains of application presented in these six chapters was a source of frustration. I was forced to stretch my thinking about a theory I thought I knew. But the exercise was rewarded because I gained a much greater appreciation for the flexibility and utility of attribution theory. It is much more than causal explanations (situational and dispositional) for unexpected and negative events. It is a fundamental element in the sense-making process. These papers indicate that attributions are both conscious and unconscious, antecedent to behavior and prompted by behavior, done mindfully and mindlessly. What specific insights into attribution processes might we take away from a synthesis of these chapters?

First, these chapters suggest that attributions carry two types of judgments. The first is a judgment about the cause of an action or event; this judgment provides an answer to the question "Why?" In the classical rendering of attribution theory, the answer to this question lies in the assumed locus of cause, external to the actor or internal. Thus, circumstantial or dispositional attributions can be made. The second type of judgment evaluates the valence of an action or event, its propriety, morality, justifiability. Social codes of proper and right conduct guide this level of judgment. These two levels of judgment are evident in the attributions that seropositive individuals offered for disclosing and not disclosing their HIV status, for example: "I'm a private person" (dispositional causality and appeal to the right of persons to maintain privacy boundaries); "She began talking about her son's cancer" (situational opportunity and norm of reciprocal disclosure or vulnerability). These two levels of judgment are evident in the reasons people imagine or express for having affairs: "The marriage was emotionally unfulfilling" (cause external to self and emotional fulfillment a highly valued goal); "I had an affair to get back at my spouse" (external cause and rule exemption allowed for victim of prior transgression). We even see the second level of judgment presented explicitly to conversational partners in such dimensions as competitive versus cooperative, friendly versus hostile, calm versus emotional. Had participants been asked why they made the assessments they did, we might well have seen systematic patterns of situational and dispositional causality to correspond with the evaluative judgments.

Second, these chapters suggest that attributions are not only retrospective sense making about events that are unexpected, negative, or both; they are also anticipatory, prospective sense making. For example, a conversational partner who wonders "Why didn't I say that?" can account for the omission after the fact, but the on-line editing decision was guided by anticipated responses from his or her partner. Likewise, a person who decides not to reveal an HIV diagnosis relies on anticipated responses for the person in question. Indeed, it is probably true that abusive parents and abused children could describe the projected attributions that guide their behavior, for example, "Well, I have to spank him because it is the only way to get his attention"; "I always say something gross to my mom because I know she will hit me anyway so I might as well make it count."

A third insight provided by these chapters is the fact that attributions are not isolated cognitions but rather are part of larger mental structures. We might call these information processing structures, relationship schema, sex role scripts, and so forth. Whatever label is given to the larger structure, it is important to note that attributions both contribute to the formation of these mental structures and reciprocally become channelized by these structures (Planalp & Rivers, 1996). For example, attributions about a media personality might invoke preliminary relationship schema, which in turn facilitate certain types of subsequent attributions. Similarly, attributions about parental abusive behavior might lead to the formation of an adaptive attachment style such as avoidant or anxious-ambivalent (Hazan & Shaver, 1987). It is important to explore the role of attributions in the formation of larger mental structures, and that brings me to my final point; a note of caution.

A NOTE OF CAUTION

These chapters help us understand the links between cognition and human behavior from the perspective of both actors and observers. They demonstrate well the theme of this section – new directions and new contexts. They have done their job and done it well. On the other hand, I believe that a note of caution is in order. Sometimes a good theory can be asked to do so much that its original coherence is lost. It becomes fragmented in the sense that its terminology is used independently of its core assumptions. This becomes problematic when data begin to accumulate within the rubric but are not aligned systematically within the parameters of the theory (see Spitzberg, this volume). Cumulative and systematic research becomes more difficult for interested scholars, particularly when they are attempting interdisciplinary investigation.

To avoid this possibility for attribution theory, it might be wise to pause long enough to demarcate the boundaries of attribution theory and to distinguish it from its several kindred terms. For example, is it sufficient to equate attributions with reasons? Can they be counted up as reasons can? Do they have to refer only to internal and external causality? Can they be as much about the speaker's world view as about the event? The chapters in this section indicate that one possible point of comparison is how attributions resemble or differ from accounts.

Some years ago Goffman (1967) observed that orderly social life depends upon the ability of social actors to maintain their own and others' face during interaction and to account for untoward behavior. This essay was followed by detailed typologies of the types of speech actions (e.g., excuses and justifications) that would serve this purpose and what conditions would apply (Scott & Lyman, 1968). More recently, however, accounts have been conceptualized as narratives or stories about a "fall from perfection," which are motivated as much by the need to come to terms with the circumstances of one's personal life as to restore social order (Harvey, Weber, & Orbuch, 1990). It might be a useful exercise for attribution scholars to enter the accounts' conversation, looking for ways in which attributions might be compared with or distinguished from accounts. This exercise need not preclude continued research in the innovative directions charted by the chapters in this section. However, given the remarkable legacy and promise of attribution theory, it is worth pausing to look at the terrain on each side even while moving enthusiastically forward.

REFERENCES

Antaki, C. (1987). Performed and unperformable: A guide to accounts of relationships. In R. Burnett, P. McGhee, & D. D. Clarke (Eds.), *Accounting for relationships: Explanation, representation and knowledge* (pp. 97–113). New York: Methuen.

Baxter, L. A., & Widenmann, S. (1993). Revealing and not revealing the status of romantic relationships to social networks. *Journal of Social and Personal Relationships, 10,* 321–337.

Burnett, R., McGhee, P., & Clarke, D. D. (1987). *Accounting for relationships: Explanation, representation and knowledge.* New York: Methuen.

Duck, S. W. (1990) Relationships as unfinished business: Out of the frying pan and into the 1990s. *Journal of Social and Personal Relationships, 7,* 5–28.

Goffman, E. (1967). *Interaction ritual.* Garden City, NY: Anchor Books.

Harvey, J. H., Weber, A. L., & Orbuch, T. L. (1990). *Interpersonal accounts: A social psychological perspective.* Cambridge, MA: Basil Blackwell.

Hazan, C., & Shaver, P. (1987). Romantic love conceptualized as an attachment process. *Journal of Personality and Social Psychology, 52,* 511–524.

Metts, S., Manns, H., & Kruzic, L. (1996). Social support structures and predictors of depression in person who are seropositive. *Journal of Health Psychology, 1,* 367–382.

Murray, S. L., & Holmes, J. G. (1997). A leap of faith? Positive illusions in romantic relationships. *Personality and Social Psychology Bulletin, 23,* 586–604.

Planalp, S., & Rivers, M. (1996). Changes in knowledge of personal relationships. In G. J. O. Fletcher & J. Fitness (Eds.), *Knowledge structures in close relationships: A social psychological approach* (pp. 299–324). Mahwah, NJ: Lawrence Erlbaum.

Rusbult, C. E., Yovetich, N. A., & Verette, J. (1996). An interdependence analysis of accommodation processes. In G. J. O. Fletcher & J. Fitness (Eds.), *Knowledge structures in close relationships: A social psychological approach* (pp. 63–90). Mahwah, NJ: Lawrence Erlbaum.

Scott, M. B., & Lyman, S. (1968). Accounts. *American Sociological Review, 33,* 46–62.

Watzlawick, P., Beavin, J. H., & Jackson, D. D. (1967). *Pragmatics of human communication: A study of interactional patterns, pathologies, and paradoxes.* New York: W. W. Norton.

PART FOUR

A DISCUSSION OF ATTRIBUTION THEORY AS A THEORY FOR CLOSE RELATIONSHIPS

CHAPTER SEVENTEEN

The Status of Attribution Theory *qua* Theory in Personal Relationships

Brian H. Spitzberg

If there is any basis for the Kuhnian notion of paradigms, strong theoretical models can so dominate the *zeitgeist* of scholarly thinking that alternative models find it difficult to gain a foothold in the precious and limited landscape of the academic press. Of all the theories proffered throughout the social sciences, few seem to succeed in infecting the body academic, much less in transforming the organism. In part, this is because new theories compete with extant theories, many of which have grown tendrils deep into the instructional corpus of the discipline itself.

One such theory that has survived and, at least in some domains, thrived is attribution theory. This chapter considers the status of attribution theory *as* a theory in general and in relation to theorizing about communication and personal relationships in particular. The chapter makes no claim to offer a comprehensive review of the expansive literature on either metatheory or attribution. The chapter, in other words, is highly selective. It proceeds by establishing definitions of theory, examining different criteria for the evaluation of theories and the research programs they support, and finally applying these definitions and criteria to a selective review of attribution concepts as they have been applied to the study of personal relationships.

A SCHEMA FOR THEORY EVALUATION

Despite intensive philosophical forays into the issues of what constitutes a good theory, a satisfactory prolegomenon for theory evalua-

Correspondence should be addresses to Brian H. Spitzberg, School of Communication, San Diego State University, San Diego, CA 92182-4561, spitz@mail.sdsu.edu.

tion seems elusive. The 20th century has seen substantial growth and evolution of metatheory and metatheoretical perspectives for organizing and stimulating social scientific knowledge (see Laudan et al., 1986; Suppe, 1989). The only established perspectives that claim a method for cumulative and increasingly valid general knowledge claims are variants of the received view and hypothetico-deductive system (e.g., Bostrom & Donohew, 1992; Chow, 1990, 1992; Gilman, 1992). Indeed, there is reason to accept even the "soft" sciences as capable of precision and generality on much the same order as the "hard" sciences (Hedges, 1987).

The analysis that follows presumes that the purpose of science is the systematic process of understanding the world as it is. This presumption is understood as contested ground (e.g., Gergen, 1973, 1979, 1986; cf. Wallach & Wallach, 1994). Regardless of this, a set of criteria for theory evaluation is developed in the following discussion with the presupposition that there exists a body of potentially accumulative, reliable, and progressive explanatory propositions regarding human action.

DEFINING AND EVALUATING THEORY

A theory is a verifiable conceptual system of interrelated propositions explaining conditionship among a set of phenomena. The term *explain* may be understood in a primitive sense as to offer an account that renders an event, a set of events, a phenomenon, or a process comprehensible. The subsuming criterion for theory evaluation is *quality*. A theory is higher in quality to the extent that it furthers accumulation of general and precise knowledge over time. More specifically, a theory's quality may be evaluated in terms of intrinsic and extrinsic characteristics. *Intrinsic* qualities are those that can be evaluated as internal to the theory itself or within the domain of scholarly activity directly relevant to the theory. Intrinsic criteria can be categorized as either necessary or desirable. Necessary characteristics are those functions a theory must fulfill in order even to be considered a theory (vs. a primitive metaphor, a story, a description, a taxonomy, etc.). Desirable characteristics are those features of the theory that connote generally higher quality the more the theory possesses of these characteristics (e.g., parsimony). *Extrinsic* qualities are those characteristics of the theory that are applied and assessed by the relevant school, invisible college, discipline, paradigm (in Kuhn's "collective practices" sense), and/or society that represent the audiences to which the theory is addressed.

The intrinsic and extrinsic criteria for theory evaluation are summarized in Table 17.1. These criteria are not exhaustive, original, or even entirely consistent (Blalock, 1979; Eysenck, 1987; Freese, 1980; McClintock, 1985). They also do not reflect many of the larger metatheoretical issues involved in theory construction (e.g., Turner, 1985, 1990, 1991). They do reflect much of the content of traditional approaches to the aesthetics of theory evaluation. A brief foray into these criteria will facilitate the examination of attribution theory.

Intrinsic Qualities

Necessary Conditions

A theory must explain a process, events, or phenomena. To do so, a basic understanding of the concepts relevant to this explanation and of their interrelationship must be provided. This explanation must be more abstract than the referent. In providing an abstract explanation, a theory must apply equally across its intended domain or scope. A theory of attributional influence that does not apply to marital decision making, for example, would not in fact be a theory of attributional influence. A theory's propositions must also avoid direct contradiction. A theory should not claim that in context C, stimulus S produces internal attributions (X) and external attributions (Y), if X and Y are defined by the theory as mutually exclusive categories.

Desirable Conditions

Generally speaking, the more specific a theory's propositions, the better it is. Prediction is a desirable aspect of propositions but not a necessary one. For example, Darwin's theory of evolution is highly explanatory, but it cannot predict the "direction" or form of evolutionary changes. Further, the more observable the content of the theory is, the easier it should be to assess its validity. The more a theory identifies its scope conditions, the better it is. Theories that subsume more concepts are generally considered preferable to those that subsume fewer. However, theories that are simple and "elegant" are generally preferable to those that are complex and conceptually extensive. These latter two criteria often produce tension, but they are not logically incompatible. At its core, for example, $E = mc^2$ is universal in scope and also parsimonious.

Table 17.1. Criteria for Evaluating Theories

I. Intrinsic qualities
  A. Necessary conditions
    1. Explanatory power: A theory must provide an account of the phenomena of concern.
    2. Conditionship: A theory must describe the nature of concepts and the propositional relationships among at least some of these concepts.
    3. Abstraction: A theory must be cast symbolically at least one level higher than the phenomena it purports to explain.
    4. Intraboundary generality: A theory must provide statements of conditionship that hold across all phenomena claimed within its scope.
    5. Internal consistency: A theory's propositions must be deductively compatible (or, the propositions must avoid deductive incompatibility).
    6. Verifiability: A theory must be potentially verifiable, such that it is
      a. Partially or potentially operational: A sufficient number of theoretical concepts must be capable of being (eventually) observed.
      b. Partially or potentially falsifiable: Conditions under which propositions derived from the theory can be assessed in terms of their verisimilitude must be (eventually) possible.
  B. Desirable conditions, *ceteris paribus*
    1. Conditionship specification: The more the theory specifies the nature (i.e., necessity, sufficiency, generality, parameters, functional form, etc.) of its propositions, the better the theory.

(continued)

2. Precision: The more the theory predicts phenomena, the better the theory.

3. Observability: The more concepts of the theory that are observable, the better the theory.

4. Boundary specification: The more the theory specifies its scope, the better the theory.

5. Breadth: The larger the domain of generalization of the theory, the better the theory.

6. Parsimony: The more concise the theory, the better the theory.

II. Extrinsic qualities

A. Control: The greater the potential for intentional manipulation of the phenomena of interest, the better the theory is judged to be.

B. Progressive heurism: The more suggestive the theory of new concepts and scholarly endeavors, the better the theory is judged to be.

C. Synthesis: The more the theory subsumes previous theories and concepts, the better the theory.

D. Empirical success: The more a theory survives scholarly tests, the better the theory is judged to be (the "money in the bank" principle: "a theory has high verisimilitude when it has accumulated 'money in the bank' by passing several stiff tests," Meehl, 1990, p. 115).

E. Empirical novelty: The more a theory makes novel predictions, the better the theory is judged to be (the "damn strange coincidences" principle: "the main way a theory gets money in the bank is by predicting facts that, absent the theory, would be antecedently improbable," Meehl, 1990, p. 115).

F. Ontological appropriateness: The more a theory metaphorically resonates with human self-conceptions, the better the theory is judged to be (Boyd, 1979; McClintock, 1985).

G. Aesthetics: The more the theory satisfies the *zeitgeist* of narrative and stylistic quality, the better the theory is judged to be.

Extrinsic Qualities

To a large extent, one may apply the criteria above to a theory knowing little else beyond the theory itself and the available research relevant to the theory. However, as Lakatos (1970), Feyerabend (1970, 1975), and Kuhn (1976) have established, theories are rarely actually adopted, retained, or rejected purely on the basis of their own intrinsic merits or empirical confirmation. Instead, any given theory is evaluated in part by the disciplinary matrix within which it is applied and within which it is competing for acceptance. This matrix applies practical, cultural, and ideological criteria to the evaluation of these theories. Extrinsic criteria, in other words, concern qualities of performance and aesthetics from the perspective of the research culture that uses the theory rather than on the basis of strictly formal or rational characteristics.

One of the cultural preferences for theories is that theory should permit control of the phenomenon. For example, to the extent that attribution theory guides improvements in marital therapy, it would be desirable. Theories that are heuristic, that is, suggestive of future questions and applications, are also viewed as preferable. Theories that are efficient in subsuming existing theories are also generally preferable. In addition, science may not have access to *the* truth as a reference point, but scholars nevertheless can collectively make theoretical predictions that are supported and replicated. The accumulation of supportive hypothesis tests, especially when these tests are strict or concern parameters or intervals, represents "money in the bank" (i.e., empirical success) in which the coin of the realm consists of "damn strange coincidences" (i.e., empirical novelty) (see Meehl, 1990).

Finally, a theory is generally better to the extent that it reflects the core metaphorical self-images and esthetic preferences that a culture upholds. "A good theory is a plausible theory, and a theory is judged to be more plausible and of higher quality if it is interesting rather than obvious, irrelevant or absurd, obvious in novel ways, a source of unexpected connections, high in narrative rationality, aesthetically pleasing, or correspondent with presumed realities" (Weick, 1989, p. 517).

ATTRIBUTION THEORY *QUA* THEORY

What is Attribution Theory?

Attribution theory has a relatively clear early history, and several useful reviews of theoretical and research issues in attribution research are available (e.g., Bell-Dolan & Anderson, 1999; Bradbury & Fincham, 1990; Harvey & Weary, 1984; Kelley & Michela, 1980; Ostrom, 1981; Seibold & Spitzberg, 1982; Shaver, 1981; Sillars, 1982; Thompson & Snyder, 1986). Fritz Heider (1958) articulated the initial framework as a conception of naïve psychology. This work was later extended by Edward E. Jones and colleagues (Jones, 1979; Jones & Davis, 1965; Jones & McGillis, 1976; Jones & Nisbett, 1971), Harold H. Kelley (1967, 1979), and others (e.g., Weary, Rich, Harvey, & Ickes, 1980; Weiner, 1986). "In its simplest form, attribution work is concerned with attempts to understand the factors involved in perceived causation" (Harvey & Weary, 1984, p. 428).

There are at least three prominent domains of attribution theory (Fletcher & Fincham, 1991, p. 8): the attribution of *general* characteristics (e.g., traits) to a person (or environment); the attribution of *explicit causation* to an event or outcome; and the attribution of *responsibility*, involving issues such as blame, normative judgment, or both. Furthermore, some research projects can be considered localized extensions of attribution theory for the interpretation of a given set of findings or hypotheses. Such efforts can be considered attributional. Other projects are explicit efforts to develop a theory of attribution processes as they affect and are affected by individual and interpersonal processes. Such efforts can be considered attribution theory proper.

The fact that attribution theory has branched off from its main trunk in so many directions makes it is difficult to evaluate the theory *qua* theory. There is no single or core theory to evaluate. From a Popperian perspective (Popper, 1959, 1980) this is problematic because any given research project can select only those particular theoretical elements that are most consistent with any given set of findings, rather than committing to a singular attribution theory. Despite the lack of a particular target, there is enough common ground among attribution theory approaches to assess some of their theoretical qualities.

Necessary Conditions: Is Attribution Theory Even a Theory?

The explanatory power of attribution theory begins with the primitive metaphor of humans as "naïve scientists." Such primitive metaphors in a theory's ontology attempt to make the theoretical system coherent at an intuitive level. In attribution theory, the metaphor provides a basic cultural conception of "what people are doing" when they perceive events and at least some insight into how and why they proceed in these perceptions.

Conditionship Specification

Issues of conditionship are more problematic. Certainly, attempts have been made to formally extract and extend the propositions from the seminal attribution theorists, including the foundational axioms or assumptions of these theorists (Jones & McGillis, 1976; Medcof, 1990; Seibold & Spitzberg, 1982). Formal theories of attribution in particular contexts have been deduced from attribution theory (e.g., Kaplowitz, 1978; Schopler & Layton, 1974), and elaborate path models have been developed for a variety of phenomena (e.g., Bradbury & Fincham, 1990; Weiner, 1986, 1995).

The generation of hypotheses from attribution theory has become a veritable cottage industry in certain areas of investigation. Attribution theory has been a platform for extensive hypothesis generation in the study of shyness and loneliness (e.g., Lunt, 1991; Peplau & Perlman, 1979; Spitzberg & Canary, 1985); conflict (e.g., Canary & Spitzberg, 1990; Kilmann & Thomas, 1978; Orvis, Kelley, & Butler, 1976; Sillars, 1981; Vangelisti, 1992); relational satisfaction and the differentiation of distressed from nondistressed couples (e.g., Fincham & Bradbury, 1987; Manusov, 1990); accounts (e.g., Fincham, 1992; Harvey, Orbuch, & Weber, 1992; Weiner, Figueroa-Muñoz, & Kakihara, 1991); the study of abuse, coercion, and negative affects such as anger and shame in close relationships (Byrne & Arias, 1997; Cantos, Neidig, & O'Leary, 1993; Holtzworth-Munroe, 1992; Wilson & Whipple, this volume); and relationship dissolution (Grych & Fincham, 1992; Harvey, Weber, & Orbuch, 1990; Sprecher, 1994).

Despite such vigorous research, there are at least three vexing problems in the explication of conditionship in most attribution projects. First, attribution theorists have yet to agree on the nature, number, and exact function of the basic attributional dimensions themselves. McAuley, Duncan, and Russell (1992) argue for the dimensions of locus, stability, personal control, and external control. Wimer and Kelley (1982) found evidence for good–bad, simple–complex, enduring–transient, internal–external, and conscious–unconscious dimensions. Weiner (1995) argues for the primacy of the personal–impersonal (i.e., locus) and controllable–uncontrollable dimensions. According to one extensive review, attribution studies investigate as few as one and as many as eight attributional dimensions, suggesting "that the basic features of attribution have not yet been agreed upon" (Bradbury & Fincham, 1990, p. 17). Despite the general lack of consensus, some theorists have drawn their lines in the sand. As Bradbury and Fincham

(1990) conclude in reference to the marital literature, "it appears that the dimensions of locus, stability, control and globality are necessary and sufficient for assessing attributions in marriage" (p. 17).

Second, attribution theory propositions tend to be statements of simple linear or moderating effects, and it is rare to find attribution theorists making predictions regarding nonlinear relationships or anticipated effect sizes. Research, however, suggests highly contextualized and nonlinear effects in attribution judgments (e.g., Boon & Sulsky, 1997). Attributions may only be relevant at certain levels of arousal, mood, or perceptual novelty; furthermore, causal ascription itself may reflect nonlinear form. For example, Forgas (1994) found that stability attributions tended to be moderate for happy and neutral subjects and higher for sad subjects, but only for serious conflicts. The pattern was different for simple conflicts. As for effect sizes, as Meehl (1990) has emphasized incessantly, strong hypothesis testing tends to occur only when specific predictions are made regarding the ranges within which effects are expected. Is attribution theory a theory of small, moderate, or large effects? There is surprisingly little discussion of this aspect of "power" in discussions of attribution theory, and yet it seems a most rudimentary concern.

Third, the very connection between attribution processes and behavior is itself largely a *tabula rasa* in the attribution theory literature. This problem seriously hindered persuasion research (Miller & Burgoon, 1978), and the cognition–behavior link is at least as vital to the eventual progress of attribution theory. It follows that attribution theory has focused too much on the psychology of attribution and not enough on the action, and especially the interaction (e.g., Hilton, 1990; Weber & Vangelisti, 1991), resulting from attribution processes. It may seem obvious from attribution theory, for example, that abusive husbands would tend to make self-serving excuses rather than justifications or apologies in accounting for their violence (Wolf-Smith & LaRossa, 1992). However, it is unclear what predictions attribution theory can make for such accounts over time, much less how such accounts would be negotiated by the couple. If this relative silence regarding interaction process continues, attribution theory will have limited implications as a theory of personal relationships. Relationships are chains of sequential and coconstructed enactments. Until attribution theory pays more attention to the ongoing, sequential coconstruction of interaction, it will remain only an interesting "minitheory" of perception in personal relationships rather than a theory of personal relationships (Newcombe & Rutter, 1982).

Abstraction

Attribution theory is clearly cast at a more abstract level than the phenomena it conceptualizes. It also has received considerable attention in terms of its intraboundary generality (and its boundary specification). Some scholars are examining the pancultural generality of attributions (e.g., Choi, Nisbett, & Norenzayan, 1999), whereas others simply claim victory in the generality of their propositions (e.g., Weiner, 1995, p. 260). Still others are attempting to identify those conditions under which attributional processing is most likely to occur or to have a significant influence. Fletcher and Fincham (1991), for example, extend Weiner's work to claim that attributional processing tends to occur under the conditions of negative events, unexpected outcomes, and affective arousal.

Internal Consistency

Internal consistency is a difficult criterion to assess in regard to attribution theory. At the level of core assumptions and propositions, attribution theory seems consistent within given metaphors and projects. However, as any given project extends its basic assumptions to more exotic contexts, the consistency of predictions may become more problematic. Two projects extending attribution theory to the study of power provide an illustration. According to Schopler and Layton (1974), given an interdependent relationship between persons A and B, A is less likely to attribute any change in self-outcome(s) to B than is an outside observer (H_1). Kaplowitz' (1978) theory predicts that the frequency with which A is perceived to have received his/her preferred outcome(s) is positively related to perceptions of A's exercised power (H_2). Presumably, H_2 is qualified by H_1. As A receives more preferred outcomes, A is likely to attribute such outcomes to self rather than to B. However, an outside observer would be more likely than A to attribute some of the change to B. Both predictions are claimed to extend from attribution theory, but their logical compatibility is difficult to interpret. As in a Victorian garden maze, the point of entry, as well as the destination, becomes easily obscured.

Verifiability

Is attribution theory verifiable? This question leads to another. When will someone who finds nonsignificant results in a study of attribution-based hypotheses come forward and claim that attribution theory is flawed and needs revision or rejection? For example, in a number of studies, attribution processes have been found to affect women's relational satisfaction in certain ways, but not men's (Byrne & Arias, 1997; Cantos et al., 1993; Fincham & Bradbury, 1987). Despite such inconsistency, there does not appear to be a rush of theorists claiming that attribution theory is invalid in explaining men's activity in personal relationships.

Two very relevant findings emerge from Bradbury and Fincham's (1990) review. First, certain dimensions receive more consistent empirical support than others (e.g., globality for negative events), whereas others are at best questionable. For example, despite the authors' claim that locus is one of the necessary and sufficient dimensions for assessing attributions in marriage, only about 40% of the studies they reviewed provided "full support" for this dimension, and between 31% and 42% of the studies reviewed provided "none." Such inconsistency of empirical support clearly does not rise to the level of necessary and sufficient. Second, by examining the statistical significance of hypothesis tests rather than examining the effect sizes, it is difficult to interpret the importance of the results one way or the other. Even if all of the studies had been significant in the expected directions, if the average effect size accounts for 5% of the variance, it would be time to begin reconsidering the value of attribution theory in the larger frame of personal relationships. As long as reviews of attribution theory rely on traditional summary techniques rather than meta-analytic techniques (e.g., Joiner & Wagner, 1997), it will be difficult to evaluate the status of the theory in terms of its verification and explanatory power.

Does attribution theory meet the basic conditions of a theory? Yes. Attribution theory identifies most of the basic perceptual conditions for attribution to occur, and it makes a number of statements of relationship among variables relevant to the explanation and outcomes of causal perception. The cracks in its surface do not appear to reach its foundation. However, the practices of those who seek to maintain the stability of the structure or to build upon its frame often have not been in the service of sound theoretical architecture. As always, it is impossible to disambiguate entirely the value of theory from the practices of those who seek to extend, amplify, and verify the implications of that theory. Those practices occur in a larger social and cultural context which creates, constrains, and evaluates many of the practices employed to construct and to disprove theories. Many of the judgments rendered in this larger context are essentially aesthetic in nature and establish bases for judgment that are extrinsic to the theory itself.

Extrinsic Qualities: Is Attribution Theory Aesthetic?

Control

A theory that offers control offers the prospect of intentional alter-
ation of the phenomenon of interest. In the case of attribution theory,
the stakes are potentially very high. If attributions play a central role in
loneliness, depression, marital distress, negative affect, conflict, and
violence, it follows that being able to alter people's attributional
processes is a potential forum within which positive relational change
can be effected (Bell-Dolan & Anderson, 1999; Carlyon, 1997;
Hendrick, 1995; Metalsky, Laird, Heck, & Joiner, 1995). Attribution theory certainly seems to identify the content and direction of change that
would most likely lead to more positive relational experience (e.g.,
Bradbury & Fincham, 1990). However, because the theory lacks an
obvious account of how behavior is connected to the attributional
process itself (see discussion of conditionship above), it is relatively
mute with regard to *how* interventions might alter attributions.

Progressive Heurism

In terms of progressive heurism, attribution theory seems to be succeeding admirably. Although attribution theory still is not prominent
in some social scientific fields (Beniger, 1990), it maintains a high level
of scholarly activity. In 1984, Harvey and Weary noted that the field
was "alive with controversy and issues" (p. 453). They realized that
this was a double-edged sword. Despite its apparent "waning" in the
face of more computational information-processing models of cognitive psychology (Berger, 1988) and its more recent competitors in the
relationship literature (e.g., attachment theory, sociobiology theory),
there seems to be a very healthy level of activity in extending, refining,
and reinterpreting attribution theory.

The table of contents for the present volume reveals a vibrant and
diversified level of activity in the areas of personal relationships and
communication. Recent efforts reveal fruits of formal theoretical work
that intentionally have not fallen far from the tree of the original theory
that gave them life (e.g., Hilton, 1990; Medcof, 1990; Weiner, 1995). The
cognitive paradigm is far from dead, and attribution theory seems
securely ensconced within the hold of this ark (see Johnson et al., this
volume). The only question with regard to progressive heurism is how
regressive some of this scholarly progress is. To the extent that questions continue to be raised and rehashed about the basic dimensions,

terminology, and assumptions of attribution theory, the program of work is at risk for becoming intractable and regressive.

Synthesis

In regard to the ability of theory to synthesize existing knowledge, attribution theory appears to have a curious contextual synthetic property. It has been applied to numerous contexts, particularly those that appear uniquely and appropriately suited to its boundary conditions. If negative, unexpected, and arousing situations are those that are most likely to produce attributional processing, then attribution theory has certainly done its duty to these contexts. However, attribution theory is increasingly serving as an intermediary "box" in path diagrams of larger social information-processing models (e.g., Bell-Dolan & Anderson, 1999; Fletcher & Fincham, 1991; Weiner, 1995). In a recent book on *Knowledge Structures in Close Relationships* (Fletcher & Fitness, 1996), attribution theory reveals only a scattering of entries in the index and represents entirely subordinate discussions in the text. Nonattribution theories appear to be synthesizing attribution theory, rather than the reverse. In other words, attribution theory is becoming something synthesized by other more comprehensive models and theories, rather than providing the organizing framework itself.

Empirical Novelty

The next external criterion, empirical novelty, has been the subject of serious scrutiny. For example, Bradbury and Fincham (1990) do an admirable job of examining rival hypotheses in their review of attribution effects in marriage. Sillars (1982) attempts to assess the strength of attribution principles in light of alternative information processing interpretations in explaining interpersonal conflict. However, most actual studies still devote relatively little space to the consideration of rival hypotheses. If computationally based information-processing models continue to dominate cognitive psychology, principles such as the availability of heuristic and valence schemata may ultimately be derivable independently of attribution theory and be subordinated to models largely uninterested in causal ascriptions per se.

Ontology and Narcissus: Is Attribution Theory Us?

Perhaps the most fundamental question facing any theory is the appropriateness of its image of humans and humanity. The advent of the computer changed far more than the configuration of office furniture. In the first half of the century, metaphors for explaining human nature and behavior tended to take on engineering or hydraulic images. For good or ill, the computer eventually dislodged these hydraulic and engineering metaphors (see Shotter, 1990; Smythe, 1990; Vroon, 1987).

Attribution theory offers only a slightly more human metaphor than either computers or engineering. Humans, it claims, are naïve scientists. We seek to understand, sometimes for the sake of understanding, but more often because understanding brings with it order and control and thus an appropriate level of comfort with the world. The naïve scientist metaphor has been the subject of considerable debate, however, with most alternative candidates based on more computational metaphors (Newcombe & Rutter, 1982; Semin, 1980). Berger (1988) suggested the alternative metaphors of "persons-as-intuitive-social experimenters," "persons-as-intuitive-samplers," and "persons-as-intuitive-psychome-tricians." Fletcher and Fincham (1991) propose the somewhat more accessible metaphors of cognitive miser and naïve lawyer. Perhaps the most narcissistic metaphor that has been offered is Weiner's (1995) suggestion that "humans are godlike" in their judgment processes.

A founding agenda of attribution theory is to provide an explanation for our explanations. It follows incestuously from the fundamental attribution error that we will tend toward favorable metaphors in this process. How different might attribution theory be if the metaphors selected were not so relatively self-serving (see Fincham, this volume; Spitzberg & Cupach, 1998)? What if the naïve scientist is an evil or "mad" naïve scientist? What if, as sociobiology might suggest, we are merely animal (rather than mineral)? Perhaps, like Narcissus, we should occasionally consider the potentially paralyzing effects of the images we envision when we peer into the water's reflection.

REFERENCES

Bell-Dolan, D., & Anderson, C. A. (1999). Attributional processes: An integration of social and clinical psychology. In R. M. Kowalski & M. R. Leary (Eds.), *The social psychology of emotional and behavioral problems* (pp. 37–67). Washington, DC: American Psychological Association.

Beniger, J. R. (1990). Who are the most important theorists of communication? *Communication Research, 17,* 698–715.

Berger, C. R. (1988). Uncertainty and information exchange in developing relationships. In S. W. Duck (Ed.), *Handbook of personal relationships* (pp. 239–255). New York: John Wiley & Sons.

Blalock, H. M. (1979). Dilemmas and strategies of theory construction. In W. E. Snizek, E. R. Fuhrman, & M. K. Miller (Eds.), *Contemporary issues in theory and research: A metasociological perspective* (pp. 119–135). Westport, CT: Greenwood.

Boon, S. D., & Sulsky, L. M. (1997). Attributions of blame and forgiveness in romantic relationships: A policy-capturing study. *Journal of Social Behavior and Personality, 12,* 19–44.

Bradbury, T. N., & Fincham, F. D. (1990). Attributions in marriage: Review and critique. *Psychological Bulletin, 107,* 3–33.

Byrne, C. A., & Arias, I. (1997). Marital satisfaction and marital violence: Moderating effects of attributional processes. *Journal of Family Psychology, 11,* 188–195.

Canary, D. J., & Spitzberg, B. H. (1990). Attribution biases and associations between conflict strategies and competence outcomes. *Communication Monographs, 57,* 139–151.

Cantos, A. L., Neidig, P. H., & O'Leary, K. D. (1993). Men and women's attributions of blame for domestic violence. *Journal of Family Violence, 8,* 289–302.

Carlyon, W. D. (1997). Attribution retraining: Implications for its integration into prescriptive social skills training. *School Psychology Review, 26,* 61–73.

Choi, I., Nisbett, R. E., & Norenzayan, A. (1999). Causal attribution across cultures: Variation and universality. *Psychological Bulletin, 125,* 47–63.

Chow, S. L. (1990). In defense of Popperian falsification. *Psychological Inquiry, 1,* 147–149.

Chow, S. L. (1992). Acceptance of a theory: Justification or rhetoric? *Journal for the Theory of Social Behavior, 22,* 447–474.

Eysenck, H. J. (1987). "There is nothing more practical than a good theory" (Kurt Lewin) True or false? In W. J. Baker, M. E. Hyland, H. Van Rappard, & A. W. Staats (Eds.), *Current issues in theoretical psychology* (pp. 49–64). North-Holland: Elsevier Science Publishers.

Feyerabend, P. K. (1970). Against method: Outline of an anarchistic theory of knowledge. In M. Radner & S. Winokur (Eds.), *Minnesota studies in the philosophy of science: Analyses of theories and methods of physics and psychology* (Vol. 4, pp. 17–130). Minneapolis: University of Minnesota.

Feyerabend, P. (1975). *Against method: Outline of an anarchistic theory of knowledge.* London: NLB Atlantic Highlands: Humanities Press.

Fincham, F. D. (1992). The account episode in close relationships. In M. L. McLaughlin, M. J. Cody, & S. J. Read (Eds.), *Explaining one's self to others: Reason-giving in a social context* (pp. 167–182). Hillsdale, NJ: Lawrence Erlbaum Associates.

Fincham, F. D., & Bradbury, T. N. (1987). The impact of attributions in marriage: A longitudinal analysis. *Journal of Personality and Social Psychology, 53,* 510–517.

Fletcher, G. J. O., & Fincham, F. D. (1991). Attribution processes in close relationships. In G. J. O. Fletcher & F. D. Fincham (Eds.), *Cognition in close relationships* (pp. 7–35). Hillsdale, NJ: Lawrence Erlbaum Associates.

Fletcher, G. J. O., & Fitness, J. (1993). Knowledge structures and explanations in intimate relationships. In S. Duck (Ed.), *Individuals in relationships* (Understanding relationship processes series, Vol. 1, pp. 121–143). Newbury Park, CA: Sage.

Forgas, J. P. (1994). Sad and guilty? Affective influences on the explanation of conflict in close relationships. *Journal of Personality and Social Psychology, 66,* 56–68.

Freese, L. (1980). Formal theorizing. In A. Inkeles, N. J. Smelser, & R. H. Turner (Eds.), *Annual Review of Sociology, Vol. 6* (pp. 187–212). Palo Alto, CA: Annual Reviews Inc.

Gergen, K. J. (1973). Social psychology as history. *Journal of Personality and Social Psychology, 26,* 309–320.

Gergen, K. J. (1979). The positivist image in social psychological theory. In A. R. Buss (Ed.), *Psychology in social context* (pp. 193–212). New York: Irvington.

Gergen, K. J. (1986). Correspondence versus autonomy in the language of understanding human action. In D. W. Fiske & R. A. Shweder (Eds.), *Metatheory in social science: Pluralisms and subjectivities* (pp. 136–162). Chicago: University of Chicago Press.

Gilman, D. (1992). What's a theory to do ... with seeing? Or some empirical considerations for observation and theory. *British Journal for the Philosophy of Science, 43,* 287–309.

Grych, J. H., & Fincham, F. D. (1992). Marital dissolution and family adjustment: An attributional analysis. In T. L. Orbuch (Ed.), *Close relationship loss: Theoretical approaches* (pp. 157–173). New York: Springer-Verlag.

Harvey, J. H., Orbuch, T. L., & Weber, A. L. (1992). Introduction: Convergence of the attribution and accounts concepts in the study of close relationships. In J. H. Harvey, T. L. Orbuch, & A. L. Weber (Eds.), *Attributions, accounts, and close relationships* (pp. 1–18). New York: Springer-Verlag.

Harvey, J. H., & Weary, G. (1984). Current issues in attribution theory and research. *Annual Review of Psychology, 35,* 427–459.

Harvey, J. H., Weber, A. L., & Orbuch, T. L. (1990). *Interpersonal accounts: A social psychological perspective.* Cambridge, MA: Basil Blackwell.

Hedges, L. V. (1987). How hard is hard science, how soft is soft science? The empirical cumulativeness of research. *American Psychologist, 42,* 443–455.

Heider, F. (1958). *The psychology of interpersonal relations.* New York: John Wiley & Sons.

Hendrick, S. S. (1995). Close relationships research: Applications to counseling psychology. *Counseling Psychologist, 23,* 649–665.

Hilton, D. J. (1990). Conversational processes and causal explanation. *Psychological Bulletin, 107,* 65–81.

Holtzworth-Munroe, A. (1992). Attributions and maritally violent men: The role of cognitions in marital violence. In J. H. Harvey, T. L. Orbuch, & A. L. Weber (Eds.), *Attributions, accounts, and close relationships* (pp. 165–175). New York: Springer-Verlag.

Joiner, T. E., Jr., & Wagner, K. D. (1996). Parental, child-centered attributions and outcome: A meta-analytic review with conceptual and methodological implications. *Journal of Abnormal Child Psychology, 24,* 37–52.

Jones, E. E. (1979). The rocky road from acts to dispositions. *American Psychologist, 34,* 107–117.

Jones, E. E., & Davis, K. E. (1965). From acts to dispositions: The attribution process in person perception. In L. Berkowitz (Ed.), *Advances in experimental social psychology* (Vol. 2, pp. 219–266). New York: Academic Press.

Jones, E. E., & McGillis, D. (1976). Correspondent inferences and the attribution cube: A comparative reappraisal. In J. H. Harvey, W. J. Ickes, & R. F. Kidd (Eds.), *New directions in attribution research* (Vol. 1, pp. 389–420). Hillsdale, NJ: Lawrence Erlbaum Associates.

Jones, E. E., & Nisbett, R. E. (1971). *The actor and the observer: Divergent perceptions of the causes of behavior.* Morristown, NJ: General Learning Press.

Kaplowitz, S. A. (1978). Towards a systematic theory of power attribution. *Social Psychology, 41*, 131–148.

Kelley, H. H. (1967). Attribution theory in social psychology. In D. Levine (Ed.), *Nebraska symposium on motivation* (pp. 192–240). Lincoln: University of Nebraska Press.

Kelley, H. H. (1979). *Personal relationships: Their structures and processes.* Hillsdale, NJ: Lawrence Erlbaum Associates.

Kelley, H. H., & Michela, J. L. (1980). Attribution theory and research. In M. R. Rosenzweig & L. W. Porter (Eds.), *Annual review of psychology* (Vol. 31, pp. 457–501). Palo Alto, CA: Annual Reviews.

Kilmann, R. H., & Thomas, K. W. (1978). Four perspectives on conflict management: An attributional framework for organizing descriptive and normative theory. *Academy of Management Review, 3*, 59–68.

Kuhn, T. S. (1970). *The structure of scientific revolutions* (2nd ed.). New York: New American Library (with University of Chicago Press).

Lakatos, I. (1970). Falsification and the methodology of scientific research programmes. In I. Lakatos & A. Musgrave (Eds.), *Criticism and the growth of knowledge* (Proceedings of the International Colloquium in the Philosophy of Science, Vol. 4, pp. 91–195). London, UK: Cambridge University Press.

Laudan, L., Donovan, A., Laudan, R., Barker, P., Brown, H., Leplin, J., Thagard, P., & Wykstra, S. (1986). Scientific change: Philosophical models and historical research. *Synthese, 69*, 141–223.

Lunt, P. K. (1991). The perceived causal structure of loneliness. *Journal of Personality and Social Psychology, 61*, 26–34.

Manusov, V. (1990). An application of attribution principles to nonverbal behavior in romantic dyads. *Communication Monographs, 57*, 104–118.

McAuley, E., Duncan, T. E., & Russell, D. W. (1992). Measuring causal attributions: The revised causal dimensions scale (CDSII). *Personality and Social Psychology Bulletin, 18*, 566–573.

McClintock, C. G. (1985). The metatheoretical bases of social psychological theory. *Behavioral Science, 30*, 155–173.

Medcof, J. W. (1990). PEAT: An integrative model of attribution processes. In M. Zanna (Ed.), *Advances in experimental social psychology* (Vol. 23, pp. 111–209). New York: Academic Press.

Meehl, P. E. (1990). Appraising and amending theories: The strategy of Lakatosian defense and two principles that warrant it. *Psychological Inquiry, 1*, 108–141.

Metalsky, G. I., Laird, R. S., Heck, P. M., & Joiner, T. E., Jr. (1995). Attribution theory: Clinical applications. In W. T. O'Donohue et al. (Eds.), *Theories of behavior therapy: Exploring behavior change* (pp. 385–413). Washington, DC: American Psychological Association.

Miller, G. R., & Burgoon, M. E. (1978). Persuasion research: Review and commentary. In B. D. Ruben (Ed.), *Communication yearbook 2* (pp. 23–47). New Brunswick, NJ: Transaction Books.

Newcombe, R. D., & Rutter, D. R. (1982). Ten reasons why ANOVA theory and research fail to explain attribution processes: I. *Current Psychological Reviews, 2,* 95–107.

Orvis, B. R., Kelley, H. H., & Butler, D. (1976). Attributional conflict in young couples. In J. H. Harvey, W. J. Ickes, & R. F. Kidd (Eds.), *New directions in attribution research* (Vol. 1, pp. 353–386). Hillsdale, NJ: Lawrence Erlbaum Associates.

Ostrom, T. M. (1981). Attribution theory: Whence and whither. In J. H. Harvey, W. J. Ickes, & R. F. Kidd (Eds.), *New directions in attribution research* (Vol. 3, 405–424). Hillsdale, NJ: Lawrence Erlbaum Associates.

Peplau, L. A., & Perlman, D. (1979). Blueprint for a social psychological theory of loneliness. In M. Cook & G. Wilson (Eds.), *Love and attraction* (Proceedings of an international conference, pp. 99–108). Oxford, UK: Pergamon Press.

Schopler, J., & Layton, B. D. (1974). Attributions of interpersonal power. In J. T. Tedeschi (Ed.), *Perspectives on social power* (pp. 34–60). Chicago: Aldine Publishing Company.

Seibold, D. R., & Spitzberg, B. H. (1982). Attribution theory and research: Review and implications for communication. In B. Dervin & M. J. Voight (Eds.), *Progress in communication research* (Vol. 3, pp. 85–125). Norwood, NJ: Ablex.

Semin, G. R. (1980). A gloss on attribution theory. *British Journal of Social and Clinical Psychology, 19,* 291–300.

Shaver, K. G. (1981). Back to basics: On the role of theory in the attribution of causality. In J. H. Harvey, W. J. Ickes, & R. F. Kidd (Eds.), *New directions in attribution research* (Vol. 3, 331–358). Hillsdale, NJ: Lawrence Erlbaum Associates.

Shotter, J. (1990). The myth of mind and the mistake of psychology. In W. J. Baker, M. E. Hyland, R. van Hezewijk, & S. Terwee (Eds.), *Recent trends in theoretical psychology* (Vol. 2, pp. 63–71). New York: Springer-Verlag.

Sillars, A. L. (1981). Attributions and interpersonal conflict resolution. In J. H. Harvey, W. J. Ickes, & R. F. Kidd (Eds.), *New directions in attribution research* (Vol. 3, pp. 279–305). Hillsdale, NJ: Lawrence Erlbaum Associates.

Sillars, A. L. (1982). Attribution and communication: Are people "naïve scientists" or just naïve? In M. E. Roloff & C. R. Berger (Eds.), *Social cognition and communication* (pp. 73–106). Beverly Hills, CA: Sage.

Smythe, W. E. (1990). Mental representation and meaning: Arguments against the computational view. In W. J. Baker, M. E. Hyland, R. van Hezewijk, & S. Terwee (Eds.), *Recent trends in theoretical psychology* (Vol. 2, pp. 261–266). New York: Springer-Verlag.

Spitzberg, B. H., & Canary, D. J. (1985). Loneliness and relationally competent communication. *Journal of Social and Personal Relationships, 2,* 387–402.

Spitzberg, B. H., & Cupach, W. R. (1998). Dusk, detritus and delusion: A prolegomenon to the dark side of close relationships. In B. H. Spitzberg & W. R. Cupach (Eds.), *The dark side of close relationships* (pp. xi–xxii). Mahwah, NJ: Lawrence Erlbaum Associates.

Sprecher, S. (1994). Two sides to the breakup of dating relationships. *Personal Relationships, 1,* 199–222.

Suppe, F. (1989). *The semantic conception of theories and scientific realism.* Urbana, IL: University of Illinois Press.

Thompson, J. S., & Snyder, D. K. (1986). Attribution theory in intimate relationships: A methodological review. *American Journal of Family Therapy, 14,* 123–138.

Turner, J. H. (1985). In defense of positivism. *Sociological Theory, 3,* 24–30.

Turner, J. H. (1990). The misuse and use of metatheory. *Sociological Forum, 5,* 37–53.

Turner, J. H. (1991). Developing cumulative and practical knowledge through metatheorizing. *Sociological Perspectives, 34,* 249–268.

Vangelisti, A. L. (1992). Communication problems in committed relationships: An attributional analysis. In J. L. Harvey, T. L. Orbuch, & A. L. Weber (Eds.), *Attributions, accounts, and close relationships* (pp. 144–164). New York: Springer-Verlag.

Vroon, P. A. (1987). Man-machine analogs and theoretical mainstreams in psychology. In W. J. Baker, M. E. Hyland, H. Van Rappard, & A. W. Staats (Eds.), *Current issues in theoretical psychology* (pp. 393–414). New York: Elsevier Science.

Wallach, L., & Wallach, M. A. (1994). Gergen versus the mainstream: Are hypotheses in social psychology subject to empirical test? *Journal of Personality and Social Psychology, 67,* 233–242.

Weary, G., Rich, M. C., Harvey, J. H., & Ickes, W. J. (1980). Heider's formulation of social perception and attributional processes: Toward further clarification. *Personality and Social Psychology Bulletin, 6,* 37–43.

Weber, D. J., & Vangelisti, A. L. (1991). "Because I love you…": The tactical use of attributional expressions in conversation. *Human Communication Research, 17,* 606–624.

Weick, K. E. (1989). Theory construction as disciplined imagination. *Academy of Management Review, 14,* 516–531.

Weiner, B. (1986). *An attributional theory of motivation and emotion.* New York: Springer-Verlag.

Weiner, B. (1995). *Judgments of responsibility: A foundation for a theory of social conduct.* New York: Guilford.

Weiner, B., Figueroa-Munoz, A., & Kakihara, C. (1991). The goals of excuses and communication strategies related to causal perceptions. *Personality and Social Psychology Bulletin, 17,* 4–13.

Wimer, S., & Kelley, H. H. (1982). An investigation of the dimensions of causal attribution. *Journal of Personality and Social Psychology, 43,* 1142–1162.

Wolf-Smith, J. H., & LaRossa, R. (1992). After he hits her. *Family Relations, 41,* 324–329.

CHAPTER 18

Are There Superior Options?

Commentary on Spitzberg's "The Status of Attribution Theory qua Theory in Personal Relationships"

John H. Harvey and Julia Omarzu

Attribution is part of the environment. Whenever you cognize your environment you will find attribution occurring.

(Heider, 1976, p. 18)

I think that the very way it [attribution theory] developed—it wasn't some bright idea that somebody had, that somebody forced on somebody's data or tried to extend by brute force. It came out of a lot of phenomena that social psychologists have looked at and tried to interpret. I just can't imagine that the phenomena that are hooked into that kind of cognition will change or be modified. They'll never go away. We'll always have to have that kind of explanation.

Harold H. Kelley, 1978, commenting on the future
of attribution theory (interview between editors
and Edward E. Jones and Kelley in Harvey,
Ickes, & Kidd, 1978, p. 384).

Spitzberg has written an interesting and enlightened statement on "the status of attribution theory *qua* theory in personal relationships." In this statement, Spitzberg essentially challenges the value and precision of attribution theory in explaining phenomena such as close relationships. Spitzberg shows a sophistication regarding attribution theory and the logic of the philosophy of science undergirding theory development that is impressive and rare in these times of scholarship in the close relationships field. Nevertheless, in this paper we take issue with certain points Spitzberg makes and offer another perspective on attribution theory. We also ask the big picture question not addressed in

Correspondence should be sent to John H. Harvey at the Department of Psychology, University of Iowa, E11 SSH, Iowa City, IA 52242. e-mail john-harvey@uiowa.edu. We thank Valerie Manusov for comments on an earlier draft of this commentary.

Spitzberg's analysis: Are there superior options to attribution theory in understanding close relationships? Before raising these issues, we present a perspective that may assist this dialogue and that pertains to the above quotes.

The opening quotes define some of the early thinking about attributional processes. As implied in Heider's (1976) definition, attribution can be conceptualized as a very basic (almost perceptual) process, in which people make quick, spontaneous inferences about causality. (This idea is similar to Kelley's (1972) notion of causal schemata, in which inferences are made quickly on the basis of learned patterns of data). From the outset, attribution theory has been a highly functional theory, which many scholars have found useful in many areas of the social and behavioral sciences. Seldom has attribution theory been proposed as a be-all-end-all account of any phenomenon, nor has attribution theory often been contrasted with other theories (as cognitive dissonance theory was in the 1960s and 1970s, for example with incentive theory in explaining the effects of counterattitudinal advocacy).

If attribution theory is all that various researchers have extended the "theory" to be (often referred to as "attribution*al* theories"; Kelley & Michela, 1980), it is quite broad and may not represent a strong theory in the classic sense, which is consistent with one of Spitzberg's concerns. If attribution theory is more narrowly construed (e.g., to involve mainly focus on *attribution of causality and basic principles*), as articulated by Heider, Kelley, Jones, Weiner, Nisbett, Valins, and others years ago, then most applications do not test the theory per se (Kelley & Michela, 1980; Harvey & Weary, 1984). Spitzberg's analysis implies this point.

Attribution theory emerged and developed in its fullest forms from the fertile minds of Heider, Kelley, and Jones in social psychology. Its origin clearly is Heider's work dating back to his dissertation at the University of Graz in Austria in 1920 and published as "Thing and Medium" in 1927 (Heider, 1983). It took Heider many years to publish his seminal attribution ideas in a mainline English source, his *The Psychology of Interpersonal Relations* (1958). In the process, Heider endured considerable disdain and cynicism regarding the value of his ideas (see Harvey, 1989). Kelley and Jones were the principal interpreters and stimulators of work based on Heider's ideas and extended these ideas in their own influential versions of attribution theory.

Since those early years extending from the publication of Heider's 1958 book through the present, attribution theory in social psychology has been extended to address problems and phenomena in developmental psychology, clinical and counseling psychology, sociology, communication, family studies, sport psychology, and probably a few other fields. It has shown the reach suggested in the opening quote by Kelley. Scholars have found the theory to be a useful heuristic framework in examining and understanding diverse phenomena, not only in social psychology but also in many other fields. In addition, it has become exceedingly broad in the sense of defining what attribution theory is, what its boundaries are, and how it may be used to analyze some phenomena that are studied in the social and behavioral sciences. Spitzberg's analysis reasonably alerts us to this development.

This diminution of work on attribution theory *qua* theory and continued strong level of work on applications of attribution theory are evident in many of the chapters in the present volume. At the same time, it might be contended that the richness of attribution theory is reflected in volumes such as the present one, appearing over 40 years after Heider's (1958) seminal statement and attesting to the continued viability of attributional ideas. Most of the basic research and writing on attributional processes no longer occurs in social psychology (where it mostly has been replaced by the more general work on social cognition). As is shown in Spitzberg's ample reference section, work on attributional applications crosses many disciplinary lines.

Attribution hit its zenith in social psychology in the late 1970s and from that point to the present has diminished in explicit work being done under the aegis of the theory or using the "attribution" name. Such a reality is evident from the fact that Harvey and Weary (1984) wrote the most recent (and possibly final) review of attribution work for the *Annual Review of Psychology*. As Spitzberg notes, work such as Hilton (1990) and Weiner (1995) reflects a small strand of continued interest in basic attributional processes. Nonetheless, attribution theory has a continued more salient presence in interdisciplinary fields such as the field of work on close relationships (e.g., Fletcher & Fincham, 1991; Fincham & Bradbury, 1987; Manusov, 1990; Manusov, Floyd, & Kerssen-Griep, 1997; Harvey & Omarzu, 1997, 1999).

Whether we are considering attribution*al* or attribution theory, the theory has proved to be a beneficial explanatory conception in various areas of the social and behavioral sciences during the last half-century. It has been shown to be a useful approach for understanding close relationships over two decades. Much work needs to be done to clarify and refine the theory, however. Nonetheless, our primary argument is that the theory compares well with other conceptions broached to understand close relationships. As suggested below, we believe that the liabilities of the theory are similar to ones that could be articulated for any major conception that has been applied to close relationships phenomena. In the next section, we take up in order Spitzberg's challenges regarding qualities of attribution theory. Given the detailed nature of these challenges, we will provide only general responses to the most significant challenges raised.

SPECIFIC REACTIONS TO SPITZBERG'S IDEAS

What is attribution theory? Spitzberg reasonably raises this question and notes the attribution*al* flavor of most current work. These applications in their totality reflect a smorgasbord quality, which is not appealing to the purist but which, as is consistent with Kelley's suggestion, reflects the intrinsic appeal of considerations of how, when, and why people make causal and responsibility judgments in analyzing all manners of human phenomena.

Is attribution even a theory? Even in its extended tentacles that have minimal relevance to the attribution of causality, attribution theory is still about as much and as good a theory as we have for understanding such phenomena as close relationships. Spitzberg mentions the current popularity of attachment theory and biological (e.g., evolutionary psychology) approaches. Yet, each of these conceptions and of others that could be mentioned suffers from similar concerns, such as whether hypotheses can be readily derived, the testability of the theory, whether the conception can be falsified, and whether it leads to insights about the phenomena in question that are superior to those derived from the other conceptions. Attribution theory also is a theory, we contend, to the extent that it has been treated prominently as such: Many scholars have recognized its heuristic value over a long period and across different fields and research agendas.

Depending on the phenomena under study, attribution theory has the advantage of focusing explicitly on how people think and feel about their relationships. Theories such as evolutionary psychology and attachment theory do not share this focus, although they present different, useful foci. What other theories in the relationship field involve propositions and a deep literature such that they represent advantageous positions in understanding thinking and feeling in and about relationships? We believe that analysts and critics of attribution theory would be making a valuable contribution if they spelled out possible comparative strengths of other conceptions in analyzing various relationship questions. For example, for a particular type of relationship phenomenon, it would be a most useful challenge to attribution theory to delineate possible predictions that other theories would make as compared with those that might derive from attribution theory (similar to Bem's 1972 challenges).

As for Spitzberg's discussion of "conditionship" as a criterion of theory, while theorists may not agree on the particular dimensions of attribution, work such as Weiner's (1986) has specified a set of dimensions that have stimulated considerable research. Early attribution theory was valuable in specifying conditions that differentiate people in different attributional roles. For example, Jones and Nisbett's (1972) actor–observer hypothesis, which indicated that actors in general would attribute their behavior to external factors but that observers of the same act would attribute it to qualities of the actor, is an example of a well-tested statement of conditions, which eventually was qualified to a high degree (e.g., the actor–observer effect can depend on motivation of the actor, such as egoism, or of the observer, such as empathy with the actor). Our biggest concern is that too few similar formulations are being developed at this point in time.

The general area of social cognition has become more dominant than the area of attribution per se in the last two decades, in part because there are a variety of minitheories in the social cognition area that spell out more detail about mediation than do most attributional conceptions. As Spitzberg suggests, the computer, or computational, metaphor for human judgment also is prominent today. Yet its popularity derives from the insights it helps us gain about mediation. Thus, for many investigators a theory that deals well with mediation is indeed a useful theory. Attribution theory does that and more. When we examine the full extent of attribution literature, we see that scholars have used attribution not only as a mediation variable or construct and a dependent variable but also as an independent variable. Attribution has been used as an independent variable in research programs, the most prominent being the work emanating from Schachter's (1964) theory on how attributions may be manipulated to impact emotions (Valins & Nisbett, 1972). This latter work showed the influence of manipulated attributions on emotional states.

Spitzberg contends that there has been a paucity of work on the attribution–behavior linkage. We agree, but this concern is not new. In the early 1980s, the first author (Harvey) was involved in developing a program of experimental studies designed to investigate how attribution may mediate the relationships between cognitive sets about other people and actual interaction with them (Harvey, Yarkin, Lightner, & Town, 1980; Yarkin, Harvey, & Bloxom, 1981; Town & Harvey, 1981). Unsolicited attributions about other people were shown consistently to affect subsequent behavior on the part of the attributor. Overall, this research program provided evidence that people engage in types of verbal and nonverbal behavior with target others that are consistent with (and can be predicted by) their prior attributions toward those target others.

More generally, Bem (1972) provided important theorizing about and some evidence on attribution-behavior relationships. Bem showed that people sometimes make inferences about their own behavior based on observation of their behavior and the context in which it occurs. They essentially deduce an understanding of why they behaved as they did after observing the behavior and its environmental context. For example, a person who is induced by a friend to campaign for a political candidate for whom the person did not have a strong prior attitude may later look back at his or her campaigning behavior, decide that no one forced him or her to do the campaigning, and conclude that he or she really does like the candidate.

Is attribution theory verifiable? The one major input we would offer regarding Spitzberg's argument for this question is that literally thousands of studies very likely have been conducted and have not supported attribution theory predictions (and the present authors have produced their fair share). These studies, however, seldom have been published unless they accompany other significant evidence and interesting ideas. Spitzberg's concern about scholars reporting nonsignificant data bearing on attribution theory may not give enough due to the role of publishing practices that do not afford much space to nonsignificant findings. One of the chief qualities of attribution work throughout the 1970s and early 1980s was the frequent skepticism about and further testing of basic hypotheses such as the actor-observer hypothesis and the "fundamental attribution error" (e.g., Harvey, Town, & Yarkin, 1981). Thus, we would argue that predictions based on attribution theory have been found wanting in many studies, only some of which have found their way into the literature.

Under the question "Is attribution theory aesthetic?" Spitzberg suggests that the lack of strong evidence about the attribution–behavior link has reduced the theory's value in various areas, such as marital therapy. He is correct on that point. He also suggests that other theoretical approaches are synthesizing, rather than the reverse, as time goes on. He is correct on that point too. However, these other approaches are quite general (e.g., social cognition, social cognitive), and even in the heyday of attribution theory in the 1970s, it still was considered part of social perception theory in social psychology – and it still is by scholars conversant with that tradition (e.g., Fiske & Taylor, 1991). Attribution could be seen as part of the evolution in the 1950s of the "new look in perception" (Bruner, 1957), which emphasized the role of the perceiver in actively bringing ideas, biases and sets, and experience to bear on her or his perception of the world.

Finally, Spitzberg suggests that attribution theory's image of humans has been fairly lofty: "humans as god-like in judgment processes." At the same time, an important qualification of attribution theory has been the extensive work on attributional egoism (Miller & Ross, 1975; Weary, 1980). Importantly, attribution theory acknowledges the possibility that people's biases, decision errors, and seeming irrationalities may be based not on faulty linear reasoning or on cognitive limitations but on social experiences that transcend rational analysis. The naïve scientist metaphor implies that we have a desire to integrate motivations, past experiences, and perceptions in a way that satisfactorily explains causality. People use attributions not only to advance their own lives and help others but also to be defensive, to try to cover up misdeeds, and even to carry out and justify horrible acts of cruelty.

CONCLUSIONS

By knowledgeably challenging attribution theory, Spitzberg has rendered a valuable service to scholars interested in this theory and to work, such as the present volume, that has attribution near the apex of its focus. We find much of Spitzberg's reasoning to be tenable. At the same time, we believe that the attribution theory story is even more complex than the picture he paints. As such, attribution theory has been tremendously successful in stimulating research, theory, and critical commentary over a long period of time. It has readily fulfilled Kelley's (1978) claim that it was not a body of ideas that by brute force were imposed into our thinking about human thought, feeling, and behavior. Rather, attribution theory has been a survivor in the jungle of theories in the social and behavioral sciences primarily because of its practical appeal and its so-called common-sense psychology insights of the theory that Heider (1958) first proposed.

In its fullness, attribution theory has become something like a grand general theory of human thought, which attempts to help explain how humans make sense of a constantly changing environment. As Heider posited, the attribution process may be viewed as omnipresent in human life. Attributional processes often represent the quintessence of adaptive behavior. However, as is true with any theory, particularly a grand theory, attribution theory leaves a lot to be desired and always will be a work in progress. Just as we do not expect a large-scale map of the world to designate every scenic view, intersection, or rural community, neither should we expect a large-scale theory to explain every facet and quirk of human social cognition.

REFERENCES

Bem, D. J. (1972). Self-perception theory. *Advances in Experimental Social Psychology, 6,* 1–62.

Bruner, J. S. (1957). On perceptual readiness. *Psychological Review, 64,* 23–52.

Fincham, F. D., & Bradbury, T. N. (1987). The impact of attributions in marriage: A longitudinal analysis. *Journal of Personality and Social Psychology, 53,* 510–517.

Fiske, S. T., & Taylor, S. E. (1991). *Social cognition* (2nd ed.). New York: McGraw-Hill.

Fletcher, G. J. O., & Fincham, F.D. (1991). Attribution processes in close relationships. In G. J. O. Fletcher & F. D. Fincham (Eds.), *Cognition in close relationships* (pp. 7–35). Hillsdale, NJ: Erlbaum.

Harvey, J. H. (1989). Fritz Heider (1896–1988). *American Psychologist, 44,* 570–571.

Harvey, J. H., & Omarzu, J. (1997). Minding the close relationship. *Personality and Social Psychology Review, 1,* 224–240.

Harvey, J. H., & Omarzu, J. (1999). *Minding the close relationship: A theory of relationship enhancement,* New York: Cambridge University Press.

Harvey, J. H., Town, J. P., Yarkin, K. L. (1981). How fundamental is "the fundamental attribution error"? *Journal of Personality and Social Psychology, 40,* 346–349.

Harvey, J. H., Yarkin, K. L., Lightner, J. M., & Town, J. P. (1980). Unsolicited attribution and recall of interpersonal events. *Journal of Personality and Social Psychology, 38,* 551–568.

Harvey, J. H., & Weary, G. (1984). Current issues in attribution theory and research. *Annual Review of Psychology, 36,* 427–459.

Heider, F. (1958). *The psychology of interpersonal relations,* New York: Wiley.

Heider, F. (1976). A conversation with Fritz Heider. In J. H., Harvey, W. J. Ickes, & R. F. Kidd (Eds.), *New directions in attribution research* (Vol. 1, pp. 3–18). Hillsdale, NJ: Erlbaum.

Heider, F. (1983). *The life of a psychologist: An autobiography,* Lawrence: University of Kansas Press.

Hilton, D. J. (1990). Conversational pressures and causal explanation. *Psychological Bulletin, 107,* 65–81.

Jones, E. E., & Nisbett, R.E. (1972). The actor and the observer: Divergent perceptions of the causes of behavior. In E. E. Jones, D. Kanouse, H. Kelley, R. Nisbett, & S. Valins (Eds.), *Perceiving the causes of behavior* (pp. 79–94). Morristown, NJ: General Learning Press.

Kelley, H. H. (1978). A conversation with Edward E. Jones and Harold H. Kelley. In J. H. Harvey, W. J. Ickes, & R. F. Kidd (Eds.), *New directions in attribution research* (Vol. 2, pp. 371–388). Hillsdale, NJ: Erlbaum.

Kelley, H. H., & Michela, J. L. (1980). Attribution theory and research. *Annual Review of Psychology, 31,* 457–501.

Manusov, V. (1990). An application of attribution principles to nonverbal messages in romantic dyads. *Communication Monographs, 57,* 104–118.

Manusov, V., Floyd, K., & Kerssen-Griep, J. (1997). Yours, mine, and ours: Mutual attributions for nonverbal behaviors in couples' interactions. *Communication Research, 24,* 234–260.

Miller, D. T., & Ross, M. (1975). Self-serving biases in the attribution of causality: Fact or fiction? *Psychological Bulletin, 82,* 213–225.

Tolman, E. (1932). *Purposive behavior in animals and men.* New York: McGraw-Hill.

Schachter, S. (1964). The interaction of cognitive and physiological determinants of emotional state. *Advances in Experimental Social Psychology, 1,* 49–80.

Town, J. P., & Harvey, J. H. (1981). Self-disclosure, attribution, and social interaction. *Social Psychology Quarterly, 44,* 291–300.

Valins, S., & Nisbett, R. E. (1972). Attribution processes in the development and treatment of emotional disorders. In E. E. Jones, D. Kanouse, H. Kelley, R. Nisbett, S. Valins, & B. Weiner (Eds.), *Attribution: Perceiving the causes of behavior* (pp. 137–150). Morristown, NJ: General Learning Press.

Weary, G. (1980). Examination of affect and egotism as mediators of bias in causal attributions. *Journal of Personality and Social Psychology, 38,* 348–357.

Weiner, B. (1986). *An attribution theory of motivation and emotion.* New York: Springer-Verlag.

Weiner, B. (1995). *Judgments of responsibility: A foundation for a theory of social conduct.* New York: Guilford.

Yarkin, K. L., Harvey, J. H., & Bloxom, B. M. (1981). Cognitive sets, attribution, and social interaction. *Journal of Personality and Social Psychology, 41,* 243–252.

Index